Auth

Ti

Basic Speech Improvement

UNDER THE ADVISORY EDITORSHIP OF J. JEFFERY AUER

BASIC
SPEECH
IMPROVEMENT

HORACE G. RAHSKOPF

University of Washington

HARPER & ROW *Publishers New York, Evanston, and London*

BASIC SPEECH IMPROVEMENT

C-1

Library of Congress Catalog Card Number: 65-13474

This book is gratefully dedicated to all those who through the years have encouraged my study of speech, with special acknowledgment to four great teachers—Albert Craig Baird and Della Crowder Miller, and the memory of Samuel Silas Curry and Charles Henry Woolbert.

CONTENTS

IV. *Forms and Uses of Speech*

PREFACE

This is a textbook for speech improvement. The aim is to study speaking as a distinctly human activity, which, though varied in its different forms and uses, consists always and basically of certain characteristic processes. These elements are both psychological and symbolic, both mental and organic, both covert and overt. Together they constitute a uniquely human function.

The student's attention is directed primarily to the task of improving these elemental speech processes. Part I provides a general explanation of the speech act, describing the interacting roles of speaker and listener, and outlines methods of study, practice, and criticism. Part II is addressed to the psychological and logical processes which are inherent parts of speech activity—motivation, attitudes, knowledge of facts, inference, organization, imagination, emotion, and memory. The foundation for this treatment is laid in the symbolic nature of thought. Part III is devoted to the symbolic processes involved in body action, voice, articulation, pronunciation, and use of words, all of which enable a speaker to put his thought into definite, visible, and audible form.

No attempt is made to study systematically the various kinds of speaking, although several types are recommended as exercises. Those speech forms have been chosen for practice which most directly develop the primary elements of speech and which are most easily adapted to classroom use: conversation, discussion, oral reading, and the short talk to an audience. To provide guidance for these speaking exercises, their most important characteristics are sketched in Part IV.

Throughout the book the author strives to make clear that the visible and audible aspects of speech—the bodily movements, vocal modulations, and articulate word forms—are not merely overt expressive processes, but their silent and implicit, as well as visible and audible forms, are the media in which a speaker achieves the creation and formulation of thought—for himself as well as for a listener. Thinking does not occur in a vacuum; it requires formulation in some kind of action, and for the speaker that action is speech. The traditional concept that "content" is more or less independent of the "delivery," that overt manner of speaking is merely added to thought as a means of communicating it to others, is here challenged as a false and misleading concept. The visible and audible processes of speech are not merely external techniques superimposed on thought; they are an integral part of the act of thinking itself. This book is written on the principle that thought and overt utterance are but two ways of looking at the single, unified process by which nascent response is brought into tangible, symbolic form. This duality of language forces us to treat in distinct sections (Parts II and III) the psychological and symbolic aspects of speech, but they are nevertheless only two ways of looking at one process.

The subject of this study, we remind our readers, is *basic speech improvement*. We concentrate on that objective, and strive constantly toward unification of the psychological and technical, of the "inner" and "outer" processes. Such unification is the foundation of any truly expressive artistry or effectiveness in communication.

Acknowledgments

My debts are too numerous to record completely. In the background, of course, are all those who taught me, especially the four great teachers to whom the book is dedicated. More immediate gratitude is due Lousene Rousseau, former college editor for Harper & Row, who first suggested the work and encouraged its early stages. Later J. Jeffery Auer gave valuable advice as consulting editor. I also acknowledge gratefully the assistance of Thomas R. Nilsen and Dominic A. LaRusso, each of whom not only prepared a chapter of the text but also served as generous and untiring critic. To Dr. LaRusso I am further indebted for his extensive contributions to the exercises and practice materials, and for his advice in the choice of illustrative material. Many other colleagues should be named for their useful comments and suggestions along the way: Barnet Baskerville, Bert Browne, Clair Hanley, Michael Hogan, Oliver Nelson, John Palmer, Robert Post, and all members of the teaching staff for the course, "Basic Speech Improvement," given at the University of Washington. Of course, none of these colleagues should be held accountable for any shortcomings of the work. The blame is mine, especially since I have not always followed the advice so generously given.

Special acknowledgment is due Professor Vernon Mund of the University of Washington and Professor Alethea Mattingly of the University of Arizona for their advice on specific details, and Robert D. Monroe of the University of Washington Library for invaluable assistance in preparing Chapter 6 and the Appendix on Sources of Information. Frances E. King gave far more than routine service in checking and typing the final manuscript. To the University of Washington Office of News Services, and especially to James O. Sneddon, supervisor of photography, I am indebted for most of the photographs which illustrate chapter themes and for helpful advice in their selection.

A final word of gratitude should go to my wife, Frances, and our daughter, Melinda, who have endured vicariously the struggles of authorship.

I fear that this list of acknowledgments is incomplete, yet I would not overlook anyone who has helped. To all those colleagues, students and friends, both named and unnamed here, who have given encouragement and advice—my heartfelt thanks.

H.G.R.

Seattle, Washington
January, 1965

INTRODUCTION
for the STUDENT

Throughout this course bear in mind that your object is to achieve the greatest possible degree of speech improvement. Every bit of speaking you do, therefore, whether in the classroom or anywhere else, should be regarded as part of your practice and training. Mumbling, incomplete phrases, half-formed sentences, use of "uh" and its near relatives "and-uh," "but-uh," "well-uh," and similar evidences of disordered and incoherent thinking are never acceptable. Your instructor may frequently call on you to answer questions about a previous day's lecture or material assigned for study. In all such cases your responses should be in definite, well-phrased, complete statements. No less will be acceptable. Nor is inattention to the reading or talking of others to be condoned. Speaking is interaction between people, and you and all your colleagues are to be active participating members at all times.

In order to carry through the series of classroom speaking exercises to the best advantage, you should begin at once to study your resources as a speaker and to develop a list of subjects and materials you would like to use in oral practice throughout the course. Ask yourself the following questions:

> What stimulating and informative experiences have I had (in work, travel, previous study, sports, music, hobbies, community organizations, or other activities) which point toward subjects worth thinking and speaking about in a college or university setting?

> What have I read (novels, poetry, plays, science fiction, or essays) which suggest topics challenging and likely to interest my fellow students in this class?

> Which of the courses I have taken or am now taking deal with subjects I would like to talk about—science, literature, history or other social studies, the various arts, philosophy?

> On which of these various subjects, if any, am I now well informed?

> Which subjects offer the most substantial values for further study and research?

As you think about these questions, you should be able to

xiii

develop a list of topics for extempore speaking, materials for reading aloud, and problems for discussion, which may surprise you by its length, variety, and challenge to further study. Your speech class is a place where you should put to use some of the knowledge gained from other sources.

Throughout the course every exercise in oral communication should be in accord with college and university standards. For reading aloud you are expected to choose selections of good literary value; for discussion, problems of real significance for campus, community, or nation; for talks or conversations, topics of intellectual value or importance to society. In a college class there is little excuse for casual talks on such topics as, "My Summer Vacation" or "A Fishing Trip," if, as is often the case, they call for no depth of preparation and result in nothing more than rambling narrative. Any value which talks of this kind may have as "ice breakers" at the beginning of the course is likely to be outweighed by their superficiality. You are competent to speak and read about matters of real and valuable content; otherwise you would not have been admitted to the college. The processes of research by which to gain information are part of the discipline which basic speech improvement requires.

The topics suggested under the headings which follow are intended to stimulate you to develop your *own* list of materials out of your *own* interests and studies.

Reading aloud. Make a list such as the following of a few speeches, essays, and poems which challenge your thinking and from which you would like to choose selections for reading aloud to the class.

> John F. Kennedy   "Inaugural Address"
> Robert Frost   "Mending Wall"
> Thomas Huxley   "The Method of Scientific Investigation"
> Ralph Waldo Emerson   "Self Reliance"

Problems for discussion and subjects for conversation. Make a similar list of topics on which you would like to join in discussion with some of your classmates. For guidance refer to the section on problem-solving patterns in Chapter 9 and to Chapter 19. Observe the following examples:

> How Best May We Define an Educated Man?
> What Should Be Our Attitude on the Civil Rights Issue?
> How best may We Help Individuals to Become Economically Efficient?
> How Should College Curricula Be Reshaped to Meet the Needs of the Atomic Age?

Expository talks.   Assemble groups of topics for several different types of expository talks. Consult the material on expository speaking in Chapter 20.

Description of a structure
   The Structure of a Neuron
   The St. Lawrence Waterway
   Organization of the United States Congress

Explanation of a process
   Bookbinding
   Preparation of Blood Samples
   The Manufacture of Cheese

Analysis of the outstanding qualities of a person
   Horace Mann, Educator
   George Clemenceau as Statesman
   Woodrow Wilson, Idealist

An account of an historical event
   The Battle of Waterloo
   The Founding of Your University
   The Trial and Death of Socrates

Explanation of a concept or general idea (see Chapter 6 for discussion of concepts)
   Existentialism
   Aristotle's Concept of Rhetoric
   Progressive Education

Persuasive arguments.   Choose a few problems or controversial issues on which you would like to make talks. Refer to the material on persuasive speaking in Chapter 20. Select subjects about which you hold positive convictions which you can support by factual and logical reasoning. The following general topics may suggest more specific themes which are relevant to your campus or area and fall within the range of your interests and convictions:

   Student Government
   Requirements for Graduation
   The Grading System
   Regulation of Broadcasting
   Liquor Control
   Juvenile Delinquency
   Civil Rights
   Government Support of the Arts
   Religion in the Public Schools
   Support of the United Nations
   Foreign Aid
   State Income Taxes

In constructing a list of subjects and materials you may find special value and interest in developing continuity of themes. For illustration, let us suppose that you have an interest in the study of biology or zoology. After the introductory talk and the first discussion exercise, you might present a *series* on related topics:

1. Oral reading from Darwin's *Origin of Species*
2. An expository talk on the structure of a simple life form, e.g., amoeba or euglena morpha
3. A process talk on cellular division
4. A biographical talk about a famous scientist, perhaps Charles Darwin or George Mendel
5. An account of a significant event in the history of science, such as Darwin's voyage on H.M.S. *Beagle*.
6. An explanation of the concept, "Heredity"
7. A group discussion of the impact of the doctrine of evolution on thought in America
8. An argument on some disputed scientific theory

Similarly, if you are a student of American Literature, you might choose Ralph Waldo Emerson, for example, and build a series of exercises like the following:

1. Oral reading of an excerpt from one of Emerson's essays
2. Structure or process talk on analysis of Emerson's style as a writer
3. Biography concerning his career as lecturer
4. Poetry reading of "Each and All" or "The Rhodora"
5. Historical event talk about his journey to Europe in 1833 or the address on "The American Scholar" in 1837
6. Concept talk on individual freedom or transcendentalism
7. Discussion on an appraisal of Emerson's influence on thought and life in America

Or if you are interested in military science and training, you might like the following sequence:

1. Oral reading of an excerpt from one of General MacArthur's speeches, such as his address to the United States Congress, April 19, 1951, "Don't Scuttle the Pacific," or his speech at West Point, May 12, 1962, "Duty, Honor, Country"
2. Structure talk on the organization of the United States Army
3. Process talk on the training of a recruit
4. Biography of a great military leader, such as General Douglas MacArthur
5. Historical event talk concerning the defense of Bataan or the Inchon Landing
6. Concept talk on the meaning of leadership
7. Group discussion on the relationship of civilian and military authority

8. Argumentative or persuasive talk on the unification of the armed forces

For a student of law, such a series as the following might be challenging:

1. Prose reading of a paragraph from some famous legal argument as Jeremiah S. Black's plea, "In Defense of the Right of Trial by Jury"
2. Structure talk on the organization of the Federal judiciary
3. Process talk on admission to the bar
4. Biography of the life and work of any great lawyer or jurist
5. Event talk about the court martial of Lambdin P. Milligan, in October, 1864
6. Concept talk on the right of trial by jury

Since you are a student of speech, you might wish to develop some topics about a phase of communication:

1. Structure talk on the sound system of the English language
2. Process talk on the origin and development of the phonetic alphabet
3. Biography of Alexander Graham Bell
4. Event talk on the invention of the telephone
5. Concept talk on the meaning of communication
6. Discussion concerning how we can best achieve communications control in the United States
7. An argument on some phase of the policies of the Federal Communications Commission

If you decide to use a series of topics related to a central theme, research in each of the subjects will enrich the content of all the exercises in the series. Whatever lists you actually develop, hand them to your instructor for his evaluation and comment. He will give you any further help or guidance you may need in making final selection of a subject or problem for each classroom speaking exercise.

I

PRELIMINARY
VIEW

1

WHAT IS BASIC
IN SPEECH?

Improvement in any activity must proceed on certain basic principles. In order to direct our efforts adequately, we must know what is most fundamental in speech activity. In other words, we need to understand the nature of this process we hope to improve. What does speech involve? What factors are basic in it?

The most important concept that should guide our efforts in speech improvement is this: *Speech is a primary and distinctive human process or activity.* Man alone of living creatures speaks; his speech is the central feature of his humanity. The words *primary* and *distinctive* are crucial to our theme and will bear some examination.

Primary Nature of Speech

Our daily lives revolve around speech. We talk with people to pass the time of day, we ask them to do things, we raise questions and give information, we express our opinions and feelings, we discuss problems, we plan group activities, we seek to influence others to accept our beliefs or follow our courses of action. It is plain that nearly everything we do involves some kind of oral communication. We carry on very few activities by ourselves. All of us want to be liked and respected. We want our opinions and ideas to have an impact on others. We want to be recognized by our employers, to succeed in our jobs, to deal effectively with people who work for us, to gain an adequate education, to develop our personalities. In short, we want to live effectively; and we accomplish these things largely through the medium of speech. Individual success in any area depends largely on talk, and any man who cannot speak his thoughts effectively is severely handicapped.

There is, moreover, a larger sense in which speech is primary in our lives. Modern social scientists have asserted that speech is the principal medium for social interaction or, as Grace A. de Laguna phrased it some years ago, "Speech is the great medium through which human cooperation is brought about."[1] In other words, speech is an essential process in the maintenance of an orderly and stable society.

[1] *Speech: Its Function and Development*, Yale University Press, 1927, p. 19.

This relation between speech and society is many sided of course, but two aspects of it need emphasis here. On the one hand, the ability, as well as the freedom, of each person to speak is a product of social life and institutions. Speech is not innate in the individual. A child acquires the speech patterns of the adult world into which he is born, and he tends to use them largely in accord with the traditions and institutions—linguistic, cultural, and political—of the society in which he matures and lives. These facts largely account for the stability and continuity of a society and its culture. On the other hand, the essential pattern of any society is made up of the complex lines of communication between individual men and speech is one of the most

Ancient Athens began the study of speech.

The Acropolis

important, if not *the* most important, medium in which these lines of communication are established. Most social institutions—family, school, club, church, legislature, courts, and even the press—operate by means of spoken communication among their members. These facts indicate a vital role for the individual citizen in any society. He is not merely a creature of that society; he is also a dynamic force in its continuity and evolution for better or worse. For free men in a free society, this responsibility is especially significant. Since they are not henchmen of a dictator or blind preservers of tradition, they are entrusted with the evolution and continuing improvement of society. They can make or break the world in which they live, and they can do so largely through the kind of spoken communication they carry on together.

Through speech, our institutions not only develop and operate, but also achieve continuity and a degree of permanence. Members of

Rome nurtured the study of speech.

The Forum

groups and communities respond to their environments in varied ways, and the inevitable result is a widened range of social exploration. By means of speech we explore, and plan with foresight; we announce our intended responses in advance, and influence our neighbors' conduct. Although the visual or written symbol is the primary means of permanence, the speech symbol contributes to permanence in at least two ways: (1) It is the most basic and frequently used form of symbolic action in which the continuity of everyday social life is carried on. (2) The spoken word is a principal means of transmitting from generation to generation those legends, folkways, and rituals which are necessary elements in the stability of any society.

These social values of speech are based primarily on its function as response. For each of us, talking is a way of interacting with our environment, primarily, of course, with other people. Sometimes our utterance is an independent form of action in its own right, for instance in conversation and in artistic expression such as oral reading and acting. More often talk is a substitute for direct, overt action, as we shall see later. In any event, whether original or substitute, speech is a major form of response to others.

For each individual, however, the innate aspects of speech are even deeper than its social aspects. Deeply hidden within the private mental life of each of us is a constant flow of inner talk. The act of speech, silent and incomplete, serves as the medium in which much of our thinking is carried on. Thinking is a process of analyzing and evaluating people, things, and events—not as in direct action when we shake hands with a friend, drive a nail, or sign a check—but in terms of inner

5

substitute action, indirectly and tentatively, as though to prepare for overt action. All of us use speech silently in shortened and implicit form as the principal medium in which we formulate our thoughts. In other words, speech is more than a means of communicating ideas already realized; it is our principal medium for creating and formulating ideas. These inner subjective uses of speech probably attain their highest significance in the purposeful planning of future action and in objective self-evaluation, which is the foundation of personality development.

Finally, because speech is the principal medium for both social interaction and thinking, we use it as a primary means of individual release and adjustment. Speech responses, when abbreviated and transferred to the inner forum of subjective processes, are not only a primary medium for thinking, but, if properly nurtured and developed, may become an important phase of our aesthetic enjoyment and emotional participation. This inner speech activity, by its very nature is a basic preliminary for overt expression. Outward expression, moreover, completes our thought and thus may further enhance emotional release and aesthetic satisfaction. Self-expression is one of the deepest satisfactions of life. All speech affords us this satisfaction; but its aesthetic uses, as in oral interpretation or acting, are especially valuable means of artistic creation and enjoyment which enrich our lives and develop our personalities.

Let us now summarize the functions of speech in daily life. For individuals speech is a means of:

1. Response to environment
2. Formulation of thought
3. Expression of thought
4. Emotional release
5. Aesthetic enjoyment
6. Growth and development

For our society speech is a means of:

1. Exploration
2. Cooperation
3. Persuasion
4. Control leading to stability
5. Continuity leading to a degree of permanence

To summarize in more general terms: For individuals the functions of speech are self-expression and development; for society the functions are communication and organized continuity.

Distinctive Nature of Speech

The fact that we use speech constantly may lead us to think of it as a very commonplace kind of action. We often take it for granted, yet a little thoughtful observation will show us that speaking is not like any other human function. Listen to anyone speaking at any level of performance for a few moments. What you observe is unique.

Notice, for example, the differences between speaking and writing. Most of us have been taught to look upon these activities as basically similar forms of linguistic expression. Educators have been so eager to correlate instruction in them (together with the related processes of listening and reading) that their similarities have been stressed and the differences too largely overlooked. It is true, of course, that the spoken sounds and written letters of any word are parallel (even though our English spelling is notoriously nonphonetic) and that any given facts or ideas may be represented in both writing and speaking. Study of each process helps to improve the other. Our work in this course will necessarily include much writing, but we should not assume that speaking is merely an oral counterpart of writing. The opposite is more nearly true; writing is the visual counterpart of speaking.

Nevertheless, speaking and writing are not merely two forms of the same process. They differ in significant ways. In speaking we tend to use simpler words, more rambling and loosely constructed sentences, and a greater degree of repetition. Writing tends to be more formal, speaking more casual; although some writings, such as stories or personal letters, are often less formal than sermons or ceremonial orations. Writing produces symbols in the form of marks on a surface appealing directly to the eye. Speaking, on the other hand, produces symbols in the form of sound and movement which appeal to both eye and ear. Writing is primarily a coordination of eye and hand in relation to thinking; speaking is primarily a coordination of both eye and ear with organs of breathing, phonation, and articulation in relation to thinking. The two processes involve widely different patterns of inner action.

Because of these differences in symbolic form, speaking and writing serve partially different social functions. The written word is a relatively permanent and unchanging means of representation which any man thousands of miles or years away may read. Writing and its counterpart, printing, thus provide a relatively permanent record of the accumulated knowledge, culture, and history of nations and societies. The spoken word, on the other hand, is a fleeting and perishable means of representation, addressed to immediate listeners and dying when the perceived energy of the transmitting sound waves and light waves is spent. The spoken word, if you remember the old adage, is one of the four things which come not back. It is a day-to-day, in fact a moment-to-moment, activity; but nevertheless an indispensable part of the dynamic processes by which a society develops knowledge, culture, and a history. Modern methods of recording, of course, have given us means of making relatively permanent records of both the sounds and bodily movements of speech. The writing materials, however, whether paper, stone, wood, or even sand, are indispensable to the process;

whereas film and tape are not essential materials of speech but merely convenient supplements to it. In this way speech is a language process which utilizes no materials external to the body of the speaker.

General Description of Speech

These contrasts, though important, do not fully describe the act of speech. We must search for more fundamental ways of characterizing it. Let us look directly at the process itself. The comparisons we have just made suggest that the uniqueness of speech does not rest in any one of its aspects such as voice or bodily action. Other kinds of human behavior have similar features. As a matter of fact, the nature of speech is not to be explained in terms of any one characteristic but in terms of its wholeness of pattern: (1) the interactions between speakers and listeners, (2) the processes that go on within a speaker, and (3) those that go on within a listener. We shall examine each of these aspects of speech to see what we can discover about them.

For the present, we are not trying to give a complete description of the act of speaking, but only to describe the *characteristic and essential processes* of any act of speech, no matter how or where used, good or bad, effective or ineffective. Evaluation will come later.

INTERACTION—THE SPEECH SETTING

First, let us look at the processes that go on between speaker and listener to see what is characteristic of speech. Here our viewpoint is social. We are looking at what goes on between man and man, and even more broadly at the total setting in which an act of speech occurs. Common to all speaking situations are certain basic factors:

1. Speaker
2. Listener
3. Location—time and place
4. Things meant or things which have potential meaning—objects, properties of objects, actions, experiences, ideas which come within the range of experience of the people involved
5. A body of commonly understood symbolic processes—words gestures, vocal modulations

An act of speech, therefore, may be defined as interaction between these forces. They, like the elements of the act itself, interact so closely that they enhance and emphasize the unique wholeness of speech as a function of human life.

Speaker and listener are almost always the most dynamic factors in a speech situation. Although they are stimulated by all other factors (time and place, facts and ideas known, available linguistic processes), each provides the primary stimulation for and the main responses to the other. Occasionally time or place may determine some features of the speech process, but such influence is exerted through the people involved. In like manner, the content or meanings of utterance and the language processes used, though they exist independently of any particular speech setting, operate within a given situation entirely through the behavior of speaker and listener. Our main interest, therefore, is in their interactions.

A more detailed account of this process of interaction is provided by the following causal sequence:

1. An event provides
2. stimuli affecting the sense organs of an individual and resulting in
3. nerve impulses which pass over afferent nerve pathways to his brain, where
4. organization and integration take place, out of which are formulated patterns of motor activity including speech responses stimulated by
5. outgoing nerve impulses which travel to muscles and glands so as to produce
6. the specialized patterns of verbal, vocal, and gestural behavior characteristic of speech. These activities of response produce
7. sound waves organized in more or less standardized word forms and light waves reflected from surfaces of the body, which are
8. transmitted through space to provide
9. stimuli affecting the sense organs of another person, the listener, in whom
10. nerve impulses pass over afferent pathways to the brain where they are
11. translated into patterns of motor response which may include verbal, vocal, and gestural formulations.
12. These speech responses of the second person in turn produce sound waves and light waves which are transmitted back to the speaker and to any other people in the setting. In other words, the responses constitute a new event which, like the one with which we started, stimulates further cycles of interaction.

THE SPEAKER

Next let us consider the speaker in more detail. Here we are looking not at what happens between man and man, but at the behavior of one individual. When you speak or when a companion speaks, do you know what kinds of processes are going on in you or in him? Some of them you can see and hear, but some phases of the action are hidden from view; they go on inside and not even the speaker himself can be aware of all of them. Nevertheless we can outline the main elements, or processes, of speech behavior.

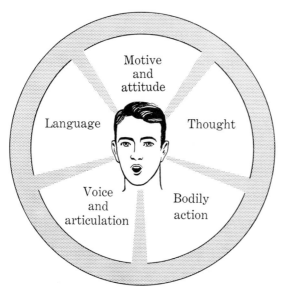

The elements of speech behavior.

First let us consider *attitudes,* and with them motives which are inseparably related. An attitude is a covert process going on within an individual in such a way as to make him ready to respond in a characteristic manner to particular kinds of stimulating situations. Attitudes are incipient actions constituting readiness for more complete outward action. Motives are the basic drives or needs which impel us to act, while attitudes are inner forces which help to determine the particular kinds of responses we make. Both motives and attitudes, of course, are closely related to emotions. In a speaker, as we shall see later, three kinds of attitudes are important—his attitudes toward the listener, toward the subject matter, and toward himself.

The second essential phase in every act of speech is *thinking.* Much of our casual everyday speaking is relatively thoughtless. Nevertheless, in a general sense, some degree of thinking enters into every act of speech worthy of the name. Certainly perceiving and knowing, drawing inferences from facts, forming judgments, and preconceiving purposes are in some degree present in every typical speaking process.

The third phase or element of speech is *bodily action,* not just any bodily action, but patterns of movement that are precisely coordinated in certain more or less standardized ways for the symbolization of meaning. We understand bodily action to include everything from a gesture of the hand and the expression of the face and eye to the subtle empathy of a speaker's responses.

The fourth phase of every act of speech consists of the processes of producing sounds: *respiration*, which provides the motive power; *phonation*, which produces the vibratory movements of vocal tone; *resonance*, which amplifies and reinforces the sounds; *articulation*, which forms the various sound elements of the oral words; and *modulation*, which is the expressive variation in the characteristics of tones. Note that all these processes involve highly specialized kinds of movements of the sound-producing parts of the body.

The last essential phase of every act of speech consists of *words* and their use—language in its audible and oral form. Here, as in the old sea captain's definition of swearing, two processes are primary— knowing the words and knowing how to put them together. Under these headings we meet such important considerations as vocabulary, grammar, syntax, and oral style. In these areas the speech student is on common ground with all students of language.

Now a listing of these elements of speech is not in itself an adequate description of its distinctiveness. In fact, such a hurried listing of elements may be misleading. The act of speech is not a conglomerate of several processes. It is true, of course, that many of the names of these elements are also names of other more or less independent areas of action. There are bodily movements and sounds that have no part in speech. Words exist in written or visual form and in other forms too. Social attitudes and thoughts may be formulated in media other than gestures and words. Nevertheless, though each of these processes has a certain independence of its own, speaking involves specialized aspects of all of them; and when they occur as phases of speech, they are parts of each other, utterly interdependent and inseparable.

Perhaps this interdependence of the elements of speech may be suggested by reviewing them in reverse order. Let us begin with the spoken words. They are standardized patterns or combinations of certain sounds or phonemes. These sounds of speech in turn are the result of, or are produced by, certain localized or special patterns of bodily action centering in what are called the organs of phonation and articulation, although of course the activity of these organs is dependent upon the coordinated participation of the entire body. In speech the more visible phases of bodily action are usually called gestures. Bodily movements, of course, are stimulated and controlled by patterns of innervation. These patterns of innervation arise in the central nervous system, and in any complex activity like speech, function under the control of the highest levels, that is, under control of the association areas in the cerebral cortex.

Now these activities in the cerebrum are the central and distinctive factor in what we ordinarily call thinking. In a complex activity like speech the activities of response involved in bodily movement, sound production, and use of words are directly stimulated and controlled by activities in the central nervous system. These higher levels of neural action, however, are dependent upon and fed by constant processes of perception. In speech a large part of these processes of perception is social in origin—that is, the stimuli are provided by people in the immediate environment; and continuous social stimulation throughout the life of the individual creates in him certain characteristic patterns of readiness to respond. These we call social attitudes and place them first in our list of the elements of speech because they represent a primary aspect of the inner mental life of the individual which largely determines and conditions his processes of knowing and inferring and forming judgments—that is, his thought processes, and, hence, his overt speech processes.

We have gone through this rather laborious review of the elements of speech in order to emphasize their dependence upon each other. In the act of speech they constitute one pattern of action. Let us illustrate the point by a comparison. A molecule of water is composed of two atoms of hydrogen and one atom of oxygen. In that molecule of water, however, the hydrogen and oxygen have lost their separate identities. They cease to be hydrogen and oxygen as such and have been merged in a new unit—the molecule of water. Now this molecule may be broken down and the hydrogen and oxygen released to their own separate and distinctive existence, but then we no longer have water. In like manner, the elements or phases of speech, though they may have their own distinct identities, lose those identities and become parts of each other in the act of speaking.

THE LISTENER

The third distinctive characteristic of speech is the presence of a listener. Of course, we sometimes talk to ourselves, but we are able to do so only because we have talked to others. Speech is an interpersonal act and its solitary use, whether internal or overt, is derived from its social use. As surely as speech is interaction, the listener is an indispensable part of the process. If we are to understand the place of listening in speech behavior, we should know the answers to the following questions: What is listening? What is a listener doing? What does listening contribute to the act of speech? What is a listener's part in speech?

A listener is primarily one who is responding. If he is a complete and adequate listener, he is wholly absorbed in the process of reacting to a speaker. Sometimes we listen only to understand what a speaker says. At other times we may listen to reorganize, to appreciate or act, to reinterpret or evaluate; or we may listen to be entertained or inspired. In every case, however, a listener is one who thinks or does something because he is stimulated. Whether he sits quietly, applauds, approves, or protests, a listener is in every case one who is responding.

Although we usually attribute the functions of speaker and listener to different people and observe their exchange of roles as statements and replies follow each other in rapid succession, yet we should also recognize that in a sense both functions are combined in each participant at every moment during which interaction goes on. A listener tends to go along with the speaker in a silent flow of action, primarily inner but sufficiently overt to communicate something back to a speaker. In other words, a listener is also inevitably something of a speaker, or at least a communicator, even as he listens. In like manner, a speaker is also constantly a listener. Though a speaker is seldom, if ever, able to observe himself as objectively as others can, his listening to himself is nonetheless a vital factor in the continuity and control of speech. Part of the total pattern of stimulation under which a speaker operates at a given moment comes from his own action at that and preceding moments. Interaction is a process not only of mutual exchange of roles, but also of mutual interdependence. As human beings we are members one of another, and the processes of speaking are of the essence of our humanity.

Forms and Uses of Speech

We should not conclude this introduction without noticing that there are many forms and uses of speech which are as variable as the situations in which we find ourselves in this social world. We converse, discuss, and address audiences; we read aloud, tell stories, and act, according to the demands of time and circumstance. In more specialized situations we telephone, interview, read poetry, persuade, and speak to microphone and camera in a broadcasting studio. Each of these arises in a different kind of situation, each meets a definite social need, each involves a distinctive pattern or interplay of forces in the setting. Each is significant in its own right and each involves problems requiring special study, as we shall see in Part IV.

Nevertheless, even casual observation of the many types of speech activity shows that they are fundamentally alike. All of them occur in situations which involve the same general kinds of forces—stimulating speaker, receptive listener, time and place, body of ideas both immediate and potential, and available symbolic processes.

All the forms of speech involve a similar pattern of interaction among these forces, centering in the mutual stimulation and response of speaker and listener. In all of the forms the same basic pattern of individual behavior occurs, i.e., every speaker and every listener in whatever situation use a distinctive, integrated action involving certain inner phases of attitude, thought, and emotion and certain outer phases of action, voice, and words. In every act of speech the coordination of bodily movement, audible phonetic patterns, and chosen word forms follows in some degree the accepted customs and standards of the social and cultural area. We are using the term *speech* to refer to these fundamental and common processes. All the various social activities such as conversation, discussion, public speaking, reading aloud, and acting are but adaptations of a fundamental pattern of behavior common to all.

In our study of the basic abilities essential to all of the forms of speech, we shall give more attention to attitudes and motives, to fact-finding, inference, and organization, and to the processes of imagination, emotional participation, and thought assimilation, than to the finer elements of skill in discussion, platform reading, or persuasion.

We shall also be more interested in the basic principles and conditions of bodily action, voice, articulation, and use of language, than in the finer nuances of gesture, vocal modulation, and rhetoric. We mean to cast no adverse reflections on the more advanced or specialized aspects and problems of speech. High degrees of skill in gesture, vocal expressiveness, and oral style have their place and importance in the study of speech. We shall give some attention to them here, but they are not our primary business in this beginning course. We shall deal with the most elemental forces common to all speaking situations and the most fundamental abilities required of participants.

From all these considerations we derive a list of the most important aspects of speech for our study:

1. Objective attitude, emotional adjustment and self-command
2. Concentrated listening
3. Thought which is purposeful, factual, logical, and enriched by imagination and emotional participation
4. Orderly sequence and organization of ideas
5. Poise and freedom in bodily action
6. Responsiveness and control of voice
7. Articulation and pronunciation which contribute to effectiveness in communication
8. Increased command of language

We cannot hope to master all of these processes in a beginning course, but we can hope to get some understanding of our speech problems and make a start toward improvement. These gains should provide a basis for further study and a lifetime of development and growth in this fundamental human activity we call speech.

EXERCISE

In a brief talk introduce one of your classmates to the entire group. At the discretion of your instructor the class may be seated in an informal circle or half-circle, and may engage in a preliminary survey of the kinds of information members should know about each other. If time is not allowed during the class period for conversation with the colleague you are to introduce, you will need to arrange to talk with him (or her) as part of your preparation outside class.

The purposes of such a simple first exercise as this are (1) to provide an easy "ice-breaker," (2) to develop the spirit of good fellowship and rapport so necessary to the common enterprise of speech improvement, and (3) to furnish information which each student will need in order to understand the classroom audience to which his later oral exercises will be presented. As an alternative the instructor may prefer to have each member introduce himself to the class.

SUPPLEMENTARY READINGS

Black, John W., and Wilbur E. Moore, *Speech: Code, Meaning and Communication*, McGraw-Hill, 1955, chap. I.

McBurney, James H., and Ernest J. Wrage, *The Art of Good Speech*, Prentice-Hall, 1953, chap. I and II.

Sarett, Lew, William Trufant Foster, and Alma Johnson Sarett, *Basic Principles of Speech*, 3rd ed., Houghton Mifflin, 1958, chap. I.

Weaver, Andrew T., and Ordean C. Ness, *Fundamentals and Forms of Speech*, Odyssey, 1957, chap. I and III.

2

YOU, THE SPEAKER

We have been thinking about speech and speakers in general. Now let us think a little more definitely about you as speaker. We shall first consider the way in which you learned to speak. This knowledge will help you observe the abilities which characterize an adequate speaker, discover your own problems, and develop an effective program of study and practice for speech improvement.

The Development of Your Speech

You began learning to speak in infancy because you were born in a human community, a speaking community. Your speech development was an inherent part of your growth as a person, a unique individual in this social world.

You learned to use sounds and movements meaningfully. At first you were simply active—kicking, squirming, babbling, and needing food, cleanliness and warmth. As you grew, your random behavior gradually became organized; it was directed toward the satisfaction of your basic needs. In the vague sensibility of your early infant life you discovered that certain cries, uttered spontaneously at first, brought certain kinds of services. As your nervous system matured, certain sounds became meaningful, i.e., you associated them with the people and objects that met your needs. The sounds were associated also with the satisfactions which people and things provided. Thus it became possible for you to anticipate your satisfactions by uttering the associated sounds or combinations of sounds, and the attentive adults around you took these as requests and moved at your service. As a result you learned to use certain sound patterns to get desired attention; you began to make noises purposefully.

The adults further helped to establish the significance of certain combinations of sounds by repeating those which were parts of the established language pattern of the community. The sounds which were not repeated or which had no relation to your needs fell gradually into disuse, and those which were repeated tended to become fixed in your growing repertoire of utterances. Your early noises and cries thus developed selectively and gradually into stable combinations of

16

sounds which stood for actions, things, and people in your expanding world. You developed a set of activities by which you could respond to things around you and demand their manipulation for your advantage even though you yourself could not manage them at all.

You became a grammarian.   Consider the importance of simple name words in this process. You saw your first smooth round object and heard someone respond by calling it "ball." In course of time you saw and handled other objects of the same kind and heard them also called "ball." Although they differed in size, texture, color, and weight, they all had the common property of roundness, and eventually the name *ball* came to stand for all objects having that property. You learned to speak the combination of sounds, *b-a-l-l*, as a way of responding to that thing.

Your utterance of the name accompanied other kinds of action such as looking at, pointing to, handling, throwing, or otherwise using the object. You learned the names for these various ways of dealing with the ball, so that you could try out different kinds of activity verbally without physically changing anything and without committing yourself to any particular overt action. By means of words, for example, you could accept the ball without actually moving it. You even learned to respond to the idea or mental image of a ball without having one actually present. Your noises thus developed into a form of behavior which you could substitute for more direct responses to the object. As your range of experience widened and your nervous system continued to mature you learned from adults the names for many objects and for various ways of dealing with them. Thus you were able to respond to a wider and wider range of things in your environment.

The use of names, moreover, helped you to discriminate the various characteristics or qualities of objects such as their size, shape, and color. The word *round,* for example, was a name by which you could single out the quality of roundness and recognize it as a distinct element of experience. Of course you no doubt perceived roundness as a purely visual experience before you knew its name. The word, however, did something to sharpen your awareness. The act of speaking fed additional elements of stimulation back into your perception so as to enhance its clarity. No other form of response can do this quite as well as spoken words. Bodily movements by themselves are seldom as discriminating. When you look at or point to an object, for example, no one can be sure which of its several features you mean to indicate. Probably anyone would assume that you are referring to the object as a whole. Without the name for roundness, it must have remained in some degree a vague and inchoate experience, poorly distinguished from your total perception of the ball.

Later in your growth you learned the grammatical classifications of these names as nouns and adjectives—the nouns standing for substantive elements of experience such as people and things, the adjectives representing their qualities. The significance of names also extended to other phases of your experience. In your early speech development you learned to recognize and name not only objects and their properties, but also movements and processes. You learned to discriminate and name their various characteristics such as speed, direction, range, and acceleration. Again you learned from adults around you the grammatical classifications of verbs and adverbs—the verbs expressing actions or processes, the adverbs representing their qualities. In short, you learned to use several kinds of words as responses which helped you to perceive your world with increasing discrimination.

You classified and organized your experiences.   While this was going on, you were also developing a sense of relationships. The units of your experience—i.e., objects and their properties, movements and their characteristics—were arranging themselves in relations of space and time, causation and sequence, coordination and subordination, comparison and contrast. Things, movements, and ideas gradually were recognized as *above* or *below, toward* or *away from, for* or *against, more* or *less, equal* or *subordinate, alike* or *different, because of* or *resulting in.* You could not have recognized such intangibles clearly without these very words to name them. The adult world into which you were growing again provided these names and classified them grammatically as prepositions and conjunctions and in some instances adjectives and adverbs—classes of words which stand for various kinds of relationships.

Your realization of such connections and contrasts enabled you to organize specific experiences into larger units and patterns. Recognition of similarities and differences, for example, enabled you to classify things and ideas into groups; and the recognition of equality and subordination among groups of things enabled you to arrange them in orderly systems. These classifications became generalized into abstract ideas. The idea of *ball*, for example, became absorbed into the larger class of toys, and this into the still larger class of gifts, and this perhaps into objects of sentiment, and so on into larger levels of generalization. As you grew and matured, you developed more and more of these generalized ideas or concepts. In each case the word became the tangible representative of the concept, which without a name would have remained in some degree vague and indefinite.

Your thought (i.e., the way in which you perceived, analyzed, organized, and understood your world) and your command of names (i.e., your spoken language) developed together. Some scholars regard language as the result of thought; others contend that thought is dictated by linguistic custom. Probably both points of view are in part correct; but the basic truth is that speech and thought are inseparable. For you as an individual this is true because they developed together as you grew from infancy to maturity.

Because words and the things for which they stand were so closely related in your experience, you learned to use words as a means of extending the range of your knowledge. Names helped you analyze into finely discriminated units the various objects, processes, and situations which you perceived. By means of names you learned to bring abstract ideas out of vagueness into clarity. By means of names you learned to deal with past and future as well as present. By means of names you were able to bring to definite form and focus a wide range of subtle elements of experience which otherwise probably would have been lost in the dim mazes of forgetfulness. Inevitably as your command of names grew and your world of experience became differentiated and organized, you learned to use words in relation to each other. You developed skill in predication; you became a user of sentences.

You became aware of yourself.   The crowning feature of this development was that you learned to recognize yourself, your own person, as a functioning unit distinct from the environment. You first recognized the various parts of your body as belonging to you; you learned their names. You, yourself, acquired a name. Then you learned to use personal pronouns as substitutes for your name and the names of other people. As your self-awareness grew, you also learned to recognize and name many of your inner mental and emotional processes. By means of word symbols you developed some capacity to project these inner processes into the future, and thus you were able to direct your behavior toward goals. You emerged as a distinctive person, aware of himself and able to act purposefully. You became a symbol-using creature, a thinker, a human being. If you had not grown up in a social world of spoken symbols which you learned to use, you would never have attained this status.

You became a thinker.   You not only learned to use word symbols socially as a means of interaction with other people; you learned also to use them privately to yourself. Under social pressure you learned the wisdom of inhibiting or delaying your verbal responses. You used the processes of utterance silently. The movements which produced overt gestures and sounds were abbreviated or reduced to subtle and implicit changes of muscular tension. Some of your movements became localized in the smaller and more delicate muscle systems such as those of face and throat. As a result of this reduction and localization of overt movements, your verbal activity tended to center more largely in your sensory and neurological processes. The subtle inner actions became substitutes for the overt symbolic utterances which you had previously substituted for direct responses; silent utterance became a substitute for a substitute.

As the behavior patterns became more localized and implicit and retreated farther into the inner recesses of your nervous system, you were learning to think in more and more specific and discriminating ways. We are not saying that your thinking occurred only in the form of implicit speech, but we are saying that implicit verbal response was one of the most important, if not *the* most important, medium in which your power as a thinker developed. As you became a symbol user and learned to internalize those symbols, so you became a thinker.

Summary. Speech as symbolic activity has been an indispensable factor in the development of your self-realization and your capacity to think:

1. The naming of units of experience (such as objects and their properties, movements or processes and their properties, ideas and concepts) helped to sharpen and clarify your awareness of them.
2. Because of this the use of names became a necessary part of the analysis and organization of your world of experience.
3. Words enabled you to respond effectively to "things" not actually present.
4. The use of words provided you with an indispensable means of developing generalized ideas or concepts, especially abstract ideas.
5. The use of names, especially proper names and personal pronouns, was an important factor in your development of self-awareness.
6. The silent internalizing of word symbols throughout all these phases of your development was an important factor in your growth as a thinker.

The Bases of Speech Improvement

All the directing influences which have shaped your life have also helped shape your speech. Much of this influence has been casual and indirect, although of course some part of it may have been planned. Your parents and some former teachers perhaps gave some thoughtful guidance to your speech development even though you may not have realized it. Possibly you participated in speech activities in high school or even took a course in speech. Some passing attention may have been given to your grammar or articulation in an English class. The greater likelihood, however, is that the speech aspect of your development was left to accident. Like Topsy, it just grew without conscious guidance and without much awareness on your part. By good fortune you may not have developed any specific bad habits. Nevertheless without systematic and planned guidance your speech growth probably fell short of the degree of maturation you might have achieved.

So now you come to make a more mature and purposeful approach to your speech improvement. You are not here merely to tinker

Speech is personal.

with your habits of articulation and gesture or to learn a few devices for successful persuasion. We do not mean to say that these matters are unimportant. Certainly you should study methods of persuasion. You may have some inadequate habits of articulation or gesture which need to be recognized and dealt with rigorously. These, however, are only partial aspects of our work. Any attempt to improve your speech is necessarily a process of trying to improve you as a human being—your attitudes and emotional control, your understanding of yourself and the world in which you live, your responsibility and integrity, your purposes. The symbols you use—your movements, sounds, and words—are the media in which these human attributes find their formulation and expression. If your communication is to be improved, your growth as a human being and your ability as a user of symbols should move forward together as one development. In fact they can move in no other way than together, for as we have seen, they are but two aspects of the process by which mind and personality develop and function. You improve as a communicator in proportion to your improvement as a person and a thinker.

Self-improvement, however, is no easy task. This seems to be more true of speech than of many other aspects of our lives. Human nature is so complex that we have difficulty seeing ourselves objectively and in perspective as others see us; yet such objectivity and perspective are essential for us as communicators. In that role we also need a wide range of knowledge and experience. No one can study speech in a vacuum. We must have ideas to talk about and an impelling purpose. Of course we should also practice the techniques of utterance (i.e., bodily action, voice, articulation, use of words), but there is no such thing as practicing delivery if you have nothing to deliver.

The improvement of our techniques of utterance requires some understanding of them, and in Part III we shall study action, voice, and language in detail. These visible and audible aspects of speech perform a two-sided function: (1) They serve as media in which our thought is created and formulated and (2) they reveal or communicate that thought. Each aspect of this double function depends on the other. If you refer back to our description of the way in which you first learned to speak, you will recall that one of the later phases of the process was the abbreviating and internalizing of utterance. Silent inner speech became a medium in which you created and formulated ideas. In simple though not quite accurate terms, most of our thinking is silent talking to ourselves. Without some formulation of ideas, of course, there would be none to communicate. When the formulation is made in silent or covert speech, the overt speech of communication follows directly from the inner formulation. Both the inner thought process and the outer communicative process are enhanced when they are carried on in the same medium (i.e., in the techniques of speech—action, vocal changes, uttered words). Speech then becomes one continuous process from inner creation to outward revelation.

This principle is especially significant for our study. Most of us are familiar with the communicative function of speech, but we tend to overlook its function as a medium for thinking. We have a deep-seated habit of regarding thought and its means of utterance as two processes—closely related, of course, but still two. In fact, the very language in which we must discuss this matter is dualistic. Yet the communicative process would be empty without thought and thought would be vague and fleeting were it not formulated in some tangible kind of action. Later we shall discuss these matters more at length.

The Process of Speech Improvement

Our task now is to set up a program for improving speech which recognizes its depth in our past growth and present life, and at the same time gives specific and immediate procedures by which our maturing as speakers can be advanced.

In view of what we have already said, the first and most basic requirement is that you should bring to bear upon your study of speech the widest possible range of knowledge. Review your past reading and experience for subjects to talk about, problems to discuss, and stimulating literature to read aloud. Examine your background of information, not only for topics on which to discourse, but also for materials to enrich that discourse. Be alert also in all your present studies for material you can use in speaking exercises. Speak about topics from your other courses; in that way you can put your knowledge to use. As surely as speech is the distinguishing characteristic of mankind, the speech classroom ought to be an integrating and enlivening factor in your entire education (see Introduction for the Student).

The broad scope of knowledge we have suggested should serve as a general framework within which we can outline a program of study and practice. The following steps are minimum essentials for your approach to speech improvement:

1. Discover the qualities or abilities which characterize an adequate speaker.
2. Analyze your own problems and abilities. To what extent are you an adequate speaker? What aspects of speech ability do you need to develop? Define the specific goals of your study of speech.
3. Develop a method of study and practice. Establish procedures for improving those phases of speech in which you are deficient.

THE ADEQUATE SPEAKER

Look around you on the college campus, in your home town, or in any other community. What qualities and abilities characterize the adequate speaker? We are not thinking of people who are heard most often or achieve a temporary notability, but of those whose influence is pervasive and substantial. Let us anticipate some of your observations:

The adequate speaker is *thoughtful and intellectually honest*. He knows what he is talking about, and he talks about real and important things. He locates his referents and verifies his facts. He never goes off half-cocked. He does not make unsupported statements nor far-fetched comparisons. He examines his assumptions and premises critically and reasons logically. His ideas march in orderly sequence. He is willing to accept facts and inferences even though they may contradict his desires and preconceived ideas. His is the kind of reserved and sober judgment in which you and all your neighbors can feel confidence.

The adequate speaker is *socially responsible*. He chooses his goals not alone for their immediate results, but also for their long-range values. He has a keen sense of ethics. He pauses to consider how his utterance will affect the group, the institution, the community in which or for which or to which he speaks; and he tries to forecast the influence for tomorrow or next year as well as for today. He is the kind of man who hopes to be present tomorrow or next year to face the outcomes of his words today.

The adequate speaker is *well balanced emotionally*. He has keen sensibilities and deep convictions, but they do not overmaster him. He is not highly excitable nor easily embarrassed. He is neither conceited nor self-depreciating, neither lethargic nor hurried, neither bombastic nor reticent. He is not self-conscious in the presence of the mighty nor condescending to the lowly, but meets all men with poise and a pleasant and tactful firmness. Whether his audience be a single friend or a vast crowd he maintains an objective view of himself, of the situation, and of his task as speaker.

The adequate speaker is *motivated and purposeful*. He is a dynamic force with a goal clearly formulated and critically evaluated. Whatever his purpose—whether to arouse interest, give information, entertain, stimulate belief, or influence action—it will be relevant to the situation and the people involved. The motives which activate such a speaker are constructive and broadly human, and his purposes well defined.

The adequate speaker is *aware of his listeners*. He tries to understand them and adapt his discourse to their needs and level of knowledge. He is as considerate of their convictions and prejudices as intellectual honesty will permit. Such a speaker looks at his listeners, is sensitive to their responses. In brief, he is keenly aware of his communicative relationship to other people and of the mutual processes of interaction.

Finally the adequate speaker is *skillful in use of symbolic processes*. His bodily action is well coordinated, his voice easily heard and thoughtfully modulated, his articulation distinct, his pronunciation understandable, his use of words exact and meaningful, and his style in general appropriate to the occasion and the listeners. The adequate speaker has disciplined and trained himself to use effectively the media in which his thought is formulated and expressed. In other words he is a master of speech techniques.

Obviously the fully adequate speaker is capable and thoroughly disciplined.

SELF-ANALYSIS

Now the important question is: How do you measure up to such an ideal standard? To what extent are you an adequate speaker? What must you do to become more adequate?

Thoughtful and continuing self-analysis is required to take stock of your capacities and resources as speaker. You cannot do this quickly nor can you depend on any one method of procedure. The speech class, however, is a good place to begin. Here you have the help of an instructor who understands speech and a group of fellow students with problems and purposes similar to yours. Working together in cooperative spirit is necessary for improvement of a social process like speech.

This principle of mutual help has a broad social foundation.

Everyone of us tends to evaluate and judge himself in terms of the responses of others. This is a many-sided process. Its more overt forms consist of comments and evaluations your friends and comrades make directly to you. They may, with varying degrees of insight and accuracy, tell you the "truth about yourself." They may argue for or against your cherished beliefs or openly campaign for or against you in the various groups where you meet. The reactions of your companions and neighbors may also be less direct. They may evaluate you in subtle, almost indefinable responses. Certain movements and sounds, such as a slight shift of stance, a turn of the head, the look in the eye, curl of the lip, change in muscular tension, modulation of vocal pitch or quality, and variation of tempo and rhythm, may reveal another person's evaluation of you. Even though we may be only vaguely aware of the process, we weigh and choose and integrate all the various and different responses others make to us, and out of them build a self-evaluation.

For this process of self-study many supplementary aids are avail-

Speech is thoughtful.

able. You should, for example, make recordings of your speech which you can listen to objectively. Some of your abilities, such as intelligence, social attitudes, emotional control, vocabulary level, mastery of grammar and usage, can be measured in quantitative terms by various written or manual tests. Some of these can be effectively administered only by trained psychologists; others you can administer to yourself. Many colleges give such tests to entering students; you probably have taken several of them and already know your scores.

Of course, some of these tests may not be entirely valid (i.e., they may not measure what they purport to measure) nor ideally reliable (i.e., they may not measure accurately). Some may not apply directly to speech. Nevertheless if thoughtfully interpreted, the results often give useful though indirect clues to the understanding of your speech abilities. This may be especially true of vocabulary and grammar tests, and in some degree also of measurements of intelligence and emotional control.

Test scores and impressions other people signal back to you are only the bases of your self-appraisal. The truly significant part is your own understanding and interpretation of these materials. Ultimately you must be your own critic. If understanding your problems is to have real value, it must be *your* knowledge. If motivation is effective, it must be *your own* drive. If practice is to bring results, it must be *your* effort. Your own insight and industry are the keys to your progress. You should, therefore, ask yourself many questions based on the concept of the adequate speaker we have been discussing. (See also discussion of attitudes in Chapter 5.) You should not expect to answer all these questions easily or quickly. Effective self-evaluation requires a high degree of objectivity and should be a continuous process. Study these standards and apply them to yourself repeatedly as our work progresses.

1. Am I a thoughtful and intellectually honest speaker? Do I take time to understand fully the situation, subject, and material about which I speak? Do I verify my information? Am I willing to accept facts and inferences which contradict my desires or preconceived notions? Am I open minded? Are my inferences logical? Do I think in orderly sequence?

2. Is my speaking socially responsible? Do I speak primarily for the good of the social group or for my own advantage—i.e., are my values altruistic or self-centered? Is my thought worth communicating? Are the form and manner of my utterance appropriate to the occasion? Am I willing to accept the results of my utterance? Will they be constructive or harmful? To the community? To others? To myself?

3. Do I maintain emotional balance in speaking situations? Do I maintain an objective view of myself as a communicator with a job to do? Do I maintain balance between self-confidence and fear, egotism and humility, dominance and reticence? Do I keep my poise and self-confidence in interviews, small group meetings, large assemblies, social hours, broadcasting studios, etc.? Do I meet disturbing or opposing factors in a situation calmly? Am I too easily excited? Or too phlegmatic?

4. Am I a purposeful speaker? Do I clearly determine my goal or intent each time I speak—i.e., do I know definitely what response I want from my listener? What motives impel me to seek this outcome? What are my reasons for speaking? Do I examine my purpose critically in relation to the situation? How will my utterance influence my listener or change the situation?

5. How well do I relate myself to my listeners? Have I tried to discover their degree of knowledge about and attitude toward my pur-

pose and material? Have I proper respect for their beliefs and view-points? Do I command their respect for my beliefs and viewpoints? Do I speak with a keen awareness of my relationship to them? Am I constantly sensitive to the interactions between us?

6. How competent am I in using the symbolic processes of speech to formulate and reveal my thought? Are my bodily movements well coordinated? Are my gestures meaningful? Is my voice adequately controlled and modulated? Are my words distinctly understood? Is my command of verbal language adequate?

If you are thoughtful about these questions, you will develop the outline in more detail and with greater discrimination as you study. These are tentative standards by which we can set up our goals and evaluate our progress. At the same time they are high ideals not easily attained. Like everyone else you have some limited potentials which you cannot surpass. Your self-analysis as well as your improvement in speech will be a gradual and, we hope, continuing development.

METHOD OF STUDY AND PRACTICE

Finally, with these preliminary standards and goals before us we come to the practical business of developing a method of study and practice. Three main levels of procedure are necessary:

Study to understand the nature of the speech process. Practice will be of little value if you do not know what you are trying to improve. See the speech act as a whole. Study its various elements but understand also their interrelation and unity. Think about the different ways of looking at the speech process. According to one's point of view, speech may be regarded as a form of behavior, a phenomenon of sound, a type of symbolism, a medium of thought, or a social process. Be alert for information about all these points of view.

You will find such knowledge scattered through many areas of learning, but especially in psychology, logic, linguistics, aesthetics, biology, anatomy, and the physics of sound. Examine all your studies, even those which may seem farthest removed, for insights which will guide your efforts toward speech improvement. Consider also the various forms and uses of speech and analyze their common elements as well as their distinctions. Some of these aspects of speech study we have already suggested. All of them we hope to develop in one way or another before our work is concluded.

Organize the over-all sequence of your study and practice. Establish the conditions which underlie speech action. Athletes know what we mean by "conditions which underlie action." They work, sometimes for years, to build up certain types of strength and coordination fundamental to performance in their particular sports, e.g., the stride of the sprinter or hurdler, the lay-up shot of the basketball player, or the blocking technique of the lineman. If thoroughly established, the basic strength and pattern of movement tend to function automatically even in the stress of competition. Perhaps the performing arts furnish even better examples. Musicians must develop their auditory concepts and the kinds of muscular coordination peculiar to their instruments before they can perform successfully. Painters need certain forms of visual imagery and skill in handling brush and palette before they produce masterpieces.

In all human functions conditions are basic to techniques; and although speech is primarily neither fine art nor sport, it partakes of the nature of both in requiring mental and physical foundations for its patterns of action. The habit of emotional control, for example, influences the nature of thinking and helps regulate all our gestures and voice modulations. Good posture and normal muscle tonus are conditions which underlie effective gesture. Clear and accurate auditory images of speech sounds are basic to distinct articulation. An established habit of breath control and the muscular strength required for achieving control with ease are necessary conditions for expressive voice modulations. Conditions such as emotional control, good posture, normal muscular tonus, accurate auditory impressions, and breath control are relatively stable and enduring habits or capacities for action which underlie the more specific and temporary processes of utterance.

Develop specific techniques. As fundamental conditions become stabilized you can concentrate more on specific skills. For example, as you gain better emotional poise in speaking situations, you can turn attention more effectively to problems of phrasing and orderly sequence of ideas. As your body acquires improved balance and freedom, you may profit by some study of gesture. As your breath control becomes stronger, you will have a more adequate foundation for developing expressive vocal changes. As your ear learns to recognize certain sounds and modulations more clearly, you can utilize drills on articulation and vocal variety with less danger of developing artificiality.

Technique, in speech as in any human function, is not necessarily superficial or mechanical. It acquires such a character only when separated from its mental and organic foundations. When technique proceeds from basic conditions, it fulfills its true function of formulating and communicating a speaker's meaning. (This principle is developed especially in Part III on the visible and audible aspects of speech.)

Adapt your techniques to the various forms of discourse. Although for beginning study we shall concentrate on those conditions and techniques which are basic to all speech, adaptations of basic techniques for the special requirements of the various forms of speaking, e.g., conversation, group discussion, public speaking, oral reading, acting, may well begin in your work here. Their full emphasis and development, however, are the primary business of more advanced courses.

Develop specific methods of practice. Of course practice in

itself is no guarantee of progress. If it were, you would now be an effective speaker, for you have had twenty years, more or less, of speech exercise. Unguided practice is as likely to develop bad habits as good habits. We should, therefore, look for some specific principles which we can use in developing the basic conditions and techniques we have been discussing.

We shall use three principal kinds of exercises.

Psychological: Exercises that direct your effort to various phases of thinking and emotional control.

Technical: Drills on gesture, voice, and articulation.

Communicative: Various speaking performances in class, such as discussions, talks, and oral reading with your fellow students.

These three kinds of exercises are not mutually exclusive. They support and even tend to merge into each other. Every bit of your practice, for example, should be in part psychological; it should be motivated by thought. Every exercise, even routine drill, should involve some hint of communicative purpose; and of course your practice of communication before the class should use adequate techniques of action, voice, and language.

All exercises have certain basic principles in common. If you are to succeed in replacing old and inadequate speech habits with new and improved habits, your practice should have at least three characteristics: It should be purposeful, systematic, and realistic.

Practice should be purposeful. Know what you are trying to achieve. Four aspects of practice are essential.

1. Understanding of goal. Effort to be purposeful must be based on specific knowledge of the result desired. If you undertake to practice vocal exercises, for example, decide in advance whether your main objective is to improve quality or power or pitch variety. If you read aloud to your classmates, you should not only know the ideas you are to communicate to them, but also whether your own learning experience is to be concentrated on stimulation of imagination, analysis and phrasing of thought, distinctness of utterance, or some other goal. If you are to engage in round-table discussion, you should know before you begin whether your main purpose is to improve your attitudes, develop the functions of leadership, or master the steps in problem solving.

2. Deliberate effort. Purpose implies drive toward the expected result. Anticipate so vividly the satisfaction of achieving your goal that you will be impelled to your practice with enthusiasm. Set yourself to work.

3. Evaluation of results. Purposeful practice requires that you know whether your work is leading toward the intended goal. This im-

plies ability to take a role as observer of your own performance. Some-times your observation may be nearly simultaneous with the action you are doing; but it is actually retrospective, i.e., a looking back and evaluating what you have just done. Such retrospection may operate from moment to moment, from one practice period to the next, from day to day, or over longer periods of time. Some types of practice, such as talks or readings before the class or perhaps exercises in tone production, can be recorded and listened to. In any case evaluation as a phase of purposeful practice is a form of self-feedback which re-quires a high degree of objectivity. Earlier in this chapter we mentioned self-diagnosis and the need for insight into the nature of your prob-lems. What we now propose is a continuation of the same principle: As you practice, observe which of your responses lead most effectively toward your goal.

4. Reinforcement.   Purposeful practice involves repetition of actions which point toward improvement. Every effective response in your practice should become a stimulus for its own repetition. Acts which are repeated tend to establish stable patterns of nerve control and thus to become permanent. You must eliminate from your practice all those responses which are not part of the desired or ideal speech behavior. You will not attain perfection quickly, if indeed at all; but you can improve by selecting the elements of good speech and making them habitual.

Practice should be systematic.   This requires three procedures:

1. Alternation of work and rest.   Psychological experiment has shown that spaced practice is more effective than continuous practice. Whether the activity is drill on technical exercises or rehearsal before performance, it should be continued long enough to pass through a warm-up phase and reach maximum efficiency, but not so long as to bring on excessive fatigue. Rest periods should occur often enough to minimize fatigue and boredom. The exact timing will vary for dif-ferent individuals and for different kinds of exercises; each one of us needs to work out his own most useful schedule. Probably few of us can practice with maximum efficiency for more than half an hour at a time, or find more than three or four such periods in the busy schedule of a day.

2. Regularity.   Habits of thought and action are not built successfully by spasmodic effort. Speaking opportunities in class should have an approximate regular frequency, although differences in types of assignments require some flexibility. For your own individual drill or rehearsal outside of class, set up two or three definite periods each day. Regularity also implies that during each practice period you should be free to work without interruption and with a minimum of distraction. Interferences diminish the return on your investment of time and energy.

3. Progressive development.   Systematic practice should begin with the simplest elements and build gradually toward the more complex and difficult. For example, if you are working on a problem in articulation, you may need to begin with the single defective consonant before you practice its various combinations with other sounds and ultimately master it in words, phrases, and sentences. If you are struggling with language problems, you may need to enlarge your vocabulary before you can make sentences more precise or enrich the vividness of your style.

Begin with basic motivating and causal elements and then take up processes based on these causal elements or resulting from them. Your practice of articulation, for example, may need to begin with auditory training to establish clear and accurate concepts of speech sounds before you practice the tongue and lip movements which produce those sounds. If you are preparing a talk, determine your purpose before you search for supporting material or try to organize a thought sequence. If you are engaging in problem-solving discussion, locate and define the difficulty before you attempt to evaluate possible solutions. Whatever kind of discourse you are using for practice, analysis and assimilation of thought sequence should precede overt rehearsal.

The rehearsal itself should be progressive too. If you are scheduled for an extemporaneous talk, begin oral practice after plan and outline are complete and four or five days before you are to speak. Practice at first with the detailed outline before you, and space the rehearsals in two or three short periods each day, gradually reducing your dependence on notes until at your last practice (perhaps the evening before you are to speak) you can use your notes as a guide but be free enough of them to speak directly to listeners. Such procedure helps to fix the sequence of material thoroughly in mind. If your assignment is to read aloud from text, thorough analysis of material should be followed by oral practice sessions spaced so that you will gradually assimilate thought without necessarily attempting to memorize words. Then you can be free enough of book or paper to speak directly to your listeners even while you are using the page as a stimulus and guide to your utterance of the author's lines.

Practice should be realistic.   Practice sessions should be as much like real life speaking situations as possible. Because complete similarity is seldom possible, you will need to use your imagination. Visualize your listener or audience; anticipate his or their relation to you. Are you to be sitting together at a fireside or talking face to face in an office? Is your audience to be seated informally around a conference table, or facing you in an auditorium? How large is the group likely to be? What may be their attitudes toward you? Toward your theme and purpose? What degree of reserve or freedom in voice and action will be appropriate? What kinds of material? How much time will you have? Who else will be speaking, and will he or they precede or follow you?

Such a list of questions, of course, could be expanded indefinitely. The main point is to try to analyze and anticipate the situations in which you speak, and determine thought, action, and word accordingly. Amount of time available is often of special importance; speakers who do not time themselves accurately are in danger of failing to achieve their purposes. This is as true of a conversationalist, sales interviewer, or lecturer as it is of a radio broadcaster. Whatever form of practice you use, whether for general improvement or in preparation for a specific occasion, speak with the greatest possible sense of reality. If you are to sit or stand when you speak, practice in that same posture. Even routine vocal exercises should be done as if to communicate to an imagined listener (see Chapter 14). Let your entire manner of action, voice, and language be adapted to the intended situation.

This, of course, cannot be applied literally to those conditioning exercises which use actions not part of the speech process but preliminary to it. Musicians, for example, practice scales and take exercises to strengthen the fingers even though such activities are no part of musical performance but preliminary to it. See Part III for further discussion of this principle as applied to speech.

Summary

Your speech has developed as an inherent part of your social and intellectual growth. Its visible and audible aspects are symbols by which we name the elements of experience and thus are able to respond to and deal with the world around us.

Speech improvement, therefore, is as broad and deep as the whole process of self-development. For so large a task a broad background of knowledge and experience should be brought to focus in a definite program of study and practice. For our preliminary thinking three major steps have been suggested: (1) Discover the characteristics of an adequate speaker. (2) Analyze your own adequacy as a speaker. (3) Outline a method of study and practice which you can follow throughout the course and in all your later speaking experience.

EXERCISES

1. Prepare a written summary of your past speech experiences to hand to your instructor in whatever form and at such time as he directs. As a basis for your statement review the following questions:

What is your earliest recollection of speaking or being spoken to by anyone? Why was the experience memorable? Was it pleasant or unpleasant?

Were any of your early speech experiences embarrassing or in any way unpleasant or painful?

Was conversation in your childhood home frequent or limited? Were you encouraged to talk or told to keep silent in the presence of adults?

What were your early school speech activities, if any? Were you called on to recite or to speak before the class? Do you recall whether discussion was used in any of your classes? If so, did you participate much or little?

What was the first public speech experience you can remember? Was it pleasant or unpleasant? Did you feel at the time that you were a success or a failure? Can you give reasons for that judgment?

During your elementary and high school years did you participate in speech activities such as debating, play-acting, declamation?

Did you take a speech course in high school? What was the nature of the course? What phase or phases of speech study did it include? What kinds of speaking did you do in class? Did you enjoy the course? Was it helpful to you? Why or why not?

Have you had any college speech courses prior to this one? If so, what were they? Did you enjoy them? Were they helpful?

What speaking experiences, if any, have you had in social or community life outside of school? Describe them briefly. Were they in public speaking, debating, discussion, play-acting, or some other form of speech?

Why are you taking this course? What do you expect to gain from it (besides the credit toward graduation)? What relationship do you expect it to have to your major study, to your personal development, and to your possible future vocation?

2. With the class divided into small, informal "buzz" groups of five or six members each, join in a round-table consideration of the concept, "The Adequate Speaker." Think with the colleagues in your group to analyze and clarify the detailed characteristics and abilities which enable an individual to meet the various speaking situations of daily life adequately. Each group should choose that one ability which they consider most important. Your instructor may ask the groups to select spokesmen to report their thinking back to the entire class, and may wish to organize these reporters in a panel. Such a panel may be used to introduce a general class forum summarizing the learnings of Chapters 1 and 2.

3

YOU, THE LISTENER

If speech is interaction between people, as we have said, then listening is as important as utterance in the total process.

Every stage in the process of speech development involves listening or its elementary basis, hearing (see Chapter 2). As an infant you heard your own random utterances and this feedback restimulated you to further utterance. You heard adults repeat those sound patterns of yours which were parts of the established language, and so they became stable parts of your repertoire of sounds. You heard names for objects and movements, and you thus learned to analyze and name their characteristics and relationships. As you learned to direct your hearing purposefully, it became an integral part of your speech development.

As a result, listening to others and yourself is now an integral part of your every act of speech. Your perception of your own speech is a necessary part of the feedback by which you maintain its continuity and control. This is also essential to your thinking. "The speaker and listener within the same skin engage in activities which are traditionally described as 'thinking.' "[1]

Definition of Listening

A speaker provides stimulation; a listener responds. Meaningful interpretation by a listener usually goes on quietly within the inner thought life, although it may and often does involve overt behavior such as looking at a speaker, sitting or standing still, refusing to turn toward some distracting event, and changing facial expression or posture in ways which indicate comprehension. In any event, whether the response be overt or covert, *listening is interpretation of the meaning of symbols.*

The ear serves a series of functions of increasing refinement. Most of us can *hear*, and the acuity of hearing can be measured objectively by an audiometer. When we direct this auditory sensitivity purposively to perceive certain definite sounds, we *listen*. This distinction between hearing and listening may perhaps be sharpened by

[1] B. F. Skinner, *Verbal Behavior*, Appleton-Century-Crofts, 1957, p. 11.

recalling that we often hear without listening or listen without hearing. When we use our listening capacity for the purpose of recognizing, understanding, and interpreting spoken language, we are using an activity more complex and specialized than simply listening to recognize sounds in the world around us. But here our names are inadequate to suggest the distinction. We use the word *listen* for the process of recognizing sounds in general and also for the recognizing and interpreting of spoken language. We hear, we listen, we_____. What discriminating word, comparable to the word *read*, do we have to fill this blank?

In answer to this question a new term has been suggested— *to aud*, i.e., to perceive and interpret spoken language, just as to *read* is to comprehend written language. The syllable is the root of the Latin word *audire*—to hear, which is the ancestor of our series of English words, *auditor, audition, auditorium, audiometer*, etc. *To aud* distinguishes a higher linguistic use of listening, just as *to read* distinguishes a higher linguistic use of looking. This distinction between auding and ordinary listening is sharpened by the fact that some aphasics recognize spoken words as words without comprehending their meaning. One of the originators of the term has said that a person whose hearing is normal, who listens attentively, who can recognize and interpret the significance of nonlanguage sounds, and whose general mental ability is relatively unimpaired, but who is unable to comprehend any spoken language, illustrates the difference between listening and auding. For us as students of speech *listening is interpretation of the meaning of the symbols of speech*. The attachment of meaning to words is the primary way of responding to speech.

The listener's behavior, both inner and outer, tends to follow the pattern of the speaker's behavior. Have you ever noticed, when listening to a raucous voice, that your throat ached because you were repeating the muscle tensions of the speaker? Listening is in part an overt action, but the subtle processes of internalized and abbreviated behavior are more significant in listening than is outward behavior. Within the listener are incomplete and silent patterns of nerve impulses and incipient muscle tensions of the speech-producing organs which repeat the essential pattern of the speaker's action. In so far as a listener genuinely understands a speaker's message, he is recreating similar attitudes and thought processes and is doing so in patterns of bodily, vocal, and verbal activity fundamentally like those of the speaker. We do not mean to imply that listeners merely imitate speakers nor that they must always agree. Every listener has full liberty to challenge, reject, or bluntly oppose any part of the messages he receives. However, the primary process by which he receives and understands those messages is a subtle inner repetition of the speaker's symbolic action.

The elements of listening, therefore, are in general the same as those of speaking. As we have seen, they consist of attitudes, thought processes, bodily actions, sounds and words, integrated in a single pattern. Speaker and listener, each in his own way, are engaged in a common kind of behavior. This is the basis of their mutual understanding. This is the foundation of interaction.

The Purposes of Listening

We listen to speech for three primary reasons.

First, we listen to be stimulated, i.e., to share the experiences of others, to enjoy, to appreciate, to be inspired. As an expression of simple interest in other people, we greet our friends and inquire about their health. At a slightly higher level this interest in others operates as a willingness to listen sympathetically to their frustrations and problems. At a more complex level this need for stimulation functions as a desire for entertainment; we need to be diverted and amused. At the highest level of stimulation we listen to be inspired, to be carried beyond our everyday selves into a world of creative imagination, noble sentiments, and ideals. This is the primary reason for much of the listening we do in church, theatre, and lecture hall.

Second, we listen to evaluate, weigh, and consider ideas. At this level decision is the typical outcome. We respond to argument and persuasion and so formulate beliefs and decide on courses of action. This probably is the type of listening used most deliberately. We become self-appointed critics. The great danger of this kind of listening is judging before we have fully understood an issue. Take time to let your understanding of a speaker's ideas mature; then apply standards of truth and logic. In addition to evaluating the worth of a speaker's ideas, we may also judge the way in which they are formulated and expressed, i.e., the speaker's effectiveness in action, voice, articulation, and linguistic usage. The two kinds of evaluation, of course, are not separate: Thought becomes definite only as it finds tangible form in some technique or medium of expression; and techniques which do not express thought are but empty and insignificant forms.

Finally, the most important kind of listening, that which underlies both the others, is listening which aims to understand. To understand, we should see a speaker's thought through his eyes, follow his inferences, sense the feeling tone of his attitudes, recreate something of his experience. Until we have tried to understand in this deep sense of recreating a speaker's mental processes, we are not really qualified to evaluate what he says to us. Psychologists, labor mediators, and men in business have pointed out repeatedly that the greatest single barrier to effective communication is the tendency we all have to judge an idea or proposal or point of view before we really understand what it means.

It has been demonstrated in many areas of life that when disputants or people of different cultures really understand each other and are able to see an issue or problem from each other's points of view, barriers tend to fade away and arguments can be resolved.

Potential Effectiveness of Listening

Numerous studies have shown that listening far outranks other language processes (speaking, writing, reading) in daily use. As long ago as 1926 a committee of the National Council of Teachers of English reported that oral language, which of course necessarily involves listening, was used much more in daily life than written language. The report was verified and made more explicit in 1929 by Paul Rankin, research director for the Detroit public schools, who asked a group of 21 adults to keep careful record of their communicative activities during a period of 60 days. Analysis of the results showed that whereas writing occupied an average of 11 percent and reading 15 percent of total waking time, talking occupied 31.9 percent and listening 42.1 percent of the time.

More recent studies tend to confirm these findings. Dr. Harry Goldstein pointed out that a very large percentage of our learning activity depends on our listening, and the research of Charles Goetzinger and Milton Valentine confirms estimates that 80 percent of our communication is oral. This means, of course, that listening goes on during 80 percent of our total communicative time as compared with 20 percent devoted to writing and reading.

Our educational system has emphasized the undoubted values of reading and writing to such an extent that the values of listening as a medium of instruction have been underrated. The elements of visual appeal and the movements of the eye have been studied extensively. The superlative value of the ear as a receiving instrument has been overlooked. As Nichols and Lewis point out, the sensitivity of the ear at any given time covers a wider range of space than the eye, requires a smaller amount of energy in the stimulus, responds with a faster reaction time, and appears to have greater capacity for continuous use than the eye. With such a foundation of sensitivity on which to build, our listening could be a highly effective means of perception and learning.

Nevertheless, we are notoriously inefficient in this basic language process. One investigator found that college students whom he tested immediately after 10-minute classroom lectures recalled only little more than half of what they heard, and that after 2 weeks they recalled only 25 percent of the information given. Daily experience in the classroom seems to give informal confirmation to such findings. How often do we gather wool, or perhaps goat feathers, while the lecture or discussion goes on! How much of what we hear in all our daily communication passes "unlistened."

These observations and findings present a serious challenge. If we are only half or less than half efficient in a process which is half or more than half our total communication, what happens to our learning? And to our human relationships, our minds, and our personalities? What might we become if our listening could be made more effective? For us as students of speech there is even a more pointed question: With inefficient listening what happens to the feedback on which our critical self-awareness and hence our improvement so largely depend?

We do not mean to overlook the problems which often attend our listening. We may be afflicted with a hearing loss, or on a given occasion be tired. Distractions of noise, poorly controlled temperature, uncomfortable seating, extraneous events may interfere. The speaking may be poorly projected or indistinct. Unfamiliar words may be used. Speaking, unlike reading, is usually a one-time process. Unless recordings are made, we seldom have opportunity to relisten in the same sense that we can reread. These matters are not excuses to be offered, but difficulties to be overcome. They emphasize our need for a careful study of the means of improving our listening efficiency.

For you the important question is, how good a listener am I? How much more effectively could I learn if all my listening, especially in the classroom, were more efficient? Of course none of us hopes to remember all we hear, and we would not want to. We need to remember important and useful knowledge and avoid cluttering our minds with random and incidental information. The facts indicate, however, that most of us listen far below our highest potential level.

The Improvement of Listening

Many of us have assumed, more or less casually, that effective listening is merely a matter of paying attention, and that any intelligent person with normal hearing needs only a little effort of will to become a good listener. Recent research shows, however, that something more is required; the most intelligent people are not always the best listeners. Some people have thought that even if direct training in listening is necessary, improvement of reading ability will carry over to its oral counterpart. It does not always follow, however, that good silent readers are good listeners. Reading and listening involve some of the same factors of ability, but training in one is not a substitute for training in the other. Although our knowledge of these matters is still incomplete, there is reasonably clear evidence that listening ability is a distinct function which needs some degree of direct instruction for best improvement.

As with all other phases of the speech process, listening is conditioned by the entire range of our personal qualities and abilities. The more effective listeners, as we might expect, tend to be those with large vocabularies and understanding of correct English usage. The good listener knows how language is put together; he has high verbal aptitude. Certain factors of intelligence are also fundamental. Among these are ability to make logical inferences; skill in differentiating between main and subordinate or supporting ideas, and between both of these and specific facts; and facility in discovering and reconstructing a speaker's plan of organization (see Chapters 6–9).

Underlying these verbal and logical skills are important attitudes and motivations. The good listener has a wide range of interests, or at least an interest in the subject discussed. If he does not have such an attitude, he knows how to bring the subject into relation to interests already established. The good listener knows how to avoid emotional blocks and the closed mind. He knows that either strong convictions on a subject or vacillating indecision will tend to interfere with effective listening. He gets himself set for listening and builds up a mental attitude anticipating the speaker's message. He is cooperative, curious, and open-minded. He knows how to concentrate, to generalize, to discriminate, to structure thought, and to relate it to his own past experience.

You, the listener, can take specific measures to sharpen the keenness of your perception of speech. Put the following methods into everyday use:

Establish the best possible conditions for listening. Observe the situation. Are such factors as ventilation, temperature, noise levels, acoustics, proximity of speaker, and seating arrangements conducive to good listening? If not, see what can be done to correct them. If they cannot be improved, make the best adjustment possible and determine to overcome the limitations. In the less formal, impromptu kinds of speaking situations you may have no opportunity to adjust the physical conditions.

Get set to listen. As far as possible be rested and alert, especially if the communication you are to receive is important. Develop an attitude of anticipation. Determine your reason for listening; is it primarily to be stimulated, to gain information, or to evaluate? Ask yourself what you expect to get from the speaker. Clear purpose has a favorable effect on listening. If the subject is known in advance, you may examine your previous knowledge of it. Try to anticipate the speaker's probable message, so that as you listen you can compare your forecast with the actuality.

Accept responsibility for the act of communication. Remember that you are one part of a two-way, or possibly even multiway, cycle of interaction. Transmission is worthless if receivers are not working effectively. Your participation should be active. Even though you sit at ease and appear relaxed, the concentration of your inner forces of response requires energy. Work at the job.

Give the speaker your complete attention. Let him know that you are an active participant by attending to him from the moment he appears. See that your posture is alert and orientated toward him. Occasionally a principal distraction may be some mannerism or peculiarity of the speaker himself. If so, refuse to be disturbed; overlook the personal element and let your entire orientation be toward the speaker's thought.

Search for the speaker's purpose and main idea. Of course you may have trouble finding a central purpose if your speaker is the kind of person who drifts at random from point to point or does not state his goal clearly. Nevertheless the effort to find his purpose is one of the best ways to analyze and understand his thought and maintain an open, exploratory mental attitude. It will help you withhold evaluation, at least until after you know what the speaker is trying to accomplish, and see his goal within his frame of reference. If you do not discover a statement of theme or purpose in his first remarks, see whether you can find any continuity in the succeeding flow of thought or in the concluding remarks. Wherever or whenever you find the indication of purpose, pin it down in a single concise statement which you formulate for yourself.

Use a speaker's pauses to fix his ideas in mind. In his intervals of silence try to catch up with him and pin down his ideas. Most of us think several times faster than anyone can speak. We are tempted to go on little side trips thinking about other matters, and so we often miss parts of a speaker's thoughts. One remedy is to make these excursions relevant to his theme. Repeat each successive idea silently to yourself. Search your own experience for facts or ideas which will amplify or clarify his meaning. Summarize, weigh the evidence, look for implications, anticipate. See whether you can interpret the trend of thinking so as to forecast the next idea or the conclusion.

Build the structure of a speaker's thought as you listen. Distinguish between purpose, central idea, and main supporting ideas. Look for their interrelationships. Does the central idea directly contribute to the attainment of the speaker's purpose? If he talks at length, there may be a series of main ideas that contribute equally to his purpose. Does the sequence of ideas unfold in an orderly manner? Examine also the relationship of subordinate ideas. Notice the transitions. Words such as *first, second, now again, furthermore* are principal signposts of progression from one idea to another. Bodily movements and voice modulations may reinforce or even provide major clues to the pattern of thought.

Do not try to remember everything, but build the framework

To listen is to think.

of important ideas as you listen. Notice especially a speaker's summaries; if he does not use them, try to make your own for each major thought sequence. When discourse is informal and random, you may not be able to find and reconstruct its pattern of thought, but the attempt will add to the effectiveness of your listening. Thought implies organization; if a speaker does not provide it, do your best to make up for his deficiency.

Control emotions which might distract your attention. Forget your worries. Perhaps your girl is angry with you, but you cannot help that now. Better concentrate on the listening of this moment. The information you gain might even be useful in winning her again. When you have a job of listening to do, nothing is to be gained by mulling over irrelevant problems. Furthermore be on guard against your prejudices, especially when you are listening to controversial ideas. All of us have some special sensitivities toward which a speaker's references may act like springs to snap shut the doors of the mind. Try to face your prejudices frankly. If possible, rationalize them by free discussion with your friends. Recognize and adjust to emotionally charged words. Concentrate on their objective matter-of-fact meanings instead of their emotional connotations.

The most important aspect of your emotional control is delaying evaluation of your neighbor's ideas until you understand them fully. Remember that a good listener tries to place himself within the other fellow's frame of reference and see things from his point of view. If you become excited and start planning a reply before you have heard the man out, you may miss an essential part of his thought. Courage and patience are required since real comprehension of a viewpoint you oppose, or think you oppose, might possibly change some of your most cherished prejudices.

Use the principle of follow-up. After a speaker has finished, repeat and summarize his thought in discussion with friends or to yourself. Restate the central theme or purpose, its outline, the inter-relation of the various ideas. Recall the most important supporting facts and illustrations. Look up unfamiliar words. Put the ideas to use in conversation, in searching for solutions, or in making decisions about some of your problems. If you find no use for the material, write the listening off as idle pastime and forget it. If the ideas are important and useful, you may want to make notes of them for future reference.

Note-taking. Note-taking is often an important aid to listening for information especially when you may not have opportunity to hear it again. No single method of taking notes is necessarily better than any other. Nevertheless certain suggestions may be useful:

1. Write down only the important ideas. This usually will call up essential details if systematic review of your notes is not postponed too long after they are taken. Excessive writing may interfere with your listening and in some informal situations might inhibit your speaker or even be considered discourteous.

2. Develop different systems of note-taking for different occasions, types of material, and speakers. Outlining shows thought structure (see Chapter 8) and should be used often. It may be too cumbersome or even impossible if a speaker's material is not well organized. A brief summary or a discursive series of items may sometimes be more useful.

3. Use abbreviations and short cuts. Minor words such as articles and conjunctions may sometimes be omitted. Key words which occur often may need to be written out in full only once and then abbreviated. Incomplete words and phrases can be filled in later if necessary. The importance of various terms and ideas may be indicated by a system of supplementary devices such as underlining, starring, capitalizing. Cross-relationships may be shown by arrows. Subordinate ideas should be indented under main ideas.

The Listener as Critic

Just as surely as speech is a process of interaction, so surely is a speech class a cooperative venture. Your progress will depend in part on the sympathetic understanding of your colleagues. When others are speaking, therefore, you have an obligation to participate not only as listener but also as friendly critic. You and your classmates may not be good critics at first. Nevertheless your critical function is indispensable and deserves careful study.

Criticism in the classroom has at least three areas of significance: First, your comments can help your fellow students create accurate images of themselves as speakers. Second, their comments can help you achieve a realistic image of yourself. Third, the practice of evaluating others should improve your understanding of the communicative process and thus help make you more objective about the qualities of your own utterance. In criticizing others you can build up a systematic set of standards and learn to apply them to yourself more effectively.

If we are to be effective as critics, we should understand the nature of criticism. *Criticism is comparison of actual achievement with an ideal.* It is not fault finding or voicing of the critic's dislikes or prejudices. Neither does it consist entirely of praise or flattery. True criticism is evaluation. It aims to show a speaker the faithful image of himself and to compare it with the ideal he might attain. In setting up standards of judgment, we must consider the sources from which they are derived.

SOURCES OF JUDGMENT

Human nature. The first source of critical judgment is the critic's understanding of the speaker. What are his problems and his ideals? From what background has he come? Has it been frustrating or encouraging? What are his present greatest needs? What is he trying to achieve? Is it what he should be striving for? What is his image of himself as speaker? How true to reality is the self-image? In what ways should it be changed? To what extent can it be changed; in other words what are the speaker's potentials? Such questions are not easy to answer. They involve careful investigation and insight. Nevertheless they must be faced if criticism is to be adequate.

Knowledge. The fully adequate critic understands speech behavior in all its aspects. He has analyzed the attitudes which activate it and the thought processes which are its substance. He knows the symbolic processes which are its media and how they are formed. His understanding of speech is enhanced by knowledge of such related areas as linguistics, psychology, physiology, and logic.

Aesthetics. The third source of critical judgment is the taste of the critic. This is not primarily a matter of what he happens to like or dislike, but a test of his ability to distinguish between artificial, pretentious effort and thoughtful creative effort. Technical perfection, i.e., well-coordinated action, distinct articulation, and correct language, is not always indicative of creative effort and socially useful thought. The good critic knows how to distinguish between technique for communication and technique for display. He can identify the fourflusher, the dilettante, and the pretender, and in contrast can recognize the sincere thinker even though he be imperfect.

Social and ethical values. What response did the speaker get from his listeners? Was it the response he desired? Was it appropriate to the situation? Was it constructive and socially useful? Was it honest? These questions are among our most important sources of judgment. However, criticism in terms of immediate results should be applied with caution because the effects of any given utterance may not appear at once. The influence of a quiet word in conversation or an opinion spoken casually in group may not appear in the life of individual or community until long after utterance. The reading of a piece of literature or a dramatic characterization may re-echo for years in the memories of all who heard it, and may shape conduct in ways which could not have been foretold. The thoughtful critic's judgments will be based on cautious estimates of value well tempered by time.

STANDARDS OF JUDGMENT

Our primary task is to help fellow students see themselves objectively as speakers and so improve their speaking. Each person is a unique individual with his own special needs and problems. The discerning critic will try to discover these and shape his standards and methods of evaluation to meet personal needs. At the same time the discerning critic knows that certain principles are fundamental for all personalities and problems. These considerations suggest some basic methods of procedure for all criticism:

1. Criticism should be realistic. It should *begin* with the speaker as he is in actual performance, not with some ideal hope of what he might be. The vision of his potential achievement and of the ideal toward which he should work is important, but it should come after his limitations and needs have been frankly acknowledged.

2. Criticism should be definite and to the point. It should deal explicitly with specific qualities of a given speech performance. The qualities of the act rather than the person should be the focus of attention. The student should derive from criticism a clear and definite picture of himself as speaker.

3. Criticism should be balanced. This implies a mingling of intensity and reserve. Balance requires a combination of frankness and tact. We do a speaker no service if we are less than honest with him, but too blunt a comment may close the door of receptivity. Even the most thick-skinned person has some sensitivity about his efforts. The well-balanced critic, therefore, looks for strength as well as weakness. He knows there is some excellence in everyone, and seeks to make virtues as evident as faults. Discussion among several honest critics may help avoid the sting of adverse comment and at the same time yield a

breadth and depth of judgment not otherwise possible. This may be especially true if the speaker himself is a participant.

4. Criticism should be constructive. Constructive criticism requires that the critic, after he has gained an understanding of a speaker's problems, (a) think in terms of that speaker's needs rather than faults, (b) analyze the causes of his difficulties, (c) suggest specific methods of removing the causes and meeting the needs, (d) seek insight into the speaker's potentialities, and (e) try to motivate and inspire him to achieve his highest potential.

Criteria for Evaluation of Speech

We should try to implement the broad principles we have discussed by formulating some definite standards. The following questions, based on the concept of the adequate speaker in Chapter 2, are designed to serve as a guide for your first assignments in evaluative listening.

The listener's preliminary self-examination: Have I established the best possible conditions for effective listening? Am I approaching my task as a responsible participant in the communicative process? Am I ready to give the speaker my undivided attention—with open-minded objectivity and emotional balance and willingness to postpone evaluation until I am sure I understand his message?

Attitudes and motives: Is the speaker objective toward himself? Is he overconfident or bashful? Does he maintain a communicative attitude toward his listeners? Is he open-minded or prejudiced? Does he rationalize? Does he declare his motives? Do you discover any hidden motives? Does the speaker reveal a contagious interest in and enthusiasm for his subject? Is his emotional participation vital and well controlled?

Thought processes: Are the ideas significant? If the speaker is a student, are his subject and material worthy of college or university effort? Does the speaker reveal a sense of purpose? Is it significant and useful? Are his theme and materials of development well adapted to the listeners, i.e., is the material interesting, impressive, convincing? Does it satisfy me? Is it likely to satisfy the members of the audience or community generally? Are the ideas clearly stated? Are transitions between ideas clear? Are statements adequately amplified? Adequately supported? Is the reasoning valid? Is the sequence of ideas orderly and well organized? Does the thought pattern have unity and coherence?

Bodily action: Is the speaker well poised? Is he at ease? Is his action purposeful and well coordinated? Are his movements spontaneous and well motivated? In general is the bodily action an effective medium of communication?

The sound elements: Can the speaker be heard easily? Is the pausing adequate? The phrasing definite? The rate appropriate? Is there adequate *variety* in pitch, rate, and loudness? Is the voice quality pleasing? If not, how would you describe the faulty quality? Is the articulation distinct? If not what sounds are faulty? Does the pronunciation conform to accepted standards? If not, list the questionable pronunciations.

Language: Are terms used which are unfamiliar to the listeners? If so, are they adequately defined? Are words used accurately? Are cliches and slang avoided? Is sentence structure clear and easy to follow? Is the grammar correct? Is there variety in the use of language? Are synonyms well used? Is vivid figurative language used? If so, does it contribute to effectiveness? Is the use of language adequate to the occasion and consistent with purpose and theme?

Complete understanding of all that is involved in these evaluative questions will require extended thought and study. You are not expected to apply them fully at first. They are a forecast of the topics of our further study, and should serve not only as a basis for critical listening but also as a bridge to carry us forward into the chapters which follow.

EXERCISES

1. Take the Brown-Carlson Test of Listening Comprehension, as administered by your instructor, and consider the significance of your score. What procedures for the improvement of listening, given in this chapter, do you especially need to follow?

2. At the close of an oral reading or short talk before the class, restate *in a single sentence*, either oral or written, the central idea or theme of the material presented. The speaker and class will judge your statement, and you should be required to revise it until everyone, especially the speaker, is satisfied with its accuracy.

3. Using the criteria of this chapter, evaluate the speaking exercise of a classmate or the speech of a citizen of your community. Hand to your instructor for his comment.

BIBLIOGRAPHICAL NOTE

The following sources have been useful in the writing of this chapter: For general background B. F. Skinner's *Verbal Behavior*, Appleton-Century-Crofts, 1957; and Carl R. Rogers' and J. F. Roethlisberger's "Barriers and Gateways to Communication," in the *Harvard Business Review*, July–August, 1952. Material on the new term *aud* is from the studies by John Caffrey, "An Introduction to the Auding Concept," *Education*, December, 1949; and Donald P. Brown, "Auding as the Primary Language Ability," Ann Arbor University, Microfilms, 1954, publication No. 10, 347.

Material on the frequency and importance of listening are from John M. Clapp's *The Place of English in American Life*, The National Council of Teachers of English, 1926; Paul Rankin's "The Importance of Listening Ability," the *English Journal*, October, 1928, and his "Listening Ability: Its Importance, Measurement and Development" in the *Chicago Schools Journal*, January, 1930; Harry Goldstein's *Reading and Listening Comprehension at Various Controlled Rates*, Teachers College Contribution No. 621; and a study by Charles Goetzinger and Milton Valentine, "Communication Channels, Media, Directional Flow and Attitudes in an Academic Community," *Journal of Communication*, March, 1962.

Any work on the effectiveness and improvement of listening is indebted, of course, to the pioneer studies of Ralph G. Nichols, which have been set forth in *Listening and Speaking*, William C. Brown Co., 1954, written in collaboration with Thomas R. Lewis; in his more recent *Are You Listening*, McGraw-Hill, 1957; and in articles published in *Speech Monographs* and *The Quarterly Journal of Speech* in 1948, and *The Speech Teacher* in 1961. H. E. Jones included some tests of listening in "Experimental Studies of College Training," *Archives of Psychology*, 1923. More recently an important series of articles appeared in the *Journal of Communication* written by Thomas T. Blewett, Kenneth O. Johnson, Maurice S. Lewis, Allen G. Erickson, Clyde W. Dow, and James I. Brown, 1951, 1953, 1954, and 1958. Other useful studies were published by James I. Brown in *College English* and the *Educational Research Bulletin* in 1954; and Charles T. Brown in *Speech Monographs* in 1959. The material on note-taking was strengthened by Paul I. McClendon's "An Experimental Study of the Relationship Between the Note-Taking Practices and Listening Comprehension of College Freshmen During Expository Lectures," unpublished doctoral thesis, State University of Iowa, 1956.

II

LOGICAL
AND PSYCHOLOGICAL
ASPECTS
OF SPEECH

4

THINKING AND SPEAKING

Our discussions of the nature of speech thus far have mentioned two important relationships between thinking and speaking. First, thought is a necessary element of speech. Noises and gestures which carry no meaning are not speech no matter how complex or pleasing their visible and audible features may be. Second, the visible and audible aspects of speech (i.e., bodily actions, sounds, and words) are media in which our thinking is formulated and in which it may achieve an outward form evident to other people. We should now explore these relationships more fully.

Psychologists have not agreed fully about the nature of thought. The term *thinking* has been used to include many activities from simple perception of an object to complex bodily movements, from random daydreaming to analysis of a complex problem or situation, from manipulation of objects to the most abstract reasoning. Traditionally, thought has meant the more intellectual processes described as knowing, inferring, generalizing, forming concepts, and making judgments. In this sense thinking is limited to the inner subjective aspects of our behavior and is considered to be distinct from outer, more easily observed behavior.

Where in this complex of meanings shall we find the concept of thought most useful to us in developing our mastery of speech? Ideally a speaker should be a person for whom there is no gap between inner thought and outer action, who can use speech as a means of formulating ideas and making them effective in action. Thinking begins when we are stimulated by perception of something in the world around us; involves activity of the central nervous system, especially its higher levels in the brain; and leads to some degree of muscular action or movement which completes a response or adjustment to the stimulating object or situation.

Physiological or life-sustaining processes certainly do not involve thinking, although it may sometimes control them and increase their efficiency. Random and highly emotional behavior could hardly be called thoughtful in any strict sense. Perhaps the surest way to distinguish between thinking and other behavior would be to call attention to its usefulness in promoting our welfare. In a general sense thinking includes all those processes by which we change habits, control emotions, and develop solutions for our problems. Thinking is the process of reacting to the world around us in ways which make adjustments to environment.

Thinking is adjustive behavior, but only the tentative and preliminary kind of adjustment which is in contrast to direct overt action. By means of thought we can analyze things, events, situations, and problems without actually manipulating or changing them; and can describe and experiment with various alternatives of action without committing ourselves to any one alternative. By means of thought we can generalize and classify our experiences, relate them to each other, and form attitudes, concepts, beliefs, and judgments, which provide a basis for overt conduct. Thinking is what happens inside us between our perception of a situation or stimulus and our overt response. Thinking is the formulation of the response. Thinking, in short, is a kind of internal behavior which is a preparation for overt response and is often used as a substitute for direct overt action. These considerations may be brought to focus for our purposes by the following definitions: "Thinking is the broad term that includes all symbolic behavior";[1] it is "that relationship of the organism to the situation which is mediated by sets of symbols."[2]

Thought as Symbolic Behavior

In human behavior, simple movements indicate things in the environment or may reveal attitudes and ideas of the person using them. Bits of behavior serve as substitutes for larger and more overt responses because they were formerly parts of those larger responses. Pointing, for example, seems to be an incomplete form of reaching and grasping. The negative gesture of shaking the head is probably a reduced form of turning to avoid something. Turning the body is always in some degree involved in running away. Situations like those which have caused us to grasp, to turn the head, or run away will occur again and again. At such times simpler or partial activities like pointing, shaking the head, and stepping aside may replace the larger responses.

One unit of behavior replaces another. These substitute units of behavior we call *symbols*. A *symbol*, as we shall use the term, *is a form of human behavior which takes the place of a larger and more complete behavior pattern and which, therefore, represents the referent to which the larger action has previously responded*. A *referent* is any unit of experience—material object, movement, situation, quality, class of objects, concept—to which a symbol refers or for which a symbol stands.

[1] J. P. Guilford, "Some Recent Findings on Thinking Abilities and Their Implications," *The Journal of Communication*, vol. III, No. 1, May, 1953, p. 51.
[2] George H. Mead, *Mind, Self, and Society*, University of Chicago Press, 1934, p. 125.

WORDS AS SYMBOLS

It is obvious that these definitions apply to units of experience and forms of behavior that are complex as well as simple. They apply, therefore, to the spoken word. Names, as we have seen, are often uttered as parts of larger responses to objects or situations or people. We name the food as we taste it. We repeat a man's name as we shake his hand. Few of us would journey to a country whose name we do not know and use. How natural, then, that words may become independent responses to be used instead of the actual tasting or hand shaking or traveling.

Although words represent things, a word is not the thing for which it stands. The moving vocal folds, the tongue, and the vibrating air waves are independent of the shapes, colors, and noises of the world we see and hear. This independence gives to the spoken word a vast flexibility. Speech is by all comparison the most flexible form of symbolic behavior. It can represent almost any form of reality, present or absent, subjective or objective, particular or general, simple or complex, personal or social. The spoken word can refer to the past or anticipate the future. It can represent things absent as well as things immediately present. It can refer to actions and processes as well as to objects and the qualities of objects, such as form, size, and color; and to the characteristics of movements such as direction, speed, and acceleration. The referent may be an abstract idea or concept. Symbols enable us to formulate clearly and represent outwardly our own inner attitudes, emotions, motives, understandings, inferences, concepts, and judgments. Whether the reference is directed outward to physical realities or inward to psychological realities, the use of symbols is the essence of the act of thinking. Our speech is freed from dependence on the environment of the moment and can explore the universe.

SIGNIFICANCE OF SYMBOLS

Roaming the universe verbally is useless and may be disastrous to mental and social life unless we use our symbols with awareness of their meaning or significance. What factors determine the meaning of a symbol?

First, a significant symbol is one whose referent can be definitely located. The wide range of possible meanings of words multiplies the danger that referents may not be clearly understood. This is especially true of broad generalizations or other intangible psychological processes. The danger persists even when we speak of material objects. Without a clear and definite referent a word stands for nothing and thus ceases to be truly symbolic.

Second, a significant symbol is one whose referent is valuable to the user. Things which contribute to our welfare, ideas and beliefs which determine the standards of the community and influence our happiness, attitudes and judgments which affect our employment and income acquire tangible meaning. As the referent influences our lives, its symbol becomes significant.

Finally, a symbol is significant in so far as its user is aware of its meaning for others. A speaker who communicates effectively must select and use words as his listeners understand them; he must interpret his own symbolic processes as his listeners interpret them. Strangers in a community, especially if it is isolated, will often hear words or see gestures which they do not understand because they have no common background of experience with those who live in the place. Laymen untrained in a technological field do not understand its terminology. Unless speaker and listener have some common background of experience in the use of a word, it has no meaning for them. Even if they have grown up in the same culture they may easily misinterpret each other's gestures or voice modulations. If words or gestures or vocal changes do not have community of meaning, speech tends to become empty jargon, a barrier to communication instead of its vehicle.

Thinking in its larger and more inclusive meaning may be carried on in a variety of symbolic forms. Scientists think in mathematical symbols, artists in terms of line and color, architects in images of form and mass, musicians in tone sequences. Daydreamers probably think in random visual images, and deaf mutes in images of their manual sign language. Some of these media can be translated into verbal utterance, but some of them—for example, the visual images of the painter or the tone images of the musician—are not reducible to words. Every expressive or communicative medium has its own special kind of message; every expressive medium embodies and sets forth its own distinctive kind of thinking. In every communicative medium we say something which can be said adequately in no other way. In like manner, speech embodies its own special kinds of messages which cannot be adequately formulated in any other medium.

The Essential Processes of Thinking

To describe the thought process as it goes on in the act of speaking, we need to analyze thinking in functional terms. In the preceding section we discussed three qualities which make our symbolic processes significant or meaningful—definiteness of reference, value in meeting life's needs, and community of meaning. Now we need to know the processes by which our symbols acquire these qualities, the mental operations necessary to give the symbols of speech their significance. We need to know what mental processes are typical of all our speaking, without which it would tend to become meaningless jargon and cease to be speech in any true sense.

Every individual has his own personal mental habits which differ from those of his neighbors and which grow and change with varied experience. Thinking for speech is often casual and sometimes humorous, now devoted to artistic expression and at another time to problem-solving. Our immediate concern is to locate and understand those processes of thought which are part of the core and essence of every act of speaking.

Perhaps we can approach such a description by eliminating the aspects of thinking that are not always or typically involved in speaking. Certainly random day-dreaming and the overt manipulation of objects as a method of problem-solving, for example, are not necessarily involved in utterance, although they may be accompanied by a running commentary of speech either silent or audible. Much of our speaking is casual, without definite and serious motivation; yet all speech, like other behavior, involves some element of drive and a sense of goal, however dimly it may be formulated.

We should observe also that not all utterance uses logical reasoning, although verified knowledge and reasoned inferences are basic to any meaningful speech. Not all speech needs extensive assembling of information or evidence; but all speech does require some development of thought in the form of fact, illustration, opinion, or argument, depending on the purpose and nature of the discourse. Not all talk requires close-knit organization of thought, yet an elementary sense of order based on relationship of ideas is a characteristic of all utterance worthy to be called speech. Not all talking involves problem-solving although such basic elements of problem solution as analyzing situations and evaluating ideas always enter into thoughtful speaking.

Still further observations will show that not all speech is creative in thought, although it typically employs some of the personal aspects of creative effort such as imagination and motivation; that not all speech involves critical evaluation and constructive planning, although the processes of judgment, whether good or bad, will always be involved in some degree; and finally that not all speech must have finished perfection of style, although care and accuracy in choosing symbolic forms are indispensable in meaningful speech.

From these observations we draw the positive conclusion that the following processes of thought are in some degree essential for every act of meaningful, purposive speech:

1. Perceiving and knowing
2. Inferring or drawing conclusions

3. Relating items of knowledge to each other and organizing them
4. Enriching and personalizing knowledge by means of imagination and emotion
5. Recalling or remembering so as to give some degree of permanence and stability to thought and make it a ready resource for speaking
6. Choosing adequate symbolic processes to complete the formulation of thought

Underlying the entire speech process is the motivating influence of needs to be met and goals to be achieved.

The Sequence of Thought and Utterance

In the more formal kinds of speaking, speakers have advance notice and can prepare with maximum thoughtfulness. The delayed response gives time for silent rehearsal to bring the thought into as clear and precise a form as possible. For interpretative kinds of speaking, such as acting and reading aloud, actual overt vocal rehearsal is usually indispensable. Public speakers too, especially student speakers, often practice their speeches out loud, and for some occasions may even write out an entire address which they memorize verbatim or read.

Thought is also antecedent to speech in the less formal kinds of speaking such as conversation and discussion. In these, overt rehearsal is seldom, if ever, necessary or even useful; yet who among us has not talked out, or perhaps written out, in advance the ideas and main forms of statement to be used in an important interview or group discussion? Even in spontaneous discourse we draw on accumulated reserves of knowledge and judgment which we have talked out to ourselves to some extent at previous times. Such talking to ourselves is a kind of informal, inner rehearsal which helps to prepare a storehouse of thought for quick use when occasion requires.

For every kind of speaking, some degree of antecedent rehearsal is an important practical means of establishing and maintaining the close connection which must exist between thought as an element of speaking and its overt expressive media of bodily movement and sound. Do not misunderstand this principle. Excessive preliminary rehearsal can lead to a fixed and stilted kind of performance which lacks spontaneity and creativeness, especially in immature and inexperienced speakers. The kind of preliminary rehearsal we are describing, whether silent or vocal, retains freedom and flexibility at the same time that it develops a firm base of thought. It gives a speaker thorough mastery of his purpose and sequence of ideas and perhaps also of some aspects of his symbolic formulations, but leaves him free to adapt his communicative processes to the actual needs of the situation as the interaction with his listeners goes forward (see Chapter 12).

Thought is also part of and simultaneous with overt utterance. This second temporal relation follows from the antecedent position of thinking for speech. The actual business of speaking is a process of recreating the dynamic patterns of expressive-communicative action which have already been tentatively formulated. Actually there is no such thing as completely impromptu speaking or reading. We draw on established habits of response, familiar interpretations, and knowledge already acquired. Even the most careless or thoughtless speaking is not entirely devoid of thought because some degree of perception and inner neurological organization must always precede overt action. The inner phases of our thinking are recreated, perhaps with some elements of newness, at the time of utterance, and follow through immediately to the visible and audible activities which complete the process and make it genuinely communicative.

If we stopped to measure the infinitesimal sequences of time required for nerve impulses to pass from sense organs through the central nervous system to the muscles which complete the overt responses of speech, we would not find thought and vocalization strictly simultaneous; but in practical terms an act of speech is an unbroken unit from perception of the speaking situation through formulation of thought to overt response.

Speech reveals the thinker.

Thoughtful Speech Is Orderly

Thoughtful utterance is (1) phrased in definite units, which are (2) separated by adequate pauses, and (3) connected by transitional elements which show the continuity of successive units. Let us consider each of these.

Discourse should be phrased in definite units. Most of our statements of any length are made up of a series of smaller, more detailed ideas. Orderly speech requires that these "atoms" of thought be so clearly distinguished that the "molecules," or larger units, can be understood fully and in detail. Utterance should fall into a series of distinct phrases which follow each other without haggling and without the all too frequent use of "uh, uh, and-uh." Such a systematic sequence of details is the result of analysis, which breaks down our experience and hence our knowledge into single items (see Chapter 8). In orderly discourse each of the detailed items takes form in a phrase. The phrase is the unit of utterance as truly as the visual word is the unit of writing. We write words separately but we do not speak them separately. If we spoke words singly, our speech would be laborious and artificial. We do not say, for example, "In—the—morning," but "Inthemorning."

We are using the word *phrase* here in a specialized sense to indicate *any group of words making up a single unit of a speaker's thought.* Such a unit may sometimes be the same as a grammatical phrase, or it may be a grammatical clause or even an entire sentence. Phrases may be long or short, few or many, depending on the complexity of a speaker's thought, i.e., on the way in which he organizes the flow of ideas in his discourse. In interpretative speech, such as oral reading or acting, the pattern of phrasing will depend on the way in which the reader analyzes and interprets the lines to be read. Whatever the kind of discourse, however, *phrasing is the process of grouping words according to the sequence of thought units.* Every speaker must decide for himself how detailed and finely discriminating his phrase units are to be and with what rapidity they should follow each other.

Nevertheless certain obvious principles should be noted. First we know that any complete sentence is in itself a unit of discourse. If the sentence is short enough to be fully comprehended as one unit, it can properly be spoken as a single phrase. If it is long or complex, it may need to be broken down into two or more phrases in order to be fully understood. Next, we know that the most basic method of dividing a sentence distinguishes between subject, the thing talked about, and predicate, that which is asserted about the subject. For example, consider the following:

A symphony orchestra consists of two basic elements.

This can be spoken as a single unit, and in some situations such phrasing might be entirely adequate. However, if the statement is to be made more incisive, a speaker would need to give special point to each part in turn as though answering the implied questions, "What am I talking about?" and "What do I assert about my subject?" The result would be more detailed phrasing:

A symphony orchestra // consists of two basic elements.

Ordinarily any attempt to break such a statement down into more than two subunits would contribute nothing to meaning, in fact might create a disjointed and artificial effect. More complex statements, however, would permit or even require more detailed phrasing. Consider the following:

The Salem witch trials // were a dramatic episode in the early history of America.

The basic distinction is between the subject, "The Salem witch trials," and the assertion which follows. However, a further division into secondary phrases might be appropriate if one wanted to make a special distinction between the dramatic nature of the event and the period in which it occurred.

The Salem witch trials // were a dramatic episode / in the early history of America.

Possibilities of more detailed secondary phrasing may be seen in the following statements:

A symphony orchestra // consists of two basic elements/—the artist or conductor / and his instrument, / the group of musicians.

The admission of Red China / to the United Nations // would be a gross violation of its charter.

Epicureanism // is a philosophy / which gives greater depth / to our understanding of pleasure.

Samuel Adams // was a leader in the American Revolution / and in the founding of our government.

The Fabian Society // was organized in England / in 1884 / to improve the condition of the poorer classes.

What can we do / to reduce academic cheating /at the University?

Of course there is nothing final or absolutely correct about any of the phrasings suggested. In some of the statements further subdivision might be possible, and in other statements small units might be combined depending on the way in which they are analyzed. The important principle is that our speech should be uttered in distinct phrase units.

Phrases should be separated by adequate pauses. The diagonal lines we have drawn in our illustrations indicate pauses in speaking. Usually we need to pause much more often than ordinary punctuation marks alone would indicate, especially if we wish to make the detailed units of our thought clean-cut and penetrating. Notice that very few punctuation marks occur within the illustrative sentences we have quoted.

The length of our pauses is fully as important as their frequency. Be careful not to make them overly deliberate and artificial, especially when the connection between successive phrases is very close. There is no surer way to make your speech sound stilted and labored than to pause so long that you break the continuity of thought. Completion of a major thought sequence often calls for a silence long enough to enable the speaker and listener to realize fully that they are moving to another main division of the discourse, and long enough also to let the listener realize fully what has just been said.

These are matters determined by a speaker's temperament and purpose, the attitudes of his listeners, the nature of his material, and indeed the entire speaking situation. Whether the phrasing is slow or impetuous, generalized or detailed, monotonous or varied, pauses are the principal means of dividing phrases from each other and giving them definite significance in the flow of discourse (see fuller discussion in Chapter 14).

Relationship of thought units should be shown by transitional cues. Listeners need to be carried along step by step. They need to know when a speaker finishes one major sequence of thought and begins another. They need to be aware of the differences between main and subordinate points, and between items of equal and inferior rank. The cues which indicate such relationships and distinctions are verbal, bodily, and vocal.

All good speakers use such transitional words as *moreover, next, however, first, second, third;* or even transitional sentences such as, "This concludes the first main point," or "Now I turn to another matter." These verbal cues, however, do not function by themselves. In fact if they are used alone, their significance is limited. There is a story about two professors, one of mathematics and the other of speech, who talked of these matters as they walked across the campus. The mathematician scoffed at the statement that bodily and vocal cues are at least as important as words. When the two men reached their building, the professor of speech opened the door, stood aside, bowed, and in deferential voice said, "*Before* you, my friend." The mathematician murmured his thanks and entered ahead of the other. He responded to the voice and gesture instead of the actual words. The point of this story is not that words are unimportant, but that we should not minimize the significance of bodily action and vocal modulations, and that consistent use of all three is necessary for the most effective communication.

Inevitably if a speaker makes a significant pause at a major transition point in thought, some kind of bodily action will be part of the change. It may be a shift in stance, a turning of torso or head, or perhaps even nothing more than a lift of the eyebrows or a gesture of the hands. No specific and binding rules about the kind of action can be laid down; every person has his own ways of responding, and every utterance is unique in its behavior patterns. In similar manner the voice which follows a pause has some part in giving tangible form to the change in thought. The vigor or mildness of attack and subtle changes in pitch and quality serve as symbols of change in meaning. We shall consider these three kinds of symbols or cues more fully in Part III.

The important point now is that progression in thought is indicated by bodily, vocal, and verbal actions which occur when a speaker pauses to renew his thought. Usually if our thinking is purposeful and well organized and our phrasing definite, the transitional cues will be present in some degree. Training can make them more effective, but the visible and audible signs of transition are inherent in thoughtful speech behavior. On the other hand, if we hurry or pause in the middle of phrase units, or chop them up with "er" or "uh" or "and-uh," we transmit to a listener the confusion and disorder which are present in our own thought.

The sum of the matter is that orderly thought finds its communicative outlet in utterance which is characterized by adequate pausing, clean-cut phrasing, and full use of all three kinds of transitional processes—bodily, vocal, and verbal.

Summary and Forecast

We began this chapter by defining thought as adjustive behavior which goes on in symbolic form, and symbols as units of human behavior which are substitutes for larger and more complete responses and thus represent the many and varied elements of our experience.

We recognized that thinking may be formulated in many different media; but that *thinking for speech* is an inner kind of behavior formulated in implicit speech symbols. The aspects of thinking which are essential to meaningful speech include knowing, inferring, organizing, imagining, feeling, and remembering. Such inner behavior, we said, is both antecedent to and simultaneous with the visible and audible aspects of speech; and should take form in an orderly sequence of phrases, separated by pauses, and connected by transitional elements. This overt utterance, of course, usually leads to other kinds of action, but our immediate concern is about the relationship between thinking as inner speech and speech as overt thinking. They represent two phases of one dynamic process of responsive behavior.

In chapters which follow we undertake to study the various phases of this dynamic process. Our concentration will be primarily on its inner, psychological aspects. Then in Part III we shall study more specifically the kinds of symbolic action which complete these inner processes in visible and audible form.

BIBLIOGRAPHICAL NOTE

In the preparation of this chapter the following references were especially stimulating: Ernest Dimnet's *The Art of Thinking*, Simon and Schuster, 1928; George H. Mead's *Mind, Self, and Society*, University of Chicago Press, 1934; C. K. Ogden and I. A. Richards' *The Meaning of Meaning*, Harcourt, Brace & World, 1956; Robert Thomson's *The Psychology of Thinking*, Penguin, 1961 (paperback); Lev Semenovich Vigotsky's *Thought and Language*, M.I.T. Press, 1962; W. Edgar Vinacke's *Psychology of Thinking*, McGraw-Hill, 1952; and Harry L. Weinberg's *Levels of Knowing and Existence*, Harper & Row, 1959.

5

MOTIVES AND ATTITUDES IN SPEECH

Speech improvement requires an explanation of the forces which make us want to speak. We have been considering speech as a form of responsive behavior. Now we seek a deeper understanding of the inner personal sources from which such behavior springs. These sources are of two general kinds: (1) motives which impel us to respond and (2) attitudes which determine the particular kinds of responses we make.

Motives

Knowledge of human motives is necessary for a speaker's understanding of himself and for adaptation of discourse to the needs and backgrounds of listeners. Probably no one ever understands fully the motives of his own actions, yet some insight into our motives is necessary if we are to control and direct our behavior adequately and maintain objective attitudes toward ourselves as speakers.

In all our face-to-face communication, moreover, we need to know what responses we can hope to arouse in our companions and what kinds of appeals will stimulate those responses. Plato recognized this when he said, ". . . he who would be an orator has to learn the differences of human souls." The admonition applies not only to orators but to all who speak in whatever kinds of situations.

A motive is a basic need or drive which impels an individual to make responses of a given kind. The word *need* ordinarily suggests something a person should seek or have. In relation to motive, however, it indicates a reason why he behaves in a certain way. Needs are imbalances within the organism, such as hunger or thirst, which stimulate activity or release of energy until a response is found which restores balance or meets the need. The naming of a motive seldom specifies the exact kind of response to be expected. A motive is an underlying drive toward action, but the particular response an individual makes is usually determined by influences which are derived from the standards and conventions of the society in which he lives.

63

Motives are not the only ways of explaining behavior. Lapse of memory can explain behavior that is inept or poorly adapted to a situation. Habits determine some of our conduct, but are more sharply defined than motives and more rigidly fixed in goal and pattern. Habitual behavior is automatic, thoughtless repetition of former responses. Traits of character are obvious and consistent modes of activity. They describe the *how* of behavior or the qualities of an individual.

SOURCES OF MOTIVES

Motivation is a broad concept which includes "every form of impulsion from the simplest physiological drive to the most elaborated, sophisticated, and intellectualized idea."[1] Motivation has its primary basis in organic conditions. In the process of restoring organic balance, sense organs are not merely passive receptors but active agents in determining the organism's relation to its environment. They select, i.e., are sensitive to, those stimuli which meet the body's needs. A response which results in satisfaction (equilibrium) tends to be repeated when the same stimulus occurs again, and continued repetition of these responses gives them permanence in the individual's behavior. An organic need is a basic motive which impels the body to seek a stimulus leading to an effective response.

Some motivations are based on psychological needs such as our craving for affection and self-realization. Most of these develop from the basic organic needs. Repetition of a response which meets an organic need makes the organism more sensitive or more ready to respond to the stimulus, so that other stimuli associated with it may become effective in producing the same or similar response. Stimulating objects thus may acquire interest in their own right. A mother's presence, for example, is associated with the satisfactions which result from restored balances in the child's organic processes. In time the mere sight of her may be enough to bring satisfaction. As the higher levels of the nervous system develop and take command, the primary organic responses evolve with the passing years into deep-seated affection for the mother which becomes a motive functioning independently of organic need. In similar manner our early organic need for gross muscular activity may develop with increasing maturity and discrimination into psychological drives toward achievement, creative expression, and self-fulfillment which seem to function without immediate dependence on the original organic impulses.

Psychological motives typically involve a basic social element. Our entire development depends on the influence of other people; our needs for food, shelter, and clothing bring us into widening circles

[1] John F. Dashiell, *Fundamentals of General Psychology*, 3rd ed., Houghton Mifflin, 1949, p. 141 n.

of social contact We are subjected to social conventions and rules to which we conform for our own welfare because we cannot live apart from other men. So we develop a set of drives based on social norms of conduct. We seek approval, affection, and security. As we assume adult responsibility, our group and community relationships acquire a larger place in our motivations and we care about status and reputation. As our emotions mature we seek the secure relations of family life. All these social drives are bound up with types of behavior which qualify us to earn a living; the desire for economic prosperity is a powerful social force. Social and cultural needs acquire a distinctive and often controlling place in motivation of our behavior.

As we mature and awareness of self increases, we become more and more conscious of the results of our various responses. As these tend to be repeated in typically similar situations, we organize the memory of past experience so that we are able to anticipate in particular cases the outcomes of certain forms of behavior. We deliberately choose responses which contribute to our psychological satisfaction and social welfare; we establish goals toward which our activity is directed. We begin to see the importance of distant goals and to develop sustained programs of action. Our preview of the outcomes of behavior may then become a source of drives which motivate our activities toward those anticipated outcomes. In all the aspects of our lives we judge the relative importance of goals in relation to our needs, reject some, and put others in a controlling position to motivate our behavior. We formulate purposes and commit ourselves to them consciously.

CLASSIFICATION OF MOTIVES

We have reviewed these facts of our growth and maturing in order to point out the wide variety of drives which activate our daily conduct. Psychologists have attempted to classify motives and to determine which are most basic. Complete agreement has not been reached, although certain needs, such as survival, love and affection, social acceptance, and self-fulfillment, are generally recognized as among the most basic. Sometimes acquisitiveness and love of power are added. All these are analyzed and described, and even named, in many different ways. The number listed by different authorities varies from one, an all-inclusive "self-actualization," to more than twenty. One of the most interesting classifications is that by A. H. Maslow; it attempts to show relations between motives and arranges them according to their dominance—physiological needs, safety, love, esteem, self-actualization— with the comment that each successive need becomes effective only when those which precede it have been satisfied.

The simplest and most frequent classification, however, places motives in two large groups: (1) the biological or life-sustaining needs and (2) the psychological or socially derived needs. A brief listing of the more important needs under each of these headings will serve to summarize this part of our discussion:

1. Biological or life-sustaining needs:
>   Activity—metabolism, response to stimuli
>   Nourishment—food and water
>   Elimination—defecation, urination, sweating
>   Protection—shelter, clothing, control of bodily temperature
>   Mating and procreation
>   Safety—avoidance of danger
>   Comfort—freedom from pain and illness
>   Relaxation—relief from tension

2. Psychological and social needs:
>   Social acceptance—group membership
>   Love and affection—courtship, marriage, home and family
>   Respect and esteem in the community
>   Encouragement and praise
>   Personal freedom—lack of confinement and frustration
>   Adventure, excitement, change
>   Information—satisfaction of curiosity
>   Employment—economic prosperity, acquisitiveness, desire for property
>   Entertainment—enjoyment of beauty
>   Power and authority—leadership, dominance
>   Self-realization and self-mastery—constructive achievement, personal growth, creative activity

The speaker who would move others must not only understand these forces as they operate in himself, but also recognize and appeal to similar forces operating in his listeners. Eventually (and sooner rather than later) you will want to think about methods of motivating other people, but your first and most important task as speaker is to understand your own motivations. Although some of our everyday speaking is casual and not deeply motivated, certain biological needs, such as safety, comfort, relaxation, and mating, may serve as direct motivators of utterance and as motivating appeals for specific listener responses. Much of our talking in selling, interviewing, and persuasion is a direct or indirect striving for economic welfare, which is an expression of our need for survival.

Our social and psychological needs usually are more direct motivators of speech than are the physiological needs. The most casual conversation is an evidence of our need for social acceptance and companionship. Much of our participation in discussion of group and community problems involves desire for the respect of our neighbors, the authority of leadership, and the satisfaction which comes from constructive achievement. The artistic speech activities, such as story telling, reading aloud and acting, grow out of our needs for entertainment, information, and creative activity, and for adventure and excitement in vicarious form. Our needs for personal freedom and self-realization underlie all our speaking.

With this general background we turn to some analytical exercises for observing motives in speech.

EXERCISES

1. Recall the setting and nature of two or three instances of the most significant speaking you have done recently outside this class. Analyze your speaking to answer the following questions:

What response did you want from your listener? What motivated you to seek such a response, i.e., what were your own basic motives? (See pp. 65–66.) To what motives of your listener did you appeal?

2. Observe an informal group discussion. Can you tell what motives are dominant in the group as a whole? in the various individual members of the group?

3. Why did you choose the particular selection of literature you last read aloud to the class? Why did it challenge you or arouse your interest? To which of the social-psychological needs of your listeners did you think it would appeal? Can you tell what motives prompted the author to write the selection?

4. Analyze a public address of some significance, either a speech made by some prominent member of your community or a published copy of an address of national significance (the magazine *Vital Speeches* is an excellent source):

What was the purpose? Was it clearly stated? Can you tell what motives impelled the speaker to choose that purpose? Analyze paragraph by paragraph the motives appealed to in the listeners. What relationship, if any, do you find between the speaker's motives and the appeals he used?

Attitudes

Motives and attitudes are inseparably related. In fact they are parts of the single process by which an inner drive emerges as a definite, overt response. Motives are an earlier stage, attitudes a later stage in the dynamics of behavior. An attitude is a controlling force which channels the impulse toward a definite kind of response.

An attitude is a subjective element of personality, an inner readiness to respond in some characteristic way. When we say that someone has an attitude toward something, we mean that he is already set for a given kind of response whenever that something appears or is mentioned. In its most elemental, organic sense an attitude is a posture or stance of the body from which certain kinds of movement may follow. In its more complex psychological meaning an attitude is a figurative posture or stance; the person is poised for a certain kind of response. The necessary pattern of neurological control is already organized and set to go into action whenever its particular stimulus is presented.

The resulting action has a definite social significance or value. Attitudes are always "toward" something. We develop attitudes toward such diverse things or stimuli as baseball and political parties, coeds and professors, foreign dialect and philosophy, fly-casting and poetry, grandmothers and African Bushmen, smoking and the Supreme Court. In every case the attitude is a tendency to respond in a definite way toward some aspect or part of our world. Attitudes can be described from two main points of view: first, in terms of structure, as mental set or state of mind; second, in terms of function, as inner process or activity.

From the standpoint of structure, an attitude is a relatively stable mental organization based on our knowledge of the object or person toward which the attitude is directed. Knowledge is the result of the ways we see and interpret things in the world around us. Perception, therefore, is the foundation of attitudes, but they also include some part of all those subjective forces, such as emotions, traits, habits, and beliefs, which give direction to our thought and action. Any particular attitude is a complex state of mind regarding the social value of a given stimulus and involves readiness to act in a certain way in response to that stimulus.

This brings us to the second or functional way of describing attitude. It is an internal psychological process, a preparation for action, in fact a kind of covert symbolic action already in progress, which has the capacity to break out in overt behavior whenever a stimulus is present adequate to call it forth. Attitudes may or may not be formulated in definite names or word forms, but they are nevertheless basic mental processes which precede and determine our overt responses.

Not every state of readiness to respond, however, nor every incipient kind of behavior, can properly be called an attitude. Innate and instinctive tendencies to action, reflexes, and physiological drives are not included. Attitudes are learned responses, developed as a result of rewards and penalties administered by society in accord with its mores and standards of evaluation. The learning goes on as part of our increasing differentiation of people and things in the world around us. We respond to them in distinctive ways. Repetition of a given response establishes a pattern which persists in our neurological and muscular organization. The pleasant or unpleasant value of our experiences and the reinforcing effects of the standards of our group or community tend to establish a stable and continuing relationship between the stimulus and our basic drives and motivations.

An attitude is a readiness to respond.

This relationship may be developed in several ways. Very often an individual's tendency to a given response is adopted from his family or social group as a result of suggestion or social pressure. We do what "is done" in our community. In our earlier years especially we tend to believe as our fathers believe and to accept what our teachers tell us. The response may thus be a matter of uncritical imitation. At other times a single experience may be so highly charged emotionally as to reorganize an entire behavior pattern.

Attitudes, however, are not necessarily rigid and inflexible nor automatic and routine; they can change as new influences are brought to bear upon us. Objects and people appear in different settings; no two situations or events are ever exactly the same. Our tendencies toward certain responses, if we are normal persons, develop a comparable degree of flexibility. Overly rigid patterns of behavior are maladjustments and in extreme form give evidence of mental abnormality or derangement. Normal attitudes combine stability and consistency of response with a flexibility which makes them adaptable to the varied experiences of our lives.

We shall define an attitude, therefore, as *a complex and well-established mental process or incipient response in an individual which is developed out of social experience and constitutes a readiness or predisposition to make a consistent though not inflexible kind of overt response to a given type of stimulating object or situation.*

69

KINDS OF ATTITUDES

Many kinds of attitudes can be observed in daily life. Interests, for example, are the kinds of attitudes which refer to classes of things. The small boy who first takes his father's watch apart has an attitude of curiosity, but he develops a genuine interest in watches only after repeated experiences with them in relation to their social values. When we are interested in something, we have a readiness to respond to all objects of a given kind in certain ways. We want to study them further, examine them more carefully, associate ourselves with them more frequently, or make more use of them.

An opinion is a complex group of attitudes integrated into readiness for response to a given doctrine, policy, or situation. Opinions prepare us for response to problems of belief or conduct. They refer to the social values which are associated with various kinds of stimuli such as persons, groups, ideas, customs, laws, standards of conduct, events, institutions, and situations.

Attitudes may refer to a wide range of areas such as race, politics, religion, education, economics, philosophy, and matters rural, urban, state, national, and international in scope. Attitudes may be characterized in many different ways. Some involve attraction or repulsion, favorable or unfavorable response; they may be individual or collective, public or private, humanitarian or selfish, personal or social, liberal or conservative.

Attitudes may also be false or truthful. Some involve distortion of our perceptions and judgments. We often see what we want to see, not what is actually present; and classify people and things arbitrarily without careful and critical examination of their real characteristics. We assign arbitrary labels. All lawyers, for example, may be branded as dishonest, all church members bigoted, all philosophy dull, all prize fighting brutal, all Japanese sly and tricky, all audiences frightening, and so on through an almost endless catalogue. Such labels applied without discrimination are stereotypes which brand people or things uncritically on the basis of limited experience and with little or no reference to the specific facts of the case. A stereotype is a verbal label which is generalized and oversimplified; it is the result of arbitrarily classifying some new stimulus object into an old familiar category.

When such a judgment involves strong emotional bias, we call the attitude *prejudice*. We should not confuse prejudice with prejudgment. In prejudice the emotion tends to freeze the attitude and close the mind to any evidence which contradicts it. A prejudgment, however, retains its flexibility and is subject to change with new knowledge. Prejudgments are unavoidable in this complex world; indeed they serve a necessary function by helping us to anticipate action.

Outward behavior does not always reveal attitudes faithfully.

For reasons of tact or social approval we often try to conceal our real attitudes. Social psychologists have developed scales for measuring attitudes, especially those falling within political, social, and religious areas. The responses measured are usually verbal and may or may not reveal the actual controlling forces of our behavior.

VALUES OF ATTITUDES

Attitudes channel our responses and thus regulate behavior so as to assure some order and stability. Without established and enduring tendencies to action our conduct would be unpredictable or even chaotic. Moreover, the inner symbolic processes in which attitudes are formulated enable us to try out our responses in preliminary form, and thus to some degree, select and control them. The subtle overt activities in which attitudes are usually expressed also serve as signals which announce our intended behavior to our companions. Without such advance cues, cooperation among people would be impossible. Unless we know what the other fellow is about to do, we cannot adjust our behavior to his. Attitudes, therefore, are not only products of social influence, but when outwardly expressed are also necessary foundations for the processes of cooperation and control on which orderly and flexible social life depends.

ATTITUDES AND SPEECH

For speech behavior even more than for other kinds of activity the consistency and control which attitudes provide are indispensable. The most important objects of a speaker's attitudes are (1) himself, (2) his listeners, (3) his subject and material. Let us consider each of them.

The speaker's attitudes toward himself.   Self-command is basic to mastery of thought and subject matter and to stimulation of listeners. Self-control is the primary qualification of a speaker. We do not mean a negative and limiting kind of control but such a positive self-discipline as frees the individual for purposeful and dynamic thought and action. Control in this larger and constructive sense is founded on good mental health.

The basic requirement is self-respect, a sense of one's own uniqueness and worth as an individual and a quiet assurance that he has useful contributions to make to his companions and his community. We are not referring to the assurance that arises from conceit. True self-confidence comes from diligent search for information and its use in formulating ideas, convictions, and purposes. The truly self-confident man, as opposed to the egotist, is not only aware of his abilities, but knows also his limitations, faces them honestly, and strives to overcome them.

Another important aspect of a speaker's view of himself is his

. When we speak, we should be able to see ourselves as rating in relation to other forces in a situation, i.e., to the o the dynamic and changing features of the setting, and to deas or assumptions implicit in the situation. The objective speaker realizes the impact of these forces upon himself and is able to direct his impact on them with conscious purpose. He is fully aware of himself as an individual with a job to do, but avoids the stultifying effect of self-consciousness by concentrating on his task instead of on himself. Such objectivity is a large factor in what we often call a sense of humor, a kind of detached attitude which enables us to meet life's problems as they arise, control our emotions, and keep ourselves in perspective.

The results of such attitudes can be seen in balance and flexibility of behavior. The objective person is freely outgoing and sociable, but can be self-contained and thoughtful. He is gregarious, but knows the resources which come from quiet meditation. He is positive and self-assured, but tempers his aggressiveness enough to avoid egotism and bombast. He knows what he wants to say, and can maintain his sense of purpose clearly without being dogmatic. He recognizes his dependence on others for stimulation and evaluation, but thinks his own thoughts and forms his own conclusions. He affirms these conclusions but is willing to think cooperatively when group or community decision must be sought.

In short, the quality of our speech is basically influenced by our self-respect, self-confidence, and objectivity; and by the fundamental balance we maintain between aggressiveness, confidence and sociality on one hand, and cooperativeness, humility, and reserve on the other hand.

The speaker's attitudes toward his listeners. Since the listener is an equal partner in the communicative process, our attitudes toward him are of major importance.

Let us recall that attitudes are based on perception, and that perception implies knowledge and understanding. One very important readiness for speaking, therefore, is some knowledge about our listener. What background influences in home, school, and community have shaped his mind? What kinds of experiences has he had in work, travel, sports, or group and community activities? What is his command of language? His capacity for artistic appreciation? His degree of imagination? His sense of humor? What motives might impel him to action? Such background knowledge can help a speaker choose purposes with realistic possibilities of achievement, and methods of discourse which are most likely to attain desirable ends.

In addition to general knowledge about a listener's background, we should inquire into his probable response to the particular purpose for which we speak or the specific theme and type of material. What stereotypes or prejudices might block his acceptance of the theme or point of view? What kinds of evidence will impress him? Is he familiar with any special vocabulary the subject may involve?

Since the time of Aristotle students of public speaking have been analyzing audiences. The ancient Greek analyzed the Athenian audience of his day, describing the emotions which motivate men, the influence of fortune, and the characteristics of youth, middle age, and old age. Modern textbooks on public speaking have followed and even extended the method. The public speaker is advised to determine in advance the probable size of his audience; the age, sex, and occupational characteristics of its members; their educational and cultural level; their political, social, and religious beliefs and commitments; their knowledge about and attitudes toward his particular subject; their probable attitude toward him as a person; and in all these matters the extent of variation or difference among the listeners. Such considerations are important not only for the public speaker, but for all of us who seek to communicate by any of the various forms of speech. The exact applications of such information will depend on the specific situation and kind of speaking, e.g., whether it is conversation, public speaking, discussion, reading aloud, or acting.

The depth of understanding gained through such knowledge should enable a speaker to meet his listener with an active awareness of relationship to him. The sense of readiness, the predisposition to speak in a certain way, should be based on an inner realization that the person here before us with whom we are to communicate is a human being like ourselves who is therefore entitled to our respect. Such an attitude is the forerunner of speech which is considerate of the listener's knowledge and convictions and, if not sympathetic with his viewpoints and problems, at least tolerant and courteous in manner.

By active observation of listener responses, a speaker directs and shapes his continued utterance. For us as social creatures and communicators no quality or technique of discourse can take the place of a genuine interest in people—an active readiness for friendly response to them based on sensitivity to their reactions, mutual respect and tolerance, and objective concern for truth.

The speaker's attitude toward his subject and material. The adequate speaker surveys his world of knowledge eagerly and is especially interested in all kinds of social objects and processes. Cicero's concept of the speaker as a man broadly educated with the widest possible range of knowledge and experience is still useful as an ideal, even though our world of knowledge is expanding so rapidly that no man can master more than a fraction of it.

The most important demand a listener can make of a speaker is that he know whereof he speaks. Real verification of knowledge implies a high degree of intellectual honesty. Stereotype and prejudice should have no place among the attitudes of the adequate speaker. Distortion of information is so common a human frailty that we must be constantly alert to its dangers (see Chapter 6).

The speaker whose interests range widely, who is open-minded and intellectually honest with himself and all his communicants, and who does his best to see the world in its true form and perspective has an adequate basis for conviction and earnestness. Only when he is sure of his facts and tempered in his inferences can he afford to be vigorous or vehement in communication. Sincerity is a quality to be highly esteemed; but when it is the spawn of a little mind distorted by narrow self-interest and emotionality, earnestness turns easily into arrogance and swagger, a fountain source of buncombe and bluff. The adequate speaker avoids such shallow foundations and builds his discourse on the rock of a scrupulous concern for truth.

A final virtue follows inevitably: The speaker whose thought is thus based needs only to study and assimilate the plan of any particular discourse until its material has become truly part of himself; he has the quality of quiet assurance. The whole man speaks not just what he has heard or studied, not merely what he believes, but some part of what he is as a human being.

In chapters which follow we shall consider further the processes by which speakers acquire information and verify, interpret, organize, weigh, evaluate, enrich, personalize, and assimilate it; and thus finally bring it to bear in the processes of communication.

EXERCISES

Development of those attitudes which enhance the quality of our speech is a constant, life-long quest calling for the highest degree of objective self-analysis and balanced judgment. We shall now present some of the principal ways to achieve the insight and self-discipline involved in such personal growth.

1. Select a person whom you know only slightly or casually, but whose dominant attitude toward other people seems undesirable or maladjusted. Name for yourself as accurately as possible just what this attitude is (e.g., self-centered, insincere, tactless, conceited, overly aggressive). See if you can discover and describe exactly what the person does or says that gives this unfavorable impression. Can you describe the effect of the maladjustment on his (or her) speech?

2. Make a list of two or three, or more if you like, of your most cherished and deeply held convictions or beliefs. You may choose them from any phase of your life and experience, although usually we find our deepest convictions in the areas of religion, politics, and social relationships. State each belief in a single concise sentence. Now examine each statement

to see whether you can determine its source. Where in your experience did it originate? Was it in one striking event or in a series of events? Did you accept it from some older person or persons whom you much admired? Did you acquire the belief as a result of your own study and investigation? What emotional involvements, if any, are related to it? Whatever the source, is the foundation of the belief sufficiently broad, typical and well verified to justify it as a general principle?

3. Analyze the situations and problems of groups to which you belong and the community in which you live in order to discover your attitudes toward them. Are these attitudes objective, well balanced, responsible?

4. Study your attitudes toward speaking: Do you speak too much or too little? Are you willing to listen to others? For what purposes do you most often speak? What is your relationship to listeners? How do they typically react to you when you speak? What do these reactions reveal about your own attitudes when you speak? What kinds of speaking do you most enjoy—public or private, practical or artistic, original or interpretative, individual or group? Can you tell why you like one or another type more than others?

5. Take whatever tests of critical thinking, attitude scales, and/or personality inventories may be administered by your instructor and consider carefully the implications of your scores for further speech improvement.

6. Map out for yourself a long-range program for developing more adequate speech attitudes. Consider the following methods, apply those which meet your needs, and seek to discover still other methods which will aid your development.

    a. Cultivate wide acquaintance with other people.
       Try to understand their viewpoints and problems.
       Ask yourself how you would feel and what you would do if you were in their circumstances.

    b. Strive to be intellectually honest with yourself and with other people.
       Try always to be factually orientated.
       Check your information for accuracy and validity; examine its sources (see Chapter 6).
       Undertake to explain only what you understand; frankly recognize and admit your areas of confusion and vagueness.
       Advocate only what you really believe and are ready to act on.
       Hold your mind open to new information and revised convictions.

    c. Try to achieve balance between the positive and negative, dominant and submissive, the outgoing and introverted, the confident and humble kinds of responses.

    d. In every kind of speaking situation concentrate on thought and communicative purpose.
       Prepare your material as carefully as circumstances permit.
       Think to and for other people, your listeners.
       Keep the communicative job to be done at the center of your attention.

7. On the basis of all the background thus far developed, prepare an analysis of your speech abilities and problems. You will find guidance for this self-analysis in the following sources: (1) list of elements of speech behavior in Chapter 1; (2) account of speech development and description of the adequate speaker in Chapter 2; (3) criteria for evaluation of speech at the end of Chapter 3; (4) discussion of thought and speech in Chapter 4, especially the last section on orderly pausing and phrasing; (5) suggestions for analysis of your motives and attitudes in this chapter; (6) comments of your instructor and fellow students. You should study carefully the recordings of your speech (see Chapter 21, Exercise 1). You may also find helpful your scores on relevant entrance and placement examinations (such as tests of vocabulary, English usage, social attitudes, and intelligence).

Consider the following questions: How well do you measure up to the concept of "The Adequate Speaker"? In what aspects of speech ability are you most proficient? In which elements of the speech process do you most need development? Are there particular handicaps or limitations you will need to overcome? Do not overplay the old familiar "line" about being nervous when you speak. Of course you are nervous. So is every other sentient human being (see Chapter 11).

Write your analysis and present it to your instructor as a basis for personal conference.

BIBLIOGRAPHICAL NOTE

Materials from the following sources have been used in developing this chapter: Gordon W. Allport's *Personality: A Psychological Interpretation*, Holt, Rinehart and Winston, 1937, and *The Nature of Prejudice*, Doubleday, 1958; John F. Dashiell's *Fundamentals of Psychology*, 3rd ed., Houghton Mifflin, 1937; Kurt Goldstein, *The Organism*, American Book, 1939; E. R. Guthrie and A. L. Edwards, *Psychology: A First Course in Human Behavior*, Harper & Row, 1949; A. H. Maslow, *Motivation and Personality*, Harper & Row, 1954; Henry A. Murray, *Explorations in Personality*, Oxford University Press, 1938; and Bernard Notcutt, *The Psychology of Personality*, Philosophical Library, 1953. The reference to Plato is from "The Phaedrus," 271; to Aristotle from *The Rhetoric*, Book I, 5; and to Cicero from *De Oratore*, Book I, 6.

6

FACTS: THE MATERIALS OF THOUGHT

If John Smith tells you he burned out the brakes of his car, if you read in a newspaper an account of an explosion, if you see in a history book a facsimile of the Declaration of Independence with its signatures, you have learned some facts indirectly from the experience of others; you are dependent on the accuracy of what they have said, reproduced, or written. If you actually smell the burning rubber, hear the explosion, or see the Declaration of Independence in Washington, you have learned some facts by direct personal experience. If for any reason you doubt the accuracy of your own observation or the statement of another, you cannot be sure that you have learned a fact.

Facts are the raw materials which thought assembles, organizes, interprets, and applies to life's problems. They may refer to real things, to statements about reality, or to interpretations of it. A statement of fact must be a true and objective description of the real object, event, or idea and free of stereotype, prejudice, and any kind of distortion—or as free as is humanly possible. *A fact is an accurate and verifiable unit of knowledge derived from experience.*

The Kinds of Facts

There are four basic units of knowledge, or kinds of information: specific details, statistics, concepts, general principles. We shall first discuss each of these separately and then consider the relationships among them.

SPECIFIC DETAILS

These are the most direct and easily observed kinds of facts. They may be single objects, events, or qualities such as color, size, speed, and direction. In discourse specific details appear usually as examples or illustrations each of which is one unit of an individual's conscious experience. Such experience is a continuity in which the event of each moment tends to blend into those which precede and follow it. The result of such continuity would be a blur of vague impressions except for our ability to break experience down into a series of discrete items, a process which seems to be completely natural and spontaneous.

This distinction between items of knowledge is often the result of different sensory processes. The recognition of one detail may be primarily a matter of sight, the next detail may be perceived through hearing or perhaps touch. We do not mean to suggest that the awareness of any given moment can be confined to one kind of sensation, but one or another may be dominant at a given moment. In so far as the dominant sensations change from moment to moment we have tangible means of recognizing successive experiences as distinct.

Again, the distinctions between successive items of experience may be found in movement or action. From this standpoint the detail of each moment's awareness is a functional unit or event. In practical terms of everyday experience we find little difficulty setting the boundaries of such events. We designate their beginnings and endings quite easily, almost inevitably. In fact we must do so in order to bring our perceived world into any kind of sensible order. Consider the simple business of shaking hands with a friend. In terms of bodily movement handshaking is not set apart from the continuity of an individual's action. Yet we recognize it as a discrete incident by regarding the lifting of the hand as the beginning and its release as the end of the action. Or consider a baseball player making a hit. At no time do his movements cease entirely as he approaches the plate; yet we mark the beginning and end of the events so inevitably that describing them seems almost a ridiculous attention to detail. We know when the swing of the bat begins and when the player arrives at base ahead of the ball.

Specific details are derived by analyzing the continuous flow of experience into distinct units. This depends on our ability to recognize boundaries between actions and so to break experience down into definite units of knowledge.

STATISTICS

Numerical, or quantitative, facts constitute our most definite and objective kind of information. The simplest figures are usually derived from a compilation of many details. We count or compute specific items in various ways to show different kinds of relationships among them. Typical of such figures are simple totals and percentages and the more technical measures such as means, deviations, and correlations. These are important in descriptive research and are indispensable in the more advanced types of experimentation which investigate causal relationships among events in order to predict or control results. Statistical information is often presented in tables, charts, or graphs which arrange systematically many figures dealing with a single topic or having a close relation to each other.

Statistics differ from the specific details or events of our casual everyday lives in that numerical facts are usually gathered purposefully and systematically. The pollster tabulates opinions, the market analyst surveys the demand for goods of a certain type, the census taker counts numbers of people and records their various kinds of possessions and characteristics. The techniques for such research are highly developed and specialized. Social scientists and members of the business community use these special methods extensively. Students of speech who discuss social, economic, and political problems should have some familiarity with statistical concepts and methods. Every student of public speaking, discussion, or debating should take at least one course in statistics.

CONCEPTS

Concepts are abstract ideas formed by generalizing from specific details. When we say concepts are "abstract," we mean that they are derived by the process of abstracting. This is the recognition of essential details and the ignoring of nonessentials. Consider, for example, the concept of *chair*. All of us have seen hundreds of chairs from the wooden straight-back to the folding beach gadget and the elaborate chaise longue. Some differ widely in details of structure, types of material, shape, size, color, and specific utility. Yet all are alike in essential features—a seat supported above the floor by posts or base and having on one side an upward extension against which one may lean for support while sitting. When we recognize these features as constituting the essence of what we think of as chair, we are abstracting, i.e., singling out the typical features and ignoring the incidental. When we do this as a means of comparing the similarities of perceived objects and classifying them, we are building general ideas or concepts.

We develop more complex and intangible concepts, such as *home, justice, democracy, immortality,* by integrating the common elements in given areas of our experience. Idealists consider such intangibles to be more real, or at least more significant, than the things we can see and touch. The essential point for us is that concepts are vastly important facts of life which are formed by processes of abstracting and generalizing and serve as materials for continued and more complex mental activity, such as the formulation of principles.

PRINCIPLES

Broad and general interpretations of human experience are usually formulated as statements of fundamental truth. Such principles are of many kinds—statements of belief, assumptions, laws, social mores, ethical standards, rules of conduct, axioms, and scientific generalizations. A principle relates concepts to each other and thus gives us a rule of conduct. The right to vote, for example, is a concept basic to the democratic way of political life; but "Every citizen should exercise his right to vote" is a principle. Love is a concept; the statement "Love your neighbor" is a principle of human relations. Gravitation is a concept of the force which holds the universe together; the principle or law of gravitation states that the force of attraction between objects is directly proportional to the product of their masses and inversely proportional to the square of the distance between the two centers of mass. We define and explain concepts; in respect to them our primary need is understanding. Principles are not only to be understood but also evaluated, argued about, believed or disbelieved, acted upon or ignored. In this way principles are not only broader, but also more dynamic and purposeful than concepts. You will notice that a principle constitutes a unit of knowledge or fact because, even though broad and general, it relates to one definite kind of experience, area of knowledge, or activity.

Principles, when broadly based in human experience, have a practical usefulness. For better or worse they are the foundations of conduct since a man usually does as he thinks. Consider the influence of our beliefs, ethical codes, laws, and social mores; they govern our behavior. Remember that most of our thinking proceeds on the basis of assumptions; even the quantitative methods of the mathematician are based on certain axioms. Some principles are amenable to scientific confirmation; others are based on human nature and validated only in terms of belief or faith. Some are established by investigation; others are assumptions based on general experience. Whatever the nature or scope of general principles, however, they underlie in some degree all formulation of thought, as we shall see when we study methods of inference.

In discussing these four kinds of knowledge—specific details, statistics, concepts, and principles—we have gone beyond the usual definition of the term *fact*. Most of the time we think of facts, do we not, as specific, observable objects or qualities or events. This common understanding does not include the less tangible kinds of knowledge such as concepts and principles, which involve the processes of abstraction, generalization and interpretation. In the ordinary view these are of quite different stuff from specific details or statistics, which are more objective and usually can be verified by direct sensory experience or computation. Concepts and principles are more subjective; they involve primarily the development of relationships among items of knowledge and personal interpretations of broad ranges of experience. Details and figures are more subject to measurement and quantitative treatment. Concepts and principles are more amenable to qualitative consideration in relation to human values and social effects.

These distinctions, although true and important, are by no means all the truth about the nature of facts. The four kinds of knowledge have more in common than may appear at first sight. All of them are inseparable from the processes of inference. Indeed, we derive all four kinds of knowledge in some degree by methods or applications of inference. Statistics, for example, are compilations which generalize details; concepts too are generalized from specific items of experience; principles are developed out of complex relationships of details and concepts. Even the details themselves are derived by means of analysis or the breaking down of experience into discrete units. Again, all four kinds of facts serve as bases for further inference. Specific details are the materials which we use in such inductive processes as generalization and analogy. Principles are general statements from which deductive reasoning proceeds. Hence all four kinds of knowledge, although different in degree of direct and immediate observation, are fundamentally similar in at least two respects: (1) All of them necessarily combine processes of knowing and inferring, and (2) all of them serve in various ways as bases for more complex processes of inference such as reasoning and judgment. We shall refer to these relationships again in our study of inference.

Sources of Facts

In our definition of a fact we referred to it as derived from experience. From what kinds of experience do we derive the various kinds of information which enter into the formulation of our thought? What are the origins of facts? Four basic sources are in common use among thinkers and speakers: (1) observation, (2) experiment, (3) interview, and (4) reading.

OBSERVATION

Observation is the direct perception of things in the world around us. Just as specific details are the basic kind of facts, so observation is the primary method of obtaining them. Consequently the essence of the process of observation is our ability to analyze experience into clearly recognized and differentiated units, thus to bring items of knowledge into the focus of attention and make them definite. Keenness of perception is based on efficient functioning of sense organs, although sensitive receptors by themselves do not guarantee keen perception. Much depends on the way we use our senses. In Chapter 3 we saw the differences between seeing and looking, and between hearing and listening. Looking and listening require intelligent and purposeful direction of their respective sensory processes. The same principle applies to all observation. It is a thoughtful as well as a sensory process, and its improvement depends on our previous knowledge, our ability to discriminate and synthesize, and our purpose (see also Chapter 12, the section on learning).

Previous knowledge provides a necessary basis for effective observation. The casual observer of the inside of a watch sees the works as a whole; they are to him just a complex of wheels and springs which make the hands go round. A skilled watchmaker, on the other hand, has been trained to see each part of the mechanism as a unit which has its own particular function in the whole operation. He is able to distinguish the movements of these parts as distinct but nevertheless part of the whole process. The watchmaker performs at a higher level of observation because of his previous knowledge. He knows *what* to look for and *where* to find it and *when* in the progress of the operation he is most likely to find what he needs to see. His knowledge was derived in part from the learning and experience of those who trained him, but in part also from his own long experience. So it is with any observation. The background of previous knowledge, whether acquired directly or from others, is a primary factor.

Ability to discriminate is another of the differences between that watchmaker and the casual observer. He notices a dozen details, or perhaps a hundred, which may escape our attention entirely. This power to discriminate is the key to all effective observation, because it is the power by which we break down the continuity of experience into specific events or distinguish the fine details in larger units of perception.

Ability to synthesize also adds an element of effectiveness to observation. Here again our watchmaker is superior. He understands the relationship of all the parts of the watch so that he can see its wholeness. He has not only discriminated and analyzed; he has put the pieces together again so that he can trace the transmission of energy from mainspring through the various controls in the system to the moving of the hands around the dial. All effective observation is thus patterned into a wholeness. Causal connection is not always involved. Sometimes synthesis is a classification of things in the world on the basis of such relationships as likeness or difference, size, shape or utility, as we noted in our discussion of concepts above (see also Chapters 7 and 8). No matter what kind of relationships are involved, however, the processes of classification and synthesis enhance the richness of observation. Until we have seen the thing (or event or idea) in its complete setting and traced all its relationships, we have not completely observed and understood it.

Purpose is the crowning ability which draws together all the other elements of skill in observation. The observer needs to know *why* he is looking; he needs to know not only *what* he is seeking but something about the intended usefulness of the facts he finds. Again the watchmaker teaches us a lesson. My purpose in observing the watch is relatively casual. All I need to know is the time of day, and so I look merely at the hands moving around the dial. My elementary aim motivates only an elementary kind of observation. The wheels and springs

*A good speaker assembles
his foundation of facts.*

inside are only a curious puzzle to me. The watchmaker has a higher purpose. He aims to restore disrupted relationships and mend the broken transmission of energy. This more elaborate purpose motivates him to analyze and synthesize more carefully and completely. His observations are directed toward a definite outcome. He begins with a more complex problem and, therefore, has a higher level of purpose. The problem and the purpose require more careful observation of the watch and thus motivate him to analyze its features with more discrimination and to see their relationships more clearly. He does not search for facts in general. He knows that the assembling of facts for their own sake or just for general interest is usually an ineffective and wasteful operation. The watchmaker is looking for the facts which will clarify the difficulty and lead to solution. His observations are directed toward a given problem and purpose. All effective observations are of this kind. They are motivated by a problem and brought to focus by definite purpose to solve that problem.

Now that we have listed the abilities or skills which determine the effectiveness of observation, we should pause to note that to a certain extent every man must be his own observer; he must develop and use these abilities himself. There is no substitute for first-hand experience. The student who has dissected a dogfish, collected rock specimens in the mountains, or observed discussion processes in groups actually at work in the community has learned some things about these matters that no one else can possibly tell him and that he cannot read in a book. Observation is still the ultimate source of knowledge. We should recognize of course, that any person's direct experience is inevitably limited. If we are to comprehend our world broadly and deeply, we must depend on other people's reports of things which we shall never have time or opportunity to see for ourselves.

EXPERIMENT

Experimentation is essentially a kind of observation, subject to all the conditions of ordinary observation and requiring all its abilities in even greater degree. An experimenter, however, operates under controlled conditions. As scientist he is not content merely to observe the isolated fact nor to wait until conditions for its repetition arise in the sequence of natural events. In some areas, of course, this is inevitable; but whenever possible a scientist establishes the conditions which will produce the phenomenon he wishes to observe, and then records and measures the results for whatever number of repetitions may be necessary to verify the findings. Observation in the experimental sense is more than the recording of events. It involves such control of events that particular kinds of relationships, especially causal relationships, can be studied.

For some types of problems, particularly those in the social sciences, the investigator may be content to describe, i.e., to gather, record, systematize, and interpret the facts of a situation. For some problems, the historical method, critical inquiry into truth about the past, is necessary. These are highly developed and specialized methods of observation. When causal relationships of forces or events are to be investigated, however, the experimental method is basic. The experimenter studies the variable factors in a situation and attempts to discover their effects upon each other. He analyzes a difficulty or area of ignorance, formulates his problem and goal of investigation, develops methods of procedure, sees that the variables are changed or controlled according to the procedure he has designed, records the effects, organizes and interprets these recorded data, traces causal connections, and generalizes conclusions or principles. He wants to find out what forces produce any given event or complex of events and what effects follow or may be expected to follow. Exact prediction is seldom possible but the degree of probability that certain results will arise from given conditions can be predicted. By the use of statistical methods the probabilities can be stated in such quantitative terms as correlation and deviation figures, or perhaps in even simpler terms of distributions and averages.[1]

If all factors in a situation can be managed so that only one of them is changed while others are held constant, then any change in

---

[1] For an explanation of these statistical concepts see any basic text on statistics, such as Oliver L. Lacey, *Statistical Methods in Experimentation*, Macmillan, 1953; and Allen L. Edwards, *Statistical Methods for the Behavioral Sciences*, Holt, Rinehart and Winston, 1954.

results may be attributed to that single changed factor. In simple forms of laboratory experimentation such direct one-to-one relation between a cause and its effect is often possible. In complex life situations, however, the factors are usually so closely interrelated that designation of one as cause and another as effect is no more than relative; any change anywhere in the system involves the entire system. If a different variable, or complex of variables can be changed for each of a repeated series of observations, a broad view of the interrelationships of all factors in the situation may be obtained. In most life situations fully adequate control is seldom possible; indeed the presence and activity of an observer is itself an additional complicating factor in an already complex pattern of activity. Experimental method, however, aims to create situations in which some degree of control is possible; and to observe the controlled variables to discover their interacting or causal relationships.

We should not assume that experimental method is the exclusive province of trained scientists operating in laboratories nor of statisticians computing their quantitative data. Laboratory and statistical methods no doubt represent a very high level of scientific activity, but even the common man in his everyday observations can use the most basic processes of experimental method. Seldom can we exercise the high degree of control possible for the laboratory scientist; but we can analyze situations and define problems, develop hypotheses, select and define the units or events we wish to observe, record the observed changes, and then compare and analyze the results of our observations. Organization and interpretation of data should follow inevitably. In other words, experimental method does not depend on any particular set of technical gadgets or statistical devices, even though these are highly useful adjuncts. Experimental method is a function of man thinking; it involves orderly processes of fact-finding and problem-solving which all of us can learn to use.[2] We shall consider these processes further when we study inference.

INTERVIEW

Direct face-to-face conversation is often the best method of getting specialized information and opinions from experts. Interviewers often seek advice as well as facts; and frequently bear the responsibility of making decisions. Interviews are used for a wide variety of purposes from the fact-finding of the reporter or pollster to the therapy of the psychoanalyst; they serve in educational guidance, job placement, and social welfare. For the moment, however, our interest is in the interview used as a source of knowledge by students. For this purpose it has wide possibilities.

[2] For a more complete discussion of experimental method, especially as it applies to research in speech, see J. Jeffery Auer, *An Introduction to Research in Speech*, Harper & Row, 1959, chap. VII.

The authority or expert in any given subject-matter area may often give you firsthand information or insights which you will not find in print anywhere, he may direct you to little-known sources which you might otherwise overlook, and he may help you resolve conflicts between the findings of others. Valuable interviews, however, are not limited to experts. Ordinary citizens, friends, and neighbors, may often help you acquire a broad background of knowledge, especially on subjects of wide interest or common experience. Interviews, in fact, are not always planned; your conversations and discussions in casual meetings with other people may be a continuing source of knowledge. Whether formal or random, interviews give us the benefit of other men's experience vitalized by personal contact with them.

If your interviewing is to yield best results, certain principles and methods should be observed:

1. Determine the purpose and scope of the interview and decide exactly what information you need.

a. Analyze the subject and the nature of any difficulty or problem.

b. Survey your present knowledge. Investigate and read to discover what sources of information are already available to you. You should not waste the time of a busy man asking for information you can find for yourself.

c. Examine your preconceived ideas and assumptions. Are they factual or based on emotional bias and prejudice? Try to approach the interview with as open a mind as possible.

d. Formulate your questions on the basis of your analysis and investigation. Of course, you may need to revise, cut short, or extend your questions during the actual interview, but careful thought beforehand will give you greater assurance and increase the possibility of useful results.

e. Give careful attention to the wording of your questions. Their form can influence the answers you will get. Avoid "loaded" questions in which a certain answer is suggested or implied. For example, the negative form, "Is it not true . . . etc.?" seems to imply agreement. The more positive form, "Is it true that . . . etc.?" seems not quite as much "loaded." However, a wording on the pattern, "What is true?" is less liable to distortion than either of the others. Even so subtle a difference as use of a definite article may sometimes be important. A question such as "Was *the* committee report . . . etc.?" implies that a committee did in fact exist and did indeed make a report. If there is any uncertainty about these facts, the indefinite form, "Was *a* committee . . . etc.?" or "Was a report . . . etc.?" may avoid a minor possibility of misunderstanding. Of course, there are times when an interviewer may need to use loaded questions, but we should do so with caution and full awareness of the dangers involved.

2. Plan the approach to the interview.

a. Choose the best qualified person for the particular kind of information you need. Has he had opportunity to know the facts? Would he have any reason to conceal what he knows?

b. Do his attitudes, interests, and viewpoints suggest particular modes of procedure, order of questions, or methods of statement?

c. Consider the possible effect your own appearance and manner might have on him.

d. Determine whether you have any common interest which you can use as a means of approach.

e. Consider the most opportune time and place to hold the interview. Perhaps an advance appointment might be wise. Does the man have any special office hours you should use? Plan for a reasonable length of time; be careful not to impose unduly on a busy man. Perhaps when you make the appointment you can determine its length.

f. Decide whether you should try to take notes during the interview. Would pencil and notebook tend to check the flow of talk? On the other hand can you remember what is said if you take no notes?

3. Organize the procedure of the interview.

a. Determine the order of importance of your questions. Usually it is wise to begin with a general statement of the kind of information you seek or a general question which will encourage your respondent to give a free report according to his own knowledge and experience. More specific questions may follow to bring out certain points of information which he may not have mentioned. In any event raise the most important points first and follow with more detailed inquiry as time permits. Balance your list of questions against the total amount of time available.

b. Control the progress of the interview as well as you can without interrupting your respondent unduly. Suggest frankly the information or opinions you need or do not need, but bear in mind that he may have a better understanding of what is relevant than you have. If he rambles, bring him back to the subject as tactfully as possible.

c. Listen carefully. Be alert to all that is said. Try to get the full meaning of each statement (see Chapter 3).

d. Distinguish between the facts your respondent knows and the opinions or interpretations he believes. Tactfully seek to learn the sources of his information and to probe the bases of his opinions.

e. Do not hesitate to ask for recommended sources of additional information.

f. Give some thought to the conclusion of the interview. Speak an appropriate word of gratitude for help received. Perhaps you may want to ask if some statement or statements may be quoted, or if you may use the man's name as source. This would be especially important if he is a recognized authority in the field of your inquiry. Leave promptly when your time is up or you see that further questioning is useless.

READING

Written and printed materials make available vast ranges of the learning and experience of other men the world over, past and present. Whereas observation provides a general background of knowledge, we depend on reading for the specific bodies of fact which form much of the substance of our everyday thought and speech.

Every speaker, that is to say every one of us, should be a constant and avid reader. Next to serious conversation there is no better way to keep the fountains of thought flowing freely. The printed or written page awaits our convenience as people seldom will do. We should read widely, critically, purposefully, and accurately, adjusting our method always to the value and usefulness of the material. Speed in reading is highly important, especially when a wide range of material is available, but depth of understanding is even more important.

We are all aware of the several forms of published materials. Books are valuable because they give broad and comprehensive views and systematic treatment of subjects and problems. Periodicals keep us in touch with current affairs and are especially useful when we are looking for material on a special topic or related to a given date or period. Encyclopedias are valuable for quick overview or summary of a topic. Documents and special reference books are usually our most basic sources. When a problem is technical or calls for direct use of primary material, publications of government agencies and of research institutions and universities have great importance. Unpublished material, such as theses, letters, diaries, and manuscripts, are the most original sources. We should use all of these kinds of materials according to the daily needs of our discourse.

Some of our general reading may be casual or even random, and may not require a precise and systematic method. Nevertheless, if you want to maintain a rich storehouse of knowledge you will need to choose with discrimination the materials to which you devote your time, give special attention to those items of knowledge which are most challenging or useful, record them and their sources systematically, and assimilate them into the orderly structure of your thought.

When you read to gather material on a definite topic or problem, your method should include four steps:

1. Make a list of the probable sources of information on the subject with which you are dealing.
2. Scan these sources to see whether they contain any of the information you need.
3. Select and record those facts you need or can use.
4. Keep a bibliography of the sources from which you secure useful information.

Make a list of probable sources of information.   The completeness of this listing should be adjusted to the time limits and purpose of
your work. Ideally every search for facts should be exhaustive; but
subjects deserve time and energy in proportion to their importance. Get
as much information as is necessary with the most efficient expenditure
of time and energy.

Every library contains four kinds of aids for this listing of
probable sources: (1) the card catalogue, (2) magazine and newspaper
indexes, (3) bibliographies and book lists, and (4) reference works,
both general and special.

1. A card catalogue lists all the material in a library. The cards
give author, title, publisher, date, and usually the size and nature of
each publication; and are arranged alphabetically according to their
headings. There are several kinds, the most important of which are
author, title, and subject cards. Most works are listed on all three. The
examples given here are reproductions of cards issued by the Library of
Congress. Libraries commonly use these instead of trying to make their
own.

```
149.9
W43L
          Weinberg, Harry L.

                Levels of knowing and existence; studies in
          general semantics.  New York, Harper  1959

                274 p.    22 cm.

                Includes bibliography.
                1.  General semantics.  I.  Title.
          B820.W38              149.94              59-12676

          Library of Congress   25
```

Author Card

An author card, of course, has the name of the author of a work
first. If it is written by more than one person, an entry is made for each
author's name on a separate card. Works published by organizations are
listed on author cards under the name of the organization. Official
government publications usually are catalogued on author cards under
the name of the nation or political unit. Publications of colleges,
libraries, and museums are usually listed under the name of the institution. State university publications are often given under the name of
the state. Sometimes works are listed not only on author cards but also
on cards headed by the name of the editor, translator, compiler, or

illustrator. In such cases the name is followed by the proper abbreviation, *ed., tr., comp.,* or *illus.*

```
Title Card

149.9    Levels of knowing and existence.
W43L
              Weinberg, Harry L.
                  Levels of knowing and existence; studies in
              general semantics.  New York, Harper  1959

                  274 p.    22 cm.
                  Includes bibliography.


                  1.  General semantics.  I.  Title.

              B820. W38        149.94              59-12676

              Library of Congress      25
```

The title card is headed by the title of a work followed by the name of the author. For magazines this is often the only card and it gives a list of the volumes which the library holds.

```
Subject Card

149.9    General semantics

              Weinberg, Harry L.
                  Levels of knowing and existence; studies in
              general semantics.  New York, Harper  1959

                  274 p.    22 cm.

                  Includes bibliography


                  1.  General semantics.  I.  Title.
              B820. W38        149.94              59-12676
```

The heading of a subject card consists of a word or phrase which indicates the subject-matter area. The subject card reproduced here, for example, has the heading, "General semantics." Sometimes a book will be catalogued under several subject headings. These different headings, if any, will then be given on all cards. Works of fiction, plays, and poems in most cases are not listed on subject cards. For biographies or works of criticism the heading of the subject card is the name of the person discussed. If a specific work is criticized, the heading includes also the title after the name of the author. Magazines on definite subjects are listed under the name of the subject—e.g., "Political Science, periodicals."

In addition to these three main types of cards—author, title, and subject—there are several other types such as analytical, cross-reference, and bibliography cards. An analytical card lists part of a work. When a book includes writings by several authors, an author analytical card may be made for each person, giving the title of the part he wrote and its place in the entire volume. A book which deals with several subjects may have several subject analytical cards. Cross-reference cards have subject or author headings and instruct one to "see" or "see also" other cards listing works related. Such cards are used for author's pseudonyms, for subjects which have two or more headings, or for references to related subjects. Bibliography cards are for publications which list works on specific subjects or within certain fields.

You will notice that all these cards except the cross-reference type have a series of numbers and letters in the upper left hand corner. This is the call or shelf number, which is the key to the classification of a work and indicates its location on the shelves of the library. There are several methods of classification. Under the Expansive and Library of Congress systems letters of the alphabet are the primary symbols. Notice that on the sample cards reproduced here the call number of the Library of Congress cataloguing system is given in the lower left hand corner as supplementary information. The main call number, which is according to the Dewey Decimal System, consists of two and sometimes three series of symbols. The first series gives the classification of the work according to subject. The field of knowledge is divided into ten classes, each of which is divided and subdivided as much as may be necessary. Each main class or division is represented by numbers of one centile. The main outline is a follows:

000–099	General Works	500–599	Natural Science
100–199	Philosophy	600–699	Useful Arts
200–299	Religion	700–799	Fine Arts
300–399	Sociology	800–899	Literature
400–499	Philology	900–999	History

The second series of symbols in a call number indicates the author and title of the work. The capital letter which stands first is the first letter of the author's surname, the numbers which follow indicate the relative position in the alphabet of the remaining letters of the name, and the small letter at the end is usually the first letter of the first word (except the articles a, an, or the) in the title of the work. Sometimes if a work has more than one volume or a library has more than one copy, there is a third line of the call number which gives the volume or copy number.

Any call number, therefore, indicates one and only one book, and every part of the number has a definite meaning and importance. Accuracy in writing down call numbers is imperative.

When you first consult a card catalogue, look at all the related subject headings you can think of. For example, if you are seeking information about speech, look up also public speaking, oratory, conversation, discussion, articulation, radio broadcasting, and even that much abused term *elocution*. When you find cross-reference cards, look up the subjects to which they refer. Early reference to author cards will also be useful. If you know or find names of persons or organizations putting out material on your topic, look them up.

Continue your search through all headings and cross-references until you feel that you have found and made note of every work which might have useful information on your problem. You will save much time and effort later if you inspect each card carefully for information about the work listed, i.e., date of publication, number of volumes, nature of contents, and whether the book includes a list of other titles on the same subject. For more extensive research projects or highly specialized subjects you may wish to consult the Library of Congress Catalogue or to utilize the resources of interlibrary loan. Librarians are always ready to assist you with these or any other problems which may arise.

2. Magazine and newspaper indexes are catalogues of articles which have been published in periodicals during a given period of time. Such indexes are issued in pamphlet or book form and list articles alphabetically by author, title, and subject. In the front of each number or volume there are usually directions for use and lists of the periodicals indexed. You will need to become acquainted with the abbreviations and symbols used in such lists. Some indexes also summarize the contents of a few books.

The card catalogue of your library will include subject or title cards for all magazines of which it has volumes. In some libraries periodicals are catalogued in a special file. When you have found the reference to a particular article which you wish to read, look up the call number of the periodical and ask for the issue or volume at the library desk.

Newspapers are especially useful in fact-finding because of day-to-day reporting and detailed coverage of events in their particular localities. The better and larger papers also contain articles of general interest. Most newspapers make no attempt to index their contents, but the index of *The New York Times* serves as a general guide to newspaper sources. In addition to indexes, directories of magazines and newspapers also provide important clues to sources of information. Such directories give lists of periodicals with information about their publication. (See the Appendix for a list of the more important indexes and directories of magazines and newspapers.)

The use of such guides should be systematic. Consider first the time during which the problem you are studying has been important enough to be a subject of research and publication. Next, for that period of time consult those indexes which deal with the subject field. All that we have said about systematic coverage of sources and accuracy in noting references applies with equal force to use of periodical indexes. Examine all cross-references and make exact note of those items which might have useful information. In writing down periodical references, however, careful distinction must be made between titles of articles and titles of the publications in which they appear. The standard method is to use quotation marks for the articles and to underline the titles of magazines or newspapers. Leave space in the upper left-hand corner for the library call number. Each of your reference cards should have a format like that shown below. Such notation means that an

---

808.5
SM

    Scheidel, Thomas M., Laura Crowell, and John R.
    Shepherd.

    "Personality and Discussion Behavior: A Study of
       Possible Relationships."

    Speech Monographs, XXV, 4. November, 1958, 261-267.

---

article entitled, "Personality and Discussion Behavior: A Study of Possible Relationships," by Scheidel, Crowell, and Shepherd, was published in *Speech Monographs*, Volume XXV, Number 4, dated November, 1958, pages 261 to 267.

While we are talking about periodicals we should remark that in addition to using the indexes for research on particular topics, all of us need to make a regular practice of reading some magazines and newspapers of general scope on the political and social problems of the day. A few of the more useful magazines for this purpose are:

The American Scholar
The Atlantic

Fortune
Harper's Magazine
The Nation
Newsweek
The Reporter
Saturday Review
Time
United Nations Review
U.S. News and World Report
Vital Speeches

Some of the most important newspapers for general reading are:

The Atlanta Constitution
Chicago Daily Tribune
The Christian Science Monitor
London *Times*
Manchester *Guardian*
New York Herald Tribune
The New York Times
Portland *Oregonian*
St. Louis Post-Dispatch
The Wall Street Journal

As students of speech we should know some of the more important journals which deal with various phases of our subject:

The Quarterly Journal of Speech
Speech Monographs
The Speech Teacher
Educational Theatre Journal
Journal of Speech and Hearing Disorders
Journal of Speech and Hearing Research
The Journal of Communication

3. Bibliographies and book lists also help us find probable sources of information. Nearly every subject of any importance has had its major sources catalogued in some way. Library card catalogues always record any published bibliographies the libraries hold. Textbooks make a practice of listing the more important sources in their fields of study. Articles in encyclopedias and special reference books often include short bibliographies of the most important works on the subjects with which they deal. Local libraries sometimes prepare bibliographies on subjects of special importance in their communities. (See the Appendix for lists of professional and trade books, including special speech indexes, and bibliographies issued by government agencies.)

4. Reference works are useful in compiling a list of possible sources on a given subject and are also in themselves major sources of information on a wide variety of topics. Such works are not designed to be read through, but are useful for ready and frequent consultation on specific points. There are all kinds of reference materials: general encyclopedias in many volumes, dictionaries, small handbooks which deal with limited and specialized fields of knowledge, pamphlets, documents, books from every level of government and every type of organization, yearbooks and almanacs, biographical works, and such special sources as collections of speeches, handbooks, microfilms, and manuscript materials (see Appendix).

Libraries usually shelve reference materials in a specially designated section or room. You will find them listed in the card catalogue just as any other books, except that the cards are marked, "Reference," or in some libraries simply "R." A working knowledge of reference material is indispensable for anyone who wishes to be well informed.

Scan the sources. While you are scanning such lists of sources, you should be jotting down every title or reference which seems to promise useful information. Each item or title should be on a separate card or slip of heavy paper with name of author, editor or compiler (usually last name first), *exact* title, publisher, place and date of publication, edition if more than one has been issued, number of volumes, and any other information about the work which might be useful to you when you refer to it later. If you use cards of uniform size (preferably 3 x 5), they can be sorted and classified more easily as you work.

Some, possibly all, of these cards will later become your bibliography or list of source materials actually used. The efficiency of all your study will be greatly enhanced if you adopt a careful and uniform method of notation. People differ in such matters and each one of us should develop whatever system is most convenient for himself or herself. The following suggestions, however, have been found generally useful:

1. Leave space across the top of the card (perhaps 3/4 of an inch) where you can write a word or phrase giving the subject or classification or nature of the material.
2. The upper left-hand corner of the card should be reserved for the library call number or other clue to where the book, periodical, pamphlet, or document can be found.
3. Write each main item of the reference, i.e., author, title, publisher, etc., on a separate line.
4. Use any space at the bottom of the card or the back for annotations about the nature of the material.

If you follow these suggestions, your bibliography card will appear very much like the sample shown below. If all this seems overly

```
370.973              Contemporary              E12
                      education

     Peet, Harriet E.

     The Creative Individual

     New York, Ronald Press, 1960.

     Discusses change in educational thinking.
     Bibliographies are given.
```

laborious and you grow impatient because of the time required, remember that with a little extra care now you can avoid the need to recheck your references later.

Scanning and listing sources, and even the taking of notes, may be carried on to some extent together, especially if one is working under time limits. How can one tell from brief, preliminary examination whether a given book or article contains useful information? There is no ready formula, but the following suggestions may help:

1. Scan the table of contents, preface, and introduction to determine what the work contains. If there is an index, it may indicate whether your particular topic is discussed.

2. Look for subtitles or paragraph headings which show the nature of the material.

3. Notice the date of publication. Material issued at the time of an important event or shortly afterward may have special value. A most basic requirement is that information should be up to date. Research which is five years old or a year old, or sometimes only a month or a week old, may be of little value. Much depends on your purpose and the nature of your subject. A book on the government of Germany under the monarchy, published before World War I, would have the advantage of contemporary knowledge of that era; but a book on the same subject published now would have the value of perspective and historical research. The most recent facts about any subject are always needed.

4. Finally consider the reliability of the author and his sources. Does the work you have in hand record its author's own findings or has he drawn information from other observers, experimenters, researchers,

thinkers? In any case you should apply the tests of authenticity which are discussed later in this chapter. In every matter we need the most reliable sources available.

Record the information.   Memory is an important storehouse of knowledge (see Chapter 12), but most of us need systematic notes to ensure definiteness and accuracy of our facts. Make a practice, therefore, of writing down every challenging and interesting idea or fact you meet, especially if it relates to a particular subject or problem which you have decided to study. For handy reference, a card file is convenient or a loose-leaf notebook.

We cannot emphasize too strongly the value of a definite and systematic method of taking notes. This applies not only to reading but to all kinds and sources of information. Recall that we are discussing facts as units of knowledge derived from experience. Whether the units are specific details, statistics, concepts, or principles and whether they are derived from observation, experiment, interview, or reading, the reliability and breadth of our knowledge are enhanced by systematic taking of notes.

The recording of your own experiences and observations, if they need notation at all, merely requires a concise statement of the events or ideas and of times, places, and circumstances of occurrence. For an interview leave space at the bottom of a card for the name of the person, time, and place. If your interviewee is an important person with a considerable list of qualifications or if your interview resulted in many items for notation, you may wish to make a separate bibliography card for him. Space should be left at the top of every card for a subject or title and possibly a code number as we suggest for bibliography cards (see below).

The making of notes from reading usually requires a more detailed and exact method, especially in the recording of sources. The particular form of notes is unimportant so long as they are legible, can be easily sorted and classified, and give exact sources. Here again people differ and each should develop the method most convenient for him. The following suggestions, however, may be useful:

1. Make your notes on cards or pieces of heavy paper of uniform size, usually 3 x 5 or 4 x 6 or half sheets of paper. You may find the large card more convenient because it gives space for brief summaries of entire articles and because it will be easily distinguished from bibliography cards.

2. Write only one unit of information on each card. This gives greater flexibility in classification of material as your work proceeds. Sometimes this advice is difficult to apply when you have a series of closely related items. How does one distinguish between units? Perhaps the controlling principle should be: Will the items ever need to be used separately, i.e., in relation to different subjects or discourses or for

different aspects of analysis or inference? All items on a single point or subtopic should be put on one card. If they apply to different points, put them on different cards.

3. Leave space at the top of every card for a heading or classification mark which you may wish to add later.

4. Be sure to use quotation marks for any verbatim quotations. Indicate omissions by means of elipses (three periods), and if you insert your own words of explanation inside a quotation, enclose them in brackets, not parentheses.

Notes made according to these rules are illustrated in the three accompanying sample cards.

Ancient Greek Political Concepts
　　　Meaning of "Polis"

Polis--a small political and religious unit in ancient Greece and Crete. Though economically and geographically distinct, each polis was not so much a city-state as the body of people making up an intimate democratic community--or more exactly the polis was the "whole communal life of the people." (p. 75)

Aristotle's Poetics demonstrated that the polis was the only framework within which man could fully realize his spiritual, moral and intellectual capacities. (p. 78)

Kitto, H. D. F. The Greeks. Penguin Books, London and Baltimore, 1951. Ch. 5, pp. 64-79.

Keep a bibliography. As you read and take notes, assemble your bibliography. When you have recorded the important and useful facts and ideas from any piece of material, include the reference card in your list of sources.

As your study proceeds and the number of useful references increases, you should find them falling into some kind of classification. Actually there are many ways of organizing bibliographies. Some are alphabetical (either by author or title), some are chronological, some topical (i.e., by subdivisions of subject matter), some according to kinds of sources (whether magazines, documents, reference books, etc.). Choose a method of classification which will enable you to refer to your sources most easily.

No matter what method of organization you use, your bibliography cards will be most easily identified if you label them by a simple

Bacon on Forms of Address

Bacon recognized the traditional kinds of rhetorical address
first set forth by Aristotle: deliberative or political speech,
forensic speech aiming at justice, and occasional speech of
praise or blame. In addition Bacon referred to preaching as a
kind of rhetorical endeavor and seemed to recognize private
conversation, particularly in diplomatic negotiations as a form
of persuasive discourse.

Wallace, Karl R. "Bacon's Conception of Rhetoric," Historical
Studies of Rhetoric and Rhetoricians, Raymond F. Howes (ed.).
Cornell University Press, Ithaca, N.Y., 1961. P. 117.

Voice for Speech
      Racial Differences

"The pitch characteristics of three groups of southern Negro
males were investigated by means of the phonellegraphic technique.
These groups were composed of six ten-year-olds, six fourteen-
year-olds, and six eighteen-year-olds, considered to represent
pre-adolescence, adolescence, and post-adolescence. The data
obtained were compared with results reported by Curry [E. T.
Curry, "The Pitch Characteristics of the Adolescent Male Voice,"
S M, VII (1940), 48-62] for three similar groups of northern
white males. It was found that the southern Negroes exhibited
lower pitch levels and experienced an earlier onset of adolescent voice change than did Curry's white subjects. Because of
certain uncontrolled variables, however, there is some question
whether the reported differences actually were due to race."

Hollien, Harry, and Ellen Malcik. "Adolescent Voice Change in
Southern Negro Males," Speech Monographs, XXIX, March, 1962,
No. 1, p. 53.

---

system of numbers or symbols. For this purpose reserve the upper right-
hand corner of each card. Notice, for example, the symbol "E 12" on
the card headed "Contemporary education" (see p. 96). This is
an imaginary symbol such as anyone might use to signify that this

card represents reference number 12 on the subject of education. If you were to make notes from this particular book, you could easily identify the source by writing this classification symbol on each note card (preferably in the upper right-hand corner) instead of writing over and over on successive cards the full statement of author, title, publisher, etc. Of course, if you later cite the material in a manuscript, you should give the complete reference in full and accurate detail; and even in oral discourse you should refer to sources in accurate though perhaps less detailed terms, unless you are giving information to students for whom your completely detailed sources might be important. The use of a code number for identifying bibliographical references is merely a temporary time-saving device for the note-taking process.

Verification of Facts

We defined a fact as an accurately known and verifiable unit of knowledge derived from experience.

Methods of verification will depend partly on the kind of facts to be tested. Reliability of specific details depends on effective observation. Reliability of statistics depends on the methods by which the figures are assembled and computed. Reliability of concepts depends on breadth of experience and the insight and consistency with which similar elements of experience are recognized and integrated. Reliability of principles depends on logical judgments based on breadth of knowledge. In spite of these differences, however, certain general principles are essential to the testing of any and all kinds of information. Whether you are using your own observations and experience or drawing on someone else's knowledge, very similar basic questions or tests apply. In either case we are evaluating the reliability of people.

CONCERNING THE PERSON AS OBSERVER

Is he competent on the subject or problem under consideration? Has he had enough experience and training to understand the situation and the kinds of information needed? Has he had adequate opportunity to observe and know the facts? Does he know where and when to look? Is he accurate? Does he perceive clearly? Are his methods of observation and study systematic and purposeful? How reliable is his memory or his method of recording his observations? Does he know the difference between observed facts and opinions derived by interpretations of facts?

Is he a person of integrity? Is he intellectually honest? Does he face the facts as he finds them? Has he ignored or concealed any significant information? What are his motivations? What special interests, if any, influenced the findings? Is there anything in the man's background of social, religious or political affiliations which might prejudice his observations? Does he have an active sense of social responsibility?

CONCERNING THE PERSON AS REPORTER

What do we know about his material?   Does it have significant chronology in relation to events? Is it up to date? Is it sufficiently inclusive and adequate in scope? Is it well organized and systematic? Is the report consistent within itself? Are the observed units clearly defined? Do you notice any contradictions among various items? Is the report logical? Does it show relationships among specific details and integrate them into meaningful concepts and principles? Are statements clear and to the point? Are special and technical terms properly used? If there is statistical material, are the units of measurement clearly defined and consistent? Do the figures actually measure what they appear to measure?

Do the observations agree with the reports of other observers? (In view of the frailty and inaccuracy of human observation and memory, corroboration by several people is an important, sometimes indispensable, method of verification.)

Does the material have a workable relation to real life situations and problems? Or to a larger body of information? Does it help to clarify a situation, solve a problem, or complete a body of related knowledge? Does it lead to a satisfying belief or an effective course of action?

Probably no set of facts can meet all these tests. Not all of them are applicable to every body of knowledge. Some of the questions are undoubtedly difficult to answer. Some, as in the judging of statistics, require study of special methods. Nevertheless the entire list points to a standard by which we can maintain a constant check on our sources of knowledge. Whether the source be a single investigator, research team, committee, court, or larger social group or institution, these questions should guide you in judging the qualifications of the reporters and in determining whether the report is truly fact or merely opinion.

OPINIONS

Opinions are convictions or beliefs which lie primarily in the areas of concept and principle and which have not yet been fully verified.   They are tentative formulations of the more subjective kinds of knowledge consisting primarily of personal interpretations of experience. We have already pointed out (see Chapter 5) that opinions are complex attitudes which prepare us for response to problems of belief or conduct. They are the result of social stimuli and refer to human and social values. In addition opinions are tentative judgments based on limited or apparent information. Opinions are not as easy to verify as direct observations, nor as fully accepted as beliefs. In situations where complete and reliable information is not available, opinions are substitutes for verified knowledge and confirmed beliefs. Seldom do we have all the essential knowledge about matters on which we must form judgments or about situations in which we must act. Inevitably, therefore, we form conclusions which actually can be no more than honest and educated guesses.

This principle was recognized as long ago as the fourth century B.C. when Aristotle in his *Rhetoric* pointed out that argument and persuasion deal with probabilities, i.e., with contingent matters which cannot be settled by completely scientific investigation but about which some decision or action must be taken. No man of sense argues about problems which can be settled by research; but when the limits of investigation have been reached and areas of uncertainty remain, then the processes of judgment move to the front and men formulate opinions. On the deeper issues of life even judgment is often feeble and men resort to intuition and faith. The dividing line between fact and opinion is forever tenuous. We shall do well, therefore, to regard opinion as tentative fact or truth and to strive diligently toward its ultimate verification and reliability.

The processes of inference and interpretation enter so largely into formulation of concepts and principles that there is a wider latitude for differences in judgment and a greater margin of error. When these more subjective and personal kinds of knowledge become well established and verified by wide ranges of human thought and experience, we call them truths; but as long as they retain any considerable element of uncertainty, we call them opinions. We should continue to distinguish carefully between facts as accurately known and verified units of knowledge and opinions as potential facts not yet fully verified and perhaps not verifiable at all.

This brings us to a final question: How should we evaluate opinions? Obviously by the same standards we apply to facts, although just as obviously we cannot expect opinions to measure up to the same rigorous standards of authenticity. If they did, they would be facts. Opinions are useful only in so far as they present the greatest possible nearness to truth. If an expert who states an opinion has had wide experience in the given subject-matter area and is a man of high personal and intellectual integrity, and if his statement meets the standards of good reporting; then we may accept his opinion as valid and useful even though it may not be ultimately conclusive.

EXERCISES

1. Analyze any of the examples of outlining in Chapters 8 and 9 (choose especially from Examples 23, 26, 28, 30, 32, 33, or 34) to determine what types of factual material are used—whether specific details, statistics, concepts, or principles.

2. Begin to analyze conversations and discussions in which you engage and to observe the conversations of other people. To what extent do you observe, both in your own speech and that of others, use of the various types of factual material as contrasted with vague and unsupported assertions? How often do you find alleged facts verified? The object of this suggestion is not to make you a hypercritical nuisance among your friends, but to increase your awareness of the different kinds of information and the importance of its verification.

3. Analyze the kinds of information used as supporting material in a public address of some significance. (See the Appendix for a list of speech anthologies; others are available in your library.) Do you discover any relationship between types of information used and the kind of subject the speaker is considering—whether expository or persuasive, and whether dealing with process, structure, biography, historical event, concept, or principle?

4. In order to become familiar with some of the sources of information listed in the Appendix, find the answer to each of the following research problems or questions. Your answers will be judged on the basis of their accuracy, completeness of citation, and conciseness of statement. For every item *list all sources used.*

a. Find the title of an important public address by Edmund Burke, one by Daniel Webster, and one by Abraham Lincoln. Give the date and place of delivery of each address, and at least one anthology or collection in which it is published.

b. In March, 1964, the Senator from Arkansas delivered an address in the United States Senate. State the title and exact date of this address and the name of the speaker. Give the source in which you found a verbatim published copy, and cite at least one newspaper or magazine comment on the speaker's point of view.

c. In 1935 D. W. Chapman and H. E. Brown conducted an experiment on a psychological problem. Cite the exact source in which this experiment was reported, and summarize the conclusions reached. To what phase of speech ability do these conclusions apply?

d. On August 15, 1947, a nation became free after 346 years of intermittent rule by a colonial power. What nation was this? From what colonial power did it gain its freedom?

e. In 1940 an article was written on "Better copper made by plastic conversion under high pressure." Where can this article be found?

f. What article appears on page 33 of the *Atlantic Monthly* for March, 1947?

g. Who is Louis B. Seltzer? Marcel Marceau?

h. What is the meaning and derivation of the word *sophisticated?*

i. Who won the men's shot-put event at the Olympic games in 1932?

j. Who wrote the article on the Sophists in the *Encyclopaedia Britannica?* What were his qualifications for such authorship?

k. Report on the background of each of the following persons, including place of birth, school or college attended, religion, early work experience, and primary occupation or position for which chiefly known:

Clare Boothe Luce	Westbrook Pegler
Walter Winchell	Lowell Thomas

Mark Hatfield   Alben Barkley

l. Locate and state the voting record of each of the following members of the so-called "infamous" Eighty-first Congress on all military issues:

Joseph McCarthy   Wayne Morse
Harry Cain   Scott W. Lucas

m. When running for the office of Vice President of the United States, Franklin D. Roosevelt in a speech described the Republican platform as a "Hymn of Hate." What was the title of the speech? Where was it delivered? On what date?

n. What happened to the gross national product of the United States in 1963? Where did you find this information? Cite completely and exactly.

o. List the lead articles in the two most recent issues of the *Federal Reserve Bulletin*. How often is this publication issued? Name the current members of its editorial committee.

p. In 1962 a well-known American psychological journal published an article entitled, "On the relation between logic and thinking." Determine the name of the author and the journal, the exact citation of the article and its main thesis. Where did you find the information? Describe briefly the nature of the publication and the way in which it is organized.

q. In 1948 Helene Blattner wrote an article on pronunciation. State its correct title, place and date of publication, and the author's professional position at the time. In what sources did you find the information?

r. What was the total number of broadcast stations (AM, FM, TV), operating in the United States on January 1, 1962?

s. In 1960 Random House published a pamphlet of travel information about the city of Rome, Italy. Report the title, size, nature of contents, and price of this publication. Where did you find the information?

t. In 1879 Robert G. Ingersoll delivered the famous "Oration At His Brother's Grave," which has been included in several anthologies of public addresses. List at least two sources in which it is published. In what reference work did you find this information?

7

INFERENCE

Knowing facts and making inferences from them are activities which imply and depend upon each other. The moment a man becomes aware of any kind of information, he begins to interpret or apply it or draw conclusions from it. Knowing tends to be an earlier phase, inferring a later phase of one continuous process of thinking; neither part of the process could occur or be meaningful without the other.

The term *inference* refers to both process and result. In its primary meaning inference is a process—the drawing of a conclusion from known facts (or opinions), a forward movement in thought from what is already known (or believed) to some new formulation of knowledge. Inference is a process of relating units of knowledge to each other. Illustrations occur every day, indeed every hour, of our waking lives. If I have heard the siren every Wednesday at noon for many months, I confidently expect to hear it again next Wednesday. My belief that all men are brothers will influence my attitude toward any individual man. If twenty of my fellow students tell me that Professor Dunderhead is a rigorous teacher, I may decide to take his course.

We also use the word *inference* to name the newly formulated knowledge or result of the mind's action. As a process inference occurs and is done before we can stop it or pin it down; but it brings into view a conclusion, a tangible unit of thought, which can be known, tested, and related to other facts and conclusions in our world of experience.

Types of Relationships

First, what kinds of relationships are basic to our thought for speech? Actually the possibilities are as numerous and varied as our experiences. To catalogue all of them would be utterly impossible, but we can recognize the main classes into which they fall. The classification will depend on the way we look at our world of experience. There are at least three possible viewpoints:

1. Substantive viewpoint: We look at objects and situations.
2. Functional viewpoint: We look at events, processes, and movements.

3. Subjective or conceptual viewpoint: We look at our own inner mental processes.

Representative relationships.   Fundamental to all our ways of looking at our experiences, whether substantive, functional, or subjective, are the sign-object relationship, in which a sign stands for external things or events, and the symbol-referent relationship between the word and that for which it stands.

Words symbolize not only tangible things in our experience but also such intangibles as the relationships among our units of knowledge. As you consider the meanings of words, you will realize that words such as *above, beside, larger* refer primarily to relationships between objects or substantive things; words such as *toward, after, into* refer chiefly to relationships between events or movements; and words such as *therefore, because* refer especially to subjective relationships or concepts.

Comparative relationships.   These also are common to all three viewpoints. When we compare situations or objects, we look at such elements as size or extent, shape, number of parts, colors, textures. When we compare events or movements, we consider speed, direction, acceleration. When we compare subjective processes, we analyze them in terms of kinds of perception, units of knowledge, and levels of abstraction. Comparison of all these kinds of elements transcends space and time. The keen observer discovers similarities and differences even in widely varied units of experience. When we emphasize the similarities, we have an important basis for grouping our observations into classes, for reasoning by analogy, and for an orderly and systematic world of experience. When we emphasize the differences, we have an important foundation for discrimination and analytical thinking, and for a varied and richly imaginative world of experience.

THE SUBSTANTIVE VIEWPOINT

We look at and talk about the world in terms of its objects and situations. Such a view, of course, is limited and inadequate, for the world is in ceaseless change. Nevertheless objects and situations do have a relative stability and permanence. We perceive things this way as a part of our common daily experience. From this point of view we can recognize at least three kinds of relationships:

Spatial relations.   Objects and situations are related in terms of distance and relative position. Some are near, some far. Some objects belong in the same setting; others are at opposite ends of the universe. Some are above, some below. Some are east, west, north, or south of others; some to the right, others to the left. We also see spatial relationships in the form of things. Front and back, top and bottom, central body and appendage, are spatial arrangements which help to determine the distinctive appearances of objects. Such relationships may change, of course, but for any given moment of time they constitute one of the basic patterns in which we observe the world around us and organize our observations.

Part-whole relations. We often perceive things in terms of their complexity, i.e., we observe the various parts or divisions in any given object or situation. The wall is a unit made up of bricks and is at the same time an integral part of the house. The mast is recognized as a distinct unit, but is also seen as part of the ship. All observation, as we have seen, involves analysis of things into smaller units and their synthesis into larger wholes. Recognition of part-whole relationships is essential to a well-organized awareness of the world around us.

Relationships of substance and quality. Every tangible thing which we perceive may be analyzed in terms of its various qualities. When we first see an object, it appears as one indivisible unit. There it is before us in its wholeness. In course of time we learn to recognize various properties: the shape or roundness of a ball, its diameter or size, its color, its surface texture, its flexibility or bounce. Most if not all of the situations and objects of our experience are analyzed into a series of such elements, with the result that each element or quality becomes a distinctive unit of perception in its own right. Nevertheless the object does not lose its unique wholeness. Throughout all this perceptual analysis we retain the impression of substance; the object remains before us as a solid thing to which the sensory qualities belong and which is more than the sum of those qualities.

THE FUNCTIONAL VIEWPOINT

We also look at and talk about the world as a continuity of process or movement, a sequence of things happening. From this point of view we can recognize at least two kinds of relationships:

Sequence in time. Events precede and follow each other. We think in terms of past, present and future and mentally arrange our experiences as "prior to," "simultaneous with," and "afterward." Any distortion of these relationships makes our world of experience disordered and confused.

Causal relationships. A causal relation is a connection between events such that one can be said to lead inevitably to the other. The first event is the moving force which produces the second.

This gives us a clue to one important distinction between description and explanation. Simple description of an event requires no more than orderly presentation of its setting and the series of movements involved and perhaps some comparisons and contrasts with other events. In order to *explain* the event, however, we need to point to the forces which produced it. Description of the symptoms of a disease, for example, does not explain its origins or nature. The skillful physician not only observes symptoms, but conducts extensive tests in his search for the causes and conditions which really explain an illness.

If we wish to give a full-rounded explanation of an event, we should also point out the effects it has produced or may produce. The past experience of a doctor often enables him to predict the future course of a disease and the probable extent of its damage to the body. Observation of results is as necessary as the search for causes if we want to understand any event fully.

Having observed a given event, we may wish to find its antecedent or the forces which produced it. If we can trace a direct line of influence back to its origin in an earlier event or series of events, we have discovered an *effect-to-cause* relationship. Or we may wish to trace a connection in the opposite direction and predict the probable future result of a present incident or course of action. A doctor must be able to predict the probable outcome of a given treatment. In such cases we are dealing with the functional significance of the earlier event or with *cause-to-effect* relationships.

Sometimes after we have discovered the cause or causes of a given event we may observe other effects of the same causes. A child's poor record in school, for example, may lead to discovery of an illness or injury in infancy, which when understood will explain some baffling health problem. Discovery of such a chain of relationship has been called *effect-to-effect* reasoning: We observe an effect, discover its cause, and then find that cause producing another result which, of course, is thus related to the event we first observed.

Every event is both cause and effect. In order to understand its full significance we should explore both its dynamic origins and the results or potential results which have followed or may follow from it in the future. In fact, causal relationship is seldom a one-way process. If one event can cause another, the second can very well react on the first so as to change its nature or operation, as when the low grade which results from neglect of study can bring about a change in study habits. In complex situations every single event or condition can influence or change every other event or condition so that causal relations become processes of interaction with many and varied lines of influence among the elements of a situation.

In most of life's events causal connections are not easy to observe. A virus may cause an illness but we cannot locate it or see it at work; medical researchers may labor long to find it. The reasons why one student fails while another succeeds are often complex and obscure. The tides of public opinion which win or lose elections are not easy to follow. Causes do not operate singly or in isolation; effects do not follow singly or in isolation. Causes operate in situations which are always changing, always partly new. Sometimes causes may be prevented from operating. A disease may be caused by a certain kind of bacteria, but they may not actually produce the illness in a given person unless the resistance of his organism has been lowered by circumstances of his environment and habits of living.

Because of these complexities certain elementary facts or conditions must be established before we can be sure that there is a causal connection between two events. We must be sure that the alleged cause actually preceded the observed effect, or that the alleged effect did in fact follow after the observed cause. We must be sure also that the antecedent event was adequate to produce the event which followed, and that related events neither displaced the alleged cause nor prevented its operation.

We shall consider in more detail the methods by which general conclusions about causal relationships may be established later on in this chapter.

THE CONCEPTUAL OR SUBJECTIVE VIEWPOINT

We may turn our attention inward to our own private mental processes. By analyzing, classifying, and organizing, we interpret the facts of direct observation to form generalized concepts and principles. The kinds of relationships among these more complex orders of knowledge are as varied as our experiences and mental processes. Some of them are most important in our thinking for speech.

Continuity. The continuity with which images, attitudes, and concepts follow each other in our inner thought processes is analogous to the time sequence of outer events as we perceive them. Psychologists of an earlier day used to speak of the stream of consciousness; and some modern novelists (such as Katherine Mansfield and Virginia Woolf) write detailed descriptions of this inner flow of ideas. All of us have observed such continuity of thought in ourselves, sometimes in simple form and again in more complex patterns.

In its most elementary form this succession of ideas is illustrated by the random associations of daydreaming. In more complex forms the flow of our ideas consists of generalizations, concepts, beliefs, and judgments. Many of these may be vague and nascent; others may attain definite formulation in words. In all its forms, whether elementary or complex, the sequence of our units of knowledge is an important relationship which underlies the orderly phrasing of our everyday communication with each other.

Relationships between concepts—levels of abstraction. We have defined a concept (Chapter 6) as a general idea built up by recognizing the essential items of similarity in a large number of more specific perceptions or units of knowledge. We attend to essential details and ignore the nonessential. The result is classification of items into groups according to the relationships of likeness and difference among the essential items.

Concepts are formed at various levels of generalization and analysis and with different degrees of abstraction. If we begin with the simple direct observation of chairs (chair[1], chair[2], chair[3], etc.) and form the concept *chair*, we shall almost certainly become aware that chairs are perceived and used in relation to other articles of furniture; and that in functional terms of use, all such objects belong together in a larger class of *household furniture*. This is a more complex concept than *chair* because a wider variety of objects is included. A higher order of abstraction is also involved because the characteristics which the members of the class, articles of furniture, have in common are fewer in number and more general than are the common features of chairs.

Continuing this line of thought we realize, of course, that articles of furniture have something in common with household appliances such as stoves, water heaters, and refrigerators; and that the two classes may be combined into a still larger class of *household equipment* in which the distinguishing characteristics among members of the class are even more general. In like manner household equipment may be absorbed into the larger class of *manufactured goods*, in which the recognizable features of specific things like chairs are no longer important. At this level a chair has ceased to be looked at as a seat with four legs and a back, or even as something to sit on; but is regarded, in common with all members of the larger class, as a certain kind of product. We might extend the levels of generalization and abstraction by observing that manufactured goods become *articles of commerce*, whose value may be computed as part of *gross national product*, which is a significant element of *wealth*, and so on.

We observe that the process of classification depends on discovering the essential properties of things. In other words it involves analysis. Now analysis can be extended in its own right. If we go back to the primary observation level and begin with our perception of any single chair, we can describe its characteristics at several different levels. We can recognize first its main parts (seat, back, legs, etc.); then the various kinds of materials of which these parts consist (wood, metal, leather, cloth, etc.); and then perhaps such detailed features as the grain of the wood, the weave of the cloth, the thickness of the leather. Beyond this we might take the materials into a laboratory for chemical analysis, and perhaps even describe them in terms of molecular structure. The chair, by this time, will have disappeared from our awareness as a thing to sit on, and perhaps even as a distinct sensory unit.

Probably few of us will ever have to analyze and classify chairs as fully as our illustration suggests; but we may well need to explore and develop the relationships of many other units of knowledge. Every area of study and experience requires some such systematic development of its levels of knowledge. We not only classify objects, but also events and processes and many complex, intangible elements of our experience and thought. Biologists classify plants and animals in a sequence of levels—variety, species, genus, family, order, class, phylum, and kingdom. According to the requirements of their several areas of study, chemists classify material elements, sociologists social events, economists fiscal institutions, psychologists mental processes, philosophers the basic problems of life. In daily life we all are constantly classifying the people we meet, the games we play, the kinds of food we eat, the schools we attend, in fact every aspect of our experience. We find typical common elements and so arrange things, events, or ideas in groups and hierarchies of groups. The items we classify may have no necessary physical nearness to each other; the groups exist primarily in mentally conceived relationships, and hence are primarily subjective or conceptual instead of external.

We have already observed that this process of classifying our experiences involves the dangers of stereotyping and prejudice (see Chapter 5). We can and should try to avoid these dangers; but if life is to have any coherent meaning whatever, we cannot avoid the processes of abstraction and generalization, even if we would, because of the sheer impossibility of dealing in any other way with the mass of detail in every day's experience. Our knowledge and experience are broken into units, these units are organized into generalized concepts, and these in turn into propositions expressing beliefs and judgments. All of these are levels of knowing which enter into our daily speech.

Sensible discourse requires constant interplay between these various levels of knowledge, especially between the objects and events of direct observation and the various levels of analysis and classification. Objects and events as perceived have little, if any, meaning except as we analyze them into their essential elements and organize and classify them in larger and more generalized relationships. At the same time analysis and classification mean nothing if they are not solidly grounded in well-verified information. There is no surer way to talk nonsense than to indulge in imaginary discriminations or sweeping generalizations which are not based directly or indirectly on facts of experience. Pointless discrimination is the way of the pedant; sweeping generalization the way of the fourflusher. If we are to communicate successfully, we must give detailed, first-order facts; and if they are to be meaningful, we must also analyze and classify them, i.e., single out the important elements and relate them to important elements in other observed facts. Throughout these processes we need to be aware of the changing levels of abstraction at which we may be working in order to keep our feet firmly on the solid ground of reality.

Predication.   All of us have been taught to regard a sentence as a grammatical unit. Predication is also a way of relating smaller units of knowledge to each other or of combining them in sensible relationships. We combine concepts, together with other kinds of thought units such as specific details and statistics, to form propositions or statements. The typical pattern for such combinations lays down a subject and then declares some functional or dynamic truth about that subject. By itself a concept is essentially topical, and although topics are useful and necessary, they tend to be static and lacking in dynamic force. A topic, expressed in a phrase, may suggest a great deal of meaning, but it actually declares or predicates very little if anything. When units of knowledge are combined into sentences, however, they become assertions which have vital significance in directing our decisions and activities. (See the section on principles in Chapter 6 and the section on arrangement of words in Chapter 17.) All propositional speech involves arranging and joining units of knowledge together in statements of varying complexity. In the section on inference we shall point out that propositions are derived by the processes of induction and form the bases of deductions.

Logical relationships. In its most elemental form a logical relationship is a simple connection in which one unit of knowledge implies or leads to another. In this general sense most or all of the relationships between our subjective mental processes could be called logical. In stricter or more exact meaning, however, logic refers primarily to relationships between propositions. A logical relationship is such a connection between statements that if one or more is accepted as true, another must also be accepted. One statement implies another.

Such a relationship involves closer connections than any we have so far discussed. Units of knowledge may follow each other in orderly sequence, the various levels of abstraction may be distinguished from each other, concepts may be joined in statements, and these organized in patterns of relative importance; and yet the deeper affinity of ideas for each other may be missing from our thought and discourse. Logical relationship means that one idea is derived from one or more other ideas, that the connection between them is necessary and compelling, that the forward leap of the mind from one statement or set of facts to a conclusion has an element of inevitability.

The elementary continuity of our thought, in which each idea calls up the next by a kind of free or even random association, involves no such compelling necessity. One fact or concept may imply or suggest another in a casual or topical sort of way, and concepts may even be drawn together into statements and organized according to degrees of importance with only an elemental kind of association. Logical relationship, however, goes beyond these simpler connections between single thought units. It may indeed connect single thought units, but in the truest sense it is a bond of union between statements; and moreover, such a bond that if one is true the other must necessarily be true, or if one is thought to be true the other must be accepted as true for the moment or until shown to be false. In logical relationships there is a close-knit, dynamic and forward-moving quality which characterizes all our higher thought processes.

We should not misunderstand the *necessary and compelling* nature of logical relationships. The inevitability of an inference refers to the nature of the *connection* between propositions, not to the truth or acceptability of the conclusion. When the conclusion of an inference necessarily follows from the first statement or set of facts, we say that the inference is valid. This means that the forward leap of the mind conforms to the laws or principles of logic which is the science of correct inferences.

There are many and varied degrees of the *necessity* by which conclusions follow from facts or groups of facts. Sometimes our inferences may be perfectly valid, i.e., in full accord with the laws of logic. More often in this world of uncertainties and probabilities, logical validity is only approximate. The connection between premises and conclusion, instead of being really inevitable, may involve some degree of error or lack of inherent relationship. Compliance with the laws of logic may be less than perfect, and our inferences may lead to nothing more than opinions and uncertain guesses. The principles of logic which we are to study in the next section are methods of developing inferences which are as close as possible to perfect validity.

Do not confuse the validity of an inference with the truth of the facts from which it arises or on which it is based. All the logic in the world will not produce a truthful conclusion if the basic facts are not true. An inference may be logically valid, but its conclusion false if the premises are false. On the other hand the basic facts may be true, but the inference invalid or illogical and the conclusion therefore false. Two elements must join to make our thought processes credible: (1) the basic facts must be true, and (2) the processes of inference must conform to the laws of logic. A builder can ruin a house either by choosing poor materials or by putting them together carelessly.

We have now completed our survey of the principal ways in which our units of knowledge may be related to each other. These relationships, together with our knowledge of the ways of finding and using facts (Chapter 6), provide the foundations on which we organize and develop discourse. This brings us to a second important question: By what methods may the relationships of ideas be developed into sensible discourse? In other words we are now to consider methods of inference and the laws of logic which govern their use.

Methods of Inference

The basic methods of inference are induction and deduction. These are the ways in which we recognize and develop relationships among our various units of knowledge. In their more advanced uses induction and deduction evolve into reasoning, judgment and problem-solving, which may involve any or all of the kinds of elemental relationships among units of knowledge which we have just considered. These more advanced and complex uses of inference are ways of interpreting knowledge and applying it to daily life. The center of our interest, of course, is in the application of the processes of inference to our speech. Discourse may not always be strictly logical in form, but at least it should not violate the principles of logic.

Before launching into a study of the principal methods of inference, however, we should consider hypothesis, a preliminary process

*Inference, like magic,
is a drawing out.*

which might be considered a kind of inference, but is less definite in procedure and less reliable in outcome.

A hypothesis is an educated guess, a reasonable but inconclusive statement, a tentative conclusion which requires further testing and verification. When our information about any situation or problem is uncertain and incomplete, and provides no adequate basis for a reliable conclusion, we improvise the best conclusion possible under the circumstances. We interpret the available facts to the best of our ability in order to derive a possible explanation of the situation or solution for the problem. This tentative conclusion we call a hypothesis. It is an attempt to explain the causes of a confused and difficult situation and points toward a possible remedy for the difficulty. It should account for the known facts in the simplest possible manner and with a minimum of assumptions.

Formulation of hypotheses is a basic step in the search for answers to our questions and difficulties. The tentative statement provides a preliminary explanation for such facts as are known and brings them into relationship to each other in some manner or to some degree, even though imperfect. A hypothesis thus has immediate value in providing a central theme around which further investigation may be carried on. Its imperfect or tentative quality points the need for additional fact-finding and suggests the direction further study should take.

When these processes have given any hypothesis a large measure of credibility, we call it a theory. Theories are generally believed and accepted as working principles because no better answers appear to be available. Any theory, however, is usually regarded with some reservation. When the greatest possible verification has been attained, theories move up to the status of laws or principles. Even at this level, however, the possibility of change should always be recognized. The history of science is strewn with laws once tenaciously believed but later disproved and rejected. Some well known examples are Newton's corpuscular theory of light, the Ptolemaic concept of the universe, the assumptions of the phrenologists, and the biological theory of spontaneous generation. We have no way of knowing with certainty how many of the accepted theories and principles of our own day may eventually be displaced, but recognition of that possibility is an indispensable foundation for unprejudiced and creative thought.

Our main interest just now, however, is not the history of science, but the kinds of thinking which will best serve our daily communication with other people. Hypothesis is one of the earliest steps in the slow and laborious climb up the ladder from our first distressing realization of a difficulty toward a conclusion which has the highest possible level of verification and certainty. We include it among uses of induction because it is derived from and interprets a body of facts, which are specific and challenging even though incomplete and tentative.

We now face the question, how can such a tentative conclusion be verified and made credible? For that purpose all methods of investigation and inference are or may be useful. The methods of investigation we have already considered (Chapter 6). To the methods of inference we now turn.

INDUCTION

When we derive a general statement about any group or class of objects or events from knowledge of a limited number of specific instances, we are using inductive inference. The process begins with detailed facts and moves toward a more general conclusion. We observe certain specific items and summarize some part of their essential common nature in a general statement or principle which is extended to include items we have not been able to observe. We conclude that what we see to be true of some units of knowledge must be true of all similar units.

Our inductive inferences are always open to some possibility of doubt or uncertainty and in most cases to a considerable degree of doubt. You and I have seen hundreds of cows, and all of them have four legs. Probably not one of us has ever seen a three-legged cow. It is possible, however, that such an exception has occurred somewhere outside our experience, or may occur at some time in the future. Greater uncertainties are typical in our everyday lives. Even though your professor may have been late to class every day for a week, you cannot safely assume that he will be late tomorrow. An inductive conclusion seldom has the fully compelling necessity which we have stated is characteristic of ideal logical relationship. The best we can hope for is a high degree of reliability. Seldom can we say, "All . . ."; the best we can do is to say, "Some . . ." or "Nearly all. . . ."

Even if we could examine all items or all members of a group or class of things, our general statement would perform only the first of the two functions of an inductive conclusion; it would merely summarize what we already know by observation. The second function— moving forward to a statement of new knowledge—would be unnecessary and impossible because no unobserved instances would be left to consider.

Primary forms of induction are generalization, analogy, and causal reasoning.

Generalization. The most elementary use of induction is counting of instances or items of knowledge. If we have observed a representative number of items, we feel safe in making a general statement about the entire class of things we are considering. What is a representative number? The number of instances required will vary according to the nature of the material, especially its degree of homogeneity, and according to the purpose of the enumeration. Unless the observed instances are known to be very homogeneous, one sample is almost never adequate. One spoonful from a bowl of sour cream, of course, will justify a conclusion about the contents of the entire bowl; but if we are dealing with a large and variable class of things, even several thousand cases might not be adequate to justify a conclusion about the entire group. Statisticians have developed some techniques for determining what size of any given sample is adequate; but in the casual discourse of daily life, those of us who are untrained in statistics (and sometimes even the statisticians) can only exercise all possible care that our samples are large enough to represent the entire class fairly. It is better to have too many items than not enough.

A more important kind of representation, however, is qualitative. Enumeration must be limited to items or units of knowledge which are of the same kind; and the similarities must be relevant to the purpose and point at issue. We must, therefore, face a second question:

Are these similarities the *essential* characteristics of the class of objects observed? If we want to draw a conclusion about size, color, type of organization, or functional value, our observations must be made in respect to these particular kinds of characteristics. We must find the relevant features and ignore the nonessential.

In other words we must use abstraction, and we must decide at what concept level our classification is to be made. Are chairs to be looked at as furniture, household equipment, manufactured objects, or articles of commerce? Is a cow to be classified as livestock or a mammal? At which of the several zoological levels should any animal be classified? How large a class are we to consider in any given case? Where shall we draw its boundaries? We must set the limits in such a way that the characteristics we have observed are fully typical of the entire class. The relationships of similarity must be both true and essential, i.e., related to the kind of conclusion we expect to make.

Generalization must include the two basic steps of all induction: We synthesize or generalize our observed particulars by perceiving relationships among them, arranging them in classes, forming concepts, and stating principles; then we infer that what we have generalized about the observed instances will be true also of those not observed, and so formulate an assertion broad enough to include both those which have been seen and those not seen. These steps are necessary if our enumeration is to yield anything more than a random and insignificant mass of details. Specific items of knowledge are the foundation of induction, but any single item by itself has little meaning or significance unless it is seen in relation to other specific items. Our counting of instances has limited value if it does not lead on to that leap of the mind by which we form general propositions.

Analogy. All induction, indeed all inference, has an implied element of comparison, as we have seen; but analogy makes an especially direct use of it. Instead of enumerating a number of similar objects or events, analogy is based on comparison of the qualities or characteristics of two items or units of experience. The compared units may be persons, objects, events, or entire situations. As a form of inference, however, analogy goes beyond simple comparison. If two persons or objects or events, for example, are alike in several observed characteristics, we infer that they must also be similar in another way which we can observe in one unit but are not able to see in the other.

If, for example, we know two students who come from homes of similar cultural environment, who have completed similar preparatory education with comparable scholastic standing, and who have passed college admission examinations with equally high scores; and if we know that one of these students has already achieved success in a particular kind of college course, then we might well be justified in inferring by analogy that the other student will be likewise successful. The induction is based on recognition of similar qualities or characteristics, but the mind moves forward from what is known of one to what has not been observed of the other.

Logicians describe the process as follows: If A is characterized by x, y, and z in relation to each other, and we know that B is characterized by x and y, then we infer by analogy that B is also characterized by z. We respond to B by seeing in it (i.e., inferring) the same property (labeled z in our illustration) we observed in A. In doing this we necessarily overlook any differences which are irrelevant to the purpose of our investigation. In this way analogical inference, like all induction, involves abstraction (i.e., selection of essential elements) as well as comparison and classification.

From the standpoint of behavior this recognition of similar or identical features is described as *identity of response*. We respond to various situations or objects in the same way by observing their similar features and ignoring the differences between them. You, for example, have been well instructed in the significance of the traffic light at a street intersection. You use analogy when you extend that knowledge to the general principle that a red light on radio tower, ship, or beacon is likewise a warning signal, and that a green light anywhere is a sign that you may proceed with safety. You infer that street corner, radio tower, ship and beacon are enough alike in essential properties to justify interpreting the signals in the same way in all four situations.

Such progression from the known to the unfamiliar is at once a stabilizing and a limiting influence. Thinking which is not anchored to well-established facts may easily become fanciful and extreme. On the other hand thinking which does not launch out boldly into unexplored channels discovers nothing new. This is the hazard as well as the value of analogy, as of all induction. We move from the familiar to the unknown. Our only safeguard is to be as certain as possible that the foundation of similarity between compared units is adequate to justify the inferred conclusion. The usefulness of analogy depends on tests which are similar to those for enumeration and in fact for all induction.

What is the extent of resemblance between the compared units? In how many particulars are the two actually alike? Do the similarities outnumber the differences? Such numerical tests may sometimes be important in themselves, but their real value arises in relation to the qualitative test suggested by further questions: Are the compared units alike in *essential* qualities? Are the similarities relevant to the conclusion? What is the purpose of your comparison?

If you are comparing football as played in Canada with that in the United States, for example, do you wish to draw a conclusion about the economic aspects, the entertainment values, or the effect on players? If your purpose is economic, you would want to know about cost of stadiums, traveling expenses of teams, gate receipts, and similar matters. If your main interest is in entertainment values, you would want information about style of play, scoring, and typical weather during the playing season. If you are appraising effect on players, you should compare salaries, frequency of injuries, number of years of participation, and occupational possibilities after playing years have passed. We should not make the mistake of assuming that because the two types of football are similar in one aspect they are, therefore, similar in all other aspects. The problem is one of determining whether the details of comparison are typical or representative of the area in which the conclusion is to be drawn.

How can we tell whether any given item is representative? There is no way except examination of details. If they belong together, if they fit the purpose for which the investigation is made, we conclude they are relevant. The details of comparison should be within the same classification or frame of reference as the intended conclusion.

Causal reasoning.   In the section on the functional viewpoint, we considered causal relationships between specific events, and stated some of the principles by which a speaker can test the actual existence of such connections. Now we are to study methods by which a speaker with a forecast to make or a point to prove may show that a given kind of event always or usually leads to a certain kind of result, or that a given observed effect typically follows a distinctive kind of antecedent.

Causal reasoning requires us to observe and compare numerous instances of the concurrence of such connections in as many and varied circumstances as possible. If we find that a certain kind of event or set of conditions is invariably followed by a certain kind of result, we infer that there must be a uniform causal relationship between them and that similar antecedents will again lead to similar effects. This is probably the highest and, if properly used, the most rigorous level of inductive thought. It involves three basic procedures or tests of soundness known as Mill's canons because they were given their basic formulation by John Stuart Mill, an English logician and philosopher of the nineteenth century.

1. Method of agreement.   Let us take a simple illustration close to our experience as students. We are interested in exploring the reasons why some of us fail or receive low grades. Suppose that we are to study a group of freshmen who are failing in one or more of their courses. We find a wide variety of possible causes. Some of the students may be devoting a large share of their time to campus activities; others work long hours to pay their college expenses. Some may have haphazard and disorganized study habits; others may not know how to take notes on lectures. Some may be lonesome or homesick or in some other way unhappy in the campus situation; others may have personality clashes with one or two of their professors. Some do not attend class regularly; others may not know how to participate effectively in class discussion.

Most of these possible causes are general and difficult to measure with precision, but let us assume for purposes of the illustration that we are advisors and by talking with the students and studying their records can obtain reasonably definite information. Let us suppose that even though we find a different set of circumstances for each student, some one common factor appears in every case of failure. Let us assume that this common factor is irregular class attendance. If there are no exceptions and this is the only factor which appears uniformly, then we would be justified in concluding that for this group of students there is a causal relationship between irregular class attendance and failure in a course. A situation of this kind illustrates the principle of agreement which may be stated as follows: *Two phenomena may be said to have a causal connection if occurrence of one is invariably followed by occurrence of the other in all the varied situations and circumstances in which they can be observed.*

In applying this method, however, we must consider the probability that our study of these freshmen may not reveal any one factor which always attends course failure. Entirely different circumstances may appear in each case. We should then suspect that the scope of our investigation is too narrow. We may not have included the real cause in our list of possible causes or hypotheses. Some other factor such as poor health or lack of intellectual ability may be the causal factor common to all cases of failure. Certainly these possible causes should not have been overlooked, and we should have included physical and mental examinations in our study. If all possible causes are not observed, the method of agreement is likely to prove ineffective.

We should also consider the possibility that a failing grade may be the result of more than one cause. If two factors appear uniformly in all students who fail, we might conclude of course, that both together are the cause and let the problem rest there. However, each of the two apparent causes might appear in different individual students. Some of them who fail might be unable to take adequate notes; others might be unable to engage in class discussion effectively. We might then conclude that either circumstance could be the cause of failure, but we would do better to suspect that we have not been discriminating enough in our observations. We should examine the kinds of courses in which these students fall short. We might discover, for example, a difference between lecture courses and those in which discussion is a large element. We might observe inadequacy in the notebooks of those who fail the lecture course, and inability to engage in discussion as a uniform characteristic of those who fail the discussion type of course. If so, we would conclude that there was a different cause for failure in each type of course. Successful use of the method of agreement requires careful observation and discriminating classification of the events for which causal relationships are to be determined (see sections on generalization and analogy above).

2. *Method of difference.* The difficulties and uncertainties in the method of agreement suggest that other methods may sometimes be needed to verify our conclusions. Let us return to our first illustrative situation in which we observed that for our group of freshmen, failure in a course is always preceded by irregular class attendance. This indicates that irregular attendance is a cause of failure, but it does not show that poor attendance is always and inevitably followed by failure. Some students may be found who attend class irregularly but succeed in passing. The method of agreement does not by itself establish a uniform one-to-one relationship between the two events, irregular class attendance and failure. In order to establish a greater degree of certainty in our conclusion, we should study not only the records of all those who failed but also of those who made passing grades. Was their attendance regular or irregular? In other words we need to study the negative instances—in this case the instances of nonfailure.

For the sake of the illustration suppose we find that none of the freshmen in our group who got a passing grade has been irregular in attendance. We would then have double confirmation of the causal connection. Those students who fail have attended irregularly; and all those who attended irregularly have failed. Not one who passed has been irregular. If this improbable situation should actually occur, we would have established a reasonably clear and uniform one-to-one causal relationship between irregular class attendance and failure. This second method, involving observation of negative instances, is called the method of difference. The combined methods of agreement and difference may be summarized thus: *Two phenomena may be said to have a dependable and uniform causal relationship if, in all situations in which they normally occur, (1) the occurrence of one is always preceded or followed by occurrence of the other and (2) nonoccurrence of one is always preceded or followed by nonoccurrence of the other.*

3. *Method of concomitant variations.* This is also called the method of covariation or functional correspondence. Real life situations are always complex, as we have already seen, and their elements interact in complicated ways. The illustration we have used is obviously oversimplified and hypothetical. Probably neither regular class attendance nor any other one factor by itself will ever determine a student's grade. Irregular attendance probably would be influenced by some other factors such as condition of health, or amount of time spent in campus activities or outside work. Hence even the combined methods of agreement and difference may leave considerable uncertainty about actual causal relationships. We still cannot be entirely certain that we have adequately considered all possible factors; nor can we arrive by these

methods at any measure of the relative influence of the various factors. In many cases we cannot even be sure which of the forces in a situation might be the principal cause. Some of our freshmen might be failing primarily because of home conditions, or intense preoccupation with another subject of study, or even disappointment in love.

In our illustration, moreover, the situation is oversimplified in another way. We have considered only two alternatives, passing or failing; when as a matter of fact the grading system provides for recognition of several levels of achievement. In many cases the difference between a *D* grade and a failure may not be very significant, especially if the student is already on probation; and sometimes even the difference between *C* and failure may have little practical significance, as, for example, if the student is trying to earn a place on the honor roll. The *C* might ruin his prospects with as much finality as failure. If we wish to establish a clear causal relation between two factors or kinds of events, we need to consider not just the presence or absence of each but also the relationship between levels of variation in each.

For purposes of illustration let us again suppose that different individuals in our group of freshmen attend classes with various degrees of regularity. If we find at the end of a term that those whose attendance was least regular had lowest grades, those with medium regularity of attendance had middle range grades, while those with most regular attendance had highest grades, and if after careful search we find no other factors in the situation which seem to change with grades, then we could affirm a causal relationship between class attendance and grades with even more confidence than the methods of agreement and difference by themselves would justify.

A similar method could be applied to the relationship between class attendance and grades for any single student. Suppose that Jonathan Doolittle attends different classes throughout his college career with various degrees of regularity. If we keep careful records of both his attendance and his grades, we might find a significant degree of covariation which could justify a conclusion about the causal connection between his grades and class attendance. This third method of testing or verifying causal relations can be summarized as follows: *Two phenomena have a dependable and uniform causal relationship if, in all situations in which they occur together, any variation in one is accompanied by a comparable degree of variation in the other and any lack of change in one is accompanied by a similar lack of change in the other.*

This method has special value in situations where it is possible to control the variables. To continue our imaginary illustration, suppose we could control class attendance deliberately so as to produce various degrees of irregularity and compare these variations with differences in grades. If all other factors in the situation—such as study hours, health, outside activities—could be held constant for all members of the group, we might then draw a valid conclusion about the relationship between class attendance and grades. In fact, with grade levels expressed in numerical grade points, the functional relationship between the two variables might be stated in quantitative mathematical terms such as an equation or coefficient of correlation. Such procedure is the essence of scientific method.

In situations where all variables can be completely controlled, especially in laboratory situations, exact quantitative results are often possible. In life situations, however, such control is seldom achieved. Because of the complex interrelation of factors we may not always be able to tell which of several variables is cause and which effect; in fact two or more elements of the situation may be results of another unknown factor or combination of factors. One of the so-called effects might even react upon its antecedents so as to reverse the causal sequence of events. In our illustration, for example, grades already given might influence a student's morale or his interest in his studies and thus change the regularity of his class attendance. In such situations we are no longer dealing with direct and simple causal connections, but with highly variable functional relationships between events.

It must be evident that no single method by itself is entirely adequate to verify the truth of causal relationships. Indeed all three methods together may often leave considerable reason to doubt the conclusion. Simple agreement among instances of a given kind of event is necessary as a first step. Observation of consistent differences between positive and negative cases adds a degree of assurance, but still takes no adequate account of the complexities of life situations nor of various levels of change. If two kinds of events meet the tests of agreement and difference adequately and in addition display concomitant patterns of variation, we might be justified in concluding that one is a cause of the other.

Summary. We have now completed our rapid survey of the methods of inductive inference. These are ways in which specific units of knowledge are brought into relationship to each other and interpreted so as to form general propositions. If you will now look again at our discussion of the kinds of relationships we find in the world of our experience, you will observe that almost all of them function to some extent in the processes of induction, but that comparison, abstraction, causal relations, and predication, as we have noticed, are at the core of the process. These are the kinds of relationships with which induction chiefly deals.

DEDUCTION

In its most general and popular meaning the term *deduction* is often used to include all processes of inference of every kind. Its more precise meaning, however, refers to that kind of inference which applies a general proposition to a more specific or less inclusive unit of knowledge. Deductive reasoning is a method of applying general principles to particular cases. It begins with a general statement which usually is accepted on the basis of observation or comparison, or as logicians like to say, established by inductive methods. The inference then moves toward a more specific or limited conclusion. When we have accepted a proposition as true, deduction shows what further propositions must also be accepted. Deduction, in other words, develops the implications of our knowledge and belief.

Although the deductive process involves several kinds of relationships among ideas, especially causal relationships and various levels of abstraction and classification, the primary characteristic is the logical relationship. This, as you will recall, is such a close affinity between propositions that if one is accepted as true the other probably is also true. The deductive process deduces or draws out what is already inherent in the premises; and the conclusion states explicitly what is already implied. Because of this we say that the connection between statements in a valid deduction is a necessary or perfect relationship. If the basic premises are true, the conclusion must be true. In fact, deduction has been defined as that kind of inference in which the conclusion follows necessarily from the premises.

Deduction is, therefore, the opposite of induction in at least two primary ways: (1) Whereas induction proceeds from specific items to general statement, deduction proceeds from general statement to more specific or less inclusive units of knowledge. (2) Whereas induction usually involves some element of uncertainty, a valid deduction leads to a conclusion that is inevitable and true if the premises are true.

We shall understand deduction more easily if we think in terms of the syllogism, the typical form in which deductive inferences are stated. Actually there are three principal forms of the syllogism—categorical, hypothetical, and disjunctive; but all syllogisms of whatever form are alike in consisting of three propositions, of which two are premises and the third a conclusion inferred from the premises. The hypothetical and disjunctive forms are of some importance and will be discussed briefly, but the categorical syllogism is the most basic and will command most of our attention.

The categorical syllogism. Let us consider some illustrations beginning with one which has come down to us from the early Greek study of logic:

Major premise: All men are mortal.
Minor premise: Socrates is a man.
Conclusion: Therefore Socrates is mortal.

The first statement or major premise is a general proposition which declares that all members of a given class, men, are included in a larger class of mortal beings. The second statement or minor premise brings a particular person within the scope of that first statement, i.e., within the class of men. The final sentence merely states the obvious conclusion that what is declared in the major premise must also be true of Socrates.

Notice that each of the statements in this syllogism is made up of two parts which logicians call *terms*. In the entire syllogism there are three terms of which the first two, *men* and *mortal beings*, are general concepts and the third, *Socrates*, is a particular unit of knowledge. In a valid categorical syllogism these terms must always be combined in a fixed and definite pattern:

The major premise:
   Middle term, man (all men) + major term, mortal beings
The minor premise:
   Minor term, Socrates + middle term, man
The conclusion:
   Minor term, Socrates + major term, mortal beings

The middle term occurs in both premises and serves as an agent for bringing the other two terms into relationship to each other. Having performed its function, this middle term is then dropped and the conclusion states the connection established between the minor and major terms.

These relationships can be shown graphically by a series of circles as shown below. This deduction is as conclusive as we can expect any inference to be. The two premises are universally accepted as true;

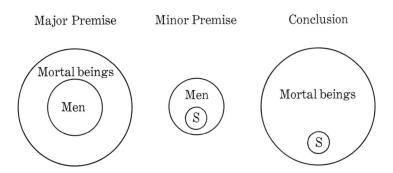

| Major Premise | Minor Premise | Conclusion |

we have no reason to doubt that men are mortal nor that Socrates was a man. Since the premises categorically place all men among mortal beings and Socrates among men, the conclusion is inevitable.

Consider now another illustration:

Major premise: Most freshmen are naïve.
Minor premise: Felix is a freshman.
Conclusion: Therefore Felix is likely to be naïve.

In this there is no such assurance as we find in the first illustration about Socrates. The wording "Most freshmen . . ." leaves some possibility that Felix may belong to that small group of freshmen who are quite sophisticated. All we can conclude is that Felix is "likely to be naïve." In the graphic illustration below the circles do not fall within each other as neatly as in the preceding syllogism.

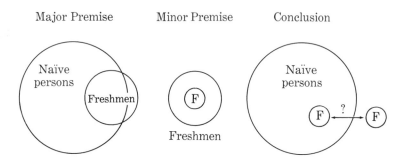

| Major Premise | Minor Premise | Conclusion |

Only some freshmen are naïve.   How should Felix be classified?

Where does Felix belong—among naïve persons or outside that class? Nothing in the premises gives us an answer. All we can conclude is that since the greater number of freshmen are naïve, Felix is likely to be among them. If we could count the number of naïve freshmen exactly, we might state the probability that Felix is one of them in a numerical ratio, for the probable truth of any assertion is the proportion of cases in which it can be verified as true.

In this example, however, we are given no such exact information; all we know is that most freshmen are naïve and that a few are not. The middle term, *freshmen,* the concept which forms the connecting link between naïve persons and Felix, is not taken in its full meaning and the conclusion is therefore in doubt. If in this second example we could say, "All freshmen . . ." with as much assurance as we said "All men . . ." in the first example, the deduction would be equally conclusive. In a valid syllogism the middle term must include all members of its class, i.e., must be taken in its full extent of meaning. As the logicians say, "It must be distributed" in at least one of the premises.

Let us take a third example:

Major premise: Any measure which helps to strengthen newly independent nations should be continued.
Minor premise: The foreign aid program helps to strengthen new nations.
Conclusion: Therefore foreign aid should be continued.

This deduction could be represented graphically, as was done for the two preceding examples, by drawing a large circle for (1) policies which should be continued, a smaller circle for (2) measures which help to strengthen new nations, and a very small circle for (3) foreign aid. The relationships among these terms are adequate for a valid conclusion. The middle term, *measures which help to strengthen newly independent nations*, is taken in its full meaning; the word *any* is equivalent to *all* in significance. The premises, if accepted as true, establish a clear logical connection between major and minor terms and the conclusion necessarily follows.

The uncertainties lie in the truth of the premises, not in their logical connections. It is not necessarily true that *any* measure that helps new nations, should be continued; some measures, in addition to the good they do, might do harm in certain unexpected ways. Indiscriminate foreign aid, for example, might undermine our own national economy. Moreover, foreign aid may or may not strengthen a particular new nation; much will depend on conditions within that nation and on the way the aid is granted and administered.

These observations emphasize the difference between truth and validity of an inference which we considered in the section on logical relationships earlier in this chapter. Statements may be true or false; but inferences are either valid or invalid. The truth of a premise can be established only by such inductive processes as observation and experiment. The validity of an inference can be established only by applying the tests of logic. A true deductive conclusion must meet a double test: Its premises must be true to fact; its inference must meet the test of validity.

Before we leave the categorical syllogism, we should observe the effect of negative premises. Consider, for example, the following deduction:

Major premise: No Republican will vote the Democratic ticket in the next election.
Minor premise: Jones is a Republican.
Conclusion: Therefore Jones will not vote the Democratic ticket.

According to the major premise, Jones as a Republican, is one of those who will not vote Democratic. This illustrates the general principle that if the major premise of a deduction is negative the conclusion must also be negative. If the minor premise is negative, however, or if both premises are negative, a valid conclusion can seldom, if ever, be drawn. If I argue, for example, that all businessmen will vote the Republican ticket in the next election, and add that Jones is not a businessman, I have failed to state whether Jones is among those who vote Republican or outside that class. All we know is that he is not a businessman; no conclusion is possible. Again, if I assert that no businessman will vote the Republican ticket (negative major premise) and point out that Jones is not a businessman (negative minor premise), I still have no way of knowing whether Jones is or is not among those who will vote Republican, and can make no valid inference. No valid conclusion is possible from two negative premises.

Let us now summarize what we have learned about the requirements of deductive inference as expressed in categorical syllogistic form:

1. A complete categorical syllogism must include three propositions: major premise, minor premise, and conclusion.
2. These propositions must be formulated by combining three terms or units of knowledge in the following pattern:

   Major premise: Middle term + major term
   Minor premise: Minor term + middle term
   Conclusion: Minor term + major term

3. No term may be used in the conclusion unless it has been used in the premises.
4. The middle term must be used in the full extent of its meaning in at least one of the premises.
5. If both premises are affirmative statements, the conclusion must be affirmative.
6. If the major premise is negative, the conclusion must be negative.
7. If both premises are negative, no valid conclusion can be inferred.
8. If one premise is limited, referring to "some" rather than "all" of a given class, the conclusion must be likewise limited; and the conclusion cannot be limited to "some" unless one premise is so limited.

Thus far we have been speaking entirely of the categorical syllogism. The two remaining forms, hypothetical and disjunctive, should be mentioned briefly:

The hypothetical syllogism. This begins with an "If . . . then . . ." type of statement. If *x* is true, then *y* necessarily follows. The "If" or conditional clause is called the antecedent; the "then" clause or statement of result is called the consequent.

   Major premise: If a student buys a ticket, he will be admitted
                     to the homecoming game.
   Minor premise: John has bought a ticket.
   Conclusion: Therefore he will be admitted.

John has satisfied the condition and will be admitted. Our statement affirms the antecedent, and the conclusion is valid.

Notice, however, the major premise does not say that purchase of a ticket is the only way to be admitted to the game. For all that the premise tells us, there may be other ways to gain admission, such as complimentary ticket or employment as an usher. Hence we cannot assert that if John does not buy a ticket he will not be admitted. We cannot deny the antecedent and draw a valid conclusion. Consider also the result of denying the consequent.

Major premise: If a student buys a ticket, he will be admitted.
Minor premise: John will not be admitted.
Conclusion: Therefore he has not bought a ticket.

This much we know from the minor premise: John will not be admitted. This means that none of the possible methods of admission, including purchase of a ticket, will be fulfilled. In short, truthful denial of the consequent makes possible a valid negative conclusion.

Now suppose that we know certain facts of the case which enable us to affirm the consequent: nothing in the information we are given tells us by what means. It could be by complimentary pass or several other methods, as well as by ticket. Hence even though we know that John will be admitted, we cannot conclude that he will purchase a ticket. We cannot affirm the consequent and draw a valid conclusion. In a hypothetical syllogism a valid conclusion is possible only if we affirm the antecedent or deny the consequent.

The disjunctive syllogism. This begins with a major premise which offers two or more alternatives, "Either this . . . or that . . . or that. . . ." The minor premise is a categorical statement which affirms one of the alternatives or denies all but one of them. If the minor premise affirms one alternative, the conclusion denies all the others. If the minor premise denies all but one alternative, the conclusion then affirms that one.

If in any given situation there are several alternatives, the task of establishing the minor premise is likely to be complicated and difficult. Disjunctions, therefore, are most useful in the simple form which involves only two alternatives. In such a case, if the minor premise affirms either alternative, the conclusion denies the other; or if the minor premise denies either alternative, the conclusion affirms the other. Consider the following:

Major premise: The accident occurred either on Highway 10 or Highway 99.
Minor premise: It could not have occurred on Highway 10.
Conclusion: Therefore it occurred on Highway 99.

or

Major premise: The accident occurred either on Highway 10 or Highway 99.
Minor premise: The report shows that it occurred on Highway 99.
Conclusion: Therefore it did not occur on Highway 10.

In this obvious form such an inference seems almost too simple to deserve comment; yet complex human events may often require reduction to such a form to bring important aspects into focus. Observe that no valid conclusion can be drawn unless the following are true:

1. The major premise includes all possible alternatives.
2. These alternatives are mutually exclusive; no one of them includes any part of the others or involves the others in its operation. Obviously no valid inference can be made if the alternatives are not true and complete alternatives.
3. The minor premise is clearly shown to be true.

Sometimes a disjunctive statement may be a concealed or poorly phrased hypothetical statement, especially if it involves causal relations. Consider the following:

Major premise: Mr. X will either increase his sales or his business will fail.
Minor premise: He cannot increase his sales.
Conclusion: Therefore his business will fail.

The conclusion seems entirely valid. Consider, however, a minor premise which affirms the other apparent alternative:

Major premise: Either Mr. X will increase his sales or his business will fail.
Minor premise: His business will fail.
Conclusion: Therefore he will not increase his sales.

The conclusion does not follow because other factors than sales might cause the failure, e.g., high costs or labor troubles.

The fault here might seem to be omission of possible alternatives such as reducing costs or solving labor difficulties; but more careful analysis shows that there is concealed here an "If . . . then . . ." type of situation. Let us state positively the effect of increasing sales on Mr. X's business, as follows:

Major premise: If Mr. X increases sales, his business will survive.
Minor premise: He is increasing his sales.
Conclusion: Therefore the business will survive.

We have affirmed the antecedent and drawn a valid conclusion. If we were to deny the antecedent, no valid conclusion could be inferred; for even if Mr. X does not increase his sales, his business might possibly survive for other reasons, such as lower costs. If the known facts were to justify denying the consequent (the business did not survive), we could conclude with validity that none of the possible causes of survival, including increase of sales, actually occurred.

It is apparent therefore that restating the disjunction so as to bring out the actual hypothetical nature of the situation enables us to see the relationships of the terms clearly and make valid inferences. The point is that we must take care to see that our disjunctive statements are not actually concealed hypothetical statements.

These forms of the syllogism—categorical, hypothetical, and disjunctive—do not always appear in the neat and compact forms we have been considering as illustrations. In our everyday discourse, as in printed or written materials, deductions are often concealed in a mass of detail. We do not always state our premises completely; one of them may be merely implied or assumed. Order of statements may be changed. The terms of which propositions are composed may be confused; their meanings may be shifted. Relationships of premises and conclusions may be obscured by illustrations and details of information. A speaker may develop one of his premises at length before proceeding to state his conclusion. We need to know how to reduce the complexities of discourse to the simple patterns of clean-cut logic, so that we can test both their truth and their validity; and thus try to detect false reasoning in our own speech and in the speech of others.

In conclusion. If now we draw together some of the various strands of our study thus far, we can see that induction and deduction operate together. Let us recall, first, that induction is the basis of deduction. The premises of deduction, unless they are matters of faith or pure assumptions, are usually derived by inductive methods, such as generalization, analogy, and reasoning about causal relationships. Induction is thus the foundation on which deduction builds. Even the formulation of an hypothesis or tentative generalization is a search for some general principle from which a conclusion can be validly inferred.

We should also recall that deduction is essential to meaningful induction. The specific instances with which an inductive process begins would have very meager significance if they were not assembled and interpreted in relation to each other and in terms of general principles. As we have said before, no single unit of observation has much meaning by itself. It must be seen in relation to other units. As John Dewey said, when knowledge is reduced to specific items of sense, connection between them is impossible unless some a priori propositions are recognized as true.

This is the distinctive function and value of deduction—to apply general propositions to single instances; or, differently stated, to see the single instance in the broad perspective of general truth. In every induction there is some implied assumption; if no other, there is at least the assumption that the order of nature is stable and dependable and that what we know to be true of some things is certain to be true also of other things. Thus deduction, the application of general principles, is always involved in any significant use of induction. Deduction is a way of testing and using our observations and generalizations and all the other kinds of inductive inference.

EXERCISES

1. Continue (as in Chapter 6, Exercise 1) your analysis of some of the outlines in Chapters 8 and 9, centering attention this time on the types of thought relationships and methods of inference. What uses has the speaker made of comparisons, spatial relationships, part-whole or substance-quality relationships, time sequences, causal relations? What concepts has he employed? Do you find various degrees or levels of abstraction? Notice the ways in which factual material is classified. Has the speaker made any use of hypothesis? Pick out examples of significant uses of induction and deduction. What form have they taken, e.g., are they generalization, analogy, causal reasoning or syllogism? Is the over-all structure of the address inductive or deductive?

2. Make similar analysis of an important public address published in one of the anthologies or in *Vital Speeches*.

3. Continue (as in Chapter 6, Exercise 2) your observations of conversation and discussion, but look now at the various kinds of relationships among thought units and the kinds of inference. As directed by your instructor, prepare an analytical report on these elements as you find them in informal speech. Do they meet the criteria of soundness presented in this chapter?

SUPPLEMENTARY READINGS

Black, Max, *Critical Thinking*, Prentice-Hall, 1946.

Dewey, John, *How We Think*, Heath, 1933.

—————, *Logic, the Theory of Inquiry*, Holt, Rinehart and Winston, 1938.

Fearnside, W. Ward, and William B. Holther, *Fallacy: The Counterfeit of Argument*, Prentice-Hall, 1959.

Mill, John Stuart, *A System of Logic*, Routledge, 1892.

Sharvy, Robert, *Logic: An Outline* (paperback), Littlefield Adams & Company, 1964.

8

ORDER AND ORGANIZATION

Orderly and well-organized discourse is the product of an orderly mind. When a speaker jumps at random from one subject to another, or rattles along without stopping to recognize units of knowledge, or haggles his phrases or punctuates them freely with "uh," he is suffering more than a surface difficulty. His disorder is confusion of thought.

We have already considered some of the most elemental and detailed aspects of orderly thinking: phrasing, the grouping of words according to thought units; pausing, which gives a speaker time to formulate his ideas in phrase units and separates them from each other; and using transitional cues to indicate progress from one thought unit to the next (see Chapter 4). Methods of organizing into orderly patterns the larger units of our discourse, such as groups of facts, supporting ideas, and inferences should be considered in two ways—first, by analyzing the broad foundations of orderly thought; and second, by considering methods and techniques of outlining.

Foundations of Orderly Thought

Orderly thinking requires at least five preliminary conditions. Control of emotion is very important, but we shall postpone consideration of it for a later chapter (see Chapter 11). Our immediate concerns are communicative attitude, formulation of purpose, analysis of subject matter, and synthesis of materials.

COMMUNICATIVE ATTITUDE

Without a desire to communicate, no definite formulation of purpose is likely to occur. Without a sense of purpose no clear statement of theme is possible. Without clear statement of theme adequate planning of a systematic pattern of supporting material is impossible. A communicative attitude, as we have already seen (Chapter 5), is founded on understanding of our listeners and rapport with them. We should do our best to learn as much as possible about those to whom we speak. This information is a necessary part of the basis on which we choose purpose, analyze subject or problem, and synthesize material.

PURPOSE

Speech purpose is a deliberate preview or anticipation of outcome. The speaker should have a clear and definite concept of the desired response and the determination to arouse it.

We learn, by generalizing past experience, that certain actions and utterances on our part tend to stimulate distinctive kinds of responses by our companions. When a given utterance has had a typical result often enough, we can say it again not only with anticipation but also with deliberate intention that the familiar result shall follow. *Purpose is the organized projection of past experience by which we can preview the end a given kind of behavior is planned to achieve.*

For most of our life activities, and especially for speaking, our purpose is to arouse some definite kind of response, whether in attitude, thought, or overt action. We speak for the following general reasons (from simple to complex):

1. To announce our presence, as in routine greetings or casual comment. The response we seek is recognition and attention.

2. To arouse interest in a subject. The response we seek is some degree of sustained attention.

3. To release pent-up emotions or overcome frustrations, as in the use of exclamations and expletives. The response we expect is usually quiet acceptance of our state of mind or perhaps sympathy. This more than any other kind of purpose tends to be personal rather than directed toward a listener.

4. To ask for information. Typically though not necessarily, this takes the form of question. The response we seek is statement of facts.

5. To give information; to explain. The response we seek is understanding.

6. To stimulate enjoyment and appreciation. The response we seek is an empathic sharing of experience.

7. To influence attitude and belief. The response we seek is agreement with an opinion or conviction.

8. To move to action. The response we seek is renewed or changed behavior.

9. To solve a problem. This is the most complex and difficult purpose to achieve, primarily because it requires not merely a given kind of response by one individual but, in group and community life, deliberate cooperation between two or more people.

These various purposes are not always separate or distinct in use. Some are more covert, others more overt; some are more emotional, others more intellectual. Yet all involve responses of an organism in action. Each successive purpose may depend in part on achievement of those listed before it. Getting attention and arousing interest, for example, are basic to any of the more advanced kinds of response. Some use of facts is necessary if we are to achieve any of the higher and more complex purposes. Problem-solving requires extensive use of all or almost all of the more elementary processes.

We should bear in mind, however, that no orderly utterance can have more than one basic goal. Whenever one of the more elementary or basic purposes is used to help achieve a larger or higher level purpose, the elementary process actually ceases to be a purpose and becomes part of the speaker's method of developing his thought. If, for example, I am to stimulate enjoyment and appreciation, I must arouse interest in my theme and give my listener some background of information. If I am to influence belief, I must not only gain the recognition and attention of my listener but secure also his understanding of my theme or proposal and an appreciative sharing of my point of view. In each case the preliminary steps are not purposes, but methods of achieving purpose.

If our speaking is to be orderly and effective, we need to know not merely what *kind* of response but exactly *what specific* response we desire. We do not in fact speak to arouse appreciation in general, but appreciation for a specific kind of achievement, or occasion, or work of art. We do not speak to convince at random, but to secure acceptance of a given definite proposition or point of view or principle. We do not speak just to motivate in general, but to stir certain people to act in definite ways in specific situations. If purpose is actually to serve as a basis for orderly thought, it must be definite.

Purpose, however, cannot be intelligently determined until we know something about the subject of which we are to speak, i.e., have done some analyzing and synthesizing of material.

ANALYSIS

The essence of analysis is that kind of discrimination which can distinguish between the qualities or elements of our units of knowledge as well as between the units themselves. This is significant at all levels of perception and thought. When applied to objects, analysis is the recognition of qualities or parts of a structure. As applied to activities or events, analysis involves distinction between their component forces, movements, or functions. At the conceptual level, analysis is the discriminating perception of those features or elements of our observations from which we generalize concepts. At the level of principle, analysis is a process of recognizing the various concepts which enter into our beliefs, assumptions, rules of conduct, axioms, and generalizations. At the problem-solving level it is the discovery and formulation of the essential questions or issues on which the solution depends. When we analyze anything, we are primarily trying to find the component parts of which the whole consists and to discover the relationships of those parts to each other as well as to the whole.

It follows that analysis is a way of reducing our experience to order. We systematize a confused situation by singling out its various parts or elements, and may reduce these further to more detailed characteristics. The level of detail to which any unit is reduced will de-

Speakers, as builders, must order their materials.

pend on the purpose for which it is perceived, thought about, and classified. Recall the chair we used to illustrate levels of abstraction in Chapter 7. If we intend to build a chair, analysis will be in terms of structural parts and materials. If we wish to enjoy its aesthetic values, we shall analyze in terms of sensory qualities such as texture, thickness, and color. If we think of the practical uses of chairs, we shall analyze in terms of size, form, weight, and durability. If we were chemists seeking to develop stronger and lighter synthetic materials from which to build chairs, we should be analyzing molecular structure. If we were physicists, we might analyze the atomic patterns of arrangement within the molecules. Any given unit of knowledge may be analyzed from many points of view and for many diverse purposes; but if we maintain clear distinctions between various purposes, viewpoints, and levels of abstraction, the elements we perceive will constitute a systematic and orderly hierarchy of knowledge.

Analysis is thus an important aspect of orderly speech. Analysis begins with search for the elemental phases of a subject or problem to be spoken about, discovers the main ideas involved, breaks each main idea down into subordinate ideas, reduces each of these to a more detailed series of statements, recognizes the component phrase units within each statement, and finally recalls the detailed facts and elements of experience which give meaning to each unit of knowledge.

Grouping is the essence of organization.

In original speaking (conversation, discussion, public speaking) we analyze our own experiences and thoughts. For interpretative speaking (oral reading and acting) we analyze the experiences which someone else has written down for us. The applications are variable, but the basic process of analysis is fundamentally similar in every case.

SYNTHESIS

While we are formulating purpose and analyzing subject matter, synthesis of our units of knowledge is also going on. Synthesis is the reverse of analysis. Whereas analysis breaks experience down into successively smaller units, synthesis restores the wholeness of the larger units and renews their relationships. It completes the structuring of experience which analysis has begun. Synthesis puts facts and ideas together in classes and relates the classes to each other. It utilizes inductive and deductive reasoning to develop the relationships among units of knowledge (see Chapter 7). Synthesis may start at any level of analysis; but if it is completely systematic, it begins with the smallest units of experience, integrates them into successively larger units, and builds them into statements which develop a theme and stimulate a desired response.

When we review our experience to discover information which may be useful in developing a subject or exploring a problem before us, we use all available sources of information—observation, experiment, interview, and reading (see Chapter 6). As the body of facts grows, we classify, organize, and draw conclusions from them. We synthesize our knowledge of the subject into an orderly pattern of thought.

Methods and Techniques of Outlining

These processes we have just discussed involve judgments about the relative importance of our various units of knowledge. Some units are more significant than others for a given purpose; these must be put in the more dominant positions in the arrangement of our material. Some concepts and propositions are central, others are marginal. Some are equal or coordinate in rank, others subordinate. Some units of knowledge are outcomes or products of thinking; others are but stages in the process. Some are thoughts to be developed; others are means of development to be left beside the way when their usefulness has ended. A generalization is usually more important than the details from which it is derived; the conclusion more important than its premises; a principle more important than any single application. We organize our discourse on the basis of judgments about the relative importance of our ideas. Such judgments involve many complex factors and should be made with care, reserve, and an open mind.

Any speaker who has realized a definite purpose and analyzed and synthesized his subject matter has laid the foundation for orderly utterance. The formulation of his thought is already well under way; and as he carries his preparation forward, his sense of order should find expression in a well-organized thought outline.

In its fullest sense an outline is a basic analysis and plan for development of a subject or problem. It may present a topical summary of information, a logical pattern of argument or persuasion, or a synthesis of orderly steps for solution of a problem. Such a systematic structure of thought may be prepared for one's own guidance or to give others a concise summary of thought on a given subject or problem. A good outline can serve both purposes at once. Outlines should be carefully prepared with precise attention to details and clarity of statement, although obviously they should receive special care when intended for someone else. The oral interpreter, of course, should analyze and outline his author's material before presenting it to a listener; and even the actor, who must memorize verbatim, will do well to analyze the logical progression of the scenes he plays and the speeches of the character he portrays.

For informal and casual kinds of speaking a complete written outline is seldom necessary. Indeed in preparing for any speaking situation a man who has disciplined his mind by years of practice in outlining and who is thoroughly familiar with his subject may formulate a plan of discourse without benefit of writing. In many informal situations a speaker may have no opportunity to write an outline in advance and may have to depend on silent inner formulation and arrangement of his thought. Even when a complete outline of a subject or problem has been written, a speaker who has mastered his material may choose to carry with him to the interview or conference table or platform only a selection of key phrases or statements to remind him of his plan of discourse. A fully mature speaker may not need notes or outline at all while he speaks. Students of speech do well to outline so carefully and master material so fully that their dependence on notes and outlines while speaking in any situation can be reduced to a minimum (see Chapter 12). In order to develop such ability we need the discipline which constant writing of outlines gives. Let us, therefore, consider in more detail the kinds of outlines, their characteristics, and the patterns of thought on which they are based.

FUNDAMENTAL PRINCIPLES OF OUTLINING

Speakers make outlines according to the nature of their material, the form of discourse they are to use, and their own convenience. Sometimes these are inductive in arrangement; more often they are deductive. All kinds of outlines, whether topical or logical, informative or argumentative, occasional or problem-solving, fragmentary or complete, should have certain fundamental characteristics:

1. Unity of subject and theme. No one can talk about, listen to, or understand more than one subject at a time.

2. Direction toward a single purpose. In some circumstances a speaker might be able to achieve two goals at once; but the odds are heavily against it. Decide what response you want and direct the entire sequence of your thought toward achieving it.

3. Coherent arrangement of material. Coherence means that the parts stick together and that the connections between them are un-

mistakably clear. This goes a step beyond unity of subject and purpose. Whereas unity requires that all parts of an outline or discourse shall be directly related to one central theme, coherence requires that the parts shall also have a consistent relationship among themselves.

4. Clear relationships of coordination and subordination among thought units.

5. Over-all progression or continuity of subject and purpose from opening statement to final conclusion. Each part should provide a basis for the parts that follow, so that the entire thought pattern is an unfolding sequence of development.

SPECIFIC DETAILS OF OUTLINE CONSTRUCTION

To implement the general principles listed above, certain details should be observed for the several parts of an outline.

Title and purpose. An outline should be headed by a title and a statement of purpose which clearly set forth the intended use or desired response (see illustrations below).

Differentiation between purpose and theme. Whereas a speaker's purpose is the response he desires, his theme is the essential thought by which he plans to arouse that response in the listener or listeners. The distinction is inherent even in a simple conversational situation in which the purpose might be to establish good rapport with a neighbor while the theme may be embodied in simple statements such as, "Good morning!" and "I am glad to see you." Study the following illustrations:[1]

Example 1.　(An explanation of a structure or plan of organization)
　　　Title:　　The Symphony Orchestra
　　　Purpose:　To inform listeners about the make-up and organization of a symphony orchestra.
　　　Theme:　　A symphony orchestra consists of two basic elements—the artist or conductor and his instrument, the group of musicians.

Example 2.　(An explanation of a process or event)
　　　Title:　　The Manufacture of Paper
　　　Purpose:　To explain the process of manufacturing paper.
　　　Theme:　　The manufacture of paper consists of four basic processes.

Example 3.　(An explanation of a concept)
　　　Title:　　Epicureanism
　　　Purpose:　To stimulate my friends to a deeper appreciation of a philosophy of pleasure.

---

[1] All sample outlines in this chapter are based on the work of students in speech courses at the University of Washington. The author is especially indebted to Patricia Brown, Carole Goplerud, R. H. Holmquist, Robert Kerslake, Walter Konde, Ted Remmert, Hiromia L. Sakata, and Hanna Schott.

Theme: Epicureanism is a philosophy which gives greater depth to our understanding of pleasure.

Example 4.   (An inspirational discourse)
Title: The Lifework of Booker T. Washington.
Purpose: To increase my listener's appreciation of the life of Booker T. Washington.
Theme: Booker T. Washington devoted his life to improving the condition of the Negro people of the United States.

Example 5.   (An argumentative discourse)
Title: Red China and the United Nations.
Purpose: To support and strengthen the conviction that Red China should not be admitted to the United Nations.
Theme: The admission of Red China to the United Nations would be a gross violation of its charter.

Example 6.   (A motivating discourse)
Title: Advantages of Fraternity Life.
Purpose: To persuade a fellow student that he should join a fraternity.
Theme: You should join a fraternity because it will enrich your college life.

Example 7.   (A problem-solving discussion)
Title: How Can Student Cheating Be Controlled?
Purpose: To think toward solution of the problem of cheating at the University.
Theme: What is the nature and extent of cheating at the University?
or
What can we do to reduce cheating at the University?

Observe that these illustrations include a variety of purposes, from simple explanation to more complex persuasive and problem-solving endeavors. Some of the subjects require much more intensive study and preparation than others. The problem-solving discussion (Example 7) would be primarily exploratory; the others assume that a body of information has been assembled or a conviction established in advance of the speaking. In each case, however, the statement of purpose is the speaker's mandate to himself; the theme is the essence of his message to his listener. Purpose may not always be declared openly in discourse, but it should be clearly stated in an outline and should be the primary directing force of a speaker's entire procedure. For a given listener or audience the statement of theme may sometimes be postponed or merely implied for reasons of tact, but failure to declare it forthrightly always involves the risk of vagueness. In most situations, especially in classroom practice, both purpose and theme should be clearly stated.

When a theme is stated, it should be a direct and simple declaration of the main idea you wish to develop, or in the case of inquiry a direct question which states the essential problem to be solved or information desired.

Example 8.

Inadequate:	I would like to discuss Emile Zola with you for a few minutes.
More definite:	Emile Zola was one of the most famous French novelists of the nineteenth century.

Example 9.

Inadequate:	Let us consider the process of manufacturing paper.
More definite:	The manufacture of paper consists of four basic processes—preparation of the wood, making the pulp, cleaning and beating the pulp, drying and pressing it into sheets.

Example 10.

Inadequate:	Solar heating begins with the sun.
More definite:	Solar heating is a method of storing and using solar energy to heat our buildings.

Example 11.

Inadequate:	Let us talk about the proposal to admit Red China to the United Nations.
More definite:	Red China should not be admitted to the United Nations.
	or
	Admission of Red China to the United Nations would be a gross violation of its charter.

Statements. Each item in an outline should be a direct statement—usually a simple declarative sentence, although for some subjects and types of speaking (as in conversation, inquiry, or discussion) questions may be important parts of a thought pattern or sequence. Predication is a necessity if speaking is to be meaningful. Outlines, therefore, should formulate thought in explicit statements. Phrases are inadequate because they do not state meanings definitely; they do not bring specific details and concepts into direct predicative relationships. Study the following examples:

Example 12.

Inadequate:	Steps in the growth of the telephone idea.
More definite:	The idea of the telephone developed gradually.

Example 13.

Inadequate:	Importance of the Bastille.
More definite:	For the people of France in the reign of Louis XVI the Bastille was a symbol of their oppression.

Example 14.

Inadequate:	What democracy was like in the Mediaeval period.

More definite: In the Mediaeval period democracy was a limited concept.

Example 15.
Inadequate: Reasons for studying literature.
More definite: We should study literature because . . . (The reasons should be stated in a series of declarative sentences. See discussion of arrangement of points and numbering and lettering.)

Example 16.
Inadequate: Causes of the difficulty.
More definite: The causes of academic cheating lie with parents, faculty, and the students themselves.

Complex and compound sentences and double statements should also be avoided. Observe the following examples:

Example 17.
Confusing: Booker T. Washington founded a school for Negroes and spoke often on behalf of their rights and duties.
Clearer: I. Booker T. Washington founded a school for Negroes.
II. He spoke often on behalf of the rights and duties of the Negro people.

Example 18.
Confusing: Daniel Webster was strictly English in his ways and appearance. This may have accounted for his comparative difference from other great men of his time.
Clearer: Daniel Webster was distinguished from other prominent American men of his time by his English appearance and manners.

Example 19.
Confusing: There are three steps in the production of copper, and without it America would not be where she is today.
Clearer: I. The process of producing copper involves three steps.
II. Copper is an important commodity in the American economy.
(These might constitute separate themes.)

Example 20.
Confusing: Cheating in college is a widely used method of obtaining good grades, and is brought about by pressures from family, employers, and the colleges themselves.
Clearer: I. Cheating is a widespread practice in our colleges and universities.
II. It is caused by pressure on students to obtain good grades.

III. These pressures are exerted on the students by family, friends, potential employers, and the faculty members themselves.

Single direct statements are not necessary (1) if a speaker carries with him a brief list of key words and phrases as reminders of important points and (2) when items are listed as subordinate to a statement which they complete, as in the following examples:

Example 21.
　　　The following chemicals may be used in the pulp-making process:
　　　　　1. Sulphite
　　　　　2. Soda
　　　　　3. Sulphate

Example 22.
　　　The principles of rhetoric as formulated by the ancient Greeks and Romans were organized in five main groups or subdivisions:
　　　　　1. Proof
　　　　　2. Organization
　　　　　3. Style
　　　　　4. Memory
　　　　　5. Delivery
（Of course if one were to develop these points, they would need to be stated in definite sentence form to give each term an explicit meaning.)

Arrangement of points.　An outline usually should follow a deductive pattern. As applied to outlining *deductive* means only that general statements or conclusions are placed first, with the more detailed supporting statements following in subordinate position. The material may involve any and all forms of inference, but every statement which directly supports or develops another statement or conclusion should be in a position subordinate to it. Statements which support the same point, or points of equal rank, should not overlap or duplicate each other but should be mutually exclusive in content. Coordinate statements should also be as near parallel or similar in form as possible.

Example 23.　Employment of Handicapped Persons.
　　　Purpose:　To create a favorable attitude toward employment of handicapped persons.
　　　Theme:　Handicapped persons, properly trained and placed, are effective employees.

BODY

I. Handicapped workers have demonstrated their effectiveness.
　　A. A few days ago I bought an insurance policy from a man who manages his business from a wheel chair.
　　B. Last week a friend of mine had his watch repaired by a man who has lost both legs.
　　C. In Albertson, New York, a company named Abilities, Inc.,

which specializes in assembling electronic equipment, employs 300 handicapped people, pays them $825,000 annually in wages, does an average business of almost $2 million annually, and sends an average of two employees to better jobs each month.

D. In Austin, Texas, the city government employed 251 people with various kinds of handicaps in 1959. These employees
   —took no more than average sick leave.
   —were less prone than others to leave their jobs.
   —had commendable accident records.

E. In Chicago the Rehabilitation Institute said that more than 300 handicapped people have proven their success since 1954.

F. A joint survey by the Department of Labor and the Veterans Administration showed that handicapped workers
   —often are morale builders and pace setters for workers without handicaps.
   —have a slightly higher production rate than others.
   —have equally good absentee records.
   —in many cases have better safety records.

II. Careful training and placement largely account for the success of these handicapped workers.

A. Under Public Law No. 565, the Federal Rehabilitation Act of 1954, free rehabilitation counseling is provided for handicapped people.

B. Handicapped persons' abilities are carefully tested.
   1. IQ performance tests are given.
   2. Educational comprehension tests are given.
   3. Adequate standards must be met before job placement.

C. The United States Employment Service and State-Federal rehabilitation agencies have placed thousands of severely handicapped persons in jobs suited to their abilities.
   1. A blind person can "see" just as well as anyone else in an X-ray darkroom.
   2. The deaf work efficiently in spite of the noise of a key-punch section.
   3. Partial paralysis from polio does not necessarily restrict a copy typist.

CONCLUSION

I. Our theme is that handicapped persons, properly trained and placed, are effective workers.

II. Certain implications clearly follow:

A. You should encourage and support any and all efforts to provide job training and placement service for handicapped persons.

B. You should look with favor upon employment of such persons.

On rare occasions an outline may follow an inductive pattern. In outlining this means only that specific details or supporting statements are given first, followed by the inferences or conclusions drawn from them, as illustrated in the following condensed format based on the material in Example 23:

Example 24.   Employment of Handicapped Persons
> Purpose: To create a favorable attitude toward employment of handicapped persons.

BODY

A. A few days ago I bought an insurance policy from a man who manages his business from a wheel chair.
B, C, D, and E as given in Example 23.
F. A joint survey by the Department of Labor. . . .
I. We may therefore conclude that handicapped workers have demonstrated their effectiveness.
  A. Under Public Law No. 565 . . . free rehabilitation counseling is provided for handicapped people.
  B and C as given above.
II. These facts suggest that careful training and placement largely account for the success of these handicapped workers.
Theme: Properly trained and placed handicapped persons are effective employees.

Such an inductive arrangement is useful primarily in speaking situations where (1) the listener is so completely ignorant of the subject that he could not understand a statement of theme until some basic information has been given, or (2) he is so opposed to the speaker's purpose and theme that he might refuse to accept them or even to listen if they were stated bluntly at the beginning. Most outlines, however, should present the logical structure of a speaker's thought in deductive form, with the understanding that he will be able to make the changes in order of points required by the attitude of the listener and the speaking situation.

Numbering and lettering.   In each part of an outline the relationships among thought units should be indicated by a consistent series of number and letter symbols. A convenient and widely used series consists of Roman numerals, capital letters, Arabic numerals, and small letters, as used in all the sample outlines in this section. The complete series is set up as follows:

Statement of theme
I. Major point or thought unit directly supporting theme
  A. First-order subpoint supporting or developing I
    1. Second-order subpoint supporting or developing A
      a. Third-order subpoint
        (1) Fourth-order subpoint
          (*a*) Fifth-order subpoint
          (*b*)
        (2) Fourth-order subpoint

          b. Third-order subpoint
       2. Second-order subpoint
    B. First-order subpoint
    C. First-order subpoint, etc.
  II. Second major point or thought unit directly supporting theme
    A. First-order subpoint
      1. Second-order subpoint, etc.
 III. Third major point, etc.

Observe that parentheses distinguish fourth and fifth orders of subpoints. For most subjects five orders of symbols will be adequate; but if additional characters are needed, they can be made with double parentheses: $((1))$, $((2))$ for sixth-order points and $((a))$, $((b))$ for seventh order. If only one additional level is needed, the letters *x, y, z,* could be used.

Notice also that the number of subpoints under any given heading will vary according to the nature of the material. In most instances, however, there should be not less than two subpoints under a given statement, if there are any at all; no unit of knowledge can be analyzed into just one subordinate part. The principal exception is in argumentative or persuasive discourse where a speaker may have only one supporting reason for a given assertion.

Subtitles. The subtitles for the three parts of an outline—introduction, body, and conclusion—should be centered over the head of their sections. They do not need symbols (see Examples 25–28).

Introduction. Here the speaker should state (1) the method by which he proposes to establish contact with his listener's interests or state of mind and (2) any preliminary information—such as historical facts, definitions of important terms, statement of issues, and forecast of the plan of organization—which may be needed to help the listener understand the theme and respond to the purpose of the speaker. Study the introductions to the illustrative outlines in Examples 26, 28, in this chapter and 29, 30, 31 and 33 in Chapter 9.

Body. The body presents the sequence of thought by which the theme is to be developed. It combines the results of sound analysis of the subject or problem with synthesis of the material by which the speaker's purpose is to be achieved. In fact the building of an outline is in itself the major part of the process of synthesis. The following illustrations are designed to show how (1) deductive arrangement of (2) a series of concise statements (3) properly labeled can be used to show the relationships of coordination and subordination in a systematic structure of thought. Observe the differences between the disorganized and well-organized examples.

Example 25. (Disorganized)
    Theme: The Fabian Society was organized in England in 1884 to improve the condition of the poorer classes.

I. At that time the British Empire was the greatest nation on earth.
  A. Never before had so few accumulated so many vast fortunes.
  B. Never before had the gulf between the rich and poor been so wide.
II. The working classes lived in filth and squalor.
  A. A sociological survey showed that only one-third of the slum dwellers were living above starvation.
  B. Drunkenness and crime were prevalent.
III. The working classes in the great industrial centers were unrepresented in Parliament because the right to vote was restricted to those who owned property.
IV. The aged and incapacitated were most pathetic; their only recourse was to live in one or two room cubicles with their children or go to the workhouse.
V. Many wealthy people and middle class intellectuals became seriously concerned about conditions of the working classes in the great cities.
  A. The wealthy contributed to various charities.
  B. Writers exposed the inequities of British society.
VI. Approximately 700 writers and intellectuals formed a Society through which they hoped to agitate for gradual social reform, old age pensions, accident, health and unemployment insurance.
  A. They called themselves the Fabian Society, after the Roman general, Maximus Fabius. Fabius harassed Hannibal but avoided pitched battle.

If you study this Example 25 carefully, you will see that point I does not directly support or develop the main theme, and that points II, III, IV, and V are not clearly related to the theme. Subpoints A and B under I, moreover, do not help to develop it; instead of showing the greatness of the British Empire they seem to show exactly the opposite. Point VI, although it obviously helps to develop the main theme, is a complex statement involving several points.

Study the following revision in which complex and overlapping statements have been eliminated and each statement directly supports or helps to develop the point under which it stands. Observe that the number of main headings has been reduced making the organization more compact. Introduction and conclusion have been added to illustrate the relationship of parts.

Example 26. (Revised)

Fabian Socialism

Purpose: To give an account of the origins of Fabian Socialism.

INTRODUCTION

I. We in the United States have recently heard a great deal about "urban renewal."

A. Urban renewal is a Federal program designed to assist the large American cities in reclaiming their slum areas.

B. We are concerned about this problem because slum conditions breed crime and disease.

II. If everyone in our city were put into an area the size of the central business district and herded into buildings about the size of this one in which our class meets, we would begin to approximate conditions which existed in London during the latter part of the nineteenth century.

BODY

Theme: The Fabian Society was organized in England in 1884 to improve the condition of the poorer classes.

I. The impetus for founding the Society was the wretched condition of the working people.

A. Even though the British Empire was the greatest nation on earth, her wealth was concentrated in the hands of a few.

B. The working classes lived in filth and squalor.

1. A sociological survey showed that only one-third of the slum dwellers were living above starvation level.

2. Many entire families, including aged and sick members, were crowded in two small cubicles or rooms.

C. Drunkenness and crime were prevalent.

D. The working classes were not represented in Parliament; the right to vote was restricted to those who owned property.

II. Remedial measures were begun by many wealthy and intellectual leaders.

A. Many of the wealthy contributed to various charities.

B. Writers exposed the inequalities of British society.

III. The inadequacy of these measures led a group of approximately 700 writers and intellectuals to found the Society to agitate for gradual reform.

A. The name "Fabian" was derived from the Roman general Maximus Fabius, who was famous for his use of gradual delaying tactics in defending Rome against Hannibal.

B. The purpose of the Society was to agitate for gradual social reform.

C. It advocated old age pensions and accident, health, and unemployment insurance.

CONCLUSION

I. The slum conditions prevalent in Great Britain's major cities during the latter part of the nineteenth century were a disgrace to a nation which had amassed tremendous wealth, power, and prestige.

II. These conditions were successfully exposed to public view by a young, idealistic, and dedicated group of writers.

III. The Fabian Society persisted in its efforts for reform and gained the ear of politician and public alike.

Examine also the disorganized outline in Example 27.

Example 27.   (Disorganized)

Samuel Adams, American Patriot

INTRODUCTION

Samuel Adams was an American patriot of the upper classes.
 I. Born in Boston in 1722, the son of a rich merchant, ship owner, and magistrate.
 II. Educated at Boston Latin School and graduated from Harvard in 1740.
   A. Wrote his master's thesis on the lawfulness of resisting supreme magistrates.

BODY

 I. In business he was unsuccessful.
   A. He lost half his capital in a business venture.
   B. He lost the other half in a loan never repaid.
   C. He became a partner with his father in an unsuccessful brewery.
 II. He was a genius at political management.
   A. A great power in town meetings.
   B. Inventor of the caucus.
   C. He was selected in 1764 to draft the town's instructions to its representatives for protesting the Stamp Act.
     1. This was the first public American protest against taxation by the British Parliament.
     2. First suggestion of a union of colonies for the redress of grievances.
 III. When the Townshend Acts were passed, he drafted the legislature's petition to the King of England.
   A. He helped to form the Committees of Correspondence to secure cooperation among the colonies.
   B. This led directly to the Revolutionary War.
     1. George III ordered the legislature to rescind it.
     2. The legislature refused by a vote of 97 to 12.
   C. The King then resolved to send troops to the colony.
 IV. Adams inflamed public spirit.
   A. He wrote articles in the Boston *Gazette.*
     1. These upheld the colonists' legal rights.
     2. He insisted on the impossibility of compromise.
   B. The Boston Tea Party was unquestionably arranged or supervised by him.
 V. Political views.
   A. He was a prominent advocate of the Declaration of Independence.
     1. He was one of its original signers.
   B. He believed in committees instead of executive heads.

C. Nationally he was an Antifederalist.
1. He opposed a strong national government.
2. He had a fear of tyranny by the wealthy class.
VI. After long hesitancy he supported the Constitution of 1787.
A. Only on the understanding that a Bill of Rights be added.
B. His voice in favor of ratification by Massachusetts saved the Constitution to the nation.

CONCLUSION

I. A man always interested in the rights of the colonists.
II. He had courage and zeal to stand firm for his ideals, no matter what the opposition.
III. Quote by Thomas Jefferson.

Notice that many of the items in this outline are indefinite phrases instead of sentences, that the distinction between introductory material and the main body of thought is not clearly drawn, and that there is no adequate statement of either purpose or theme. The actual theme, which is implied but not stated, is that Adams was a leader in the Revolution and the founding of our Government. The statement that Adams belonged to the upper classes, which appears in the position of main theme, is actually supported by very little of the material which follows it. Point I does not support the main statement at all. Other points, such as II, IV, and V, are not stated so that their relationship to the main statement is immediately clear. Several points do not even support the statements under which they stand. In the conclusion only the second point has definite meaning; the first and third items are indefinite and vague.

In the following revision observe that all units are definite statements; that purpose and theme are clearly differentiated; and that all background information about Samuel Adams' early life and abilities, which is not really part of the main theme, is placed in the introduction where it helps us to understand the theme. In the body of the outline the supporting materials have been placed under the headings which they directly support, and the number of main headings has been reduced from six to three. The larger number of main points is too many for the average listener to remember easily and clearly. As a result he probably would get a scattered and disorganized impression of a speaker's thought and a sense of vagueness and frustration. On the other hand, a limited number of main headings (probably not more than three or four) helps a listener to get a clear and unified comprehension of a speaker's message. Compare Example 28 with its predecessor.

Example 28. (Revised)

Samuel Adams, American Patriot

Purpose: To stimulate in my listeners a greater appreciation of Samuel Adams, an early American patriot.

INTRODUCTION

I. All of us feel a sense of pride in the achievements and sacrifices of the men who founded our national government.

II. Samuel Adams, like many others among the early patriots, was a member of the upper classes.

    A. He was born in Boston in 1722, the son of a rich merchant, ship owner and magistrate.

    B. He was educated at the Boston Latin School.

    C. He graduated from Harvard in 1740.

III. Early in life he showed a leaning toward political leadership.

    A. He wrote his master's thesis on the lawfulness of resisting magistrates.

    B. He became a power in town meetings.

    C. He developed the idea of the caucus.

BODY

Theme: Samuel Adams was a leader in the American Revolution and in the founding of our Federal Government.

I. He was prominent in the early protests which led to the Revolution.

    A. In 1764 he was elected to draft instructions to the representatives of Boston for protesting against the Stamp Act.

    B. When the Townshend Acts were passed, Adams drafted the petition of the Massachusetts Legislature to the King of England.

    C. Adams helped to form the Committees of Correspondence to secure cooperation among the colonies.

    D. These actions led directly to the Revolution.

        1. The protest against the Stamp Act included the first suggestion of a union of the colonies against use of the taxing power by the British Parliament.

        2. The protest against the Townshend Acts was the last major event leading to war.

            a. King George ordered the Legislature to rescind the protest.

            b. The Legislature refused by a vote of 97 to 12.

            c. The King then resolved to send troops to the colonies.

II. Adams was a prominent leader throughout the Revolution.

    A. His articles in the Boston *Gazette* made the crisis inevitable.

        1. These articles upheld the colonists' legal rights.

        2. Adams insisted on the impossibility of compromise.

    B. The Boston Tea Party was unquestionably arranged and supervised by him.

    C. He was a prominent advocate of the Declaration of Independence and one of its signers.

III. After long hesitation Adams supported the Constitution of 1787.

    A. His hesitation was the result of his political views.

      1. He believed in exercise of authority by committees instead of executive heads.

      2. He was a strong Antifederalist.

        a. He opposed a strong national government.

        b. He had a fear of tyranny by the wealthy class.

    B. His support of the Constitution was given with the understanding that amendments constituting a Bill of Rights would be added.

    C. His voice in favor of ratification by Massachusetts assured the adoption.

CONCLUSION

    I. Samuel Adams' political leadership was an important influence in the Revolution and the founding of our federal government.

   II. He had courage and zeal to stand for his ideals, no matter what the opposition.

  III. Thomas Jefferson said of him: "I always considered him more than any other member, the fountain of our more important measures . . . He was truly the man of the Revolution." (Quoted from Jefferson's manuscripts by James K. Hosmer, *Samuel Adams*, Houghton Mifflin, Boston, 1896, pp. 364–365.)

Conclusion. The conclusion of an outline should give final emphasis to theme and purpose, or desired response. This may be done in various ways depending on subject and purpose. Some of the more important methods exemplified in the various sample outlines in this chapter and the next are listed below. See Chapter 9 for Examples 29 ff.:

    1. Simple restatement of theme (Example 30).

    2. Summary of main points (Example 31).

    3. Restatement of theme or main points as modified and interpreted in the light of material presented in development of the theme (Examples 26 and 33). Such a conclusion may often take the form of a comment on the status of the subject or problem in the light of information presented.

    4. Emotional reinforcement of theme. This may be done by an appropriate illustration, an appeal to motives, or a quotation, such as the one from Thomas Jefferson in Example 28. A minor element of emotional reinforcement is also present in the outline in Example 26. Emotional appeal, as we shall point out later, should always grow out of the sincere attitudes and feelings of the speaker, and should be appropriate to subject and occasion. In a conclusion it should be brief.

    5. Reference to possible applications of material presented. In simple form this appears in Example 29, and in more complete and definite form in Example 23. Notice that the speaker in this illustration is addressing people who are not employers.

    6. Statement of questions for further study or investigation. As we might expect, this method appears most often at the conclusion of problem-solving outlines (Example 34), although any expository

discourse may well conclude with a statement of questions or kinds of additional information needed.

Conclusions should not be overly long or labored. The important truth is that any act of spoken communication should end with a sense of definiteness. An outline should indicate how this is to be done in a given case.

List of sources. Every outline, especially those prepared for classroom speaking exercises, should have appended a list of the sources of its material. These should include any pertinent first-hand experience of the speaker; any interviews, with specific indication of time, place, and person interviewed; and a bibliography of written and printed sources (see Chapter 6). Notice that an example of such a list of sources is included at the end of the outline in Example 33.

EXERCISES

1. Planning and outlining are really little more than ordering knowledge from the general to the specific. Outlining is, in fact, a way of classifying knowledge to make it more easily understood and accepted. Show how each of the following subjects may be divided and subdivided into at least three levels of subordination:

Watches	Fingers	Nails
Travel	Grass	Tables
Sports	Trees	Colleges

2. Make an outline of a public address published in *Vital Speeches* or one of the anthologies (see the Appendix for suggested sources). Observe as far as possible all details of correct outline form.

Answer the following questions: Has the speaker made his purpose and theme clear? Are major thought units directly related to the main theme? Are the relationships of coordination and subordination of the various thought units carried out consistently and clearly? Are introduction and conclusion adequately related to the purpose and theme?

If the speaker has not observed the principles of good organization so that his mistakes show in your outline, add a brief critique of his methods.

9

PATTERNS OF
ORGANIZATION

A most basic requirement is that every outline, especially in the main body of its material, should be arranged according to some consistent pattern of relationships. It is not enough that we use an orderly system of symbols, nor that each statement supports or develops the idea under which it stands, nor that coordinate units are mutually exclusive. The entire plan for developing a subject should be based on the characteristic relationship among the units of knowledge which make up the material. Look again at some of the sample outlines in the preceding chapter and you will see that those which are disorganized lack a systematic type of relationship among thought units. Example 25, for instance, begins with the greatness of Britain, shifts to the condition of the working class and the activities of the wealthy, and finally comes around to the organization of the Society. The relationships are haphazard and therefore difficult to relate to the main theme and to each other. In like manner the outline in Example 27 has no consistent foundation. The thought sequence zig-zags from early education through business failure, political management, Townshend Acts, public spirit, and political views, before the final point that Adams supported the Constitution of 1787.

By discovering the basic relationships involved in their subject matter we can systematize these outlines. Notice that the revised outline in Example 26 mentions first the conditions which motivated the origin of the Fabian Society, then some preliminary activities, and finally the actual organization. This could be described either as a time sequence or as a pattern of causal relationships. The most important fact, however, is that it is consistent and systematic. Some subjects may involve several different kinds of relationships; in such cases a speaker can choose the one best suited to his purpose. Other subjects or problems may involve only one basic kind of relationship; the speaker's task is to discover and use it. We can find the best pattern of organization for any given subject more easily if we are familiar with the common forms available to us. We shall now consider the principal types.

Nature has its own patterns.

Topical Pattern

A topical plan simply organizes a subject by breaking it into component parts. Explanations of structures or organizations, for example, might be arranged on the basis of part-whole or substance-quality discriminations. Geographical matters will fall easily into a spatial pattern. Descriptions of processes can be organized to answer basic questions: who, what, when, where, how, or why? In the realm of concepts or abstract ideas the topics might be arranged on the basis of theories or levels of abstraction. For many subjects the units could be contrasting ideas such as theory and practice, purpose and means, or structure and function. Many other patterns are possible depending on the kind of subject matter.

Although a topical plan of organization is sometimes used to convince or move to action, it is primarily useful when we wish to ask for or give information or stimulate enjoyment and appreciation. The distinctive usefulness of a topical outline is for presentation of an analytical summary of a body of facts. The basic purposes it helps to achieve are expository and descriptive. Study the following examples:

Example 29. (Explanation of a structure or organization)

The Symphony Orchestra

Purpose: To inform my listeners about the make-up and organization of a symphony orchestra.

Some patterns are man-made.

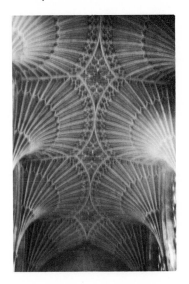

*Thoughtful discourse
has a background of
organized pattern.*

INTRODUCTION

I. All of us have enjoyed the music of symphony orchestras either by listening to recordings or broadcasts or by attending concerts in person.

II. If we have attended in person, we probably realize that the orchestra is not a random assembly of musicians.

BODY

Theme: A symphony orchestra consists of two basic elements— the artist or conductor and his instrument, the group of musicians.

I. The conductor is the artist.

A. He selects and interprets the music.

B. He determines technical details of the performance.

C. He focuses the energies of his musicians so as to bring out his interpretation of the music.

II. The musicians constitute four principal sections according to the functions of the instruments they play.

157

A. The string section is the backbone of the orchestra.
   1. It consists of two kinds of instruments:
      a. Those played with a bow—violin, viola, cello, and double bass.
      b. Those which are plucked—harp and guitar.
   2. Those played with the bow provide the most important melodic parts of the score.
   3. More than half the average number of players in the orchestra are in this section.
B. The woodwinds are next in importance as melodic instruments.
   1. They produce sound by vibration of a column of air within a tube.
   2. The members of this group include piccolo, flute, clarinet, oboe, English horn, bassoon and contrabassoon.
C. The brass instruments provide the "heavy artillery" of the orchestra.
   1. They include trumpet, horn, trombone, and tuba.
   2. Their powerful tones are most often used in fanfare or passages of a brilliant or military nature.
D. The percussion instruments contribute rhythmic life and special effects to the music.
   1. They produce sound by the vibration of stretched membranes or metallic bodies.
   2. They are of two principal kinds:
      a. Those which produce musical notes—timpani, bells, celesta.
      b. Those which produce noises—drums, cymbals, castanets, tambourine, triangle.

CONCLUSION

I hope I have given you information which will increase your understanding and enjoyment of the music of symphony orchestras.

Example 30. (Explanation of a concept)

Epicureanism

Purpose: To stimulate my friends to a deeper appreciation of a philosophy of pleasure.

INTRODUCTION

I. Most of us think of pleasure as something temporary and superficial.
II. Epicureanism was a philosophy which looked upon pleasure as the only good and the basis of morality.
III. Epicurus, the founder of this doctrine, taught in Greece during the fourth and third centuries B.C.
IV. For convenience we shall consider his philosophy in three major parts.

A. His tests of truth.

B. His attitude toward nature.

C. His concept of morality.

BODY

Theme: Epicureanism is a philosophy which gives greater depth to our understanding of pleasure.

  I. Epicurus taught that the supreme tests of truth and reality are found in the senses.

A. The evidence of reality is in the human body.

B. The soul is a bodily substance.

 II. Epicurus' philosophy of nature was based on a concept of natural causes.

A. He believed that the gods stand aloof from the world of men.

B. They take no part in creation or governing of the universe.

C. They merely provide examples of perfection for men to follow.

D. Men may glimpse these examples of perfection in dreams which enable them to see through the wall which divides the earth from the dwelling of the gods.

III. The heart of Epicurus' system was his belief that morality is the attainment of true pleasure.

A. The supreme pleasure is a tranquil and happy mind.

B. Bodily pleasures are true pleasures only as they minister to peace of mind.

C. Extremes, either of excess or of asceticism, disturb man's inner spirit.

1. Drunkenness may make us happy temporarily but does not lead to a permanently tranquil mind.

2. Fasting upsets man's inner spirit because it weakens the body.

D. True pleasure, according to Epicurus, is "the pleasure of the freedom of the body from pain and the soul from anxiety."

CONCLUSION

Epicureanism was not a philosophy of indulgence and sensuality, but a principle of higher pleasure attained by moderation and self-control.

Chronological Pattern

Sequence in time is inherent in all subjects dealing with functions or processes or events. It is especially important when we are considering historical material. The chronological plan might be regarded as a special form of the topical plan in which the time element determines the parts. Such a method is obviously very closely related to narrative, but when applied to factual or expository material does not have the continuity or free-flowing quality of narration. For expository purposes the time sequence is divided into discrete steps or phases which are more clearly indicated than in narrative.

Observe, for example, the revised outline on Samuel Adams (Example 28). The main units supporting the theme move through a sequence from his part in pre-Revolutionary protests, to his activity during the Revolution, to his work in support of the Federal Constitution after the Revolution. No'attempt is made to give a narrative of Adams' life, but the essential phases of the theme are marked off in a time pattern. For this subject some other pattern of organization might have been used, but the chronological plan is adequate to create a sense of order. For most explanations of events or processes the time order is usually inevitable. Consider, for example, the following outline on manufacture of paper:

Example 31.   (Explanation of a process)

The Manufacture of Paper

Purpose: To explain the process of manufacturing paper.

INTRODUCTION

I. Most of us would be surprised if we stopped to count the number of paper articles we use in a single day.
   A. Already this morning each of us probably has used milk and egg cartons, bread wrappers, napkins, newspapers, waxed paper, and paper bags.
   B. All of us have a variety of books and papers with us now.
II. The paper industry is one of the largest in the United States.
   A. During the past 50 years it has become the "fifth wonder of American industry." (John A. Ainsworth in *Paper, the Fifth Wonder.*)
   B. In value of shipments it is exceeded only by motor vehicles, meat, steel and petroleum.

BODY

Theme: The manufacture of paper consists of four basic processes.
I. The first step is preparation of the wood.
   A. Trees are cut and sent to the mill.
   B. They are stripped of their bark and thoroughly cleaned.
   C. The logs are cut into chips of uniform size.
II. The second stage is the cooking of the chips in chemicals to separate the wood fibres from the lignin or connective material.
   A. One of three chemicals may be used in this cooking process—calcium bisulphate, caustic soda, or sodium sulphide.
   B. The chips and chemicals are cooked with steam until reduced to a wet, pulpy mass.
   C. The pulp is cleaned and bleached.

    D. The lignin is dissolved and the fibres are separated and suspended in water.

III. The third stage is the beating of the pulp.

    A. The wood fibres are brushed and cut to proper length in the Jordan machine.

    B. During this process dyes are added to determine color.

IV. The final process is the rolling of the pulp into sheets in the Fourdrinier machine.

    A. First the material is on a wire mesh screen which may be perforated by as many as 6000 holes per square inch.

    B. The wet sheet of pulp then goes to a belt of wool felt which passes between many pairs of rollers where more moisture is pressed out and the fibres are set.

    C. Finally the sheet passes through a series of steam-heated rollers at speeds up to 2000 feet per second.

    D. The surface finishing and cutting into sheets of various sizes depends on the use to which the paper is to be put.

CONCLUSION

The principal steps in manufacture of paper are:

I. Reduction of the wood to chips.

II. Cooking the chips to pulp.

III. Beating the pulp.

IV. Rolling the pulp into sheets and finishing the surface.

Causal Pattern

Any subject which consists primarily of cause and effect relationships should be organized on the basis of those relationships. The method is especially applicable to historical subjects in which the causes of an event or series of events are to be explained, or to a discussion of contemporary problems in which an attempt is made to predict the future results of present conditions or actions. Suppose, for example, you are to make a talk on the causes of the Civil War. You would need to analyze and describe background conditions, probably including some account of the history of slavery in the United States, and would then undertake to show how these backgrounds shaped the forces which actually started the fighting. Or suppose that you attempt to predict the long-range effects of President Kennedy's quarantine of Cuba in 1962. In such a case you would analyze the setting in which the Russians established their bases on Cuban soil and would then show what impact the President's action would be likely to have on the Organization of American States and the United Nations, as well as on future Russian, Cuban, and United States policy.

Such a method is an extension and deepening of the chronological pattern; it involves not merely a statement of the continuity of events, but demonstrates that certain events lead to other events. The causal pattern of organization is not only inherent in some entire subjects; it is an important partial foundation for many subjects, especially if the purpose is argumentative or problem-solving. The first step in any problem-solution, as we shall notice later, is analysis and description of the basic difficulty, including a search for the causes of that difficulty (effect to cause reasoning). At later stages in the problem-solving process when possible solutions are evaluated, an attempt must be made to foresee their probable results (cause to effect reasoning). Since causal relationships are involved in logical reasoning, they are an important element in the logical and problem-solving methods of organization.

We can see how causal patterns are involved with other kinds of relationships if we refer back to the outline on employment of the handicapped (Example 23). The first division describes the success of handicapped workers, the second part shows the procedures which have led to that result—a development from effect to cause. The outline on the founding of the Fabian Society (Example 26) begins by describing a problem, shows next some preliminary activities which that problem motivated, and then shows how those activities led to organization of the Society—a cause to effect procedure. You will also find causal elements in the outlines in Examples 33 and 34.

Logical Pattern

As you will readily infer, this kind of outline is based on a logical relationship between units of knowledge, a connection between statements such that if one is accepted as true the other must also be accepted (see Chapter 7). One statement is said to be true *because* one or more other statements are true. Observe the following example:

Example 32.
>Theme: You should join a fraternity *because* it will enrich your college life.
>
>   I. Fraternity life will lead to the formation of lifelong friendships *because*
>   A. Every fraternity man I know has formed lasting friendships in his house.
>   B. My own experience confirms this view.
>   II. Fraternity membership will give you increased opportunities to participate in college life and activities *because*
>   A. Membership in a fraternity brings one into contact with campus leaders.
>   B. Fraternities encourage their members to become active in campus affairs.
>   III. The fraternity house will provide a pleasant and comfortable residence during your college years *because*

    A. Fraternities plan interesting and worth-while social events.

    B. Fraternities must maintain high standards of living.

Bear in mind that we are considering here logical *structure*, not necessarily conclusive logical reasoning. The arguments given, of course, should be as convincing as possible in this world of uncertainties and contingencies, but logical form in an outline merely requires that supporting reasons should be tied to their major points by the *because* relationship, i.e., by such a relationship that if the supporting reasons are true, they create some degree of likelihood that the major point under which they stand is also true. The principal kinds of supporting statements are generalizations, analogies, causal inductions, or abbreviated deductions.

Logical outlines are primarily useful when a speaker's purpose is to influence attitude and belief or move to action. With such purposes the material by which themes are developed should be motivating or at least should help to induce belief. The speaker says in effect, "Accept this belief, perform this action, or carry out this policy *because* . . ." and then gives his reasons. In discourse which is primarily informational or inspirational, the material is simply broken down into parts and details are given. Subpoints clarify and develop the ideas under which they stand; they do not attempt to prove. In contrast, speaking which aims to convince or persuade must give reasons for the theme proposed.

In the following outline the *because* relationship is dominant. Compare it with the outlines in Examples 28–31, where there are no reasons why we should believe or do anything but only various kinds of information arranged in systematic order, and where readiness to accept the facts is taken for granted. When the purpose is to convince or persuade, however, the reasons why a listener should accept the speaker's point of view must be definitely given. In the body of the following outline notice that the *because* relationship, implied but not stated, exists between every point and the supporting statements which stand under it.

Example 33. (An argument on a controversial issue)

Uncle Sam's Farm Problem

Purpose: To persuade my listeners that the present federal farm price-support program should be abandoned.

INTRODUCTION

  I. The federal price-support program for designated products operates as follows:

    A. The government will lend a farmer an amount based on the parity price of his product.

      1. Parity prices are those which will give a commodity its exchange value or buying power as computed on the basis of the immediately preceding ten years.

  B. Settlement of the loan depends on actual market price of the crop.

      1. If the price is below parity, the farmer keeps the money loaned him and the government keeps his crop.

      2. If the price is above parity, the farmer sells his crop and repays the loan, keeping the difference as profit.

  C. The main objective is to increase the income of farm families to a level comparable with nonfarm families.

II. "The nation is confronted with a serious overproduction problem in agriculture." (Lauren K. Soth, "Farm Policy for the Sixties," p. 222.)

  A. The total output of farm products in the first half of the 1950s exceeded population growth.

  B. The structure of the farming industry (more than four million small independent competitive firms) makes abundant production inevitable. (L. K. Soth, *ibid.*, p. 209–210.)

  C. Output is now 6–8 percent greater than can be consumed at present price levels. (*Ibid.*, p. 208.)

BODY

Theme: The price support program has not proved to be the best available remedy for the farm problem.

  I. Price supports have not actually accomplished their main objective—to increase the incomes of farm families to a level comparable with nonfarm families.

    A. Although there are a million fewer farm families than 10 years ago, the percentage of such families in the lowest one-fifth on the income scale has increased from 41 percent in 1946 to 50 percent in 1953 and 55 percent in 1957. (U.S. House Committee on Agriculture, figures from census reports. Cited by L. K. Soth, *ibid.*, pp. 210–211.)

    B. In 1959 the average income per person for the nonfarm population was $2,216 but for the farm population only $965. (U.S. Dept. of Agriculture, *The Farm Income Situation.* Cited by L. K. Soth, *ibid.*, p. 211.)

 II. Price supports tend to increase the problem of overproduction of food.

    A. In September, 1961, our stockpile of field grains was 85 million tons, 88 percent in the hands of the government, enough for all our needs for half a year; while our wheat surplus was 4.2 million tons, 97 percent held by the government, more than one year's needs. ("Freeman Weighs the Farm Surplus," p. 36.)

    B. "No stronger inducement to expand production can be conceived than to say to a farmer who has just marketed a big crop at a guaranteed rigid price that we will pay you

      this same rigid price for another big crop like this one."
      (Black, John D., *Economics for Agriculture*, p. 597.)

  C. Lauren K. Soth says, "The price supports of recent years
      have encouraged new investment in agriculture." (*Op. cit.*,
      p. 214.)

III. These price supports are expensive.

  A. Of $60 billion spent each year for American farm products
      about two to two and one-half billion go for increased
      prices under farm price supports. (Freeman, "The Inside
      of the Farm Problem," p. 53.)

  B. By 1961 the Commodity Credit Corporation had invested
      $7.5 billion. ("Freeman Weighs the Farm Surplus," p. 36.)

  C. The cost of storing the feed grains alone has been $500
      million a year. (*Ibid.*)

IV. Other possible remedies are available for study and trial.

  A. Lauren K. Soth says, "The logical alternative is effective
      production control which would limit market supplies and
      raise prices in the market place." (*Op. cit.*, p. 220.)

  B. John D. Black has proposed that the government control
      production of any given commodity by announcing in
      advance that it will buy in the market at a specified price
      whatever is necessary of a specified volume of production;
      and if production is in excess of this volume, will reduce its
      purchase price in proportion to the excess of production
      over the specified volume. (*Op. cit.*, p. 597.)

  C. Theodore W. Schultz of the University of Chicago has
      suggested that farm families be offered a cash payment by
      the federal government for moving to other occupations—
      a homestead policy in reverse. (Cited by L. K. Soth in
      Farm Trouble, pp. 132–133.)

CONCLUSION

  I. I do not presume to know how the farm problem can be
    solved.

 II. It seems clear, however, that the present price-support program,
    based on loans, parity prices, and restricted acreage

    —has not actually increased farm income.

    —has increased food surpluses.

    —has increased the taxpayers' burdens.

III. The price-support program should be replaced by more eco-
    nomically sound measures.

Sources of Material.

Experience: I grew up on a farm.

Interviews: None

Bibliography:

  Black, John D., *Economics for Agriculture*, Harvard University
    Press, 1959.

  Freeman, Orville, "The Inside of the Farm Problem," *United
    States News and World Report*, July 31, 1961, pp. 50–54.

—————, "Freeman Weighs the Farm Surplus," *The New York Times Magazine*, September 24, 1961, pp. 36–37 and 88–89.

Soth, Lauren K., "Farm Policy for the Sixties," in *Goals for Americans*, Report of the President's Commission on National Goals. Prentice-Hall, 1960.

—————, *Farm Trouble*, Princeton University Press, 1957.

Problem-Solving Pattern

John Dewey analyzed and described the process of problem-solving, and his formula has been repeated with minor variations by many others. He pointed out that the process begins with a "situation in which there is experienced obscurity, doubt, conflict, disturbance of some sort" and should end with a "situation that is clear, coherent, settled, harmonious."[1] In order to achieve such an outcome people who undertake to remove a difficulty or resolve a troubled and confused situation should take certain steps in reflective thinking. We present here an expanded version of Dewey's outline.

Problem-Solving Pattern

I. Awareness of the difficulty: What are the symptoms?
   A. What is wrong? What hurts? What losses are involved?
   B. Size: How big is the difficulty? Is it increasing?
   C. Occurrence: Whom is it affecting? In what ways? Under what conditions? At what times? In what places?
   D. Present efforts: What, if anything, is now being done to remove the difficulty? In what ways or to what extent are these efforts ineffective?
   E. Implications: What results can we expect if the difficulty is not removed or alleviated?

II. Analysis of the problem: What is its basic nature?
   A. What conditions created the difficulty?
      1. What are the principal causes?
      2. Are there contributing or secondary causes?
   B. What kind of remedy or solution should we seek? What criteria should govern the choice of solution?
      1. What direction must an effective solution take? An effective solution must directly attack the operating causes of the difficulty.
      2. What boundaries or limitations should an effective solution observe?

III. Suggestion of solutions: What possible solutions or remedial measures are available or can be developed?
   A. What resources and procedures would each proposed solution require?

---

[1] John Dewey, *How We Think*, rev. ed., Heath, 1933, pp. 100 ff.

      B. Exactly what would have to be done, by whom, and at what cost?

  IV. Evaluation of solutions: What is the best available solution? Each should be studied in terms of its relation to and potential effect upon the problem situation.

      A. To what extent would each available solution be effective in removing or alleviating the causes of the difficulty?

      B. What possible side effects might result from each solution?

      C. To what extent would each proposed solution preserve other values in the situation? (See II, B, 2 above.)

   V. Acceptance of best solution

      A. Which solution should be adopted as the best potential remedy for the difficulty?

      B. If no single proposal seems adequate, would some combination of potential courses of action be effective?

      C. How can the chosen course of action be put into successful operation? What steps would be necessary to implement it?

These or similar questions should guide our thinking and investigation about any problem. The order of steps, though flexible, has a basic significance. We should always begin the attempt to solve any problem by discovering the nature and causes of the difficulty which creates the disturbance or painful condition. Until the causes are understood and criteria established, we do not know what kind of solution to look for. It is equally clear that we cannot choose a solution wisely until we have considered the entire range of possible actions and analyzed each for its potential value. Sometimes the answers to one or another of the questions may be perfectly clear and require no elaboration, but no single question in the sequence can be overlooked if we are to arrive at successful solution of a problem.

Suppose, for example, the faculty of a college charges that cheating in classes is increasing and requests that officers of the student body study the difficulty and recommend a solution. Obviously the first step for any investigating committee would be to find out, as accurately as possible, how much cheating is actually done and in what forms. This, of course, would require a definition of what constitutes cheating as well as description or definition of any related processes or terms. Next, the causes should be sought. What pressures or conditions motivate students to cheat?

Out of all this information should emerge some conception of the kind of remedy which might reduce the amount of cheating and a series of specific suggestions for achieving that result. Suggestions might include such measures as change in examination methods, more careful proctoring of examinations, changes in teaching methods or grading system, and introduction of an honor system. All possible remedies should be analyzed and evaluated in terms of their probable effectiveness. Out of such evaluations might emerge a conclusion, or tentative conclusion, that one particular course of action or series of actions is most likely to remove the causes of the difficulty and achieve the desired result. When ways and means of putting this best remedy into effect have been considered, the task of preliminary thought is done and the time for action has arrived. If the chosen solution is effective, the job is finished. If not, the problem-solvers will have to re-examine their difficulty and look for other possible solutions.

The five questions or steps in thought we have outlined are a summary of the necessary procedure of any problem-solving process. They indicate, therefore, the kind of main headings which should be used in an outline of that process. As the results of investigation and thought emerge in the form of definite information and conclusions, the outline should take the form of positive statements instead of questions. These positive statements should give answers, for the particular subject or problem, to the questions in the outline of problem-solving procedure. For points on which definite conclusions have not been reached, the headings of the outline should remain as questions or in tentative form.

The following example summarizes the pattern of thinking developed by a group of students on the problem of academic cheating. They reached a definite conclusion about the best available remedy; but we shall not state it here, preferring to leave the last point of the outline open for your own judgment.

Example 34.   (A problem-solving discussion)

Academic Cheating

Purpose: To seek a solution for the problem of academic cheating.
or
To get a better understanding of the problem of academic cheating.

INTRODUCTION

I. The essential point in defining cheating seems to be the distinction between use of an aid for actual learning or merely for obtaining a grade.
   A. Cheating includes:
      1. Copying from another's paper or examination book during an examination.
      2. Use of another's report or paper as your own.
      3. Copying of published material for presentation as your own.
      4. Use of crib notes, i.e., test information written in concealed places such as cuffs or slips of paper.
   B. The following practices are not considered cheating:
      1. Obtaining another student's lecture notes to make up a lecture missed for legitimate reason.
      2. Employing a private tutor.

C. Answers to the following questions are uncertain and should be the subject of further thought and discussion:
   1. Should copying of lecture notes for class sessions which have been missed deliberately be considered cheating?
   2. Does cheating include the use of another student's report or paper as a guide or outline in the preparation of one's own paper?
   3. Does cheating include the use of test files in fraternity houses?

BODY

Theme: What can we do to reduce academic cheating at the University?

I. Academic cheating is a well-known and disturbing fact.
   A. We have the following evidence that cheating in college is a widely used method of obtaining grades.
      1. In surveys taken at many colleges and universities (e.g., University of Washington, University of Utah, Brigham Young University, Yale University), students have admitted cheating.
      2. At the University of _____, 66.8 percent of students admitted cheating and 8.9 percent of these admitted that they did it often.
      3. Although no specific survey has been made at this university, many students have expressed concern over the cheating they have observed.
   B. Cheating has harmful effects on the educational process.
      1. The prevalence of cheating undermines ethical standards by creating the impression that it is accepted or condoned.
      2. Cheating is unfair to the honest student.
      3. It is self-defeating for the cheater.
         a. Successful cheating encourages neglect of study.
         b. It robs the cheater of foundation for advanced courses.
         c. It discourages the honest student.
         d. It tends to reduce a degree to a piece of paper.
II. The causes of cheating suggest some standards or criteria which should govern our search for a remedy.
   A. Cheating is the result of pressures and motivations created by society, by the families and relatives of students, by the faculty and administration of the college, and by the students themselves.
      1. Social pressures are created by:
         a. The general tendency to condone fraud and dishonesty in community life.
         b. The demand from prospective employers for high grade records.
         c. The grade requirements of the G.I. Bill.

      d. The great influence which grades have on draft exemptions, honors, awards, etc.

  2. The families and relatives of students create pressures to cheat by:

      a. Parents' insistence on high grades.

      b. Rivalry between brothers and sisters or other relatives.

      c. Emphasis on grades for sake of status and prestige.

  3. College faculties and administrations encourage cheating by:

      a. Lax attention to teaching duties due in part to over-emphasis on research and publication.

      b. Repeated use of the same examination questions.

      c. Use of tests which require only rote memory of facts instead of rational thought.

      d. Careless arrangement of examination rooms and ineffective proctoring.

      e. Too much dependence on one or two examinination grades in determining students' final standing.

  4. Students themselves are responsible for cheating because they:

      a. Do not have adequate understanding of the nature and purposes of college education.

      b. Lack basic moral standards.

      c. Do not study adequately.

B. In the light of all the above information, the following principles are suggested as criteria for any satisfactory solution:

  1. If possible the solution should be a cooperative measure, i.e., it should include the entire campus in its operation, students as well as faculty and administration.

  2. The solution should consist primarily of actions which can be carried out by the college or university without aid from people off campus.

  3. The solution should be directed toward removal of the basic causes of cheating.

  4. The solution should, as far as possible, preserve and enhance any values inherent in present educational practices.

III. The following solutions for the problem of cheating have been suggested as worthy of consideration:

A. Reduce the opportunities for cheating by more careful and systematic classroom control:

  1. More intensive and systematic teaching with thorough review before each test.

  2. Better physical conditions for examinations—e.g., less crowded rooms, provision of blank blue books and individual copies of test questions.

  3. More watchful proctoring.

  4. Greater variation in examination questions from term to term.

B. Replace present letter or number grading systems by a system of descriptive evaluation of each student's intellectual achievement and ability.

   1. Such a system implies general agreement on a list of fundamental abilities which professors would evaluate and a general statement of standards to be used as a basis for judgment.

   2. A series of brief evaluations of each student by several professors would constitute a profile of his abilities and achievements.

C. Establish an honor system to apply to all assignments and examinations, including the following features:

   1. Thorough indoctrination in the meaning and operation of the honor system for all freshmen at time of entrance, including a pledge of honesty as a prerequisite for admission.

   2. Clear definition of what constitutes cheating, formulation of a code of personal honor, and advance statement of penalties for dishonoring the pledge.

   3. Establishment of a board to administer the system.

   4. The following question requires further thought and discussion: Should the system require students to report violations?

IV. Some evaluations of these potential remedies for the evils of cheating are as follows:

A. Reduction of opportunities for cheating by more careful and systematic classroom control seems to have the following values and weaknesses:

   1. Possible advantages:

      a. More systematic teaching and review would improve the entire educational process.

      b. Better physical conditions, e.g., wider separation of students, provision of blank blue books and individual copies of questions, would reduce facilities for cheating and help to remove temptation.

      c. More watchful proctoring could prevent most cheating.

   2. Possible disadvantages:

      a. More intensive review might tend to narrow teaching in order to prepare students for a particular examination.

      b. Tighter controls in examination rooms would increase tension and suspicion.

      c. The authoritarian aspect of the system would not enlist the cooperation of all groups of the college or university community.

      d. This remedy does not apply directly to some of the basic causes of cheating, such as social and family pressures to earn high grades.

B. Substitution of descriptive evaluation of each student's intellectual achievement in place of present systems of grading by letters or numbers seems to have the following values and weaknesses:

1. Possible advantages:
   a. Students would have no motive to cheat and little, if any, opportunity.
   b. The system would reduce tensions arising from competition for grades. Descriptive evaluations would not be as easily compared as letter or number grades.
   c. The effort to evaluate each student personally would put more emphasis on individual instruction and closer contact between professor and student.
   d. Each student would have a more definite knowledge of his strength and weakness as a scholar.
2. Probable disadvantages:
   a. Faculty members would be heavily overburdened by the requirement that they prepare individual analyses of students.
   b. This overburden would make the system self-defeating by compelling faculty members to make hasty or sketchy judgments.
   c. The cost of more individualized instruction, which such a system implies, would be enormous.

C. An honor system seems to have the following values and difficulties:
   1. Probable advantages:
      a. Such a system would reduce tensions and increase mutual respect and good will among all groups on campus, especially between faculty and students.
      b. Of all proposed remedies the honor system seems best adapted to re-educate the student in his understanding of the purposes of education, his moral standards, and his habits of study.
      c. The honor system would leave the faculty in control of the processes of instruction and evaluation.
   2. Disadvantages appear to be as follows:
      a. Successful prevention of cheating is doubtful.
         (1) The honor system will not remove the pressures for high grades, especially those exerted by society and families, nor those provided by faculty and administration.
         (2) Although honor systems have succeeded in some universities, the success seems to depend on traditions which have developed gradually during long periods of time.
         (3) In some universities honor systems have failed.
      b. If the honor system fails, the faculty will have to assume authoritarian control.

        c. The failure would increase suspicion and ill feeling among students and between students and faculty.

V. Progress toward choice of the most effective remedy seems to depend on judgment of the relative weight of various considerations.

  A. Increased control of classroom procedures:

    1. Seems to be the surest and most practical means of securing immediate reduction of cheating.

    2. But there is doubt that it would reduce the basic social causes of cheating and might even aggravate them by increasing rigidity and tension in the teaching-learning situation.

  B. Substitution of individual evaluation of student achievement for the present letter or number grading systems:

    1. Seems to give most ideal emphasis to basic educational values.

    2. But the required increase of individual contact between professors and students would place an impossible burden on faculty members and be very expensive.

  C. An honor system

    1. Emphasizes basic educational values by:

      a. Placing responsibility on students.

      b. Leaving faculty in control of instruction.

      c. Requiring cooperation among all concerned.

    2. Is of doubtful practical value *because*

      a. It depends on successful indoctrination of students and building of long-range traditions.

      b. Does not remove off-campus social pressures which are principal causes of cheating.

CONCLUSION

  I. If you have arrived at a definite conclusion on the basis of the preceding considerations, you should now state it positively and then consider ways and means of putting it into operation.

  II. If you have not reached a definite opinion, the only statement you can properly make at this point will be a tentative judgment that one of the proposed solutions, or possibly some combination of details from more than one, seems to be best.

  III. If you have not even formulated an opinion, then your only proper statement will be a recognition of the need for further investigation, thought, and discussion.

If during the problem-solving process you are called on to explain the nature of the problem to various groups on the campus, you could use the first two or three main headings as a guide for your presentation. That is, you would state whatever information is available about the kind and extent of cheating, its causes, and the possible kinds of remedial action. A more complete presentation, of course, would go on to analyze the various available solutions. If you or the committee eventually reach a firm conviction that one certain solution should be adopted, you could make a speech advocating that particular remedy. In such a case, of course, you would be adding the role of campaigner to your previous roles as investigator and problem-solver. As a campaigner you would no longer be merely raising questions and seeking answers; you would be declaring a positive point of view and giving arguments in support of it. Your method of organization would then be primarily logical. You would be asking your listeners to accept your proposal or point of view *because* of definitely stated reasons. Your choice of supporting arguments, however, should be based on the necessary steps in the process of problem-solving.

It should now be clear that (1) the problem-solving pattern of organization is primarily useful when we are exploring problems and seeking solutions, but that (2) it may also be useful when we wish to report the results of investigation or advocate a particular course of action.

Summary

An adequate outline is organized in terms of the basic thought relationship most characteristic of the subject matter. The most important kinds of relationships are topical, chronological, causal, logical, and problem-solving.

EXERCISES

1. Analyze the published versions of several significant public addresses (see note on sources in the Appendix) to determine the pattern of organization used in each; make outlines which will show the nature of these patterns clearly.

2. In like manner analyze the sequences of material in classroom lectures, conversations, and group discussions to which you listen. For each of these kinds of speaking try to determine which of the patterns of organization (topical, chronological, causal, logical, and problem-solving) is most effective.

3. Listen to a discussion group in action either on the campus or in the community, and observe the extent to which the problem-solving pattern of organization is followed. Summarize the procedure in outline form. In what respects does the group fail to follow an orderly procedure? How does this affect the outcome of the discussion?

10

THE SPEAKER'S IMAGINATION

Although imagination and emotion may sometimes appear to be the opposites of reason and good sense, we should remember that imagination and emotion are inherent qualities of life which enrich our experience and give it a warmly personal touch. Reason and intelligence are permeated through and through with emotional drives and imaginative creations, and in many instances are strengthened and enriched by them. Because we speak to each other as total human beings, our communication involves some elements of creativity and emotional drive as well as of reason. We pause, therefore, to ask how imagination and emotion can be so developed and controlled as to contribute to more effective thought and communication. We shall consider imagination first and study emotion in the next chapter.

Nature and Function of Imagination

Most psychologists as well as students of art and literature, have regarded imagery as an important aspect of the thought process, although some psychologists have insisted that thinking may be entirely imageless. Indeed a few people, chiefly scientific men and abstract thinkers, report that they experience little or no imagery. Most of us, however, create imagery of some kind.

Imagination is the mental process which deals with images, typically faint though often accurate reproductions of previous perceptions. Whereas an original perception occurs in the presence of a stimulating object, event or situation; an image occurs in the absence of an external stimulus. Its immediate stimulation arises within the body as an indirect and delayed result of former perception. Thus imagination is that aspect of mental activity which functions primarily in relation to internal needs, impulses, and processes of the individual. All of our thinking is a mingling of original perceptions and images in varying degrees. Creative thinking, especially, is a combination of realistic problem-solving processes and imaginative processes.

Apart from dream images there are four principal kinds of

175

Imagination opens wide vistas.

imagery. All of them are parts of our waking experience, although not all of us experience them in equal degree. For our present purposes the afterimage, an immediate continuation of a sensation after its stimulus is removed, and the eidetic image, an unusually vivid and almost photographic copy of an original perception, are not important. Our interest is directed chiefly to memory and creative images.

A *memory image* is simply the recall of a previous sensory experience which closely resembles the original stimulating object. The visual type is dominant in most of us. Nevertheless images of sound, odor, taste, touch, temperature and muscular tension are also important sources of that vividness which lends color and interest to our discourse and helps to make our facts meaningful and impressive.

A *creative image,* on the other hand, is in a sense a new unit of mental experience. This is the kind of imagery which characterizes artists and creative thinkers. It is built upon recall of past perceptions, but combines and rearranges them into original creations. Such creative images are a primary source of the insight by which we discover new aspects of thought, formulate hypotheses, and find solutions to problems.

Memory and creative images are aspects of one continuous process. Memory images provide the elementary materials of imagination, and the creative process gives vital impetus and enlarged meaning to these images. Each type is by itself incomplete; each supplements and fulfills the other.

Imagination is a many-sided function of mental life. In its broadest meaning it includes, at one extreme, the hallucinations of the mentally deranged; and, at the other extreme, the richest productions

Imagination creates new interpretations.

of creative artists. On a literary level imagination is often defined to include such fanciful and unreal creations as mermaids, winged horses, dragons, and griffins. On the other hand Samuel Taylor Coleridge distinguished sharply between imagination and fancy, regarding the latter as a superficial, almost mechanical, combination of fixed and rigid elements, sometimes with playful or perhaps even bizarre effect. Imagination he considered a higher creative process which assimilates experience, integrates and transforms its diverse elements, and thus creates new and original insights into some of the profound truths of life. This is a lofty concept, but it seems to limit the scope of imagination to extraordinary processes beyond ordinary human capacity. Most critics have defined imagination broadly enough to include fancy, considering the latter simply as an elementary level. In its broadest meaning, then, imagination includes not only the playful and artificial operations of fancy, but the day-dreaming of youths, the inspired "hunches" of problem-solvers, and the whole realm of metaphor and figurative language as well as creative artistry.

Obviously we are not primarily concerned with hallucinations, even though some speakers may seem to be afflicted with them. In a sense speakers should indeed see visions and should include an element of playfulness in some of their imagery. The light touches of day-dreaming and fancy have their values, especially in our more casual conversations. However, our main business here is to study those normal and constructive types of vividness and insight which enrich our daily communication and open up pathways to problem solutions, scientific generalizations, artistic creations, and the inspirations which move the mind forward toward conclusions.

Imagination functions in a broader scope, with more original and complex elements and more freedom of action that does reasoning. Whereas reasoning operates more largely with verbal materials, imagination is a spontaneous and sometimes unconscious rearrangement of concrete images. Whereas inference moves in a more direct line from fact or premise to conclusion, imagination may range the universe in search of resemblances on which to base the integration and interpretation of experience. Imagination is a special kind of inner behavior or inner perception which re-creates past experiences and gives them richer meaning and in its higher and more complex aspects reorganizes them creatively into new and original patterns.

Even an act of original perception, if it is to have really significant meaning, must involve some element of imagination to bring out its relationship to other experiences.

> . . . experience becomes conscious, a matter of perception, only when meanings enter it that are derived from prior experiences. Imagination is the only gateway through which these meanings can find their way into a present interaction; or rather . . . the conscious adjustment of the new and the old *is* imagination.[1]

Imagination is the power which sees objects and situations in their breadth and wholeness, grasps relationships between diverse elements, organizes them into new and moving concepts, infuses them with feeling, and thus vitalizes knowledge and experience so as to lift it above the commonplace of our daily routine.

Imagination and Speech

Improvement of imagination is especially important for us as speakers because it is involved in almost every phase of speech behavior. There is, in fact, a very close relationship between imagery and all bodily action. Experiments have shown that visual images, for example, involve slight tensions in the muscles of the eye; and that imagined overt actions such as lifting a weight or talking with a friend involve subtle contractions in the appropriate muscles.

Imagery, moreover, has a definite and indispensable part in the development and coordination of overt speech movements. Auditory images of sounds and words are basic to distinct articulation and

[1] John Dewey, *Art as Experience*, Minton, Balch & Co., 1934, p. 272.

expressive voice modulation. Only in exceptional cases can we produce sounds which we cannot hear or of which we do not have distinct auditory images. This fact has a definite neurological basis. Whenever we vocalize or speak, the sound waves stimulate our own ears. The auditory impulses are fed back into the central nervous system and pass upward to the association areas of the cerebrum where they are integrated with other percepts and give rise to patterns of motor impulse which stimulate and control continuation or repetition of the sounds.

In like manner, the sensory impulses arising from bodily movements play a vital part in stimulation and control of further action. Sensations arising from the contacts which tongue, lips, and soft palate make with each other and with surrounding structures during articulation give rise to memory images of touch. These together with auditory images enter into the integrated patterns of motor nerve impulses which stimulate and control further articulatory movements. Kinesthetic or muscle sense images are especially important in this process. Every time a muscle contracts, kinesthetic impulses are initiated in the nerve endings embedded in that muscle, pass into the central nervous system, and enter into the patterns for neurological control of further movement. In so far as we can see our own movements, visual images also play a part in the continuity and control of action. Usually we are more likely to be aware of the visual and auditory images than of the tactile and kinesthetic, but these more subtle kinds of imagery are nonetheless important in the control of behavior.

Images have an equally valuable function in relation to thought for speech. As communicators we need to make our ideas vivid, give a tangible quality to utterance, enrich our recall of past experience, and make our units of knowledge more specific. When we speak in terms of light, colors, sounds, odors, tastes, or movements, we add charm and subtle force to our discourse. In so far as we share common types of imagery with our listeners, we are able to re-create experiences we have in common with them and thus find a vivid basis for understanding. For most of us, word images are especially important. They enrich memory and make it more specific. They are the principal symbols in which our thought for speech is formulated (see Chapter 4). As Suzanne Langer said: "Before language communicates ideas, it gives them form, makes them clear, and in fact makes them what they are . . . Language and imagination grow up together in a reciprocal tutelage."[2]

Imagination is also essential to a speaker's understanding of himself. Most of the materials out of which we build images of ourselves are derived from remembered awareness of our own behavior and of the ways other people respond to us. Each person's formation of his

[2] Suzanne Langer, "The Cultural Importance of the Arts," in M. F. Andrews, *Aesthetic Form and Education*, Syracuse University Press, 1958, pp. 4 and 7.

own self-concept is in large part a process of integrating these memory images.

Beyond these elemental uses of imagery, we have the extended values of creative imagination which serve the processes of inference, problem-solving, and artistic performance. In everyday reasoning and problem-solving, creative thinking begins when we become sensitive to an irritating or disturbing element of dissatisfaction in a situation. Almost every phase of problem-solving involves insight and imagination (see Chapters 9 and 19). In artistic kinds of endeavor, the imagination operates with greater freedom and abandon. At this level a problem is more a matter of deep urgings toward self-expression than of external situation or difficulty. The facts are conditions of the inner spirit rather than information to be sought, and the fusion of imaginal materials is more varied and less likely to be channeled toward one particular kind of outcome. The processes may be more intuitive than reasoned. When we speak as interpreters (for example, in acting or oral reading) or when we speak under stress of intense emotion, our imaginations often reach higher levels of artistic creativity. The highest product of imagination is a perfect blending of the message with the linguistic media in which it is formulated and communicated.

Improving Imagination

After all this emphasis on the values of imagination, we should ask how it works. What can we do to enhance and improve it? Of course not all our speaking can be or needs to be inspired. The common and routine exchanges of every day call for no lofty visions. Nevertheless our simplest conversations will be enlivened by vivid imagery, and creative insights will enrich all our discourse.

How can this be achieved? Contrary to the usual assumption, the processes by which we create ideas and insights are not merely casual inspirations of the moment. They are part of our growth. They develop out of past experience as joint products of effort and intuition. Useful inspiration is always supported by knowledge and inference. Thoughtful spoken discourse is just such a growth and development. If we are to have anything really worth communicating, we must acquire a solid foundation of knowledge; and if we are to utter anything more than commonplaces, we must have some flashes of insight and inspiration. Any utterance above the commonplace is also something of a venture in faith. Though it comes up out of our past, we are required to launch out in new directions. We must have freedom from old and fixed assumptions, complete surrender to the task in hand, and willingness to accept the hazard which any new venture involves.

Many great artists and scholars have described their mental

processes in ways which we can utilize for the improvement of our spoken communication. Their descriptions have been assembled, analyzed, and found to include certain common elements of method which any thinker, whether plodding or inspired, can use with advantage. The method falls into four phases which are not sharply distinct or separate, but which constitute broad and overlapping procedures.

PREPARATION

This is a time of sustained preliminary labor, during which the thinker should expose himself to the widest possible range of information about his subject or problem. The relevant facts are assembled, digested, organized, and understood. Recall of past experience, observation, reading, and discussion are the necessary processes (see Chapter 6). They often involve uncertainty and doubt, sometimes even frustration. The mind is seeking ideas, exploring, analyzing, probing, evaluating. At this stage the creative person is especially receptive to new ideas. He is reaching out in all directions for the knowledge from which new concepts and solutions can be constructed. All his previous experience, especially his training in logic and research methods, is significant in this search. He will avoid casting his findings in old and stereotyped classifications, but will seek new relationships and categories. The amount and variety of information assembled, the extent to which it is related to vivid personal experience, and the freedom and originality with which it is organized and interpreted will largely determine the creative nature of the end product.

INCUBATION

The accumulated knowledge needs time for germination and maturing. Sometimes intensive labor leads to a kind of surfeit or mental indigestion and further effort seems to yield no results. Then a period of rest is in order which gives the mind time to digest and assimilate the assembled information. Either a change of activity or a complete rest will give the ideas time to grow and develop. Physical exercise is an excellent mental relaxer. Sometimes with a short-range problem even sleep may be an effective interlude. Whatever the type of change may be, however, nothing should interfere with a complete turning away from the problem at hand.

The length of this incubating period will vary according to the temperament of the person, the nature of his problem, and the kind and amount of his preliminary study and thought. During this time, however, the unconscious mind is reworking and reorganizing information gained during the preparatory period, until eventually new ideas begin again to crowd to the surface of conscious thought. Some will be entirely inadequate to meet the need or problem, others only partly adequate. Some will tend to appear, fade out, and reappear in modified forms. Those ideas which seem most nearly adequate will tend to appear again and again in more highly developed form. Sometimes the period of incubation will be interrupted by frequent returns to active fact-finding. The periods of preparation and incubation may recur in alternation as successive stages of work and rest, of acquisition and assimilation of material.

ILLUMINATION

Eventually comes the moment of insight. Out of periods of preparation alternated with periods of incubation, the adequate idea emerges. Sometimes as ideas take form and move into new relationships there may be advance intimation that the flash of insight is about to occur. At other times the moment of inspiration may arrive with apparent suddenness. In any case, revived past experience and new information are assimilated and integrated into new patterns of thought. Just how this happens, just what goes on below the surface in the unconscious mind is not clearly understood.

Numerous creative thinkers and artists, however, have described the kinds of situations and cues which lead to the effective solution or satisfying outcome. For Hermann von Helmholz, famous German psychologist, ideas came unexpectedly without effort, like an inspiration, particularly "during the slow ascent of wooded hills on a sunny day." The mathematician, Henri Poincaré, found his best inspirations during periods of apparent rest and unconscious work when he was unable to sleep or in the midst of an activity quite unrelated to his problem. The composer, Von Weber, would wander through the forest memorizing the words of a theme until the idea of a whole musical piece would flash through his mind. Joseph Rossman inquired of several hundred inventors and learned that their creative ideas occurred mostly in relaxed moments after awakening from sleep or following hard work or when they were daydreaming, bathing, dressing, talking with a friend, reading, or listening to a concert.

A. E. Housman spoke of the way lines of poetry would flow into his mind "with sudden and unaccountable emotion" during walks of two or three hours after lunch. Amy Lowell said that for her the initial impulse for a poem might drop into the subconscious and be forgotten for days or months, when suddenly the words were there demanding to be written down. The novelist, Henry James, has related the manner in which one of his stories began. A stray suggestion made by a Christmas Eve dinner companion, was forgotten for some years and finally "emerged from cool reclusion all suffused with a flush of meaning." Harry Emerson Fosdick, one of America's great preachers, remarked that after he had explored his subject fully, both from his own inner resources and from materials outside himself, the structural outline of a sermon would emerge "out of the material as though by spontaneous suggestion."

Such inspirations may seem to be entirely spontaneous, and in a sense they are. Yet like all true inspiration they grow out of knowledge, sustained attention, and periods of quiet maturation. Creative imagination is a dynamic process which develops out of experience and study, matures in the hidden subjective level of thought, and springs into visible life with apparent and sometimes mystifying suddenness. The moment of illumination may be attended by emotional stress, especially if long-established attitudes are upset, but ultimately it brings a deep sense of satisfaction and a feeling of quiet confidence that here is truth.

VERIFICATION AND DEVELOPMENT

The inspired idea must be developed and elaborated in terms of the situation or context in which it is to be applied. Outworn aspects will need to be discarded, fresh insights added. The new concept, if it is to live, must find a medium which clearly embodies its form and pattern of growth. When speech is the medium, we must find those symbolic forms of action, voice, and language which will formulate our thoughts adequately and communicate them clearly. The results will be judged in terms of their effectiveness in meeting the problems and situations which need to be solved or clarified.

This final period of intensive effort extends and verifies the work done during the initial preparatory activity. Together these two periods of work distinguish genuine creativity from daydreaming or psychopathic imagining. The factual groundwork for our inspirations is a means of assurance that our visions will be realistic.

What significance do these four phases of the creative thought process have for us as speakers? Not all of us are endowed with imagination of the creative sort. There are few Huxleys and Einsteins or Roosevelts and Churchills among us. Nevertheless there is a spark of creative mentality in every one of us which can be developed to bring forth ideas worth communicating, even inspired ideas. In our daily discourse we can develop our highest potentials by utilizing the methods which great thinkers and communicators have outlined. Norman Thomas, one of the most active speakers ever to appear on the American platform, said: ". . . the speaker should live with his theme or message, turning it over and over in his mind. He will be surprised at how many useful illustrations or ways of putting his case will come to him as he walks the street, or reads a newspaper, or gets ready for bed, or wakes up in the morning."[3] The advice is applicable in all our spoken communication.

[3] "Random Reflections on Public Speaking," *The Quarterly Journal of Speech*, April, 1954, p. 146.

When the moment of insight comes, we should seize the new idea quickly, formulate it definitely, and put it to work in some way which will make it tangible and enduring. Write it down, discuss it with a friend, think about its possible aspects and applications. Put it to the tests of verification, revise, develop, and expand. In this way we can make fact-finding more meaningful. In this way we can lay the basis for clearer organization of thought and more effective use of the symbolic means of communication—bodily action, voice, and language. This is the way of the creative thinker and communicator.

EXERCISES

Methods of improving our use of imagination are not exercises in the usual sense of activities to be done in definite ways at specified times. Improvement of imagination depends more on development of certain habits of mind as aspects of a continuing and permanent manner of life. Of course some degree of systematic planning and effort is essential, as we have seen, but one's philosophy of life and way of regarding the world are even more important for the development of imagination. Obviously, then, the following suggested means of improvement should be approached not as practice to be done today only or during this course of study, but as continuing habits of thought and action to be carried forward throughout one's life.

1. Endeavor to sharpen your habits of discrimination and observation (see Chapter 6, section on observation). If you are looking at an object, for example, notice the materials of which it is made; its shape, size, color, and texture; or its functions and uses. If you are considering a process or action, take note of such features as its direction, speed, complexity, motive power, controls, and effects. Effective description or explanation of objects or events depends on vivid use of such details.

2. Take every opportunity to broaden your appreciation of the various arts. Visit museums and galleries. If possible, take courses in appreciation of painting, music, architecture, as well as literature. Give special attention to poetry and imaginative literature. Notice the kinds of imagery used. If you are to read aloud, either as interpreter or actor, let your thought dwell on the lines so as to arouse the widest possible range of images and related ideas. Begin with the following selections, but extend your reading as widely as possible.

> *Oh, to be in England*
> *Now that April's there,*
> *And whoever wakes in England*
> *Sees, some morning, unaware,*
> *That the lowest boughs and the brushwood sheaf*
> *Round the elm-tree bole are in tiny leaf,*
> *While the chaffinch sings on the orchard bough*
> *In England—now!*
> *And after April, when May follows*
> *And the white-throat builds, and all the swallows!*

Hark, where my blossomed pear-tree in the hedge
Leans to the field and scatters on the clover
Blossoms and dewdrops—at the bent spray's edge—
That's the wise thrush; he sings each song twice over,
Lest you should think he never could recapture
The first fine careless rapture!
And, tho' the fields look rough with hoary dew,
All will be gay when noontide wakes anew
The buttercups, the little children's dower
—Far brighter than this gaudy melon-flower!
        ROBERT BROWNING, "Home Thoughts, from Abroad"

I thought that I dreamed a dream one night—
That I was a moth on a joyous flight,
Under a sky the west wind cools,
Over a sky of fields and pools.
Like a tinted leaf in the wind content,
Over the wonderful world I went;
Over a valley with wavering wing
My shadow flew like a startled thing.
On through the waters spread below,
I saw my delicate phantom go—
On, till a flash, and that bright world broke,
And I was a man at a sudden stroke!
        EDWIN MARKHAM, "Which Was Dream?"

Out of the Valley of Gardens, where a film of new-fallen snow lay smooth as feathers on the breast of a dove, the ancient Pools of Soloman looked up into the night sky with dark, tranquil eyes, wide-open and passive, reflecting the crisp stars and the small round moon. The full springs, overflowing on the hillside, melted their way through the field of white in winding channels; and along their course the grass was green even in the dead of winter.

But the sad shepherd walked far above the friendly valley, in a region where ridges of gray rock welted and scarred the back of the earth, like wounds of half-forgotten strife and battles long ago. The solitude was forbidding and disquieting; the keen air that searched the wanderer had no pity in it; and the myriad glances of the night were curiously cold.

His flock straggled after him. The sheep, weather-beaten and dejected, followed the path with low heads nodding from side to side, as if they had traveled far and found little pasture. The black, lop-eared goats leaped upon the rocks, restless and ravenous, tearing down the tender branches and leaves of the dwarf oaks and wild olives. They reared up against the twisted trunks and crawled and scrambled among the boughs. It was like a company of gray downcast friends and a troop of merry little black devils following afar off.
        HENRY VANDYKE, "The Sad Shepherd"

The suns of summer seared his skin,
The cold his blood congealed;
The forest giants blocked his way;
The stubborn acres' yield
He wrenched from them by dint of arm,
And grim old solitude
Broke bread with him and shared his cot
Within the cabin rude.
The gray rocks gnarled his massive hands;
The north wind shook his frame;
The wolf of hunger bit him oft;
The world forgot his name;
But 'mid the lurch and crash of trees,
Within the clearing's span
Where now the bursting wheat-heads dip,
The Fates turned out—a man!

R. WIGHTMAN, "The Frontiersman"

3. When you begin preparation for a discourse of any kind (whether conversation, discussion, or talk to an audience), begin well in advance by exploring all aspects of your present knowledge and thought about the subject. The following procedure should prove helpful: (*a*) Write down the largest possible number of related ideas. Give your mind complete freedom to wander over the widest variety of thought. Put down everything which occurs to you; do not stop to evaluate. Postpone criticism until after you have assembled a substantial list of items. (*b*) Then go back over the list to review and evaluate. (*c*) Select those ideas which seem to have most interest and value, especially those which group themselves around a single basic theme or purpose. (*d*) After you have completed this review of your own ready storehouse of information, begin the search for additional facts and ideas by whatever means are appropriate—observation, experiment, interview, reading (see Chapter 6). (*e*) Take alternate periods of rest and work until new insights and ideas begin to develop. (*f*) Elaborate and verify these ideas until they have taken form in a full-rounded, purposeful, and coherent plan for communication to a listener.

BIBLIOGRAPHICAL NOTE

Material on the artistic and creative aspects of imagination was stimulated by such writings as Samuel Taylor Coleridge, *Biographia Literaria*, London, 1898, especially chaps. XII and XIII; John Livingstone Lowes, *Road to Xanadu*, Houghton Mifflin, 1927; Lascelles Abercrombie, *The Idea of Great Poetry*, Harcourt, Brace & World, 1926; Frederick Clarke Prescott, *The Poetic Mind*, Macmillan, 1922; William Hazlitt, *Lectures on the English Poets*, G. Bell, 1880; June Downey, *The Creative Imagination*, Harcourt, Brace & World, 1929; John Dewey, *Art as Experi-*

ence, Minton, Balch & Co., 1934; Suzanne Langer, *Feeling and Form*, Scribner, 1953; Peter McKellar, *Imagination and Thinking*, Cohen and West, 1957; E. J. Furlong, *Imagination*, Macmillan, 1961; and Harold O. Rugg, *Imagination*, Harper & Row, 1963.

Development of the four stages of creative thinking in the section on improving imagination is based on Graham Wallas, *The Art of Thought*, Cape, 1931, especially chap. IV; Catherine Patrick, *What Is Creative Thinking*, Philosophical Library, 1955; and Brewster Ghiselin (ed.), *The Creative Process*, University of California Press, 1952.

The testimony of creative thinkers was gleaned from a variety of sources: Henri Poincaré, "Science and Method," *The Foundations of Science*, Science Press, 1913, Book I, chap. 3; Paul C. Squire, "The Creative Psychology of Carl Maria von Weber," *Character and Personality*, March, 1938; Joseph Rossman, *The Psychology of the Inventor*, The Inventor's Publishing Company, 1931; A. E. Housman, *The Name and Nature of Poetry*, Macmillan, 1933; Amy Lowell, "The Process of Making Poetry," quoted in Ghiselin, *op. cit.*; Henry James, Preface to *The Spoils of Poynton*, Macmillan, 1922; Harry Emerson Fosdick, "How I Prepare My Sermons: A Symposium," *The Quarterly Journal of Speech*, February, 1954.

11

THE SPEAKER'S EMOTIONS

Have you ever remarked in response to a criticism of your speaking, "I was so nervous; I could have done better if I had not been frightened." Confrontation of speaker and listener, however, is an essential part of the speech process, and your effectiveness in meeting the pressures of that confrontation is the real measure of your speech abilities. The maladjustments which we call nervousness, self-consciousness, and fear are real hindrances to our effectiveness as speakers and deserve thoughtful consideration.

Merely getting rid of nervousness and fear, however, is a negative approach. Since every significant experience of our lives is in part emotional, we should be able in speaking to replace fear with some degree of whatever emotion is in harmony with our thought. Those speaking situations are barren of meaning which arouse in us no overtones of pleasure or sadness, love or anger, hope or discouragement. The acme of effective speech combines the impetus of deep emotion with the calm and deliberate judgments of rational intelligence.

The Nature of Emotion

There are wide differences among psychologists concerning the nature of emotion. Definitions are sometimes so broad that they include all affective processes, such as organic sensations, moods, sentiments, attitudes, interests, aversions, and even temperament. A narrower definition limits emotion to acute and disorganized types of response such as anger and fear. Other theories have stressed instincts as the basic drives of emotion; sought explanation of emotion in the conflict of opposing attitudes; emphasized the physiological and behavioristic aspects, looking upon emotions as release of energy or internal bodily changes; or tried to explain entirely in terms of what happens in the nervous system. In spite of these disagreements, however, psychologists are almost unanimous in recognizing three basic elements in all emotional behavior:

First, there is some form of overt expressive action which can be seen and described, at least in part. This action may be either positive or negative, approaching or withdrawing, well-coordinated or disorganized, constructive or disruptive in pattern and effect.

Second, emotion involves a series of physiological changes chiefly in respiratory, glandular, circulatory, and excretory systems. These processes within the viscera and smooth muscles of the body are controlled by the autonomic division of the nervous system.

Third, each of the various kinds of emotion involves some psychological experience or awareness which seems to be characteristically different, although we are not always able to describe the differences clearly. This awareness includes perception of the external stimulus which gives rise to the emotion and in some degree an awareness of the organic and expressive changes which are involved.

Emotion is a complex process which begins with perception of an external stimulus (object, event, or total situation). Awareness of the stimulus leads immediately to evaluation in terms of liking or disliking, pleasantness or unpleasantness, potential threat or advantage. This evaluation is more a matter of feeling tone and connotation than of precise denotative meaning; and seems to be closely related to whatever inner organic changes are characteristic of the particular emotion, even though the relationship is not well understood. The pattern of overt expressive action which completes the response is determined by the nature of the external stimulus, the evaluation given it, and the related organic changes. Perception, evaluation, organic reverberation, and expressive overt action are inseparable aspects of the emotional experience.

From this description it follows that the internal organic changes of emotion constitute a kind of mediating activity between perception of the stimulus and the overt response. Controlled emotions activating bodily processes can help us observe and evaluate the external facts more adequately and prepare for more effective response. In itself an emotional reaction does nothing about the stimulating situation; in fact extreme and uncontrolled emotion may reduce our ability to make effective response. Emotion is a powerful driving force which impels us to overt action. If uncontrolled, the action can frustrate and hinder effective response; but if controlled, it is an indispensable part of our communicative behavior.

Emotional responses are learned and can therefore be changed by relearning or conditioning. In the earlier years of this century John B. Watson demonstrated that the fear response in a child could be transferred from one stimulus object to another and could be generalized and even extinguished by repeated presentation of the stimulus under carefully controlled conditions. Later work has shown that both visceral and skeletal organic changes can be conditioned, and that stimuli from sources internal as well as external to the body may affect visceral processes. It appears also that emotional disturbance is characteristic of early stages of learning but tends to disappear with repetition of the new material; and that responding organisms act to reduce or avoid the distress of an unpleasant situation. These facts constitute the foundation for control of our emotions.

Speech Fear

Since fright is in some degree experienced by most speakers, we turn now to a more definite consideration of its nature and remedies. Some facts have been observed and some ideas developed which may help us understand ourselves and our speech problems better.

THE DOUBLE NATURE OF FEAR

Fright is usually described as a negative and disorganized kind of behavior. Although emotions may appear, in general, to energize the organism to meet difficult situations, some recent studies indicate that extreme fear has a directly opposite effect. Strong stimulation of the sympathetic nervous system together with discharge of large amounts of adrenalin into the blood stream actually depresses muscular activity and makes mental work virtually impossible.

A primary factor in this disrupting effect of fear is the inner conflict it involves. New and strange features in any situation may create confusion in the way it is perceived and evaluated. Such confusion arouses conflicting tendencies of response. Confused perception and evaluation reduce the ability of the cerebrum to choose one response and inhibit another. The conflict may then extend from higher neurological levels to lower motor levels and thus stimulate conflicting patterns of muscle tension. Confusion and conflict in mental processes of evaluation and choice lead to confusion and conflict in muscular response. We fail to inhibit one action tendency fully and as a result leave no clear pathway for any action.

In contrast to these observations, fear may also be a means of increasing the effectiveness of our responses. Fear alerts us to the hazards and difficulties of situations. Such a prospect demands that something be done vigorously and appropriately. Fear, like other emotions, may serve as a mediating stimulus, an inner response which intervenes between the external stimulus and the overt response and plays an important part in determining that response. "Although fear, at times, may serve as a debilitating deterrent to action, ample evidence from daily experience indicates that it often functions as a potent goad to action."[1]

Moreover, fear, at least moderate fear, may help us learn new and more effective behavior patterns. As Dollard and Miller point out,

[1] Judson S. Brown, *The Motivation of Behavior*, McGraw-Hill, 1961, p. 147 ff.

fear in a new situation may serve "to elicit responses that have previously been learned in other frightening situations"; and they add, "A reduction in the strength of fear reinforces the learning of any new response that accompanies it."[2] As we launch into purposeful and thoughtful speech, we may find the tension and disorganization of acute fear draining away and better coordinated patterns of speech behavior emerging.

These two diveregnt concepts of speech fear supplement each other more than they contradict each other. On one hand, if we hope to speak with vigor and effectiveness, we cannot allow extreme and disrupting degrees of fright to overmaster us. On the other hand, we need that moderate kind of fear or apprehension of the hazards of oral communication which will make us more alert to its demands and more keyed to the kind of organized and coordinated action it requires.

SYMPTOMS AND CAUSES OF SPEECH FEAR

We have three primary sources of information about speech fear:

1. Observation of speakers. We identify fear in others by tense and awkward posture; by such poorly coordinated actions as shifting of feet and nervous movements of hands; by negative or avoiding responses, such as the averted eye or retreat behind the nearest desk or chair; and in some cases by listless movements and weak or high-pitched voice. Fright also reduces a speaker's ability to use language effectively. Studies have shown that severely frightened student speakers are less fluent and more prone to errors in grammar, while students with minimal fright have a higher verbal output and a wider variety in types of words used.

2. Speakers' own reports. As speakers we are aware of internal and organic symptoms of fright—dry mouth, tightened throat muscles, pounding heart, weak knees, cold hands and feet (literal as well as figurative), confused articulation, and anxious sweating of hands and fingers. We may also feel that our listeners are disapproving, and may have difficulty remembering what we had intended to say.

3. Measurements of organic effects. Experimental measurements indicate that during speech fright pulse and blood pressure are changed, glandular secretions increased, and digestive processes reduced. It is significant that some of these characteristics of frightened speech, including some internal chemical and visceral changes, occur also in vigorous and emotional normal speech. Primarily the difference lies in degree of coordination and control. In fright the high levels of control in the association areas of the cerebrum fail to carry out their primary function of coordinating complex behavior. As a result the frightened speaker's sense of purpose may be confused, his thought disorganized,

[2] John Dollard and Neal E. Miller, *Personality and Psychotherapy*, McGraw-Hill, 1950, pp. 77–78.

*Effective response
is animated.*

his memory vague, his gestures poorly coordinated, his articulation slurred, and his use of language limited and inept. In vigorous normal speech, on the other hand, the highest levels of the brain carry out their integrating functions with the result that purpose tends to be clarified, thought well organized, and overt behavior well coordinated. Both vigorous normal speech and frightened speech are characterized by strong emotion; but in fright the organism is unable to control and use the additional energy which increased stimulation makes available.

This generalized description of speech fright should not blind us to the fact that people differ in the extent to which it is experienced. Some of us suffer extreme distress in public situations, while others may feel no more than mild excitement. The onset of fear is not the result of environment alone nor of the individual's sensitivity alone. Both the nature of the situation and the state of the organism are determining factors. Fright, especially speech fright, is a result of interaction between the individual and the situation in which he is placed. We shall consider next the kinds of situations that are most likely to induce speech fright and the kinds of people that are most likely to suffer from it.

Kinds of situations. Speech fear is typical in a demanding, perhaps even threatening situation. We do not mean that listeners are belligerent; if they were, mere fright would be a useless defense. The danger in a speaking situation usually is no more than a threat of failure in communication with its consequent blow to our self-esteem and reputation. Many speaking situations, certainly all those which are public or which involve large groups, call on us to make extraordinary

Intense feeling energizes speech.

adjustments, to assume a kind of leadership, to clarify understanding, allay emotions, and change convictions or beliefs—in short to assert our thought or project our personalities in some positive way. Such demands are always difficult to meet and threaten failure in the realms of social success and self-esteem.

The presence of a listener or audience is a challenging factor in any situation. If that presence interferes with concentration on the message to be communicated, a conflict in thought may result and lead to conflicting action tendencies. We are torn between our desire for self-expression or communication and the fear that we may not succeed. There is conflict between the bright hope of self-fulfillment and the possibility of failure. As a result we are unable to integrate our responses into a well-coordinated pattern.

Not all speaking situations involve these hazards in equal degree. Quiet conversation, casual exchanges of greeting or comment, oral reading and discussion among close friends or in the family circle may involve no great emotional or social pressure; yet even these intimate and personal kinds of situations often involve matters of far-reaching significance in our lives. The speech situations which arouse intense strain, if not fright, and challenge our capacities for emotional adjustment are those in which important issues of personal welfare are at stake, whether they involve personal interview, small group discussion, or large audiences.

Kinds of people. Much depends, of course, on the emotional stability of the individual. It seems obvious that people with low self-confidence and a high degree of sensitivity are most likely to become

193

frightened. Extensive studies made some years ago showed, for example, that confident speech students consistently scored higher on tests of general emotional adjustment than poor speakers. A general sense of inferiority and low self-evaluation were much more frequent among fearful than among confident student speakers. Many more fearful than confident students reported sensitivity about personal appearance and social rebuffs, worry over mistakes of etiquette and grammar, and frequent feelings of discouragement and uncertainty. The fearful ones more often described themselves as being shy, sensitive and self-conscious.

Other research has indicated, as we might expect, a close relationship between amount of speaking experience and ability to adjust to speaking situations. Students with a continuous and varied record of speech activity and training from early childhood were able to meet the demands of speaking situations with better adjustments than the inexperienced. The students most susceptible to fright were not only those with least speech experience; they were also the ones who avoided participation in speech as well as other social activities. It seems clear that speech fear is not just a function of difficult situations; but part of a more extensive personal problem related to sensitivity, self-consciousness, and lack of experience. Even experienced speakers feel apprehensive in the presence of a stimulating speech situation, but they know how to control their fear and excitement.

If we can inhibit the tendency to dwell on the hazards, discomforts, and possible failures, and discipline ourselves to concentrate on our communicative task, then we might master the fright. If we do not let our fears obsess and distract us, and instead establish the image of success, our fright may be reduced to that degree of controlled excitement which any challenging situation should induce in us and which successful speech response requires.

The Control of Speech Fear

It is most significant and hopeful that emotions are subject to re-education and can be brought under control. However, the complex nature of emotion in general and of speech fear in particular should make clear that in this as in most aspects of speech improvement, no quick and easy remedies are available. Whatever your particular emotional maladjustments in speech may be, they probably are the result of many influences extending over many years. For most of us they are habitual modes of response which can be changed fundamentally only by a gradual process (we hope not too gradual) of reorientation and relearning.

What helps one person, moreover, may not help another. We

come from different backgrounds and educational experiences. We differ in sensitivity and social orientation. Our speech abilities and problems are not all the same. In this section, therefore, we shall try to discuss remedial processes so broadly and inclusively that you and every other student will find suggestions to fit your particular needs. Then with the guidance of your instructor you may achieve a clear understanding of your problem and be able to choose those procedures which apply to it.

We shall follow the main guiding principle of all problem-solving: The most effective measures are those which apply directly to the *causes* of difficulty. We shall discuss in the following sections the causal factors implied in preceding sections, and then search for appropriate methods of re-educating ourselves.

OVERSENSITIVITY AND LACK OF CONFIDENCE

To the extent that oversensitivity and feelings of inferiority are causes of speech fear, the following suggestions will be helpful:

Broaden your social contacts. Anyone who is shy and diffident should seek appropriate and modest ways of meeting and conversing with other people. Develop outgoing attitudes. Get out of the chrysalis stage, but be careful not to become just a social butterfly.

Develop an objective attitude toward yourself. Appraise frankly your limitations as well as your strengths (see Chapter 5). Study the nature of emotion and use your increased understanding as a basis for analyzing your fears and apprehensions. Whenever and wherever you have occasion to speak, look upon yourself as a person with a job to do in relation to other people—that is, as one of the dynamic forces operating in a larger process of interaction.

Fortify your self-confidence in every possible way. Act bravely and you may begin to feel brave. Your feelings can be influenced by your actions. The muscular aspect of your behavior cannot be separated from the sensory and neurological aspects. If you stand up, square your shoulders, look your listener in the eye, take a deep breath, and declare your ideas forthrightly, the feedback to your self-awareness may help to banish the inner conflict and turmoil.

If notes will help you, prepare them fully and carefully. Then throw them away, or at least maintain as much independence from them as possible. Thorough preparation is a much better foundation for self-confidence than words on a piece of paper.

Never stop in the midst of any speech activity because of fear or embarrassment. Occasionally there may be other reasons for discontinuing, but you should usually finish what you begin no matter how harassed and uncomfortable you may be. Giving in to fear "will inevitably distract a man from achieving what truly enhances his human nature . . . the perfection he could achieve given his capacities and opportunities."[3]

Build up the image of success.   Fear can be diminished by association with pleasant experience. Therefore dwell on your past successes; anticipate more of them in the future. Successful communication can be a thrilling experience because it meets two of our most basic needs—social acceptance and personal self-fulfillment. If we keep our attention centered on the image of success, we increase the likelihood of changing the distress of possible failure to the delight of a challenge adequately met.

LACK OF SPEAKING EXPERIENCE

To the extent that inexperience in speaking, especially to large groups or in public situations, is a cause of fear, the following measures may be useful:

Seize every opportunity to speak.   Some caution is needed, of course, to avoid being merely loquacious or a show-off; but if you are timid because you lack experience, move in boldly to counteract the inhibiting effect of fear.

Arrange your speech participation in a graduated sequence from simple to more difficult activities.   Begin, for example, by extending your everyday contacts and quiet conversations with friends. Make new acquaintances and tactfully explore their interests. Increase your participation in group activities, first in small groups and then in successively larger companies. Some participation in student organizations will provide opportunities. As your range of activities grows, you will find or should seek public appearances. On your campus there are forensic, interpretative, and dramatic organizations. The departments of speech and drama probably sponsor debate groups, a readers' theatre, and many play productions. With moderation join any or all of these which appeal to your interests. You will find much help in overcoming speech fear if you move as rapidly as possible from the simple, everyday speaking activities to those which are progressively more complex and difficult. The joy of success, nurtured and carried forward from occasion to occasion, is one sure means of conquering the fear which so easily frustrates us.

DISTORTED PERCEPTION AND EVALUATION

To the extent that lack of objective attitude toward the people to whom we speak and the settings in which we meet them is a cause of speech fear, the following attitudes should be developed:

Be optimistic.   Direct your attention to the encouraging features of the situation. Observe the friendly faces present. Note the

[3] Magda B. Arnold, *Emotion and Personality*, Columbia University Press, 1960, vol. 2, p. 278.

ease with which you can be seen and heard, the helpful introduction, the eager attention of the listeners. Think of the confidence implied if you came through tryouts for a place on the debate team or in the play cast or were specially invited to speak.

Rise to the occasion. Look upon the difficulties of the situa-ation as challenges to be met and overcome. If the listeners are tired, restless, inattentive; if there is competing noise; if the light is inade-quate; if the attitude and activity of your listeners distract you; what-ever the hazard, take those measures necessary to conquer it. In so doing you may be able to forget, at least in part, your own apprehension and discomfort. But if you run away, either literally or in attitude, you will eventually despise yourself as a weakling.

Keep perspective. Remember and dwell upon the idea that your listeners are human beings much like yourself and your partners in the interacting process of communication.

WEAKNESS OF CEREBRAL CONTROL

Cerebral control is the process by which the highest levels of the central nervous system dominate and coordinate complex patterns of behavior. In practical terms this means that well-organized, logical thought processes should exert a controlling leadership over the entire speech act, including its sensory and emotional phases and its visible and audible techniques. To the degree that speech fear is caused by failure of the higher levels of the brain to exert such an organized con-trol, the following means of mental discipline should be helpful:

Thorough preparation. This is the foundation on which to establish leadership of the intellect. For informal and casual occasions, of course, only informal preparation may be necessary. We may some-times anticipate conversations, review our resources, and even formu-late certain key statements; but most of our daily communication, be-cause of its impromptu nature, must depend on the ready availability of a storehouse of knowledge and insight. For situations of a more formal kind, deliberate preparation is necessary. All that we have said about understanding our listeners, formulating purpose and theme, gathering information, and organizing it in logical sequences, is relevant not only for public occasions and large audiences but for many of the smaller and private speaking occasions as well. For reading aloud, of course, selection of material appropriate to the occasion and the listen-ers, and the fullest possible understanding of the author's thought and purpose are essential. For every occasion and every kind of speaking all the processes by which we marshal and organize our thought are basic means of emotional control.

Master your material thoroughly. Many speakers and students of speech stop work with the completion of an outline. They fail to study and rehearse the thought until it is fully assimilated and made completely their own. Rehearsal, both silent and vocal, is an important means of mastery (see Chapter 12).

Allow enough time. Whenever possible begin your preparation for any speaking occasion, formal or informal, well in advance of the time you are to meet your listener or listeners; and distribute your work at intervals so as to allow time for maturation as well as inspiration.

INNER CONFLICT

In the degree that speech fear arises from conflict between divergent views or tendencies to action, we should seek means of resolving the conflicts. Firm choice of alternatives in speech purpose and methods is an essential means of establishing confidence and reducing fear. To achieve this, some additional measures of mental discipline are required.

Be definite. As much as possible without making snap judgments, let your choice of alternatives be definite at every stage of preparation—in choice of subject, purpose, theme, material, methods of development, and techniques of utterance. Take time to think carefully, but let your decisions be positive and clean cut. Those speakers are least likely to suffer from fear who come to their communicative task with sure knowledge of goals and methods.

Do not be distracted. Concentrate on your job as communicator. Adhere to your purpose, talk directly to your listener. Do not let your attention wander to side issues or to feelings of inferiority. Your listeners will care little about your uncertainties; they want to know what you have to say.

INADEQUATE TECHNIQUES

To the extent that bodily action, vocal expression and use of language are poorly coordinated and ineffective, they undermine confidence and contribute to speech fear. The remedy is practice to improve the conditions and techniques of utterance.

Practice to establish the basic conditions which underlie effective speech techniques (see Chapter 2, section on method of study and practice). These basic conditions include balance and repose of body (see Chapter 13), responsive and controlled breathing (see Chapter 14), and economy of effort and reduction of tension in all speech movements.

Practice to improve specific techniques of utterance. Study coordination in general bodily movements and gestures so that action shall be under control of thought and communicative purpose (see Chapter 13). Practice exercises for clarity of articulation and expressive voice modulation (see Chapters 15 and 16). Study to increase vocabulary and correct language usage (see Chapter 17).

Whenever appropriate use warming-up exercises just before important speech performances. Exercises in relaxation, deep breathing, and simple calisthenics are especially useful for freeing the channels of action and correcting any imbalance in release of energy which the anticipation of speaking may induce.

REVIEW

You will notice that the recommended procedures for control of fear are of four kinds: (1) general reorientation of attitudes regarding fear; (2) a continuing program of speech experience; (3) methods of preparation for speaking; and (4) improved techniques of utterance. Almost all methods for speech improvement are useful in the development of self-command and emotional control. If the fright which inhibits our action, drains our energies, and tends to "freeze" us when we speak under stress, can be converted into an energizing factor which impels us to renewed and well-coordinated action, then our speech fear can become an asset.

Emotion and Thought

The surest means of achieving emotional control is through maturation. Maturity implies moderate and well-considered behavior patterns which in turn are a sign of increased neurological integration and intelligent control. As we develop toward adulthood, we should become increasingly able to endure life's frustrations and meet its crises with less extreme inner turmoil and less explosive overt responses. We should become less self-centered and less subject to self-pity, better balanced and more moderate in our appraisal of other people and events in the world, better coordinated and more relaxed in action, and in general more objective and factual in all our behavior. This does not mean that we should cease to experience deep emotion, but it does mean that our emotions will be characterized by more accurate perception, more objective evaluation, more moderate internal organic changes, and more subtle and well-coordinated outward expression. Control of emotion, in speech as in every other phase of life, requires not only coordination of its overt responses, but integration of the total behavior.

Such integration requires that the emotional and intellectual aspects of our lives function in close relationship; they should act together as parts of one system. ". . . rationality and impulse are synergic, and strongly tend to come to similar conclusions rather than contrasting ones."[4] We have already seen that emotional experience begins with perception and evaluation of a situation; in this it has common ground with logical reasoning. In our consideration of imagination (Chapter 10) we noted that every stage of problem-solving has some emotional

[4] A. H. Maslow, *Motivation and Personality*, Harper & Row, 1954, p. 3.

involvement. Recognition of a difficulty arouses a sense of frustration and in severe cases may even arouse a disorganizing emotion such as anger or fear. The search for solutions must involve some emotional participation until the final resolving of the difficulty brings relief from tension and a sense of satisfaction. Interestingness, moreover, is based on appreciation and enjoyment of ideas, and motivation has its roots in depth of conviction. Sincere feeling reinforces logical reasoning. In fact, emotion is most useful in speech when directed to purposes and themes which are logically derived and developed; and our logical modes of thought are most impelling when founded on depth of interest and conviction. "When reason is separated from the emotions, the former is unmotivated and the latter, blind."[5]

BIBLIOGRAPHICAL NOTE

In this chapter the remarks on nature and development of emotions were influenced primarily by the following sources: M. L. Raymert (ed.), *International Symposium on Feelings and Emotions*, McGraw-Hill, 1950; A. A. Roback (ed.), *Present-day Psychology*, Philosophical Library, 1955; O. Hobart Mowrer, *Learning Theory and Behavior*, Wiley, 1960; Konstantin M. Bykov, *The Cerebral Cortex and the Internal Organs*, Chemical Publishing, 1957; R. L. Solomon and E. S. Brush, "Experimentally Derived Conceptions of Anxiety and Aversion," *Nebraska Symposium on Motivation*, University of Nebraska Press, 1956; and John B. Watson, *Behaviorism*, People's Institute Publishing Company, 1924.

For the symptoms and causes of fear in the speech situation the author relied on the well-known studies by Howard Gilkinson and Franklin Knower in *Speech Monographs*, 1942 and 1943, and in *The Quarterly Journal of Speech*, 1940. Other useful articles in *Speech Monographs* were by Milton Dickens and William R. Parker, November, 1951; Gordon M. Low and Boyd V. Sheets, November, 1951; Louis Lerea, August, 1956; and Eugene J. Britten, November, 1959. Useful sources in *The Quarterly Journal of Speech* were by Charles W. Lomas, February, 1937; and Eugene C. Chenoweth, December, 1940.

[5] V. J. McGill, *Emotions and Reason*, Charles C Thomas, 1954, p. 111.

12

THE SPEAKER'S MEMORY

$\mathbf{A}$ll that we have said about thinking for speech is useless without memory. Information is of little value to a speaker unless he can recall it. Wise choice of purpose and theme depends on remembered knowledge about listeners. Logical inference requires command of facts and premises. Imagination, even in its creative sense, is based on past experience in the form of memory images. Emotional participation depends on a speaker's ability to relate his past experience to a present situation. Even the preliminary planning of a discourse requires a storehouse of memories.

In our use of the various forms of speech we depend on memory in different ways and in varying degrees. The conversationalist and discussant need quick and ready command of a wide range of information. An extempore public speaker needs a disciplined ability to remember his speech plan and the materials for its development; he requires an organized and logical kind of memory. An oral reader, even though manuscript or book is before him, needs that kind of memory which is based on deep understanding of an author's meaning in terms of the reader's own experience. A reader should assimilate an author's message so fully as to make it his own. Actors must add to this assimilative memory a facility for exact verbal reconstruction of the dramatist's lines. For all kinds of speaking a full storehouse of memory is a continuing necessity. The organizing and disciplining of our recollections is the final and indispensable, though often neglected, stage in preparation for any formal or definitely anticipated speech performance.

The Nature of Memory

Although verbatim memory is useful and often important, our daily communication depends more on recall of facts and ideas. Indeed the attempt to recall fixed patterns of words may sometimes disrupt our thought and actually hinder our speech. Words, of course, are an essential medium of our communication, but they should be used primarily as vehicles of thought.

Memory is the process by which past learning becomes effective in the present. The conscious recall of past experience should be a creative act which accumulates experience and organizes it into meaningful units or concepts. Memory does not operate as a separate faculty of the mind, but is a complex function involving perception, logical relationships, organization of ideas, emotional participation, and indeed the entire personality: ". . . memory is the whole mind viewed as the conserver of its experience."[1] The total process includes three main phases—(1) learning, (2) retention, and (3) recall. Each of these deserves some comment.

LEARNING

Edwin Guthrie defined learning as the more lasting effects of practice. Some psychologists would add that the practice should be directed toward a definite goal. For our purposes as students of speech, of course, purpose and results are highly important. Both our learning and our remembering should aim to produce changes which accomplish better expressive-communicative processes. To achieve such results, we should remind ourselves of the basic laws of learning, which are the foundation of our efforts to improve memory.

Law of frequency. The more often a given response follows a given stimulation, the more likely will it recur when that stimulation is repeated. Experimental research has shown a "positive relation between amount of practice and the amount remembered, with diminishing returns at the higher degrees of learning."[2]

Law of recency. The time at which given stimulus-response associations are experienced is a factor in learning. If causal connections between a stimulus and two different responses have had equal reinforcement, the more recent will persist more strongly in behavior. This new response will continue as an item of learning until it is replaced by a still more recent response.

Law of intensity or vividness. This refers to the degree of stimulation or energy which enters into learning. A normal child needs to touch a hot stove just once to know and remember the painful result. All of us at some time have changed an old established habit as a result of just one startling or intense experience. Any increase in intensity of stimulation tends to modify the law of frequency by reducing the amount of practice required.

RETENTION

Effective memory requires that the results of learning shall be preserved during a latent period. Although our knowledge of what actually happens in the nervous system is limited, retention is usually

[1] Kate Gordon, "Memory Viewed as Imagination," *Journal of General Psychology,* 1937, p. 113.
[2] Ian M. L. Hunter, *Memory: Facts and Fallacies,* Penguin, 1958, p. 42.

thought of as maintenance of whatever neurological changes have been established during the learning process. The more thorough the initial learning, the more completely are the neurological patterns established. Frequent repetition of any given act tends to maintain its neurogram, but disuse leads to deterioration and possible disappearance, especially if new and more recent stimulus-response associations have been formed. We think of retention, therefore, as depending on maintenance of the neurological patterns which have been established during the learning process.

RECALL

If learning and retention are to reach their most effective outcomes, our recollection of past experience should have two essential characteristics.

First, every well-remembered thought has in some degree a quality of intimate personal experience. The memory will be even more vivid if we are aware of the time and place of its origin.

Second, recall involves creative reconstruction as well as recognition. Remembering is a reorganizing and interpreting of some part of an individual's past in terms of his present. No two instances of recall of a given event or fact are ever exactly alike. Some details which were once clearly perceived may have been forgotten, and those which are revived may often be in a changed order and relationship. New details, not originally observed but arising from later experience or even from imagination, may possibly be added. The pressure of social conventions and beliefs exerts an influence. We tend to observe and recall those elements of experience which meet with social approval. Memory is thus a complex process of selecting, imagining, and organizing elements of past experience. One of the greatest students of memory said, ". . . the past is being continually remade, reconstructed in the interest of the present."[3]

Because speaking is such intensely personal business, these viewpoints are especially important for us. The messages which we communicate should be so thoroughly assimilated into our own experience that we think of them as belonging to us. Oral communication, moreover, should be essentially creative; it should reconstruct past experience. The kind of memory which is most useful to us as speakers is not merely a routine recalling of words. It is instead a meaningful organization of concepts and principles which provides a live and flexible pattern or framework in which detailed units of knowledge find their inherent places in relation to other details as well as to concepts and principles. In this process words serve as instruments of thought. In most of our everyday discourse we do not need exact verbatim memory, but we do need to remember words, at least key words, as the media in

[3] F. C. Bartlett, *Remembering*, Cambridge University Press, 1961, p. 309.

which we formulate and recreate our ideas. *For a speaker, memory is that phase of his thought by which he recalls previous learning and thinking and uses them in communication to meet the demands of a present situation.*

Improving Memory

The improvement of memory has been a matter of concern to students of speech since the Greeks first began to study oratory in the fifth century before Christ. In its earliest beginnings Greek literature was essentially oral and depended on recitation and oral communication. This fact made memory an important art—so important, in fact, that the Greek rhetors and sophists, or teachers of wisdom, gave it an important place in their instruction. The principles of memory became one of the five basic divisions of the study of rhetoric, together with proof, organization, style and delivery. At the high point of the ancient classical development of rhetorical study in the first century before Christ, the great Roman orator, Cicero, gave memory a place in his writings; and a little more than a century later the great Roman educator, Quintilian, summarized the best of the classical instruction regarding memory.

Almost all memory systems are primarily based on organization of material by the use of artificial symbols. Such systems, though no doubt useful in some situations, are too cumbersome to be of much value to us. Speakers do not need artificial devices or patterns of organization; the process of speech has its own inherent symbols and methods of arrangement. The very form of an outline, with its numbers and letters to label points, provides a kind of location pattern by which we can recall ideas (see Chapter 8). We have available, moreover, the language symbols in which our communication is carried on. These provide direct and efficient media for remembering the content of our speaking.

Let us assume that you are anticipating a speaking occasion with time to make thorough preparation in advance. If the form of speech is to be conversation, group discussion, or address to an audience, we shall also assume that you know the subject, purpose, and theme of your remarks; that you have some knowledge about your listeners; that you have adequate information about the subject, and that you have organized your thought in a coherent and well-unified outline. If you are to read aloud or act in a play, we shall assume that the material is already chosen. What next? Whatever the form of speech, your final, basic task in preparation is to master the thought sequence you are to communicate. For acting, of course, the memorizing must be carried on to exact verbal recall. For reading from text you will not need complete verbal memory, but should master the author's message thoroughly. Whether the speaking is to be original or interpretative, the logical and assimilative phases of memory are equally necessary and fundamentally similar. The three basic aspects of remembering—learning, retention, and recall—suggest the essential processes. (1) Increase your mastery of the material. (2) Use those methods of learning which will enhance retention. (3) Create the best possible conditions for recall.

INCREASE YOUR MASTERY OF THE MATERIAL

This is by far the most important means of insuring adequate recall.

Give attention to motives and attitudes. As you approach the task of memorizing, focus your interest. The task of communicating ideas which are fully assimilated should be an exciting challenge.

Deepen your understanding. Ideas which are richly meaningful are more easily remembered than thought which is formal and routine. Take an overview of your material and relate it to your past learning and experience in as many ways as possible.

Review your plan of organization. Study the relationships between your purpose and theme and the major divisions of thought. Keep in mind the kind of organization you have used (i.e., whether topical, chronological, causal, logical, or problem-solving, as given in Chapter 9); and make it the framework within which you recall details. Concentrate first on the more important ideas. Begin by reviewing your purpose, next your theme, and then the main supporting points. Develop these into a frame of reference which summarizes your entire pattern of thought. Details can then be filled in for each main unit, and may even seem to fall naturally into place under their major headings.

Dwell on the logical relationships of ideas. Observe the facts and premises on which inferences are based. Notice the transitions. Study the comparisons and contrasts between ideas; look for similarities and differences; observe and evaluate selectively. If you are to read aloud, analyze the structure of the author's thought. Study his images and figures of speech. Whether your speaking is to be extemporaneous or interpretative, observe the unity and coherence of the thought. Understanding the inner relationships of ideas is the basis of memory. Without it practice will be of little value.

Rehearse the thought sequence. Think it through repeatedly. Practice aloud. Experimental results indicate that merely speaking the names of objects is an aid to memory, and that a combination of oral practice and silent study is a more efficient method of memorizing than silent study alone. Follow the advice given in Chapter 2 and let all your practice be purposeful, systematic and realistic. For public appearances take some practice, if possible, in the setting where you are to speak or in a place with similar characteristics of size and acoustics. If nothing else, you can at least create an imagined prevision of the situation. Let all your practice be done as if in the presence of your listener or listeners.

Use the method of wholeness.   Speak the entire discourse as planned from beginning to end. If you are preparing ideas or units of thought for use in the give and take of conversation or group discussion, rehearse each unit completely. Let the precise wording and to some extent also the order of details remain always flexible and subject to change and development. Rigid verbal memorization will rob you of freedom to adapt as you proceed, and is certainly not a means of building either confidence or effective recall. Suppose you do memorize verbally—and forget? What then? Embarrassment, perhaps panic; in any event, thought sequence gone! Better to depend on logical rather than strict verbal memory, and let yourself be a freely creative agent of communication. Even the actor, who must follow accurately the text of the play as written, can apply this principle of logical and creative memory as a foundation for his exact verbal memory.

Distribute your practice.   Relatively short periods of study and rehearsal alternating with periods of rest are more efficient than a smaller number of longer periods. Practice spread over a period of time is more efficient than short-term cramming. Research shows that in general longer intervals up to perhaps two days have the advantage. For students and teachers of speech the suggestion seems obvious: Begin preparation for a speaking exercise well in advance so that practice can be distributed between alternate periods of work and rest.

Additional experimental work has indicated, however, that overly long intervals between repetitions of material tend to decrease the accuracy of its recall; but that frequent rehearsal tends to fix the pattern and general form of a thought sequence after only a few repetitions. The advice does not apply equally to all kinds of material, but may reasonably be summarized as follows: Learning is accelerated at first by frequent short practice periods which tend to fix the essential pattern of thought; thereafter repetition at longer intervals may help to enrich details within the general framework established by the earlier practice. Work should stop whenever fatigue or any kind of confusion might introduce disorganized study habits. Bear in mind always that no two of us are alike and that every speaker should work out his own optimum methods of memorizing the various types of material he communicates.

Overlearn the material.   Experiments in memorizing have shown that for lists of nonsense syllables a certain degree of overlearning, at least 50 percent, increases retention for intervals of 2 to 28 days. The larger the interval the greater is the economy. Nonsense syllables, of course, are not propositional speech. The fact, however, that statements are usually more meaningful than unrelated words should make the effects of overlearning propositional speech even more significant than the overlearning of syllables. The more we study and repeat a given sequence of thought, the more we are likely to remember.

USE METHODS THAT WILL ENHANCE RETENTION

Study organized and meaningful material by the "whole" method with frequent repetitions of oral practice distributed between intervals of rest and carried even to the point of overlearning. A frequent type of interference with retention is the canceling out of older learnings by new activities. This is in harmony with the law of recency. The more extensive the intervening activity, the less is retained of the original learning.

The nature of the inhibiting activity, as well as its extent, is important. If the intervening thought or action is similar to that which was learned originally, the amount of interference increases, unless of course old and new materials are identical or nearly so—in which case recall is aided, as we might expect. The increased interference from similar materials is probably the result of confused mingling of old and new which blurs the distinctive nature of the original learning. On the other hand, if the intervening activity or learning is entirely different from the material first learned, the danger of confusing the two is decreased. The implication is, clearly, that after a period of learning one should resort to a totally different kind of activity in order to enhance the likelihood of remembering.

An interesting extension of this principle is found in experiments which showed better memory after a period of 6 to 8 hours sleep than after a waking period of the same length. For shorter periods, 1 or 2 hours, the difference in recall was insignificant. Even though this result was obtained with figures and nonsense syllables instead of meaningful statements, it has a suggestion for speakers, especially student speakers: If you are scheduled to do an exercise in communication on a given day, especially in the morning, review your material immediately before retiring on the preceding night. We might add that sleep during the preceding class hour will have but little value.

CREATE OPTIMUM CONDITIONS FOR RECALL

These conditions, of course, are closely related to the conditions for learning and retention. Nevertheless certain special factors should be mentioned.

Allow a warm-up period. All of us have had the experience of recalling with difficulty a past event or the lines of a poem, but discovering after continued thought that the first fragmentary recollections were increased and even grew into full-rounded memory. This suggests that during some interval of time just before speaking we should let our minds dwell on the ideas we intend to communicate so that the recall of details will be enriched and systematized by an increasing range of association.

Use any devices of association which will help recall. Relationships of number, similarities of sound or color, or even the space relationships used in ancient memory systems may be helpful as supplementary devices. Even better is the use of a system of catchwords, perhaps the key nouns or verbs of your material, to represent your points; or the use of imagined objects, persons or events as symbols of ideas to which they are related. Sometimes even bizarre or playful relationships may help to fix a series of thoughts in mind. Selective attention to the more important points in your discourse together with use of symbols to represent them will have the advantage of reducing the bulk of material to be remembered.

Memory needs effective reminders.

Fill in the gaps in learning. We have seen that our perceptions are seldom complete or accurate and are often changed in later recall. We tend to fill the gaps in a first perception or learning with details from other experiences. Imagination may thus reconstruct a memory into a concept more coherent and enriched, although possibly less accurate, than its original experience. We have already spoken of this reconstruction as the creative or re-creative aspect of memory. If carried too far, of course, it may result in distortion; but if kept within the bounds of purpose and theme, such a method can expand and enrich the development of your thought.

Maintain your poise. If after all your effort to attain a failproof memory, you find your thought blanking out, be matter-of-fact. Forgetting may be an embarrassment but is no crime. Neither is it a crime to look at your notes or turn to your outline if you must. Better yet, pause and deliberately review all possible cues which might restore your chain of thought. The pause probably will seem much longer to you than it actually is. If the empty void is not filled before your listeners become restless, speak up, take them into your confidence, and search aloud for your next idea. Many of your listeners will have experienced similar difficulties on other occasions. Maintain deliberate self-possession and they probably will join your search with sympathetic patience.

BIBLIOGRAPHICAL NOTE

In addition to works already cited in the body of the chapter, the author found useful stimulation and guidance in Edwin R. Guthrie, *Psychology of Learning*, Harper & Row, 1935; David Rapaport, *Emotions and Memory*, Meninger Clinic Monograph Series No. 2, International Universities Press, Inc., third printing, 1959; and George Katona, *Organizing and Memorizing*, Columbia University Press, 1940.

For some of the more specific topics the following additional sources were used: On the value of audible rehearsal, in addition to the books already cited by Bartlett and Hunter, M. C. Barlow, "The Role of Articulation in Memorizing," *Journal of Experimental Psychology*, August, 1928. On distribution of practice, A. P. Bumstead, "Distribution of Effort in Memorizing Prose and Poetry," *American Journal of Psychology*, 1940, in addition to comments by Bartlett and Guthrie. On overlearning, William F. C. Krueger's "The Effect of Overlearning on Retention," *Journal of Experimental Psychology*, 1929. On the interference of new learning with old, J. G. Jenkins and K. M. Dallenbach, "Oblivescence During Sleep and Waking," *American Journal of Psychology*, 1924; and Esther J. Swenson, *Retroactive Inhibition*, University of Minnesota Press, 1941.

Cicero's discussion of memory will be found in *De Oratore*, Book I, chap. V, and Book II, chaps. LXXXVI–LXXXVIII; and Quintilian's comment in *Institutes of Oratory* or *Education of an Orator*, Book XI, chap. 2. Another work of the first century B.C. which includes an important discussion of memory is the *Rhetoric to Herennius*, Book III, chaps. XVI–XXIV.

III

VISIBLE
AND AUDIBLE ASPECTS
OF SPEECH

Introduction

In Part II we studied speech from a psychological point of view. We began with the observations that thinking involves symbolic activity and that the visible and audible aspects of speech provide symbols in which our thinking reaches definite perceptual form and communicative value. Now we are to consider speech as behavior, as an activity of a sentient and responsive human organism. We shall study first the action of the body as a whole, not only because in itself it is an important communicative medium, but also because it is a basis for the audible processes of speech. Vocalization and articulation are specialized functions of specific bodily organs whose effectiveness depends on the coordinated activity of the entire organism. The sounds we produce are, in turn, the stuff of which oral language is formed; and our effectiveness in choosing and using words is based in part upon our vocal and articulate skill. These processes, of course, may be studied in whatever order seems best to meet the needs of particular students; but we shall present them in the order of their fundamental relationship: first, bodily action; then vocalization and vocal expression; next, word formation, that is, articulation and pronunciation; and finally, choice and combination of words or use of oral language.

13

VISIBLE COMMUNICATION: BODILY ACTION by Dominic A. LaRusso

The Role of Bodily Action

We have seen that interdependent action of the elements of speech produces a complex act which enables one man to "stir up" images and meanings in the mind of another. We have at our disposal audible and visible activities which we organize into patterns designed to produce understanding and action in others.

While many patterns of audible activity (sounds, words, syntax) are available for communication, we have fewer established patterns of visible activity. Because these patterns are not as widely recognized as the audible, most of us are but vaguely aware of the extent to which we are influenced by "silent" communication. Upon reflection, however, we can recall instances when we have felt a distinct dislike for a person who had said very few words to us. There was, we recall, something about him which we could not accept. And we felt this even though we know that our ability to judge emotion on the basis of facial, gestural, or vocal expressions alone is limited. While these cues may not be accurate, they are nevertheless employed by the average person. In addition to these, we utilize subliminal cues, physical actions which are not singly identifiable but which taken all together furnish substance and meaning. In the words of Ray Birdwhistell, "no unit of motion carries meaning per se. Meaning arises in context." And in context, "there is no 'meaningless' motor activity."[1]

ACTION AFFECTS THE TOTAL ACT

Although bodily action may have limited denotative meaning, it is rich in connotation. In every society there are certain nonverbal symbols which can be used to make the interaction between speaker and listener more smooth, more complete, and more meaningful. Among the Egyptians, for example, bending the arm and bowing from the waist has long been recognized as a definite sign of respect. The Italians recognize a bent right arm with clenched fist held skyward

[1] *Introduction to Kinesics,* University of Louisville, Kentucky, 1952, p. 10.

and the palm of the left hand on the right bicep as a positive sign of strong disrespect. The Portuguese look upon a tug of the earlobe as indicative of highest approbation.

This type of activity, including the more subtle actions, may help or hinder a speaker's attempts to communicate effectively because such action is assumed to be purposeful by the average member of society. Although we may often misinterpret specific acts, the fact is that every action has some definite meaning. As psychiatrists and psychologists remind us, one gets to know something of mental and organic states by noting the type, direction, and force of bodily activity. How do we recognize the brain-injured, the drunk, the tired individuals? In the absence of direct signs, and often in addition to them, we rely on evidence furnished by bodily action. The underlying neurological control of spoken communication may often be obscure, but bodily action is nevertheless an important part of the entire process.

As employed in this discussion, the term "bodily action" is differentiated from random activity regardless of the complexity involved. For us *action is that observable physical activity which occurs as the result of reflection and motive.*

A fundamental assumption of this view is that mind and body are part and parcel of each other. Today, few seriously argue the belief that mind and body are completely divorced. The majority of scholars accept the contention that the blood that feeds the big toe is the same blood which is needed to feed the brain. Moreover, as the toe needs blood to function efficiently or at all, so the brain needs a constant supply of enriched, oxygenated blood to operate properly. Without such a supply directed and initiated by the action of the various muscles of the body, the brain functions less and less well and, in degrees, begins to die; without such blood, the individual gets sleepy, becomes unconscious, falls into a coma, and dies. Hence, an active, responsive, and healthy body is indispensable to an active, responsive, and efficient brain. In this sense, bodily activity is in some degree a part of all mental activity; in turn, mental activity is a part of bodily action. It is as though, "the muscles . . . the senses, the whole physiological apparatus of man define to a great extent the form and context of his world of activities."[2]

In relation to speech we note that an absence of proper and constant activity often leads to sluggishness, depression, pessimism. Conversely, the presence of such activity is most often a large part of the sense of well-being. We have already seen that movement in the adult human being is controlled by the central nervous system which is dominated by the cerebral cortex. Perception, the early phase of

[2] Baker Brownell, *Art Is Action*, Harper & Row, 1939, p. 18.

human action, is at once a physical and mental phenomenon. It gives rise to nerve impulses which travel along prescribed pathways to spinal cord or lower brain levels.

These pathways, however, cannot guarantee recognition of such impulses by the brain. What the brain does recognize at any given moment, out of thousands of impulses directed to it, is a matter of mental set or attitude. Physiologists have long understood the fact that although a body may simultaneously experience two types of stimuli (pain and pleasure), only one will usually predominate. Do you not recall a cut or bruise received during moments of exhilaration which goes unrecognized for hours; or the headache which disappears during a party? On the other hand, under certain circumstances the most normal stimuli become painful or bothersome—for example, ambient noise, odor, or light. In either case, the attitudes of an individual are influenced by the kind and extent of bodily action employed, and, in turn, these attitudes help determine the nature of the bodily action.

In addition, bodily action plays an important role in determining the nature of our thought patterns in speech. Most obviously, the individual feeling sluggish and listless will not experience the clarity and refinement of thought which he has known on other days. The brain, in the absence of a constant and enriched supply of blood, fails to operate at maximum efficiency and the varied aspects of our thought processes (attention, memory, inference, imagination, etc.) are impaired. Prominent philosophers and psychologists have said that the various aspects of the thinking process do *not* occur without some type of organic activity. Saint Ambrose in the third century was reportedly disturbed over a prolonged attack of laryngitis because it prevented him from speaking and reading aloud and *therefore* from thinking clearly; Descartes in the early seventeenth century observed that to *think* was to be; and in our own era such men as Vigotsky, Fryer, and Mead have re-echoed the idea.

Our own observations also support the conclusion that organic aspects of speech exert some influence upon the nature of the thoughts we speak. Of all the disciplines acquired by civilized human beings, speech is the only one cultivated when the heart is innocent and the brain responsive and fertile; *it is the only one taught as concepts are being shaped.* During this period, when one corrects the articulation and pronunciation of a child, one corrects his thought. The pronunciation of *bull* for *ball*, if left uncorrected, remains much more than a mere difference between one vowel sound and another. In English, it constitutes a difference between two distinct concepts, the confusion of which can create some serious errors in communication. And so it is with distinguishing the concepts related to *coal, colt* and *cold; walk* and *walked; talk* and *talked;* and hundreds of others. As the story of Helen Keller's life demonstrates, the patterns of muscular activity developed during the critical period of youth, especially those in breathing, phonation, and articulation, do indeed affect the thinking process.

By easy transition, one can detect a somewhat similar relationship between bodily action and language. Without benefit of the gross activity necessary to the continued efficient performance of the brain, we can hardly make use of the memory, judgment, and imagination which influence our linguistic proficiencies in any given situation. Then, too, the oral symbol, wedded to early formation of concepts, depends directly upon the nervous and muscular process of articulation. Here, more than anywhere else, the influence of bodily action upon another element of speech is made evident; the importance of the neuromuscular phenomenon known as *coordination* is demonstrated. Coordination may be defined as the *process* of organizing main muscle groups into a smooth, gracefully functioning whole by employing the correct muscles at the correct time with the required amount of force.

Patently important to all of man's activities, from threading a needle or playing a violin to writing a story or delivering a talk, the process of coordination remains shrouded in mystery. For the most part, we know of its presence only as we observe it in some type of human activity; we are made aware of its importance only as a result of the dramatic effects of its absence. The artistic rendition of a song, the effective movement of a trained athlete, the complicated but aesthetically pleasing movements of a craftsman all announce the presence of coordination. In contrast, the sporadic pace of the cerebral palsied child, the frantic actions of an amateur athlete, and the comical activities of the town drunk reveal the absence of coordination. We have never been able, however, to isolate the phenomenon of coordination from its environment of total activity. What analysis is available demonstrates that coordination is a neuromuscular activity which *can* be developed but which is directly dependent upon the general and specific states of both the nervous and muscular systems. If either system is sluggish, injured, diseased or poorly developed, effective coordination is precluded.

An obvious case in point is offered by the sometimes painful experience of adolescents, particularly boys. For many years a youngster experiences success in coping with the phenomenon of growth because it has occurred in regular patterns; length, width, and strength of muscles usually have kept pace with size, sensitivity, and distribution of the nerves. All of a sudden, almost overnight, he is subjected to a body which is disproportionate; the muscular patterns he had learned to control a body 5 feet tall do not sustain him in his attempts to control one which is 5 feet 6 inches tall. Whereas earlier he knew precisely how much movement and strength were required to move his body around the edge of the dining room table without hitting it, suddenly he exerts the same amount of energy to move in the same way and with the same degree of strength, and he smashes into it. Whereas earlier he had worked out a pattern which would enable him to life an arm and a hand with the speed, strength, and direction required to place a forkful of meat into his mouth, suddenly he does precisely the same thing and finds that he has jabbed himself in the forehead instead. Is it any wonder that with the sudden growth experienced by most youths during the period of adolescence, teenagers are generally characterized as clumsy, awkward, and careless? The sudden growth helps to explain also the almost universal characteristic of the cracking voice in boys during puberty.

Of all of man's civilized activities, none requires a greater degree of coordination than speech. Considering all of the muscles which act in breathing, phonation, resonance, and articulation, vocalization involves hundreds of muscles, all of which have to be moved in split-second timing and always in relation to at least one other muscle. For example, in producing the [b] sound of English the adjustments of lips, jaw, soft palate, and vocal folds require action of no less than 19 muscles in addition to those involved in breathing; and all these muscles must act with the right amount of tension, at the proper speed, and in exactly the right sequence. No doubt many sounds require an even more complex pattern. At an average rate of 175 words per minute, with an average of 5 sounds per word, and a minimal average of 19 muscular movements per sound, a speaker produces in excess of *16,625 disciplined and refined muscular movements per minute*. It is not difficult to appreciate the importance of a sound nervous system and a healthy developed musculature to the activities of civilized man. We can understand that good coordination is a characteristic of better speakers, while ineffective speaking and poor coordination are highly correlated.

In sum, then, an individual's bodily activity plays an important role in initiating, guiding, and reflecting the nature of the other elements in his total act of speech.

ACTION AIDS THE LISTENER'S UNDERSTANDING

Properly employed, bodily action clarifies meaning and provides emphasis. A listener may often fail to grasp a speaker's meaning because of the absence of any visible cues such as facial expression or gestures. Just what does one mean by the comment that "Mr. X is a big man"? Height? Weight? Importance? An appropriate movement of the arms could easily remove the confusion. Similarly, other aspects of *description* are made more lucid by appropriate and timely bodily activity. Movement may also be clarified in this way. Direction, rapidity, complexity, and extent of movement are made more real and understandable by discreet and artistic use of the head, shoulders, arms, hands, trunk, and legs. Intricate relationships can likewise be made clearer by purposeful bodily action. Do not crossed fingers reveal an intimacy of relationship between two persons which would take many words to express as poignantly? Does not a quick roll of the eyes upward with a slight but rapid toss of the head signify hopelessness directly and with great emphasis?

Many times we fail in our efforts to communicate simply because the listener misunderstands our emphasis. Everything we say has an implicit priority which is defined by our larger system of values, the subject under discussion, the listener, and the occasion. We should make use of bodily action to ensure the degree of understanding we think proper. Mood also requires a subtle use of action if understanding is to be effected. In all these matters eye contact may help or hinder the speaker's desire to effect understanding. It hardly behooves a speaker heralded as one sincerely interested in his audience to glance at them only occasionally, while fixing his eyes on the floor, the ceiling, or over their heads.

ACTION IS IMPORTANT TO INTERACTION

In communicative interaction speaker and listener are influenced by the nature, scope, and type of bodily action employed. As with sounds (tones, particularly), bodily actions evoke memories and associations. Some actions are harsh, sporadic, even combative; others are smooth, regular, cooperative, even tender. Regardless of their nature, these actions tend to elicit corresponding actions in the observer because of the kinesthetic sense in man. This kinesthetic sense—that which enables you to know the position of your limbs without looking at them —is basic to the phenomenon known as *empathy*. Empathy, which exists in many animals but is most highly developed in man, is the imitative activity of one person perceiving a like activity in another. When we yawn as a result of seeing someone else yawn, we engage in empathic response; when we witness the spread of giggling behavior through a crowd of youngsters, we witness a display of empathy; when we note ourselves on the brink of tearful behavior while watching a poignant dying scene in a dramatic production, we demonstrate empathy.

In the very young, such sympathetic response is evoked very easily. As we become more sophisticated, more civilized, we become increasingly adept at controlling or minimizing such motor activity. "Indeed," notes I. A. Richards, "the difference between the intelligent or refined and the stupid or crass person is a difference in the extent to which overt action can be replaced by incipient and imaginal."[3] Make no mistake, however, in both the intelligent and the crass such reciprocal action takes place; the difference is merely in the extent of action. In either case, the listener becomes directly a part of the act of communication when he can perceive motor activity on the part of the speaker. This

[3] *Principles of Literary Criticism*, Harcourt, Brace & World, 1925, p. 111.

motor activity, when employed purposefully and appropriately, can make the difference between acceptance or rejection of an idea. For most listeners, bodily actions in a speaker play an important role in the completion of the communicative circuit because "words, whenever they cannot directly ally themselves with and support themselves upon gestures, are at present a very imperfect means of communication."[4] The auditor, then, is mobilized; he is swept up in the general stream of movement, intellectually and physically, so that he now has a sense of direction and the impulse to continue the movement.

Thus prepared, both listener and speaker interact profitably. The listener can begin to note the subtleties, the perspective and the color of the speaker's ideas; he can now detect more of the speaker's roots and his individuality. The speaker, alert, sensitive to and in control of the stimuli within, can turn his attention to those without; he can now detect the responses and the "closeness" of his auditors. This information, after all, is extremely important in the achievement of the speaker's ultimate purpose. Information of this sort is gathered by a system which is a part of every efficient, dynamic operation in man or machine; this system is popularly called a *feedback system*.

A feedback system, whether in thermostats, automatic pilots, proximity fuses or man, depends upon a circuit which *ensures the success of a stipulated mission by continually correcting the difference between actual and intended performance.* In all of his activities from walking to intellectual abstraction, man maintains his pursuit of an intended course only by continually controlling his actual course. In speech, then, to achieve the desired goal of understanding or persuasion, the speaker must recognize, appreciate, and utilize the information which is continually fed back to his brain; he must utilize information about his *actual* progress. You know of your actual progress during a communicative situation by the reactions of your auditors which are conveyed to you chiefly through your eyes. By watching your listener carefully, you can determine what portion of the message should be expanded or deleted, what aspect of the presentation needs to be modified, what listeners are or appear to be obstacles. Such behavior as nodding, frowns, continued whispered conversation with neighbors, or diligent note-taking helps to inform you concerning the reactions of your listeners. The absence of such signs, of course, may signify complete indifference or boredom, although indifferent and bored persons usually demonstrate their attitudes more positively by some overt bodily activity such as a roving gaze or even a yawn.

Although the sense of hearing plays a smaller role in feedback, it nevertheless serves as an important key to audience reaction. In obvious instances, your sense of hearing enables you to catch objections,

---

[4] C. K. Ogden and I. A. Richards, *The Meaning of Meaning*, Harcourt, Brace & World, 1930, p. 15.

note agreements, and acknowledge requests for additional information. In less obvious instances, excessive foot shuffling, unusual rustling, subvocal grunts all can relay important information to the sensitive speaker.

In addition to these main sources of information, there is the subliminal source to which we have already referred. Because such stimuli cannot be clearly traced or identified, they are relegated to the vague area often labeled *intuition*. Whatever the term applied to this phenomenon, it should be recognized as a distinct channel connecting speaker and listener. As such, a special effort should be made to incorporate information gathered in this fashion with that garnered by use of the eyes and ears.

Determinants of Bodily Action

ORGANIC FACTORS

Nowhere is the connection between speech and speaker demonstrated more clearly than in the element of bodily action. A speaker's general state of health is very important. Do you not find it rare indeed to experience effective speech while you are ill or feeling listless? The uncoordinated and habitually ill tend to have speaking problems more frequently and more dramatically than those who are athletic and in good health. Good health, defined as the absence of injury or disease and the presence of an optimum degree of coordination among the various systems of the body, furnishes the sound base for the smooth, sustained muscular activity necessary to both covert and overt actions of speech. With it, you have the advantage of a good foundation; without it, you work with a handicap.

In passing, then, we call attention to the need for a carefully planned and sustained program of physical fitness. A good program will make use of daily *isometric* exercises. Such exercises involve systematic flexion of the muscles against some immovable object. Compare these with *isotonic* exercises such as weight-lifting or gymnastics, which are concerned with amount of work performed. Isometric exercises can be done anytime, anywhere, under almost any conditions (see exercises at end of this chapter).

Similarly, a properly balanced diet is indispensable to good health. The fads of youth regarding food (too much, too little, too restricted) and the habit of eating too rapidly are definitely not an aid to the maintenance of good health. Alcohol affects coordination and clarity of thought; milk often poses a minor problem with some people in that it causes phlegm.

Stature influences the nature, type, and degree of movement effected by the individual. Movement of the body is a combination of activities brought about by the action of muscles working on various bones or other muscles; it is, in a word, the result of what has been called "living leverage." The skeletal system of the body furnishes the levers through which the power of the muscles may be effected. The type and range of movement is affected by the nature of the lever and the power of the muscle activated. Where the bones are small or short and the muscles short and thick, the movements tend to be quicker and more restricted; where the bones are longer and muscles longer with corresponding bulk, the movement is slower and probably more powerful. Applying this principle to the development of the body in general, we would expect to find that taller people are capable of movements with greater range, while shorter people tend to have more restricted and quicker motions.

Sex is also an important determinant of appropriate action in speech. Partly because of associations regarding stature, we have come to expect different actions of men and women. Whenever such expectations are contradicted, we may have a tendency to reject both the speaker and the message. Few people are favorably drawn to the female whose actions, particularly during speech, seem more suited to men— and uncultured men at that. Female actions are expected to be more refined, less gross, and not as forceful as those of the male. On the other hand, male speakers who continually engage in jerky, abortive, and delicate actions are helping to create a barrier against acceptance of their ideas. In sum, as you are involved in this wondrous act of simultaneous creation and communication, you are never far removed from the guides (or fetters) of your physical being.

CULTURAL FACTORS

As the individual communicates, he speaks with the combined traditions of his forebears. In addition to folk tales, as noted earlier, there are folk gestures and movements to which you fall heir merely by being born of certain parents, at a certain time, in a certain place and reared in that same environment. Years ago, there was a strong belief that certain nationalities (and/or races) manifested definite stereotypes in bodily action. Today, investigation demonstrates that cultural environment rather than nationality appears to encourage distinctive gestures and movements.

[Individuals] . . . if exposed for a period of time to two or more gesturally different groups, may adopt and combine certain gestural traits of both groups. . . . gesture and movement are a function of the communication system of which an individual is a part, and . . . a gesture can be understood only when the communication system as a whole is assessed.[5]

[5] Jurgen Ruesch and Weldon Kees, *Nonverbal Communication,* University of California Press, 1956, p. 22.

While you do carry the traits of your environment in this regard, it is important to remember that, as an educable human being, you can alter whatever habit of this sort you wish to alter. Thus, when speaking to an audience of Americans, actions which are peculiar to a particular locale will not aid your communication; in fact such actions are very often a definite barrier. Suppose, for example, you wish to emphasize that a particular person is given to gluttony. You could, of course, simply state the fact. In America today, addicted as we are to superlatives, such a statement would hardly carry emphasis. What is needed is an understatement (meiosis) or an implication underscored by a gesture which the auditors will recognize. In Italy, particularly in the Piedmont region, this could be done merely by stating that the individual had a habit which directed the course of his entire life and, following a momentary pause, placing the hand with palm down at waist level and moving it rapidly in and out near the side of the body. Would most Americans understand what was meant? Of course not. If such gestures were part of your repertoire, you would have to modify them when speaking to American audiences.

Culturally, of course, you bear the traces of certain religious influences as well. Were you a member of the Samga, a division of Buddhists, you would be forbidden to attend any dramatic, dancing, or musical performance. Since some of the gestures and actions we have alluded to could easily be classed as "dramatic" by the members of this austere sect, your activities as speaker-listener would be sharply limited. More importantly, if you were speaking to such a group, your actions as a speaker would need to be refined according to these beliefs. Other religions, encouraging great liturgy and active participation of its believers, might well cultivate freer, more open gestures and movements among their members.

Education, as I. A. Richards reminds us, is another factor of the total environment which plays a role in shaping the habitual bodily activity of a person. Training and refinement tend to encourage a controlled and coordinated set of bodily patterns. In very broad terms, we can detect the schooled from the unschooled by the nature of their bodily actions. The former, so tradition has it, engage in cultivated and purposeful bodily actions suited to time, place, people, and circumstance; the latter, untrained in the course of their development, are noted for gross and random gesticulations which are singularly unadapted.

Unfortunately, as some of our ancestors despised book learning, so some of the present generation despise physical skill of any sort. This ingrown prejudice, which has placed the bridle of "Anglo-Saxon action" upon most of us, effectively discourages a proper appreciation for *any type* of expressive gesture or movement. For fear of being branded crass, common or uneducated, people tend to be restrained and unduly reticent in bodily action, especially during speech. In the face of such opinion, it is important to call to mind the implied recommendation carried in J. Ruesch's *Disturbed Communication* and in the numerous research journals of psychology and psychiatry that *more* not *less* freedom of bodily expression is important to the health of humans. It most certainly is important to the effectiveness of our communication. Seek, therefore, to refine and cultivate appropriate bodily actions while you avoid the dangers of either suppression or exhibitionism.

PSYCHOLOGICAL FACTORS

Recent research in psychology, psychiatry, linguistics, and semantics makes us aware that the bodily actions we employ or fail to employ can be agonizingly revealing. One learns from a speaker how much he has already lived and the depth, width, and height of his life. We recall the obvious connections between bodily actions and illness, e.g., distorted facial expressions, involuntary movements (tics, blinking, twitches), uncoordinated movements of gait which accompany some states of health, abortive movements of stuttering. In less obvious instances, the habitual patterns of action employed by the "normal" individual also reveal his state of mind. Random tapping, unrelated smiles, averted eye contact, constant shifting of weight, while they fall within the normal range of action, nevertheless convey meanings concerning basic personal adjustments to the world. In addition, of course, such mobility, or nonmobility, connotes one's adjustment to the immediate situation.

Types of Bodily Action

Covert processes form the base of effective bodily action. Even the beginning student realizes that there is much more action involved in speech than that which he can view directly. In an earlier section of this chapter we called to mind some of the many muscles involved in the production of the [b] sound. To the muscles enumerated, of course, we must add all those involved in breathing, phonation, resonance and posture. Each of these processes depends upon effective, coordinated muscular action despite the fact that the results of such action may not be readily apparent to the listener.

If, on the other hand, illness or injury were to prevent the action of many of these muscles, then the listener would be made aware of their role. Note, for example, that the speaker who seeks to address an audience while experiencing the pains and discomfort attending pleurisy (inflammation of the pleura surrounding the lung cavity) will undoubtedly manifest an awkward breathing pattern as well as an unusual posture. Speakers with stiff necks, sore lips, or sore abdomens usually try to compensate by forcing additional work upon the uninjured or unaffected muscles, with the result that awkward poses or unnatural maneuvers inevitably attract attention and interfere with the effectiveness of the discourse. It is enough at this point to recall that the process of speech is rooted in the basic state of the individual which expresses itself largely in the efficacy of muscular patterns of action. These patterns, often unviewed by the audience, can work to increase or decrease the speaker's success as a communicator.

Overt activity supplies an important link in speaker-listener relations. In *Hamlet* (Act III, scene 2) Shakespeare offers some sage advice to the aspiring actor and to the discerning citizen as well: "suit the action to the word and the word to the action." As did the philosophers and rhetoricians who espoused this view some 1500 years before he was born, Shakespeare underscores the thought that every human being gives two speeches at the same time: that which is heard and that which is seen. Effective speakers mold these to form *one* which is stronger than either singly.

PRIMARY TYPES OF OVERT ACTION

As a basis for unity, good speakers use certain primary types of action, which can be observed by listeners and therefore enhance interaction and cultivate understanding. These primary kinds of action are *posture* (together with matters of grooming and dress), *gesture* (head, shoulders, trunk, arms, hands, and face), and *movement.* You will note a progressive order of scope and dependence: posture, although involving the least observable activity, furnishes the foundation for gesture and movement; gesture, using as a base the balance and readiness for activity furnished by good posture, is definitely observable; movement, based not only on the balance and readiness provided by fine posture but also on *the spirit and flow of action* offered by purposeful gesture, consists of gross and total motion.

Posture. Without doubt, the word *posture* bears as many connotations as some of our more active terms. Mention the word among a group of friends and notice the subtle adjustments that occur in their own postures as you continue to speak. This stems, of course, from the earlier pressures exerted by parents, grade school teachers, athletic directors and friends who were interested in aiding your development. As with most areas of human endeavor, however, zeal often replaces knowledge and wisdom. As a consequence, many people are made to believe that good posture means a carriage similar to the reputed ram-rod stance of the Prussian general. Contrasted with this "picture" posture there is the more functional approach, which places great emphasis upon the *relative* position of the organs and systems of the body. There is more than one kind of posture; there are various postures—for walking, sitting, standing, lying, and speaking.

All too frequently, the body is not only without conscious care and control but shamefully abused, twisted, distorted into all sorts of unproductive and even ugly shapes; it is robbed of its natural beauty and its efficiency. You are aware that the round-shoulder position creates the flat or sunken chest which, in turn, cramps the heart, lungs, diaphragm and other vital organs thereby preventing their sound functioning. But are you equally aware of the effect of poor posture upon the bones of the body? During the period of adolescence, the bones are still susceptible to the pressures of stress and strain. With all their strength and stability, they are yet capable of being shaped according to any continued influence either in the direction of deformity or of normal development. Thus, when a young lady of seventeen or eighteen insists on assuming the one-legged posture commonly portrayed in fashion magazines, she may well be contributing to the development of a deformity in the pelvic or hip region which could prove serious in later life. When a young man in his teens feels it necessary to slouch in his chair, forcing the weight of his body to be concentrated upon one joint or section, he invites distortion which could hamper future strength and coordination. While one should avoid exaggerated correctness, the importance of good functional posture cannot be overestimated.

The human body is constructed so that it is most efficient when *balanced, alerted* and *in control*. These are the elements of good posture. Whatever the activity (walking, sitting, etc.), the weight of the body must be distributed in such fashion as to maintain a balance. Balance is best described not only in terms of a nonfalling effect; it includes, also, the absence of stress, strain, and pressure which might prevent the immediate and effective use of certain parts of the body. A somewhat detailed account of one example must serve for all. If, for instance, a speaker stood before an audience leaning against a table with his weight supported by his right leg and right arm only (his left leg crossed in front of his right) and his head slung forward, he would be in a nonfalling position (technically balanced); he would however, not be in a position to engage in immediate and effective use of his hands, legs, and arms. In order to engage in such actions, he would have to reshift his weight to free his right arm and right leg. More importantly, as he stands, the muscles of his body are not provided with a sound and firm base for their contractions. The absence of such a base restricts, even prevents, effective activity. He would, then, exhibit and experience poor posture. Alertness implies a body vibrant, sensitive, and capable of responding to stimulation. It is the opposite of sluggish, flaccid, and lethargic. This quality of alertness aids in establishing a fine measure of control, which is important to good posture. Proper control carries with it the ability to make isolated, discriminating and co-ordinated patterns of action which relate directly to the entire speech situation.

In the broadest sense, matters of grooming and dress are also to be considered under the category of posture. Ruesch and Kees recognize the importance of clothes when they note that "a person's identity and taste may be established by apparel, as well as by conformity to the style of the year or the season; clothing, with its capacity for hiding defects in bones and muscles, may be regarded as a particular language in itself." Further, they observe, that "closely associated with clothing is the personal care of the face, hair, teeth, hands, and legs.[6] Discretion and sensitivity remain the effective guides in matters of grooming and dress; the wise speaker, knowing that an effective speaking habit as a whole must be well formed in the particulars, strives to remove those aspects of posture (including grooming and dress) which may serve as barriers to his effectiveness.

Gestures often specify details.

Gesture. In the course of the 2000 year history of speech studies, gesture has been the most maligned and misunderstood component. Failure to understand the interdependent nature of the entire speech act and failure to take into account the need for adapting to the specific conditions of every communicative situation were sources of the confusion and distortion. From the early Sophists who entered into what may be termed "delivery contests," through those elocutionists who believed that certain gestures carried an intrinsic cultural worth which made them eternally universal, to the popular "speech teachers" of our own time the study of gesture has often been regarded as the entire study of speech. As a reaction to this misconception, teachers of speech hesitate to undertake the study of bodily action at all. This, of course, merely compounds the error; it is as ridiculous as

[6] *Ibid.*, pp. 40–41.

refusing to study medicine because of the presence of some charlatans and quacks.

The proper study of gesture includes understanding the phenomenon as well as a concern for the effective use of head, shoulders, trunk, arms, hands, and face. Gesture includes the purposeful immobility of the speaker—a most effective gesture for emphasizing a particular point. The so-called "dead pan" delivery of some comedians is a case in point; such humor is often doubly effective.

As with sculpture, gesture has *structure*, i.e., depends upon line and mass for its form. In speech it includes the matter of timing as well. Effective gesture operates on a plane (high and middle mostly) which can be observed by the auditors because it has definite form (is not abortive, fleeting, partial) and because it is in harmony with the oral symbols offered by the speaker. In addition to structure, gesture has

Good gestures are free.

significance. It is a purposeful part of the communicative experience and signifies the unity of speaker and speech; it reveals the speaker as being a part of the thought *at the moment of utterance.* Similarly, effective gesture is characterized by a quality of purpose we refer to as *intention.* Simply stated, the good speaker intends his actions to reveal his true feelings; there are no "half-way" measures involved in his actions. Finally, good gestures manifest a degree of *universality* which makes them applicable to most speaking situations—not to the extent, of course, that they become stereotyped in terms of precise angles, definite length, or spread of motion; but to the extent that they work in harmony with our oral symbols to increase understanding and interaction.

As an average American student, you can well afford to work toward freedom of gesture since, by tradition and earlier training, you probably err in the direction of insufficient and uncontrolled gesture rather than ostentation (see exercises at end of chapter). In your exercises, work for spontaneity and avoid practicing specific motions for specific portions of your communication. In other words, while awkward and irrelevant gestures have often served to confuse or belie the meaning of your words, it does not follow that your communication will improve with improvement in and emphasis upon specific, standardized gestures. It will come, rather, from a specific endeavor on your part to (1) rid yourself of the attitude that gestures are "wrong," (2) practice for that freedom of action which is normal for you, and (3) work to refine those which are normal with you and yet are not distracting.

All this applies as well to facial expressions. The human face, which has been found to be such a barometer of feeling, contains at least ten different muscles which are used in expression. Each movement of the face, no matter how slight, is the result of the coordinated effort of two or more of these muscles; from a smile to a frown, muscular action is indispensable. And just as muscular development defines the contours and the operation of the body in general, so development of facial muscles defines the contour and the character of the face. Unlike children, older individuals commonly neglect the muscles of the face; they are predisposed to avoid such gross activities as laughing and crying while at the same time they are not inclined to think about or participate in exercises designed to maintain facial contour and sensitivity. Instead of receiving well-balanced activity, the facial muscles of the average person receive a minimum but highly specialized degree of exercise (see the recommended exercises). Consequently, the habitual expressions of a person, such as smiling, frowning, and pouting, become fixed to a point where they are as permanent as a fingerprint.

Persons who habitually pull down the corners of their mouths are believed to be expressing contempt. Persons who lift the corners of their mouths are regarded as being good-natured. . . . The interpretation of such expressive movements of the face is a universal experience; when the muscles are used excessively and remain in a semi-contracted position, they become monuments of personality structure.[7]

Eye contact, from the time of the Rhodian School of Oratory, has been considered extremely important in oral communication because the eyes are most mobile. This degree of mobility is interpreted in terms of (1) facility of movement, (2) precision of movement, and (3) degree of coordination possible between the movement and the reason for it. As with all aspects of gesture, eye contact includes the obviously specific attempt to avoid eye contact with an auditor. This will definitely be a part of the total effectiveness or ineffectiveness of your communicative attempt. Eye contact between speaker and listener provides both with an added means of interaction. Each, as a result of wise and discriminating use of eye contact, can gain valuable information concerning

[7] *Ibid.,* p. 64.

the color and perspective of ideas. Such attitudes as sincerity, concern for the other partner in the reciprocal communicative situation, and emphasis can all be demonstrated through frequent and vital eye contact.

Movement. From our previous discussion, you will recall that movement refers to the gross and total action of the body. More pronounced than gesture, it can bring support to many ideas. As with the other primary actions, one cannot offer positive advice regarding the best movement for each individual speaker. Rather, the principles of freedom and individual discretion apply here as well (see list of exercises at end of chapter). With fine posture and the momentum arising from free responsive gestures, you should find yourself moving about as you speak. Now, to be sure, you should not move, in direction, speed, or range, in such fashion as to call attention to the movement itself rather than to the concept carried by your oral symbols. For example, while it is permissible, even advisable, to take a step now and then, any random pacing is obviously unwise. On the other hand, any attempt to stand in one spot while you are speaking does not contribute to effective communication. You should be free to change your speaking position at such time as you feel the need for it; the chief requirement is that you do so easily and smoothly.

Whenever possible, you should move forward and to the side rather than backward. Avoid movements which are always at right angles to the auditor's line of vision (e.g., from one side of the room to the other) and shun attempts to get very close to the listener. In any movement bear in mind that the chief ingredients are smoothness, vitality, and purpose (even such a purpose as easing your own tension).

SUPPLEMENTARY OVERT ACTION (VISUAL AIDS)

In addition to the use of your own body, you can make productive use of visual aids to effect meaning and enhance interaction. Bear in mind, however, that in proportion as you go outside yourself in the use of aids you remove an essential ingredient of productive interaction; you begin to neutralize the important effect of your unique experience, training, and total personality.

Visual aids are intended only as supplements to a more basic phenomenon. Just as drugs applied indiscriminately without adequate diagnosis of both the disease and the patient or applied without a proper sense of timing could ruin a program of therapy, so visual aids used indiscriminately without a proper analysis of both the message and the listener or without a proper sense of timing, could ruin an otherwise sound communication.

A common and, by far, the most serious error in the use of visual material is the tendency to have it become the presentation. During these talks, the speaker has the dubious honor of serving as a glorified guide, shunted into the background on the false notion that "a picture

Blackboards, properly used, aid understanding.

is worth a thousand words." Were this true, of course, all education would devolve into a process of producing comic strips; all industry would operate with movies as chief instructors; all sales would be conducted by a reciprocal exchange of photographs. Only a moment's reflection is needed tó highlight the fact that photographs do not always convey the same message to all viewers, that one skilled speaker drawing upon the resources of experience, training and personality to meet the dynamic needs of a live audience is superior to volumes of photographs. Visual materials, therefore, serving as merely supplementary aids to understanding and belief, are only as effective as the speaker who makes and employs them.

Nevertheless, the importance of visual aids to well-ordered speaking cannot be denied. Testimony concerning their value includes the extensive use of charts, maps, films, and demonstrations through the long history of education; the more recent emphasis placed upon such material by Armed Forces training programs and various religious organizations; and the indisputable impact of television as a training medium. To the teacher they are extremely important; to the technical man they are indispensable; to the average speaker they are a very great aid.

Visual material contributes to the over-all effectiveness of well-ordered talks in at least two important ways. First, these aids tend to effect greater initial acquisition and longer retention. Various experiments have shown that material presented via combined audible and visual media is learned and retained more easily than that presented by either method singly. Such material enables the speaker to combat distractions: A listener who is exposed to pertinent, well-planned visual material cannot avoid the feeling of participation. Moreover, use of effective aids gives evidence that a speaker has taken the time and trouble to consider his listeners as people. In a word, such materials help to kindle and maintain the interest of the listener.

Secondly, visual material helps to clarify and simplify meaning. Not all ideas lend themselves easily to oral explanation. Some being more abstract or more complicated than others must be explained with the aid of visual material. This is particularly true of such items as mathematical data, engineering configurations, and complex social relations. Here, the use of visual material could serve the important function of broadening and deepening the scope of understanding without increasing the length of the explanation.

To ensure a maximum degree of effectiveness, visual aids ought to be selected and employed with care and knowledge.

Aids should be related to the message itself. Too often supplementary aids are used in a talk because someone else has used them successfully, or just because the speaker believes he must do something; so he uses various gimmicks even though they may be entirely unrelated to his task. Every aid introduced for such reasons acts to create a barrier to effective communication simply by dividing the listener's attention. If what the speaker says is not related to what is represented, confusion is raised in the mind of the listener.

Aids should be adapted to both speaker and listener. Unless the visual material is within the experience and intellectual range of the speaker, it can only serve as an obstacle to clear understanding. What the speaker cannot understand is rarely conveyed to the auditor in understandable form. Furthermore, unless the supplementary aids are adapted to the experience and intellectual range of the listener, they are of little positive value and may contribute much in a negative way. Finally, it is important to consider the visual aid from the standpoint of the speaker's stature, sex, and personality. For example, young women speakers should avoid using a huge model because of the threat of dropping it, the strain of manipulation, or unflattering reflections on the speaker's sex.

Aids should be easily seen or heard. All time, money, and energy expended in the selection of supplementary material is rendered null and void unless the material reaches the audience. Generally speaking, the smallest visual material of any value in the average 20 by 40 foot classroom is 8 by 11½ inches. This means, of course, that the main feature must be of that size. It would not do, for example, to utilize an 8 x 11½ inch map of the United States when the main feature of the visualization had to do with the peculiar size, shape, and location of the Cimarron River in Oklahoma. So also a speaker should avoid the use of auditory material which cannot be clarified or amplified to the degree necessary for easy assimilation by the audience. If ambient noise makes recognition and intelligibility of sound difficult, then that material ought not to be used no matter how pertinent or how much apology may be offered for it. Shaky easels, poor blackboard lighting, noisy projectors, and other inadequate mechanical supports which transform good aids into unwelcome distractions should be avoided.

Aids should be planned. Impromptu chalk-talks, sketches, demonstrations, and hastily improvised maps, charts, or diagrams offer more trouble than help except on rare occasions. The best and most effective visual material is that prepared well in advance of the actual presentation. Adequate planning includes consideration of the needs and capacities of the speaker, audience, message, and occasion. Planning should also include proper display to make sure the material performs its intended function. Models and charts should be brought into view only as intended by the speaker; when not a part of the immediate discussion, they ought to be covered or removed from view to prevent distraction. Such material, moreover, should be placed in such a position that the speaker can refer to it without turning his back to the listeners, obstructing their view, or diverting their eyes for too long a period of time.

Types of aids.   No single aid is uniformly superior to any other, although some media are used more frequently than others. The wise speaker is one who retains a flexible, experimental attitude toward the use of visual material because he realizes that its efficiency varies with subject, speaker, audience and occasion. All aids not furnished by the speaker's body (i.e., primary actions discussed previously) may be classified according to two major categories: *manipulable* and *non-manipulable.*

Manipulable aids include all photographs, charts, prints, pamphlets, cartoons, diagrams, maps, posters, scaled models, mock-ups and the like which the speaker handles sometime during the talk. As a result of the wide acceptance of larger aids, such as flip-charts and slides, an erroneous and unprofitable conception has arisen that the speaker ought to avoid handling things during his presentation. While it is true that you ought to avoid fruitless and aimless "toying" with materials, it does not follow that you should therefore deprive yourself of the distinctive value of special aids small enough to be handled easily. Take care that your manipulation ensures maximum value. Such small aids, for example, ought to be held chest high and approximately 12 inches from the body so that the speaker may look over the object into the eyes of his auditors. By turning, rather deliberately, from one side to the middle and to the other side, a speaker presents his listeners with a completely unobstructed view. Major obstacles are created by holding the aid to one side, cradling it in one arm, holding it too low, or moving it too rapidly from side to side. Employing the position recommended above guarantees against interference by the speaker's body while it provides for easy use. If, as speaker, you feel the need of pointing to a specific portion of the object, you merely have to turn it around, place your finger on the spot and return to the position which all can see.

Nonmanipulable aids are all materials which require some sort of mechanical supplement for their use; they are, in a word, too large for the speaker to handle. They include, of course, all photographs, charts, prints, diagrams, maps, posters, models which must remain stationary and to which the speaker must turn in order to utilize them. Movies, opaque projectors, tape recorders, and similar aids present some special problems but can be included in this list. Such aids must be employed with definite care to avoid interference and even conflict. If at all possible, large material should always be set up prior to the talk to avoid interruption of mood and train of thought. Once the display is set up, of course, you must arrange to have it properly covered until the moment of use to avoid inviting distraction.

Furthermore, when using such material you should always have your back on the same plane as the aid in order to avoid obstructing the auditor's view. As you stand in such a position, facing the listeners, you can easily use your arm to point out the salient features. Should certain points be out of reach of your extended arm, a pointer may be employed with utmost care. When possible, however, avoid the use of a pointer for it encourages the tapping, slapping, twisting behavior which serves also to distract a listener.

Summary. If you can remember that visual aids should be employed only as a supplement to oral discourse and that they should be (1) drawn from the message itself, (2) adapted to both speaker and listener, (3) physically capable of giving aid, and (4) planned—then you are in a position to take advantage of this additional support in your quest to make ideas clear and meaningful.

Characteristics of Effective Bodily Action in Speech

Purpose. Effective bodily action is purposeful, but purpose must be specifically defined (see Chapter 8). It is not enough that certain materials and actions have proved effective at other times, in other places, with other persons. There must be reason for selecting them now, for use in this place, with this audience; there must be reason for believing that they will generate an experience which is conducive to your purpose as speaker. Effective bodily action reflects motivation and a goal and demonstrates a clear measure of control. Bodily action which lacks these qualities is easily recognized: it is random, accidental, and meaningless or contradictory, confusing, and misleading.

Economy. Any unbalanced, strained, or uncoordinated action, whether it be part of a machine or a human body, wastes energy. Recall how easily a hoop rolls along the street as long as the rotation is smooth and in a straight line; as soon as the hoop begins to wobble, however, more direction and force are necessary to keep it going. Such is the case with actions of the human body. Economy of movement results from efficient movement, movement which is balanced, relaxed and coordinated. The athlete is a prime example of such efficiency, especially when his actions are contrasted with the amateur. Where the trained person requires one smooth movement, the untrained may employ three or four spasmodic actions; where the trained person is a picture of rhythm, the untrained displays great strain and awkwardness. What accounts for the difference? The less gifted person wrestles with his body while the more proficient person makes good use of it.

Economical movement must always begin from a balanced base. It requires selective relaxation, i.e., absence of contraction in those muscles not directly involved in any given act. Such muscles as the biceps and triceps of the arm, for example, need not be contracted except as they are needed to initiate a gesture of the arms. Unskilled speakers find themselves "all tensed up" simply because they are forcing certain muscles to contract unduly. This represents a terrible waste of energy; more importantly for the beginning speaker, such tension results in fatigue which sometimes results in trembling and appears to be "stage fright." You would do well, therefore, to practice selective relaxation regularly in order that you may better be able to utilize it when the occasion demands (see exercises at end of chapter).

Finally, economical action is coordinated. In the human body, especially, since no action is the result of one muscle's effort, the need for synchronization is paramount. Fine coordination includes both relaxation (as defined above) and rhythm; these aspects represent an important measure of control. With improper relaxation, with too many muscles operating to produce a certain action, coordination is not possible. Too much tension in the lips, tongue, or vocal folds during the production of all sounds easily results in unpleasant quality or poor articulation and, naturally enough, fatigue.

Appropriateness.   As with language, bodily action must always be suited to the speaker, listener, subject, and occasion. As far back as 1531, educators were warning beginning students to use bodily actions ". . . which may help intelligence, as long as they do not degenerate into the theatrical."[8] Action degenerates into the theatrical when it becomes incongruous. When men employ actions which are normally expected of women, when large individuals engage in movements which are appropriate for small persons, when light and gay motions accompany a sombre and sorrowful subject—then incongruity arises and effective communication is interrupted. Appropriateness, like other aspects of bodily action, is not a matter on which definite rules can be given.

[8] Juan Luis Vives, *Vives: on Education,* trans. by Foster Watson, Cambridge University Press (London), 1913, p. 104.

Your own knowledge, sensitivity, and judgment must control. Far from being a waste of time and thought, concern for appropriateness helps to raise you to the level of an artistic and proficient speaker.

Improvement of Bodily Action in Speech

Good health is a prerequisite. To cultivate a good state of health one should observe the following: (1) Know something of the anatomy and physiology of your body—not necessarily enough to qualify as an expert, but enough to know how to care for and use it most efficiently. (2) Appreciate the value of regular exercise—not to become a trained athlete, but to guarantee a healthy and well coordinated organism. (3) Know the value of a sensible diet; extreme dietary habits of any sort undermine health and often cause long-lasting deficiencies.

Knowledge is required. We speak here of the knowledge which makes you aware of your deficiencies, helps you to formulate a program of improvement, and enables you to carry it out. On the basis of all the information presented in this and preceding chapters you should now undertake to (1) diagnose or analyze your deficiencies of bodily action in speech, (2) determine how they can be overcome, and (3) lay out a program of practice.

In these endeavors your parents, friends, and classmates may sometimes assist; although many of them probably are not well enough informed to help greatly. Your best source of guidance, beyond what is available in this text and other books, will be your instructor. Submit the analysis of your problems and plans for improvement to him as he directs.

Practice is essential. Having analyzed your problems, gained knowledge of what is required to overcome them, and established a program of improvement, your next step is practice. A brief program of exercises is appended to this chapter. You will realize that they are not specific gestures or movements to be perfected for use in speaking. They are, instead, basic conditioning exercises designed to help establish the strength, freedom, and coordination necessary for effective bodily action. As this chapter has made clear, your total program for improvement should include an understanding of action in its relation to other elements of speech; a concern for good health; and a purposeful, systematic, and regular program of practice which shall include psychological and communicative as well as technical exercises (see Chapter 2). Your instructor will develop these with you.

We conclude our discussion of bodily action as an element of speech with a restatement of the major theme: *The adequate speaker has intimacy with an idea, a strong desire to express it, and the technical equipment honed and sharpened for translation of that idea into a meaningful, forceful and effective power.* A strong and well-coordinated body is the most basic element of that technical equipment.

EXERCISES

We, here, are concerned with practical, isometric exercises which would be of help in developing and sustaining a healthful state.

Caution: Exercises of this type should not be performed too rapidly. If in doubt, err in favor of a movement which is too slow rather than too fast. The major difficulty here is that there is a tendency to perform the movements suggested with a jerk or an exaggerated swing in which the momentum rather than the muscle is effecting the action. Muscular action should be such that the individual feels the resistance of one muscle against the other all the way through the exercise.

I.   Exercises for development of strength and basic health.
     A. General.
          1. Place the left hand over the right wrist, grasping it firmly. With the right elbow pressed against the side of the body and held as stationary as possible, and with the left arm offering definite opposition, try to flex the right arm so that the right wrist is in contact with the right shoulder. Alternate the exercise with the other arm (8 seconds duration).
          2. Clasp both hands together and raise the arms so that they are held, horizontally, opposite the chest. Now pull each arm in the opposite direction from its mate while you maintain the position of the hands directly opposite the breastbone. You may vary this exercise by starting with a position opposite either breast and pulling with the opposite arm against the force of the arm nearer to that breast (8 seconds duration).
          3. Cup the chin in the palm of the right hand and force the lower jaw open against the resistance of the right hand (8 seconds duration).
          4. In the same initial position described above, force the chin down toward the chest against the action of the resisting right hand (8 seconds duration).
          5. Keeping the jaws clamped together tightly, force the tongue up against the hard palate as positively as you can (8 seconds duration).
          6. Keeping the jaws clamped together tightly, push the tongue tip against the ridge above the upper teeth as forcefully as you can.
          7. Assume the position for the production of the [b] sound: lips tightly together, teeth slightly apart, tongue relatively relaxed on the floor of the mouth. Keeping this position, blow as forcefully as you can as though you were going to make a very loud [b] sound, but do not part the lips (8 seconds duration).
          8. Clench palms together and raise arms horizontally to a position directly opposite the center of the chest but approximately

12 inches from the breastbone. Force the hands (actually the heels of the hands) together strongly as you attempt to bring the clasped hands to within 2 inches of the breastbone (8 seconds duration).

9. Turn the head to the extreme left so that you are looking over the end of your left shoulder. Place the palm of the left hand against the right side of the face. Turn your head to the forward position, resisting the movement with your left hand and with the muscles of the opposite side of the neck (8 seconds duration).

10. Raise your head so that, without moving your back, you are looking at the ceiling. Place the heel of the right hand against the point of the chin and return the head to the forward position, resisting the movement with the right hand (8 seconds duration).

11. Extend the arms, with fists clenched, so that they are horizontal and at right angles to the chest. Keep the elbows rigid and slowly bring the arms across the body (right under left) until they they form an X, with the elbows acting as the meeting point. During the movement, be certain to resist the action as strongly as you can. If you are doing it properly, you should feel a definite tension in the chest muscles (pectoralis majors) and in the shoulder muscles (8 seconds duration).

B. Facial.

1. Purse the lips tightly and draw the mouth firmly to the left (or right). If done correctly, the right nostril will become obstructed (8 seconds duration).

2. Close mouth and inflate the cheeks as much as possible. Now alternate contraction of cheeks so the "ball of air" shifts from one side of the face to the other (8 seconds duration).

3. Close mouth and force the tongue into the right cheek firmly. Slowly pass the tongue tip over the entire cheek, across the inside of the lower lip and over the surface of opposite cheek. Remember to keep the lips together during the entire operation (8 seconds duration).

4. Yawn vigorously; open the mouth as widely as you can, raising the eyebrows in the process (8 seconds duration).

5. Pucker the lips tightly, clench the jaws firmly and shut the eyes tightly. Follow quickly by smiling broadly until the neck and cheeks feel the strain; at the same time, open the eyes as widely as possible, lifting the eyebrows as you do (8 seconds duration).

II. Exercises for coordination.

Definiteness of movement and position is extremely important in performing these exercises. Since all gesture involves rhythm, it is important to work for a spirit of "flow," which constitutes the freedom of movement we have spoken of in the chapter on bodily action.

A. Face, eyes, head.

1. At the command of a classmate turn your head up, down, from side to side. *Work for definiteness of action and smoothness of movement.* Repeat 10 times.

2. Without moving your head, follow the tip of a pencil held

about 12 inches from your nose and moved about randomly by a colleague. Movements should be alternately moderate and extreme. Repeat 10 times.

3. Without moving your head, attempt to speak to someone who is at your side and slightly to the rear. Accomplish this by twisting your face and your mouth in that direction as much as you can. Repeat to either side 5 times.

4. Read the headlines being flashed on a "moving" neon sign. Repeat from side to side for 5 times.

5. Examine a cavity located in the rear molar of each jaw; locate a sore point under either side of the tongue. Repeat 5 times.

6. Pretend that you are looking for the following:
   A four-leaf clover.
   A lost kernel of rice on a white rug.
   An exemption clause—in fine print—on a contract.
   Fleas in a collie dog's fur.
   A window with a special name in a six-story building.
   Each shot in a fast Ping-pong game.
   A hidden figure in a large painting of a forest.

7. Chew gum furiously as an excited teen-ager at a basketball game; chew tobacco as a farmer telling a tall tale.

B. Arms.

1. Push a very heavy table away from you; pull open a drawer which has been stuck for some time; open the lower half of a window sealed recently by a coat of paint.

2. Ring some very heavy, old-fashioned church bells with the aid of a bell rope; haul a bucket full of water up from a deep well.

3. Rake leaves from the lawn; sweep the kitchen floor; vacuum the living room rug; chop some wood; churn butter in an old-fashioned hand churn.

4. Lift to your shoulder a heavy sack of sugar and carry it for a few yards; row a rowboat slowly and then rapidly; paddle a canoe first from one side of the canoe then from the other.

5. Demonstrate the difference of size among the following:

Postage stamp	Elf
Sheet of notebook paper	Midget
Large newspaper	Child of seven
Regular suitcase	Young man
Steamer trunk	Tall basketball player

6. Demonstrate the actions of the following:

Wriggling snake	Skier during a slalom run
Stormy sea	Boxer, bobbing and weaving
Gliding hawk	

C. Hands, wrists, fingers.

1. Holding the arms in an extended position, chest high and parallel to the floor, raise the hands forcefully to a position signifying "Stop." With but a moment's hesitation, let the hands fall of

their own weight and repeat the entire action for at least 10 times. *During the course of this exercise, strive for a rhythm.*

2. Starting from the position outlined above, do the same thing except that you alternate hand actions. In other words, while the right hand is in the "Stop" position, the left hand is down. Again, repeat 10 times and *strive for a rhythm.*

3. Flex either arm so that you form an angle of approximately 60° and at the same time, turn the wrist so that the hand moves—quickly and smoothly—from a position of palm down to palm up. While you do this, keep the fingers as loose as you can. The effect of this will be felt most in the fingers and the wrist. Repeat 10 times, then alternate with the other arm and hand.

4. Flex the arms so that the elbows are held at the sides and the forearms are parallel with the floor. Turn the hands so that the palms face each other, as though you were holding an empty cardboard box by the pressure of your open palms against the flat sides of the box. Shift from this position, to one in which—keeping the arms and hands in the same position relative to each other—you form the palms into curved structures. In this position it is as though you were holding a large but light glass ball by the pressure of the palms against the curved sides of the ball.

5. Following the exercises outlined above, practice representing the activities listed below remembering to exaggerate position and movement while working for smoothness of flow. Remember also that an audience should be able to view and understand what you are doing.

a. Pick up a corner of a piece of material and "feel" its texture with the fingers of one hand.

b. Pick up a single straight pin.

c. Pick up and hold a tiny, young bird so that you neither crush it nor allow it to fly away.

d. Thread a needle; work the dial on a combination safe; hold a telephone during a conversation.

e. Tie a four-in-hand tie; flip a coin; crack a walnut; fill a glass of water from a tap.

f. Feel the falling rain; feel the heat from a campfire; pluck petals from a flower.

g. Grip a rope for a tug-of-war; grip the knob of a door which is difficult to open; pry open a suitcase with a stuck top.

h. Twist the screw cap off a bottle; turn a wing-nut from a very loose position to the tightest position; operate a hand fan for yourself on a hot day.

D. Trunk and legs.

1. Start with a normal standing position (feet about 8 inches apart) with hands hanging loosely at your sides. Take three steps forward, pivot and take three steps back, pivot to your original position and stop. *Work for rhythm* as well as definiteness of movement. Repeat 4 times.

2. To the command of a friend, instructor, or classmate, move

quickly for three steps in any direction called out. The key to this exercise is surprise and instantaneous smooth reaction. Repeat 10 times.

3. Walk as though you are traveling barefooted on:

Gravel roadbeds	Thick soft carpeting
Railroad ties	Oozing mud banks

4. Start to take a step forward (toward an unseen audience), but freeze in a position just prior to the completion of the step. Note the position of your body, legs, and feet and recapture this same relative position as you move to the side and to the rear. Repeat 5 times in each position.

5. Walk through:

Heavy snows	Surging water
Heavy underbrush	A mechanical maze

BIBLIOGRAPHICAL NOTE

In the preparation of this chapter the following general sources were used in addition to those specifically cited in the footnotes:

For the section on the role of bodily action: Norman L. Munn, *Psychology*, 3rd ed., Houghton Mifflin, 1956; Delwyn Dusenberry and Franklin H. Knower, "Experimental Studies of the Symbolism of Action and Voice," *Quarterly Journal of Speech*, October, 1938, pp. 424–436, and February, 1939, pp. 67–75; Henry E. Lutz, "Speech Consciousness Among Egyptians and Babylonians," *Osiris*, 1936, pp. 1–27; Norbert Wiener, *The Human Use of Human Beings*, 2nd rev. ed., Doubleday, 1954; A. I. Melden, "Action," *Philosophical Review*, October, 1956, pp. 523–541; Edward T. Hall, *The Silent Language*, Fawcett, Greenwich, Conn., 1959 (see especially the diagram on p. 92); Joseph Ratner (ed.), *Intelligence in the Modern World: John Dewey's Philosophy*, Modern Library, 1939, pp. 811–836; L. S. Vigotsky, "Thought and Speech," *Psychiatry*, 1939, pp. 29–53, and *Thought and Language*, The M.I.T., 1962; D. H. Fryer, "Articulation in Automatic Mental Work," *American Journal of Psychiatry*, 1941, pp. 504–517; George H. Mead, *Mind, Self, and Society*, The University of Chicago Press, 1934; and C. I. Hovland, I. L. Janis, and H. H. Kelley, *Communication and Persuasion*, Yale University Press, 1953, chap. 7.

For the section on determinants of bodily action: C. G. Seltjer, "Body Disproportions and Dominant Personality Traits," *Psychosomatic Medicine*, 1946, pp. 75–97; Jurgen Ruesch, *Disturbed Communication*, Norton, 1957; Ernst Kris, *Psychoanalytic Explorations in Art*, International Universities Press, 1952.

For the section on visual aids: A. L. Long, "Recent Experimental Investigations Dealing with Effectiveness of Audio-visual Modes of Presentation," *Educational Administration and Supervision*, February, 1945, pp. 65–78; H. L. Hollingsworth, *The Psychology of the Audience*, American Book, 1935, chap. VII; R. Likert, "A Neglected Factor in Communications," *Audio-visual Communications Review*, Summer, 1954, pp. 163–177.

14

AUDIBLE COMMUNICATION: VOICE PRODUCTION

Voice and articulation are not merely trimmings on the process of communication; they are indispensable media for transmitting our meanings to other people. The sounds we utter must be clearly audible if our communication is to be effective. Sounds, however, serve an even deeper function; as we have already seen, they are among the primary media in which our thoughts are formulated. This fact brings audible utterance into close relation to inner mental life and to all that we are as persons, and makes voice an important aspect of personality. People judge us almost as quickly by our voices as they do by our appearance and movement; perhaps sometimes they judge us even more quickly by our voices.

For all these reasons, then, our efforts toward speech improvement should include some attention to the sounds we utter. In order to understand voice and articulation we shall first need to review some elementary facts about sound and hearing, and then study the specific ways in which vocal organs function and variations in voice help to communicate. Articulation and pronunciation will be studied in a later chapter.

The Nature of Sound

Sound is the experience we have when vibrations stimulate the ear. These vibrations, or sound waves, arise from the oscillating motion of a solid body (e.g., violin string, drumhead) or column of air (as in a whistle or organ pipe). The waves given off by a vibrating body are essentially pressure changes in the surrounding medium. The form and frequency of the waves correspond to the pattern of movement of their source. Their power is determined primarily by the energy with which the source oscillates but may be further increased if an effective resonator is present. Resonators may be either solid bodies or cavities, i.e., masses of air enclosed in containers. Any resonator, in order to be effective for a given tone, must be of a size and type of outlet properly adapted to that tone. From their source or from the outlet of the resonator the waves of pressure move outward on a spherical wave front through the conducting medium, usually the air, until their energy is expended. Liquids and solids may also transmit the vibrations of sound. For the sake of simplicity, however, we are ignoring these media as well as electrical transmission.

If a sensitive ear is in the path of such waves, it may be stimulated by them and hearing will result. We should understand, however, that not all waves which impinge upon our ear drums give us the experience of sound. We are considering now only those vibrations which are within the range of sensitivity of the human ear. The limits of our sensitivity are not easy to state because individuals differ in this respect. All of us, however, have certain very general limits of hearing in common. Our sensitivity to frequency, for example, extends from approximately 16 vibrations per second up to approximately 20,000. This means that vibrations of frequency less than 16 or more than 20,000 per second do not usually stimulate hearing. The waves may strike the ear, but we are not aware of them; no sound is heard. Similarly our sensitivity to intensity has a range from approximately 10^{-10} (.0000000001) microwatts,[1] or a pressure of 0.0002 dynes per square centimeter, to an upper limit of 100 microwatts or 200 dynes pressure per square centimeter. The lower limit is called the threshold of audibility because vibrations at that intensity are just barely perceptible; intensities below this limit produce no sensation of sound. The upper limit is called the threshold of feeling because vibrations beyond that approximate level of power stimulate pain as well as sound and may damage the delicate mechanism of the ear.

Let us now consider these sound waves and their relation to hearing a little more carefully.

First, observe that most of the sounds we hear are of two general kinds—tones and noises. Tones are the result of periodic or regular vibrations or of vibration sequences which have an orderly pattern of change. Noises, on the other hand, consist of vibrations which are aperiodic or irregular, i.e., which have no orderly pattern; they tend to be a chaotic jumble lacking in order and harmony. Tones, as we all know, impress the ear pleasantly; noises are unpleasant, although many of the familiar noises of everyday life have neutral aesthetic value primarily because we become accustomed to them.

Next notice that the waves themselves are entirely external to the human organism. When they impinge upon the ear drum, however, the resulting auditory awareness is an experience wholly within the

---

[1] A microwatt is one-millionth part of a watt or 10 C.G.S. (centimeter-gram-seconds) units. The watt is a unit of power equal to 10^7, i.e., 10 million C.G.S. units of energy or intensity. One C.G.S. unit is the energy required to move a weight of 1 gram a distance of 1 centimeter in 1 second.

organism of the listener. The ear drum is stimulated to vibrate in the same manner as the waves which strike it, and these vibrations are transmitted to the inner ear where they stimulate the endings of the auditory nerve. Here a great change takes place. Nerve impulses are not at all like sound waves; but the normal ear is a faithful translator, and the impulses it sends into the central nervous system change as the stimulating air waves change. The characteristics of sound as perceived, therefore, are parallel to the characteristics of the vibrations in air. In other words the psychological properties of sound as heard are parallel to the physical properties of the sound waves.

Third, we should know the physical properties of the waves and the relation of these characteristics to our hearing experience. Sounds have four basic properties, all of which are important for our study of speech:

1. Duration, or time during which a sound is heard
2. Frequency of vibration, which is heard as pitch of tone
3. Intensity or power, which is heard as loudness
4. Complexity of wave form, which is heard as quality of tone

TIME AND DURATION

Every sound is the result of a series of vibrations which continue for an appreciable length of time. The minimum number of sound waves or vibrations which must strike the ear to stimulate a sensation of sound is variable for different sounds and different listeners, and in some cases may even require only one segment of a sound wave or cycle of vibration. Nevertheless the time value or continuity of any series of

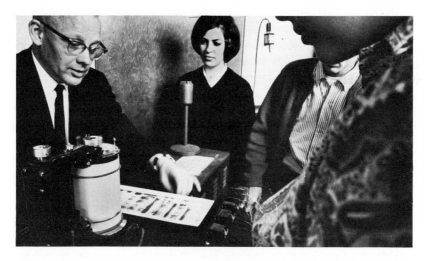

Vocal sounds can be seen—the Sonograph.

vibrations is one of its most important properties. Bear in mind, however, that the length of time a given series of vibrations continues may not necessarily be the same as the duration of the sound heard. Some parts of the vibration sequence, especially at the beginning or end, may be too weak to stimulate the ear, or the frequency may not be within the sensitivity range of the ear. For convenience we shall use the word *time* to refer to the actual vibration and the word *duration* to refer to the length of a sound as heard or the length of the auditory effect. Time, therefore, is a physical property; duration a psychological or sensory property of sound.

FREQUENCY AND PITCH

Vibrations, whatever their duration may be, are produced at a given rate or frequency. Be sure you distinguish between rate of utterance, i.e., speed with which sounds, syllables, and words are produced, and rate of vibration, i.e., frequency with which sound waves are produced. With the aid of instruments this rate of vibration can be counted in number of waves per second. Pitch on the other hand is a sensory experience, one of the ways in which the ear of an observer responds to the stimulation of sound waves. The traditional view has been that the pitch of any sound is entirely determined by the frequency of its vibrations. It is true that the ear does not ordinarily perceive a single sound wave as having pitch, but translates a series of waves into the pitch experience. Most of us have been taught to think of pitch levels in terms of the musical scale, with middle C having a frequency of 261.6 vibrations per second and C an octave higher having 523.2 vibrations per second.

These relationships are generally true, especially for the complex tones of musical instruments; but for pure tones it has been found that changes of intensity may also influence the perception of pitch. If the intensity of a low-pitched tone is increased, the pitch tends to be lower; for a high-pitched tone the pitch tends to rise with increase of intensity. In the middle range of pitch the influence of intensity is variable and slight. Hence if accurate designations of pitch in terms of frequency are to be made, intensity level should be held constant. The usual practice is to designate the pitch of a tone in terms of frequency of vibration at a loudness level of 40 decibels (db).[2]

[2] It would be accurate to say that the decibel is a logarithmic ratio; i.e., the number of decibels difference in loudness between two tones is 10 times the logarithm of their difference in intensity, or

$$db = 10 \log 10 \frac{\text{intensity A}}{\text{intensity B}}$$

The logarithm of any number is the number of times a given base number (usually 10) must be multiplied by itself in order to equal the given number. For example, the logarithm of 100 on the base 10 is 2, i.e., $10 \times 10 = 100$; the logarithm of 1000 is 3, i.e., $10 \times 10 \times 10 = 1000$; etc.

Even with this condition, however, measurement of pitch by reference to frequency does not measure it in terms of our sensory experience. As we have already pointed out, there is a significant difference between the physical properties of sound waves and the perceptual effects they stimulate. A true unit of pitch should be expressed in terms of the kind of experience it measures, and should enable us to state pitch levels in simple quantitative terms without the necessity of referring every tone to its frequency.

Attempts to develop such a unit have been undertaken by a method of fractionation. If a tone of fixed frequency is presented, and an observer is asked to adjust a second tone until its pitch appears to be half as high as the first, we have established a simple fractional relationship between the two sensory experiences. Extension of the observations to other numerical relationships between pitch levels, e.g., to find tones one-fourth as high or twice as high, provides the foundations for a sensory scale of pitch. The unit of such a scale is called a *mel*, from the first syllable of *melody*.

The mel is a subjective unit so defined that a 1000 cycle tone at 40 decibels above threshold is said to have a pitch of 1000 mels. This is taken as a starting point, and a tone which sounds half as high is given the value 500, one-fourth as high the value 250, and so on. The resulting scale of numbers, when established by consistency among a number of observers, thus constitutes a way of expressing the relative subjective magnitude of various pitches. Such a scale is designed to help us recognize and deal more definitely with the sensory experience of pitch, although it undoubtedly will be convenient to continue designating pitches in terms of frequencies.

The irregular vibrations of noise, of course, do not produce a definite pitch characteristic because their frequency is variable and indefinite; although, in so far as any element of regularity is present, a noise may have a very general and poorly defined pitch level. One may recognize a noise, for example, as high, medium, or low in pitch. Notice the difference between the rasp of a file and the hiss of escaping steam, one lower, one higher, than the other in general pitch level.

INTENSITY AND LOUDNESS

Intensity refers to the amount of energy in a given tone or noise. The degree of intensity is determined by the combined effect of amplitude and frequency of vibration. We can readily understand that any change either in extent of vibratory movement or in its rapidity would affect the amount of energy. If you could pluck a violin string so as to produce simple vibrations of a certain amplitude, and were then to increase the force so that the amplitude were doubled while the frequency remained constant, the second vibration would have four times the energy of the first. If you were to triple the amplitude, a ninefold increase of intensity would result. These physical facts are expressed in the simple formula $I = a^2$ (intensity depends on amplitude squared).

However, frequency of vibration may also change. If the violin string is shortened or its tension increased, the frequency of vibration will increase and this will also increase the amount of energy. (A common observation of daily experience is related to this fact; perhaps you have noticed that increase in loudness of voice often involves higher pitch.) If the amplitude were to remain constant, this relationship between intensity and frequency could be stated in a formula similar to that for amplitude, $I = f^2$ (intensity equals frequency squared). As a matter of fact the amplitude would not remain constant because the shorter length and/or increased tension of the string would increase its resistance to the force applied and so tend to decrease the amplitude of its motion. Changes in frequency and amplitude almost always occur together and influence each other. In order to express their combined effect on intensity or energy of vibration, we simply combine our two equations to read $I = a^2f^2$ (intensity depends on amplitude squared times frequency squared).

With the aid of instruments physicists and engineers measure the intensity of sounds in objective energy units such as dynes or ergs or watts. Students of hearing use the decibel for measuring quantitatively the difference between two intensities. If we start with a tone of known intensity and increase its power by 25.9 percent, we have produced 1 db change in relative intensity. If we again increase the power by 25.9 percent, we have produced another decibel. It is obvious, of course, that the second increase actually involves a greater number of physical units of energy because the starting point is a higher level of power; but the decibel as a *ratio* between power levels remains a constant unit regardless of the level of energy. The decibel is a unit for expressing quantitatively the difference between intensity of tones.

Since the decibel is a ratio, measurements in decibels must begin at some base or reference level of intensity. Such a starting point is usually taken at the threshold of audibility, which as we have already seen is set at a power level of 10^{-10} (.0000000001) microwatt. This is defined as zero decibels. From this base the entire range of human auditory levels has been measured and found to consist of approximately 160 units or steps, each one consisting of an increase in power of 25.9 percent or 1 db. A gentle whisper, for example, is approximately 20 db above the threshold of hearing; faint speech 40 db above the threshold; ordinary conversation is 55–65 db above; and loud speech approaches 80 db above the threshold. Very loud noises, such as those of air raid sirens or violent explosions, may range well above 100 db and approach the threshold of pain. The noise of jet engines has been measured as 160 db.

We should now consider the concept of loudness. Whereas intensity is an objective, quantitative factor, loudness is the effect of power or intensity of vibration on the ear. The energy of any given sequence of sound waves is translated by the ear into a perceptual experience of loudness. Three primary factors are involved:

1. The initial energy of the sound waves. Bear in mind that this probably will be influenced by resonance.
2. Loss of power as the waves travel from their source to the ear of the hearer. The intensity of sound varies inversely as the square of the distance from its source.
3. The sensitivity of the ear.

It is common knowledge that people differ greatly in sensitivity to energy of vibration, although it is not so well known that any single individual usually has a keener sense of loudness at some frequencies than at others. For each of us some vibration frequencies require more energy than others to stimulate the sense of hearing. The audiometer is an instrument for measuring this sensitivity. By its use one can produce tones of known frequency and intensity and record the levels at which a listener's ear responds. These sensitivity levels for a series of tones can then be plotted on a graph called an audiogram.

Although the decibel gives us a comparative way of measuring the magnitude or effect of sounds, neither decibels, dynes, ergs, or watts can be applied directly to the measurement of the *sensation* of loudness. The physical scale of decibels is commonly used but is not entirely satisfactory, because decibels are perceived differently at different levels of pitch and intensity. Here, as in the case of pitch, there is a significant difference between the physical properties of stimuli or sound waves and the effects which those waves produce in perceptual experience. Objective physical measurements do not fit subjective psychological processes.

A true unit for measuring the sensation of loudness must be derived from the experience it is to measure, and should also enable us to express loudness levels in simple quantitative terms. Such a unit is the *sone*. It has been defined as the subjective loudness level of a tone of 1000 cycles which is 40 db above auditory threshold. Frequency as well as loudness level must be specified, since as we have seen, frequency and intensity are closely related and influence each other. The sone has been developed and defined by actual experimental observation of sensation levels. If a tone is produced at a certain level of loudness and an observer is then asked to adjust a second tone until it seems to be half as loud as the first, we have established a simple numerical relationship between two sensory levels. When the observations are extended to include many observers who agree on the level of tones one-fourth as loud, twice as loud, three times as loud, and so on, the basic steps have been taken leading to establishment of a scale of equal-sounding intervals of loudness.

As we have already indicated, such a scale must have some definite level of loudness as a starting point from which the sensory values of successive tones can be judged. A magnitude of 40 db above threshold for a tone of 1000 cycles has been chosen as the unit because it correlates well with reference levels for determining both pitch and loudness and is small enough in relation to the loudness capacity of the ear to provide an adequate range for measurement.

COMPLEXITY AND QUALITY

The final characteristic of sound waves is *complexity*. Simple waves consisting of pendular movement to and fro in regular pattern can be produced under controlled conditions in a laboratory. A good tuning fork produces such vibrations, and their result is called a pure tone. You may be in the habit of using the phrase *"pure tone"* to refer to any tone which is pleasant in quality, i.e., free from noise elements. In more exact· scientific usage, however, a pure tone is the result of a simple wave form or fundamental vibration without overtones. As you listen to a tuning fork you will observe that the auditory effect is flat and lacking in the richness and variety of quality which characterize the tones of everyday life. In contrast, almost every sound we hear in the world around us is complex, i.e., the vibrating source moves in a pattern which combines several simple pendular movements. Occasionally one can see such complex vibration with the naked eye. For example, the string of a violin or cello, if plucked at the right point along its length, can be seen to vibrate in parts at the same time it is vibrating as a whole. Usually, however, the vibrations of sound waves are too complex for either eye or ear to analyze, and can be broken down into their simple vibrations only in the laboratory. There each series of simple vibrations making up a complex wave pattern can be produced and heard independently, and they can be recombined into the original complex vibration.

In such a complex tone the lowest frequency of vibration is the fundamental; the higher or secondary vibrations are overtones. All the vibrations, both fundamental and overtones are called partials. Whenever such complex waves meet a sensitive ear, the resulting experience is that of tone *quality*. The ear does not ordinarily recognize the separate components or partial vibrations but hears them as one sound, i.e., a single tone having a certain quality which changes as the complexity or combination of simple tones changes. The determining factors of quality are (1) number of overtones, (2) their relative intensity, and (3) their harmonious relation to each other. (Harmony consists of a simple whole-number relation between frequencies, for example, 100 to 200 or 261.6 to 523.2.) Just as the ear is an instrument for translating frequency into pitch and intensity into loudness, so it is also an instrument for translating complexity of vibration into the experience we know as tone quality.

The Vocal Organs

Now we need to think about the way in which our human vocal organs produce sound. Of course, a complete account would be quite complicated. Basically, the phases of the process of audible utterance involve four kinds of action:

1. Breathing provides the motive power.
2. Phonation is the activity of the vocal folds in the larynx which produce the voiced sounds of speech.
3. Resonance, defined simply in nontechnical language, is the amplification or reinforcement of tone.
4. Articulation is the process of obstructing and shaping the outgoing stream of breath and tone so as to produce the sequences of sounds which make up spoken discourse.

All the bodily organs used in voice and articulation also serve other quite different functions. We are in the habit of referring to parts of the chest, head, and throat, especially the larynx, as vocal organs; but they also serve other more fundamental purposes. The lungs and chest, for example, provide oxygen for the body. The larynx, located at the upper end of the windpipe, is primarily a valve to prevent entrance of foreign substances which would block the passage to the lungs and lead to suffocation. The passageways through mouth, nose, and throat serve for taking food and air; and the walls and surrounding parts (tongue, jaw, lips, hard and soft palates, and walls of the pharynx) act vigorously in chewing and swallowing. All these activities are life-sustaining.

On the other hand, the speech activities of these organs, though vastly important to civilized man, are definitely secondary. We call them overlaid functions because they have developed as specialized processes quite different from the life-sustaining processes. In some instances the primary and secondary functions are so different that they interfere with each other. Swallowing and vocalizing for example, cannot go on at the same time. During swallowing the larynx is tightly closed. We humans, of course, have developed great skill in using the two processes alternately at the dinner table. Again, chewing and articulating tend to hinder each other. The comment that someone "chews his words" is often an accurate description of indistinct articulation.

Each type of activity is stimulated and controlled by a special

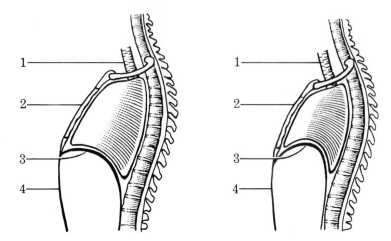

Breathing action: left, inspiration; right, expiration: (1) trachea, (2) sternum, (3) diaphragm, (4) abdominal wall. (From Marsland's Interpretive Reading.)

combination of nerve pathways, i.e., neurogram, which makes it a distinctly functional unit. The neurograms for the secondary functions have developed much more recently in the history of the human organism than the primary life-serving processes. Consequently these secondary functions are less stable and more easily interrupted or distorted than the primary functions. Our faults or bad habits in voice and articulation may be looked upon as tendencies to revert to the more elemental life uses of the organs, although many of our inadequacies are also due to inertia, excessive tension, or lack of adequate coordination. Improving these processes of voice and articulation, therefore, is primarily a matter of establishing their overlaid patterns of action so thoroughly that they will always tend to operate at maximum efficiency without interfering with the primary functions.

Effective voice depends on the coordination of three basic processes—breathing, phonation, resonance. (See Chapter 13, section on the role of bodily action, for a more extended discussion of coordination.)

BREATHING FOR SPEECH

Ordinary, quiet life breathing involves alternate expansion and contraction of the chest, i.e., alternate inspiration and expiration, in approximately equal and regular intervals of time. Inspiration of air is the result of chest expansion produced by action of certain muscles of the chest wall and diaphragm. Muscles of the chest wall lift the ribs so as to expand the rib cage. The diaphragm is a curved, partially dome-

shaped layer of muscle and tendinous tissue forming the
chest. When contracted it is flattened downward so as to
vertical dimension of the chest cavity. As this cavity incr
air flows in and expands the lungs to fill the increased s
the extent that chest expansion is maintained, the inspi
tained in the lungs. Expiration, of course, involves action directly
opposed to inspiration. The inspiratory muscles relax and the chest
cavity is contracted mainly by action of muscles in the abdominal wall
which push abdominal organs upward against the relaxing diaphragm
and pull down on the ribs so as to reduce the size of the rib cage.
Reduction in size of chest, of course, pushes air out of the lungs.

When breathing is adapted to voice and speech, this regular
alternation of inspiration and expiration is changed in two ways. First,
inspiration tends to be done more quickly and in somewhat greater
volume. This change results primarily from the increased stimulation
given by the speaker's desire to communicate. Each inspiration must
not only provide enough breath for life needs but also enough for production of the unit of utterance which follows. Second, in speech ex-

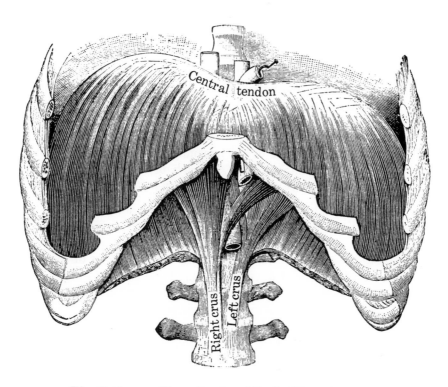

The diaphragm. (From Rasch and Burke, Kinesiology and
Applied Anatomy, *1963. Courtesy of Lea & Febiger.*)

piratory action is prolonged. The breath is kept under control and used gradually in order to give adequate power for sustained utterance. Pressure of outgoing breath, of course, is always necessary to produce the sounds of speech. Occasionally vigorous utterance will require a degree of forced expulsion, but this is easily overdone. In fact, intensity of tone actually varies inversely with amount of breath expended. Most of us waste breath during speech and do not need to develop expiratory power as much as we need to develop control and retention.

Breath control is achieved by improving the strength and coordination of the muscles of inspiration so that they can maintain the expansion of the chest and the reserve supply of air with ease and flexibility. Adequate use of breath for speech requires controlled pressure which is attained by a well-coordinated balance between expiratory action, which provides the power for production of sounds, and the controlling action of inspiratory muscles, which limits the rate of outflow so as to maintain a reserve of power. If as a result of the control any appreciable reserve of air remains at the end of a unit of utterance, there is normally some tendency to give up or release it before renewal of inspiration for the next unit of utterance.

As a result of these processes the regular two-phase alternation of inspiration and expiration characteristic of primary life breathing, is changed for speech into a three-phase process:

1. Inspiration is responsive to the speaker's purpose to communicate, and hence tends to be more rapid and greater in volume and to recur just before each new thought unit.
2. Expiration of breath during utterance is more controlled and gradual so that a reserve of power is always available.
3. Release of some of the remaining air tends to occur at the ends of thought units. (Although, of course, some reserve of breath always remains in the lungs.)

We should bear in mind that these are not rules to be followed rigidly, but norms of a basic pattern of action. Individuals differ, of course, in their movements, and each individual may use different kinds or degrees of action for various times and conditions of speaking and various purposes and ways of thinking. Every student of speech in his own way should make this fundamental pattern of breathing a thoroughly habitual part of his everyday speech behavior. Any limitation of responsive inspiration before units of utterance or any weakness in the power and control of expiration during utterance should be considered a tendency to return in some degree to the primary two-phase type of breathing which is adequate for supplying the body with oxygen but inadequate for the additional requirements of voice and articulation.

PHONATION

The larynx is a complicated structure, but in simple description might be likened to a box with walls of cartilage lined with muscular tissues and membranes and attached by muscles on its outer surface to structures of the head and neck above and chest below. This box sits at the top of the windpipe, or trachea, and is open at top and bottom to allow flow of air to and from the lungs. The passageway

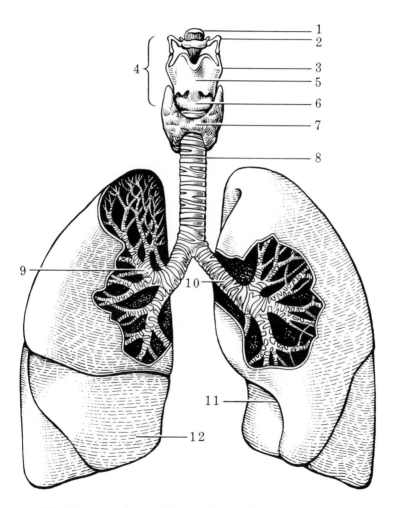

The larynx, trachea, and lungs: (1) *epiglottis,* (2) *hyoid bone,* (3) *superior horn of thyroid cartilage,* (4) *the larynx,* (5) *thyroid cartilage,* (6) *cricoid cartilage,* (7) *thyroid gland,* (8) *trachea,* (9) *bronchial tubes,* (10) *left bronchus,* (11) *two lobes of left lung,* (12) *third lobe of right lung.* (*From Oskar Guttmann's* Gymnastics of the Voice.)

through the larynx is controlled by a double valve, one part of which is at the top of the box, the other inside the box. When we swallow, the entire structure is drawn upward and the top opening is constricted so that it fits against a small leaf-shaped cartilage, the epiglottis, at the base of the tongue. In this way the upper part of the valve is closed and the substance to be swallowed is pushed past it into the esophagus which is just behind the windpipe.

The lower part of the valve inside the box consists of four small folds of muscular tissue like lips or shelves, two on each side extending horizontally from front to back of the inner passage. These folds can be brought toward each other (adducted) to close the passageway, or they can be separated (abducted), i.e., drawn back toward the walls on either side so that the passage is open for free flow of air. When closed tightly this lower valve stops any substance which may have gotten past the upper closure. This is what happens when we choke, and the cough which follows then forces the misplaced material up into the throat or pharynx above the larynx. If neither part of the laryngeal valve functions properly and foreign material gets into your windpipe, you need first aid quickly to prevent suffocation. Fortunately this rarely happens; the valves usually function perfectly.

Now compare this protective or life-sustaining action of the larynx with its function in vocalization. The lower pair of muscular folds inside the laryngeal box are the active vibrators in voice and are therefore called the true vocal folds or bands. Their edges are of connective or tendon-like tissue which is capable of a considerable range of adjustment depending on the action of the tiny muscles which make up the body of the folds. They can be made thin or rounded, tense or lax, longer or shorter. The upper or false vocal folds normally do not serve as vibrators; their primary function appears to be protection of the lower or true vocal folds.

Of course both true and false vocal folds remain apart (abducted) during inspiration to allow air to flow into the lungs, but after inspiration is completed and voice is to be produced they move toward each other (i.e., are adducted) to come into relatively near proximity in the median line of the laryngeal passage. The opening between the folds, or glottis, is thus closed or partially closed just as breath pressure from the lungs below is ready to start the folds vibrating. In speech this typically occurs at the beginning of every continuous sequence of vocalized sounds.

The degree of closure of the glottis (or amount of adduction of the folds) is coordinated with the amount of expired breath needed for various types of sounds. Voiceless sounds, for example, involve relatively more outflow of air and hence wider opening of the glottis than other sounds. Vocal tones involve relatively less outflow of air, and the movements of the vocal folds are therefore so coordinated with breath

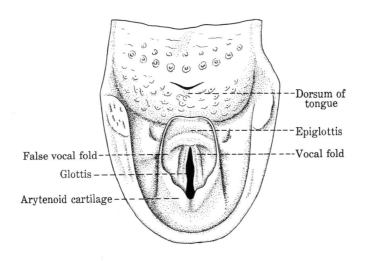

--- Dorsum of tongue

--- Epiglottis

False vocal fold --- --- Vocal fold

Glottis ---

Arytenoid cartilage ---

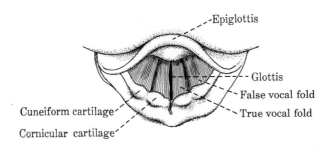

- Epiglottis

- Glottis

- False vocal fold

Cuneiform cartilage

Cornicular cartilage

- True vocal fold

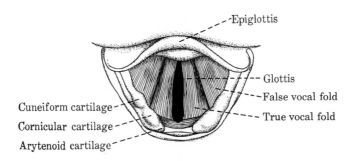

- Epiglottis

- Glottis

- False vocal fold

Cuneiform cartilage

Cornicular cartilage

Arytenoid cartilage

- True vocal fold

Top, interior of larynx (seen from above); center, the glottis in speaking; bottom, the glottis in breathing. (From Quain's Elements of Anatomy, *10th ed. Courtesy of Longmans, Green & Co. Ltd.)*

control as to bring them into closest adduction. If the folds are not closely enough adducted the tone will have an aspirate or rasping quality resulting from excessive outflow of air. If the folds are drawn together tightly so that breath pressure must force them apart in order to get vibration started, the result will be a sharp click at the beginning of

255

a tone. This tight closure of the glottis is often related to excessive tension in the throat generally. In well-controlled vocal tones the glottis is almost closed by the near contact of the inner edges of the folds, but no tight closure occurs.

For our purposes the actual movements of vibration do not need to be described in detail. It is enough to say that the action is complex (see section on complexity of sound waves above), and is the result of alternate interaction between pressure of breath and tension

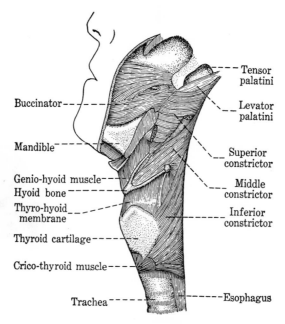

The muscles of the pharynx. (From Gray's Anatomy.)

of the vocal folds. Breath pressure forces the edges of the folds to move upward and apart, and tension of the folds causes their return movement as soon as an impulse of breath pressure has been released. The impulse of pressure thus created by each complete cycle of vocal-fold movement is transmitted from the glottis as a sound wave. As long as breath pressure is maintained against the tensed and adducted folds, so long will they continue to give off sound waves. Vocal tone is the result. Vibration stops, of course, when breath pressure ceases and the folds are relaxed and moved apart (abducted) so as to open the glottis again for free passage of air.

RESONANCE

The principal amplifiers of vocal tone are the cavities of mouth, nose, and throat. To simplify the discussion, we are ignoring chest and

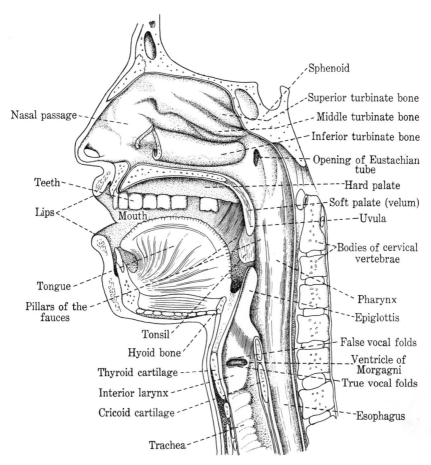

Labels on the diagram:

Sphenoid

Superior turbinate bone

Middle turbinate bone

Inferior turbinate bone

Opening of Eustachian tube

Nasal passage

Hard palate

Soft palate (velum)

Teeth

Uvula

Lips

Mouth

Bodies of cervical vertebrae

Tongue

Pharynx

Pillars of the fauces

Epiglottis

Tonsil

False vocal folds

Hyoid bone

Ventricle of Morgagni

Thyroid cartilage

True vocal folds

Interior larynx

Cricoid cartilage

Esophagus

Trachea

Sagittal view of the nose, mouth, and throat. (From Gray's Anatomy.)

tracheal resonance as well as reinforcement in solid structures of head and chest. The basic problems of improving resonance center in use of the cavities of throat and head. Bear in mind that the pharynx, or flexible cavity behind the tongue, is immediately above the voice box or larynx, and leads from the laryngeal passage upward into the nasal passages and forward into the mouth. The passageways between these various cavities may be widened or narrowed; and two of the cavities, mouth and pharynx, are highly variable in size and shape because of the flexibility of their walls and surrounding structures.

All these cavities, of course, serve equally as air passages for both the maintenance of life and for voice. The significant differences in their use lie in chewing and swallowing on one hand, the voice production on the other hand. Taking food requires vigorous action to narrow or constrict mouth and pharynx. Jaws and teeth grind, the tongue pushes food forward or back, the soft palate closes the rear entrance into the nasal passages, and the strong action of the constrictor muscles in the walls of the pharynx pushes food downward into the esophagus.

Contrast this action with the use of the same cavities for amplifying vocal tone. In this function the mouth and pharynx must be relatively open and adjusted so as to amplify effectively the vibrations of the sound waves coming up from the larynx. To achieve this, the muscles of tongue, cheeks, lips, soft palate, and pharyngeal walls must be flexible and free for rapid changes in size and shape of cavities and their outlets. These adjustments, as well as those which produce the obstructions characteristic of consonants, require complex muscular activity which, as we all know, involves muscle tension. If the resulting sounds are to be clear and accurate, however, these tensions must operate within the limits of economy of effort, without laborious and strained movement, with a sense of ease and agility. This is very different from the vigorous and constricting kind of action required for chewing and swallowing.

An important part of the process of improving voice and articulation, therefore, is the establishment of such free and facile adjustments of mouth and throat that the cavities will be effective amplifiers of tones and the obstructing organs will be precise articulators of consonants. The resulting condition of the cavities is called "the open throat" to emphasize their flexibility and openness. Maintenance of an open throat during speech also involves action of the soft palate to close, or nearly close, the posterior entrance into the nasal cavities in all the sounds of English except the three nasals (m, n, ŋ). For these sounds the palate is relaxed and lowered to permit passage of sound waves through the nasal cavities where they receive primary amplification. The resonance of other sounds of English is primarily oral. In both cases the resonance produced in an open throat has two main effects on the vocal tones of speech: (1) Amplification of the sound waves originating in the larynx increases their intensity of vibration and hence the loudness of tones. (2) Selective amplification of various partials changes their relative intensity and hence influences the complexity of sound waves and the resulting quality of tones.

COORDINATION

Now that we have discussed the basic processes of breathing, phonation, and resonance we must make clear that they operate not as three functions but as inseparable aspects of one function. Both vocalizing and articulating are dependent on breath power. The special pattern of breathing for speech probably would not occur, and certainly would have no significance or value, apart from vocalizing and articulating.

Amplification of sound waves in the cavities of throat and mouth would not occur if the vocal cords did not produce vibrations, and these vibrations would be meaningless and in fact might scarcely be heard if they were not resonated. Breathing, phonation, and resonance, therefore, are inseparable phases of one function—vocalizing.

Let us describe this unity in another way. We all know that every muscular contraction in the body is caused and controlled by nerve impulses which arise in brain or spinal cord, and are carried to the muscles by outgoing or efferent nerve fibres. As we have already seen, every complex bodily movement is stimulated and controlled by a correspondingly complex pattern of nerve impulses, a neurogram. All specialized bodily functions are served by their own special neurograms. Voice and articulation are no exception. The overlaid or secondary development of man's nervous system has provided a single complex network which integrates the speech uses of otherwise diverse organs (jaw and tongue, larynx, pharynx, lungs, and rib cage, and other parts of the body also) into one finely adjusted, synergic action.

In summary let us say that coordination is necessary in voice and articulation, for two fundamental reasons:

1. The speech activities of organs in chest and head are different from their primary life functions.
2. Speaking requires close unison of the activity of diverse organs.

Voice Improvement

On the basis of all the facts we have so far studied about the nature of sound and the functioning of the organs which produce voice, we are now ready to consider definitely the methods by which we may improve the use of voice in speech. Our purpose is to establish adequate habits of voice production so thoroughly that we shall need to give them no thought, or very little thought, when we are in a speaking situation and wish to devote our entire attention to the business of communication.

Generally, the foundations for voice improvement are of two kinds—physiological and psychological. Or to state the matter more simply, voice is a product of both body and mind. The two cannot be separated, but it is convenient to speak of them in distinct terms.

We have already mentioned the physiological factors in our study of bodily action. Health and vitality are of basic importance. Repose and ease, balance and uprightness of posture, and well coordinated gestures are important not only for visual communication but also as essential foundations for voice and articulation.

In like manner our study of thinking for speech has laid some of the groundwork for voice improvement. The definite sense of purpose, adequate knowledge of facts, orderly sequence of ideas, emotional control and imaginative enrichment which characterize the effective thinker in speech are indispensable springs from which communicative voice and articulation arise. Probably the attitudes and emotional activities of the speaker have an even greater and more direct effect on voice; at any rate they are inevitably involved in voice improvement. In this subjective realm our knowledge is less definite than in the areas of sound waves and muscle movements. It is not easy to analyze and describe the inner emotional processes which govern our behavior, especially our vocal behavior.

We should remind ourselves, however, that the well-adjusted person who has an objective attitude toward himself and toward his task as speaker has a good foundation for communicative voice and articulation. He is far less likely to be handicapped by excessive muscle tensions, slouchy posture, and poor coordination than his self-conscious or timid or overly aggressive fellow student. The person who has genuine enthusiasm for his material, who takes pains to identify himself with it fully, and who thinks in terms of his listeners, has established the foundations of meaningful sound-making in his speech. For him the motor performance of utterance is but the outward and audible completion of his inner processes of thinking, i.e., of knowing something and having a purpose to communicate the knowledge.

Perhaps we shall be able to see this relation between thinking and utterance more clearly if we refer to its neurological basis. The complex processes of speech, especially of voice and articulation, cannot be adequately coordinated by lower levels of the nervous system. It is true, of course, that some of our casual everyday uses of speech, such as routine greetings and habitual exclamations, become almost automatic habits and involve a minimum of high-level activity in the brain. Propositional speech, however, used in relation to the constantly changing situations and problems of life and involving widely diverse parts of the body, requires direction and control from the higher levels of the nervous system. One significant fact to be noted in this connection is that thousands of the nerve fibres connecting the organs of voice and articulation with the central nervous system are carried over cranial nerves directly into some of the higher levels of the brain. But these higher levels are precisely those which we regard as centers of intellectual activity; and the very highest levels, the association areas of the cerebral cortex, are distinctively the seat of the intellect, the centers in which our perceptions and memories are coordinated and organized into meaningful concepts—that is, they are the centers where thinking distinctively goes on. In short, the high-level coordinations which are characteristic of voice and articulation involve some degree of the high-level neurological activity characteristic of thought; and the audible, articulate processes of utterance are means of completing and giving form to thought processes. Improvement of thinking, therefore, is the first necessary step toward improvement of voice and articulation.

With these principles in mind we are ready to study some definite methods and exercises for voice improvement in speech.

EXERCISES FOR COORDINATION

Effective voice for speech depends on the coordination (i.e., working together) of the three basic processes—breathing, phonation, and resonance. We have also seen that this coordination depends primarily on adequate thinking, and have studied some of the general elements of thought for speech. Now we shall concentrate on a few simple and basic aspects of thinking which will most directly help to stimulate and coordinate vocal and articulate activity. Study and practice the following exercises:

1. In all your speaking of every kind, analyze the sequences of thought into single ideas or units (see Chapter 4, section on phrasing).

2. Realize the fullest possible meaning of each thought unit or phrase. Relate the idea to your experience. Make it as vivid in imagery as possible. Arouse some feeling for it (see section on duration below).

3. Direct your attention to a listener or audience. Make it your business to communicate directly to him (or her). When you are practicing by yourself, or preparing for a class exercise or a specific speech event, use your imagination to create as definite a realization as possible of your potential listener or listeners.

EXERCISES FOR BREATHING

Adequate breathing for speech is (1) responsive to thought, and (2) well controlled. Both of these aspects of breathing should be strong and definite as well as easy and flexible.

RESPONSIVENESS

Breathing is responsive when air (in addition to that required for ordinary life breathing) is inspired as a direct result of the stimulation which comes from the speaker's awareness of a situation and from his purpose to communicate meaning to someone. Observe that responsive breathing usually involves greatest expansion in the region of the diaphragm or middle of the body trunk, although in full inspiration the upper chest may also be expanded. Shallow breathing, however, in which the dominant expansion is in the upper chest seldom provides adequate power or flexibility for speech. Responsiveness may be improved by the following methods:

1. Observe breathing action in everyday experiences.

a. Sit quietly in an attitude of comfortable repose and listen intently to all the varieties of sound coming to you from near and far. Concentrate on distinguishing as many different sounds as possible. Or listen intently to quiet music. In either case notice what happens to your breathing. Does it tend to become deeper? Any greater in volume?

b. Observe what happens to your breathing when you listen to a play or concert or public address which moves you deeply. What effects do you observe on the breathing action in the middle region of your body trunk? Does meaningful stimulation tend to increase the amount of breathing activity?

c. Observe what happens to your breathing when you are surprised, for example, by a sudden noise or an unexpected meeting with a friend. Notice that increased inspiration of breath is among your first and most immediate reactions and that the greatest degree of expansion tends to be in the region of the lower ribs or middle torso.

d. Heave a sigh and notice the dominant action in the middle region of the body trunk.

e. Notice that when you are stimulated to laughter the middle region of the body is very active, and that in prolonged and hearty laughter the diaphragm often becomes tired.

2. Use these observed actions in your own speaking. Let your purpose to speak stimulate your breathing.

a. In quiet repose imagine that a friend has entered the room and asked you an important question which calls for a direct and simple answer, perhaps only "Yes" or "No." Notice that inspiration of breath is the first necessary part of your responding action. Gradually as you repeat this simple response, increase the amount of inspiration as much as you can easily without forcing the action. In other words, practice to establish the habit of adequate inspiration of breath before you speak any single unit of utterance.

b. Imagine a situation in which you urgently wish to call to someone, e.g., as in warning or command. Let the preparatory intake of breath be as free and immediate a response to your purpose to speak as possible. Repeat, increasing the intensity of purpose and amount of inspiration gradually and without forcing the action.

c. Select a subject about which you have deep conviction and prepare a brief (1 or 2 minute) extempore statement of your belief or attitude. Speak this to a friend or acquaintance with full sincerity and directness of purpose but so deliberately that every unit of your thought (i.e., each phrase or statement) stimulates a definite renewal of breath. Notice too that this frequent renewal is related to frequent release or expiration of breath after the utterance of important thought units.

d. Select from some essay or printed copy of a public address a short paragraph which arouses your interest and with which you agree heartily. Study the thought until you understand and are thoroughly familiar with it, and then read aloud to arouse in a listener or listeners something of your own degree of interest or enthusiasm for the ideas expressed. Your utterance should be so purposeful and deliberate that every unit of the thought will spontaneously stimulate an increased inspiration of breath.

CONTROL

Controlled breathing involves economical use of breath so that adequate reserve power is fully available during any given unit of utterance (i.e., phrase or sentence). Breath control may be improved by the following exercises:

1. Observe breath control in speakers who have adequate vocal power and flexibility.

a. Notice that during well-controlled utterance the expanded condition of the lower chest, i.e., the middle region of the body trunk (and to some extent the upper chest too when full inspiration has been taken), decreases so gradually and slowly that a reserve of breath power is maintained constantly. Such control is often spoken of as "supporting the tone."

b. Notice that in well-coordinated speech, control implies some tendency to release reserve breath frequently following the utterance of thought units, unless of course all reserve air has been used during the preceding utterance. The expiration should be an easy letting go of the chest expansion; air need not be expelled forcibly. In the pauses of normal speech such release precedes and prepares the way for responsive inspiration before the next unit of utterance.

2. Practice a series of simple exercises to develop or improve such control in your own speaking.

a. Inspire breath easily and responsively as though about to speak and hold the breath silently for a moment while you imagine you are speaking a simple word or phrase. Then release breath, i.e., give up the expanded condition of the chest and let the excess air flow out. Do not force the expiration.

b. Repeat the responsive inspiration and gradually increase the length of time you can hold the expansion easily without excessive muscular tension or sense of strain. Be sure to let go after each repetition.

c. Repeat the responsive inspiration and speak aloud a single word or short phrase, sensing the balance between (1) the expulsive action of the upper abdomen and the lower chest (i.e., the impulse of breath which produces power to initiate the sound) and (2) the control which prevents waste of breath (i.e., maintains expansion of the lower chest).

d. Repeat the responsive inspiration and sustain a simple tone (e.g., a hum or vowel such as ah, o, e, u,) as long as you can control the breath—i.e., as long as you can easily maintain a steady, gradual outflow of air. Stop before you lose the sense of reserve expansion in the middle region of the body trunk. Do not tense the muscles rigidly in order to maintain control. Even though considerable muscular power is actually involved in breath control, the entire action should seem easy and flexible.

e. Repeat the exercise, speaking a series of numbers in any prolonged sequence, and continuing as long as you can maintain easy control of breath. See how much you can say on one breath without giving up all your reserve air. (Note: This exercise is only a temporary device. In normal speech a person should not try to speak as much as possible on one breath, but should renew the inspiration frequently for successive thought units.)

f. Select a paragraph from an essay or text of an address, analyze its sequence of thought units, and read aloud so as to communicate to a friend or to the class, maintaining easy and flexible control of breath during the utterance of each thought unit.

g. Try to carry the habit of maintaining breath reserve and its controlled use into your conversation and all your everyday uses of speech.

EXERCISES FOR RESONANCE

Proper amplification of tone depends primarily upon openness and flexible adjustment of the cavities in throat and mouth. Our next step, therefore, is to practice a series of exercises which will help to establish the open throat as a permanent speech habit.

1. Relax neck and facial muscles.

a. Let the head sink forward until you feel it hanging heavily and unable to sink further. Let the lower jaw sag. Roll the head gently from side to side so as to feel the muscles free and flexible.

b. Relax the head sideways as far as it will go, so that you feel its weight. Let the jaw sag heavily. Repeat first on one side, then on the other.

c. Gently touch and massage cheeks and lips with the fingertips to increase the sense of freedom and repose in the face.

2. Relax jaw and tongue, open the mouth.

a. With the head upright let the mouth open with the jaw sagging as of its own weight. Notice whether the tongue is relaxed easily in the floor of the mouth with its tip resting lightly against the back of the lower teeth.

b. With jaw and tongue relaxed inspire breath easily and notice the tendency of the middle and back of the tongue to sink and the soft palate to rise, thus opening the passageway through the mouth a little wider. As a temporary test of this opening, stand so that the interior of the mouth is visible in a hand mirror and observe the movements of tongue and soft palate until you discover the "feel" of the open throat. Then lay the mirror aside and repeat the exercises, depending on your tactile and kinesthetic sense impressions to guide you.

c. Repeat the above exercise, increasing the amount of breath inspiration and relaxation of throat until the action stimulates a desire to yawn. Control the breath and keep the tongue, jaw, and throat relaxed so as to delay completion of the yawn as long as possible. Yawn when you can no longer resist and then repeat the exercise.

3. Develop nasal resonance.

a. Prepare to speak, i.e., inspire breath responsively (see section on breathing above) and open mouth and throat as indicated in the preceding section. Then close the lips and produce the sound *m* as an easy hum at your medium pitch level. Think of the tone as centered in nasal cavities, but feel the vibrations also at the front of the face and in the lips.

Maintain breath control during the sound. Note that in the nasal sounds, *m*, *n*, *ng*, the mouth passage is closed and the soft palate lowered to open the nasal passage.

b. Repeat the preceding exercise, gradually increasing both the duration of the tone and the sense of full vibration in nose and face as much as you can without strained or overly tense action.

c. Repeat Exercises 1 and 2 above, using *n* and *ng* instead of *m*. Notice that for *n* the mouth passage is closed by bringing tip of tongue against upper gums just behind the teeth, and that for *ng* the back of the tongue is raised to contact the soft palate. In these actions be sure the jaw is free and flexible and the breath easily controlled.

4. Develop oral resonance and the tonal value of vowels.

a. Initiate the nasal *m* and after sustaining it briefly let the lips fall apart and the mouth open so that the hum changes without interruption of vibration into an oral tone (preferably the vowel *ah*). This tone should seem to center at the front of the mouth, and should be free of nasal quality. Maintain easy breath control. Repeat combining *n* and *ng* as well as *m* with several vowels, e.g.,

m-ah, m-o, m-u, m-a, m-e

n-ah, n-o, n-u, n-a, n-e

ng-ah, ng-o, ng-u, ng-a, ng-e

b. Repeat the preceding exercise introducing in each syllable a stopped consonant between the nasal sound and the vowel, e.g.,

m-b-ah, m-b-o, m-b-u, m-b-a, m-b-e

n-d-ah, n-d-o, n-d-u, n-d-a, n-d-e

ng-g-ah, ng-g-o, ng-g-u, ng-g-a, ng-g-e

Notice that in each syllable the nasal and stop sounds have the same kind of mouth obstruction. In production of a stop the soft palate rises to close the nasal passage; otherwise the breath would escape through the nose and no clear stopped sound would be produced. Introduction of the stop is a means of exercising the soft palate and avoiding excessive nasality in the vowel.

c. Prepare to speak and intone a continuous series of vowels changing smoothly and without break from one to the next, e.g., *ah-o-u-a-e*. Maintain good breath control during the sequence and open the mouth freely so as to get maximum resonance.

d. Repeat the preceding exercise using various vowel and consonant combinations in a series of syllables but retaining as much of the amplified vowel value as possible in the shorter tones of rapid utterance, e.g.,

l-ah,	l-o,	l-u,	l-a,	l-e
b-ah,	b-o,	b-u,	b-a,	b-e
v-ah,	v-o,	v-u,	v-a,	v-e
d-ah,	d-o,	d-u,	d-a,	d-e
k-ah,	k-o,	k-u,	k-a,	k-e

e. Select some short piece of lively conversational prose and read it aloud to a friend or to the class, attempting to enhance the communicative value of your utterance by keeping as much of the richness of tone and distinctive vowel qualities as possible. Single out for special practice any syllables or phrases which seem to lack full freedom and clarity of tone.

EXERCISES FOR PHONATION

Adequate phonation requires (1) proper adjustment of the vocal folds in relation to each other, and (2) unhindered vibratory movement activated by controlled pressure of breath. Because we have little, if any, awareness of the complex processes going on in the larynx, improvement of phonation depends primarily on three related processes: breath control, resonance, sensitive hearing.

Excessive outflow of air hinders the proper adduction of the vocal folds and weakens the basic power or "support" of the tone. (Refer to the exercises for breath control in the section above.) The presence of a well-adjusted resonating cavity increases the effectiveness of the vibrator. (Refer to the exercises above.) All tone production depends on hearing. A speaker's auditory percepts control the complex patterns of nerve impulses which bring breathing, phonation, and resonance into coordination.

Our purpose now is to use the ear as a means of coordinating breathing, resonance, and vocal fold action so as to initiate tones freely and easily. Study and practice the following exercises:

1. Listen carefully to a recording of your speech to determine whether the tones begin smoothly or whether they begin with either a breathy rasp or a sharp break or click. The aspirate sound is caused by poor breath control with inadequate adduction of vocal folds. The click is caused by shutting the glottis (opening between the vocal folds) so tightly that breath pressure must force the folds apart sharply before vibration can begin. (See section on phonation above.)

2. Prepare for utterance (as described in the exercises for breathing) and initiate a vowel of short duration, for example, *o*, *ah*, *u*, *e*. Maintain easy control of breath (as in the exercises for breathing). Listen with special care to the beginning of the tone. Is it well coordinated and smooth or do you hear the results of poor coordination—i.e., either the escape of wasted breath or the click that arises from forcing apart tightly closed vocal folds? Repeat the single short vowel until you get the feel of the vibration starting freely and easily.

3. If you find the click occurring persistently, try using a single breath consonant before the vowel; for example, combine *ah* with *s*, *f*, or *sh* so as to make syllables *sa*, *fa*, *sha*. The flow of breath for the consonant should keep the vocal folds from closing tightly. Breath should be well controlled, of course. Next use the voiced cognate of each breath consonant; for example, change *sa* to *za*, *fa* to *va*, and *sha* to *zha*. The voiced consonant in each case starts the vocal folds vibrating before the vowel begins and so prevents their tight closure. Repeat, gradually reducing the duration of the consonant until it disappears entirely and the vowel is initiated by itself.

4. Repeat the exercise, initiating the same vowel several times in moderately rapid succession after a single inspiration of breath—for example, *ho*, *ho*, *ho*, or *ha*, *ha*, *ha*. Notice that the series of tones constitutes a kind of simplified and elemental phrase without the complex sound patterns of ordinary utterance.

5. Select a passage from some essay in which many sentences and phrases begin with vowels and read it aloud to a friend or the class, trying to carry the easy and well-coordinated tone initiation of the preceding exercises into your sustained communicative utterance.

6. Make a short talk on a subject about which you feel deeply (e.g., a tribute to a friend or an appreciation of a work of art or some heroic or humanitarian deed). Your instructor and fellow students will help you evaluate your vocal effectiveness.

7. Try constantly to carry into your daily conversation the responsiveness and control of breathing and the ease and freedom of tone which make your speech a clearer and more effective means of communication.

SUPPLEMENTARY READINGS

Anderson, Virgil A., *Training the Speaking Voice*, Oxford University Press, 1942.

Hahn, Elise, Donald E. Hargis, Charles W. Lomas, and Daniel Vandraegen, *Basic Voice Training for Speech*, 2nd ed., McGraw-Hill, 1957.

Hanley, Theodore D., and Wayne L. Thurman, *Developing Vocal Skills*, Holt, Rinehart and Winston, 1962; and *Student Projects for Developing Vocal Skills*.

15

AUDIBLE COMMUNICATION: VOCAL EXPRESSION

Our voices, as distinguished from our words, convey meaning by means of modulations or expressive changes which reveal something about attitudes, thoughts, and emotions. Words typically have a matter-of-fact, objective significance. They more largely denote—i.e., point out or name things, ideas, referents of all kinds. Vocal changes, however, connote or suggest our more subtle meanings—hidden or half-realized intentions, richness of past experience, depth of emotion, varying shades of discrimination and emphasis. Sometimes the subtle nuances of voice give us away, or contradict our words, almost as effectively as do our facial expressions or unconscious bodily movements. Insincerity or sarcasm, for example, are usually revealed in voice even if our words say something quite different. A voice deficient in meaningful changes, no matter how mellow or pleasant to the ear, has little value for purposes of thoughtful speech.

The important questions for us are these: How can we improve this aspect of our speaking? How can we make vocal modulation a more significant means of formulating and communicating our meanings? We have already studied their two primary foundations: first, adequate thinking, which involves clearer definition of purposes, better organized thought sequences, richer personal meanings, and more discriminating recognition of thought units and their relationships; second, basic vocal conditions of which the most important are command of breath, unhindered phonation, and full resonance. A speaker who has mastered these primary processes will usually find his voice tending to respond spontaneously and faithfully to the nuances of his thought.

We say "tending to respond" because vocal modulations do not inevitably and necessarily follow from improved thinking and basic vocal coordinations. Two additional capacities must be developed if we are to make the most effective use of voice: sensitivity to vocal changes and understanding of their expressive-communicative values.

Voice can change only in its essential properties—duration, loudness, pitch, and quality. Vocal modulations are of these four kinds. In Chapter 14 we studied them as physical characteristics of sound and as auditory experiences. Now we shall consider them as expressive-communicative processes. These are not unnatural skills to be acquired by strange and difficult means. They are part of our human nature and of the culture patterns of the linguistic community in which we live. All of us use some degree of these modulations but many of us are limited in our command of them. We have formed bad habits or have failed to develop our capacities to the best use. As in all other aspects of speech, constant and alert practice is necessary to restore and maintain the highest potentials in vocal expression.

Duration

The basic elements of duration in speech are pause, quantity, and rate. We begin with these because poor timing can ruin the effectiveness of all other modulations and of articulation too.

We have already seen that the pause acts as a kind of auditory punctuation separating the phrase units of utterance from each other (see Chapter 4). The pause is an interval of silence during which a speaker creates or re-creates the next step in his thinking. At the same time the pause gives him opportunity to renew the basic processes necessary for voice production. A pause not only gives one time to think but also time to respond to thinking by taking breath and opening the mouth for utterance. These simple preparatory actions increase the likelihood that the breath power will be adequate and that the vocal bands and resonating cavities will be properly adjusted for vocalization. Therefore, mind your pauses! Take your time! Think in orderly phrase units!

Quantity is the duration of the sound units of speech. Every type of speech sound has its own characteristic duration. Stopped consonants are always relatively short; they explode and are done. Voiced sounds in general tend to be longer than unvoiced sounds. Vowels require duration to build up their distinctive resonant qualities. Some vowels are characteristically longer than others. Accented syllables tend to be longer than unaccented. (These matters will be discussed more fully in the chapter on articulation.) Every sound and syllable must be given enough time to build up its distinctive nature. Especially is this true of vowels since they carry most of the loudness, pitch and quality factors we shall discuss in the remainder of this section.

If one were to measure the exact duration of all the pauses and all the syllables in any phrase, their sum would be its total elapsed time. Rhythm and rate are more complex characteristics of speech resulting in part from the way in which the more basic elements, pause and quantity, are combined.

Rate is simply the speed at which one talks. Usually it is counted in number of words per minute, although a more exact (and more difficult) measure would be number of syllables per minute. In general, a rate of less than 100 words per minute is considered slow, a rate of 200 words is very rapid. Probably a median optimum pace is approximately 120 words per minute. Speakers differ in rate according to temperament and kind of muscular coordination. Some of us are characteristically slow and deliberate, others quick and impulsive. Each of us, therefore, should study to find that rate of utterance at which he can achieve maximum communicative effectiveness. Those who are slow and phlegmatic in thought and speech may need to develop a more rapid and dynamic rate. The larger number of us, however, need to slow down by making more thoughtful use of pause and by giving sounds their appropriate quantity or time value. Our uttered thought should move forward rapidly enough to command and hold a listener's attention, but should be slow enough so that the speaker can create his meanings adequately and the listener can understand accurately and fully.

At the same time we should learn to use variations in rate according to our attitudes and purposes and the type of situation in which we speak. In some exciting situations even a very deliberate person may speak rapidly. In serious or depressing situations a quick and excitable person may speak slowly. The rate of sensitive speech usually varies from sentence to sentence or even from one phrase to the next depending on the nature of the thought. Monotony in timing, as in any other aspect of speech, lacks communicative value and usually becomes tiresome. All of us, whatever our characteristic temperament and tempo, need to develop sensitive variations in rate.

Rhythm is the alternation of silence and sound and of strength and weakness in utterance. It is not exclusively a matter of time; variable accent of syllables is also involved (see section on rhythm in Chapter 16).

From all that we have said we should now be able to list our most frequent bad habits in use of duration:

Hurrying or speaking so rapidly that our pauses are too short for adequate response and our phrasing becomes vague and confused.

Drawl or speaking too slowly: our pauses become mental blanks instead of periods of thought, and speech sounds, especially vowels, are prolonged beyond their natural length.

Jerkiness or stopping and starting in hurried jerks which distort the time values of our sounds and throw rhythm out of balance.

Monotony or tendency to use the same unvarying rate and rhythm.

Since values change with changing situations, subject matter, and temperament of speaker, we cannot lay down rigid rules but should study to develop sensitivity and insight in our uses of duration. The following exercises, done under guidance of your instructor, will help.

EXERCISES FOR DURATION

1. Listen to recordings of your own speaking and reading and evaluate your use of pause, phrasing, rate and rhythm. Join with your classmates in exchange of evaluations. First, try to determine the nature of your faults, and then their causes. For example, do your difficulties, if any, lie primarily in emotional attitudes and habits of thought, or in lack of adequate vocal response, or in both. Are you hurried, or too phlegmatic? Do you fail to analyze your thought into clear phrase units? Do you lack definite communicative purpose? Ask your instructor to evaluate your self-analysis.

2. Analyze the uses of pause, phrasing, and rate by people with whom you converse and by the public speakers, readers, and actors to whom you listen. Do you discover any relationships between effectiveness of communication and use of these elements?

3. Read aloud selections of prose and poetry of different spirit and emotional tone, and observe the ways in which the phrasing and variations of rhythm and rate reflect the emotional content and determine the clarity of meaning communicated.

4. Make a short talk on a subject about which you have strong convictions and attempt to channel your attitudes into meaningful pauses, definite phrasing, and orderly rhythm instead of hurry or jerky confusion.

Loudness

Vocal power is important for speech in three principal ways:

1. We should speak loudly enough to be heard easily. Speech that cannot be heard might as well not be spoken.
2. We should use enough energy to form the various sounds of speech clearly. Every speech sound has its own characteristic power.
3. We should use enough variation in force to produce varying degrees of accent and emphasis (see section on pitch below) and to make effective whatever type of rhythm is characteristic of our thought pattern.

In itself loudness is not a measure of the intelligibility of speech but the modulation of loudness is an important factor in effective communication.

As we have seen, the intensity of a tone, i.e., the energy of its vibration, is not the same as the loudness or level of audibility, which depends in part on sensitivity of the ear. The audibility of a speaker's discourse, however, depends on even more complex factors. Power of tone is determined by breath pressure and resonance. These processes are influenced by a speaker's depth of conviction, intensity of purpose, and degree of emotional participation. These psychological responses are often influenced by the nature of the setting, which may be highly exciting or matter-of-fact, deeply moving or commonplace. Moreover, such details as number of listeners, distance between speaker and listeners, and seating arrangements or distribution of listeners, as well as the physical features of the setting will have stimulating influence on a speaker. Even the sound-absorbing qualities of surrounding walls and the presence or absence of disturbing noises affect one's use of vocal power.

In Chapter 14 we mentioned that the power of sound varies inversely as the square of the distance from its source. Consequently any speaker's voice, especially in a large room, could easily become inaudible were it not for reinforcing reflections of sound waves from the surrounding walls. If the shape of the walls is such that the waves are reflected in conflicting patterns, dead spaces or noisy echoes may interfere with a speaker's audibility. Other noises in the setting may also interfere. Some background noise is almost always present in any speech setting, and when it becomes loud enough to interfere with audibility, a speaker's vocal power must be greater than the competing noise if he is to be heard and understood.

In general our failures to use adequate vocal power are of three kinds:

1. Weakness
2. Overloudness including waste of energy and strain
3. Monotony, or failure to adjust to the varying needs of a communicative situation

For loudness, as for all other vocal modulations, precise rules are difficult if not impossible to formulate. Sensitivity to power values and to the reactions of the listeners must be developed on the basis of experience. A necessary foundation for such sensitivity, of course, is normal acuity of hearing. The ideal way to determine whether you have normal hearing is to take an audiometric test, especially if you have any reason to suspect that you have a hearing loss. Knowledge of your level of hearing will help you evaluate and adjust your vocal power adequately.

Certain basic procedures for improvement in use of loudness can be inferred from our previous studies. First, maintain clear, definite thought and direct communicative purpose. Second, use adequate pause and orderly phrasing. Third, develop and maintain full use of the basic vocal processes, especially responsiveness and control of breath and fullness of resonance. These conditions are the foundations of flexibility and ease and should remove any need for strained shouting in order to be heard. Fourth, develop the habit of observing whether your listeners give evidence of difficulty in hearing, and learn to adjust your loudness to their needs. As you practice to improve these abilities, a few specific exercises may be helpful.

EXERCISES FOR LOUDNESS

1. Repeat the exercises for resonance (Chapter 14) with variations in loudness. For example, intone a nasal sound or vowel very softly and increase the power gradually until it is at the loudest level you can sustain easily. Again, increase the power of a sustained tone gradually to a high level and then let it diminish gradually, sustaining easy control of breath throughout.

2. Speak a simple word or command quietly as to someone close beside you; then repeat the utterance as though to someone at a distance.

3. Go with a friend or classmate into a large room or auditorium and practice making him understand you distinctly from opposite ends of the room. Success in this, of course, will involve not only loudness but adequate pausing, phrasing, and distinctness of articulation, which involves flexible uses of vocal power appropriate to the different sounds of speech.

4. Practice speaking and reading in many different kinds of situations, e.g., in private conversation and small discussion groups and to public audiences of different sizes; study the variations of vocal power required.

Pitch

As we have learned in previous sections, vocal pitch is a sensory experience which we casually speak of as "high" or "low," but which actually depends upon frequency of vibration. In vocal tones the frequency is determined by length, thickness, and tension of the vocal folds. Since these adjustments of the vocal folds are involuntary, a speaker's control of them depends on his depth of thought and emotional control, the sensitivity of his hearing, and his mastery of related voice processes (breathing, phonation, resonance).

Two aspects of vocal pitch influence communication: the average or general level and the range or variety. Let us examine each of these.

GENERAL PITCH LEVEL

The concept of average pitch does not imply one fixed level of tone but a limited band of frequencies at the approximate middle of a speaker's range. Such an average in itself is not a direct communicator of meaning. Women's voices, for example, are typically higher in pitch than men's, yet a soprano voice may be as effective in its way as a baritone. Nevertheless a speaker's pitch level is important because of its relation to emotional control and to the normal functioning of the vocal organs. For example intense emotion such as joy tends to raise pitch level. A high pitched, thin voice seems to be related to immaturity and lack of poise, while a lower or optimum pitch suggests self-assurance and confidence.

We can easily infer some of the reasons for these relationships. Lack of poise and emotional imbalance usually involve excessive muscular tensions which interfere with normal functioning of the vocal organs. The vigorous energy of intense excitement, for example, may result in greater tonicity of laryngeal muscles. Tensions in the tongue and pharynx may so constrict resonating cavities as to weaken or eliminate lower partials and amplify higher partials of the tones. In either case the result is abnormally high pitch. For some of us, excessive tensions of this type have become fixed habits. On the other hand we occasionally find a person in whom hypotension involving sluggish action of vocal organs leads to abnormally low pitch.

In contrast to both of these types a clear and well-balanced thinker speaks with greater economy of effort, his phonation and resonance are more relaxed and normal, and as a result his voice tends to find its optimum pitch level. This, of course, will be the level at which the basic vocal processes (breathing, phonation, and resonance) are well coordinated, and therefore the level at which adequate loudness, pleasing quality, and freedom of pitch variation are most easily achieved; in other words, the level at which more effective communication is possible.

To improve your pitch level use two primary methods:

1. Determine whether there is a significant difference between your habitual level and your optimum or normal level. To determine your habitual level read a short selection (200 to 250 words) of prose aloud several times. In the first reading use the full range of pitch variation you can command easily and without artificiality. Then during successive readings narrow the range gradually both from above and below, until at the end of the third or fourth reading you are chanting on the monopitch which seems easiest for you and lies near the central point of your range. Let the chant end in a sustained vowel and find its pitch by striking the nearest note on a piano. This will approximate the average pitch you habitually use.

To locate your optimum or normal pitch level begin by singing up and down the scale several times using the piano as a guide. Sing down the scale to the lowest note and up to the highest note (including falsetto) you can sustain easily. Repeat several times and check the limits of your range on the piano. Your natural or optimum pitch level will lie approximately one-fourth of your total range above its lowest note. In order to compensate for temporary variations, the test should be repeated on several successive days and the mode or most typical result accepted as your optimum pitch. This, of course, is a relative rather than an exact scientific measure. Nevertheless, if your habitual pitch differs by more than one or two tones from your optimum pitch, you should move forward from this first step to the next.

2. Practice to restore your optimum pitch level. This should involve careful review of the basic processes of voice production:

> Emphasize ease and freedom of action; relax. Be sure that breath power and control are adequate.
> Review the coordination of breathing and vocal folds in phonation (Chapter 14).
> Establish freedom of resonance in an open throat.
> Utilize deliberate pausing in order to secure orderly phrasing.
> Test the acuity of your hearing.
> Practice speaking and reading aloud at the approximate pitch level which the tests have shown to be your optimum. Recheck to find and make habitual the pitch level which is easiest and most natural for you.

PITCH VARIETY

The discussion of optimum pitch should not deceive us into thinking that we speak, or ought to speak, on one level or within a narrow range of pitch. Effective communication demands variety. During normal speech the pitch of the voice is constantly changing. You should not only establish your optimum or best average pitch level, but should study also to improve its range and variety.

Variations of pitch occur in speech in two different ways; they are of two different kinds. *Intervals* or steps are changes which occur between tones, that is between syllables, words, phrases, and sentences. *Inflections* or slides are changes which occur without interruption of phonation, that is during production of vowels. These two kinds of changes are closely related and work together to produce the complex and varied melody patterns or intonations which characterize lively, discriminating, purposeful utterance.

These intonations of speech are closely related to the more intellectual or logical aspects of our thought. We observe, for example, that questions are usually spoken with rising inflection, assertions with falling inflection, and doubt or uncertainty with the circumflex or combination of rising and falling slides in tone. Intervals are primary means of expressing discrimination between successive thought units, and the inflectional pattern of a sentence shows something about the speaker's understanding of the relative importance of its component ideas. The total pattern of pitch change in discourse reveals the relationship of its parts and hence its logical structure as understood and interpreted by the speaker.

Of course pitch does not function alone in this matter. In normal speech it is typically combined with changes of duration and loudness to express varying degrees of accent and emphasis. Accented syllables, especially in emphatic words, typically have longer duration, greater intensity, and wider pitch range than unaccented syllables or unimportant words. The extent to which these elements are blended differs for different speakers and even for the same speaker at various times and under varying circumstances of utterance. Nevertheless melody pattern remains the principal means by which speakers formulate and communicate their personal interpretations of the relative importance and relationship of their ideas.

This can be illustrated easily if we notice the way in which pitch pattern or emphasis in a simple sentence shifts from word to word as the logical meaning changes. If you speak the sentence, "I saw George this morning," the name probably would be the dominant element in your thought and hence the emphatic word; *he* was the person you saw, not someone else. Suppose, however, there is reason for emphasizing that you actually *saw* him; you did not merely hear or hear about him. If your voice is normally responsive, it will spontaneously produce a pitch change (probably combined with some increase of duration and loudness) on the word *saw* to indicate that it carries the central meaning. In like manner the word *morning* will become central if time of day is the most important element of thought, or the word *this* if the distinction between today and previous days is most important.

These differences in logical meaning cannot be shown by the words alone. If the sentence were spoken as a complete monotone with all vocal changes omitted, the relative importance of ideas would not be indicated. The listener would have to provide his own interpretation of the meaning. If logical structure of discourse is to be shown, pitch changes are indispensable. Of course a degree of emphasis might be shown by increasing the loudness and/or the duration of the important words, but such isolated use of modulation seldom occurs in normal speech. It would have to be produced artificially, and hence would be inadequate for effective communication. The distinctive function of pitch variety in speech is to give expression to the logical relationships of our thought.

We should immediately add, however, that intellectual and

emotional aspects of communicative thinking cannot be separated and that the pitch variations of speech are also closely related to our emotional attitudes. Some careful research has shown, for example, that anger is characterized by wide and rapid inflectional changes, while grief shows limited range and slow pitch changes. Fear shows a high median level and a wide pitch range; indifference a low level and narrow range.

Your own casual observation will detect some everyday relationships between pitch changes and emotion. Have you not noticed that timid, self-conscious people tend to use a chronic rising inflection? Or that egotistical, domineering people overuse abrupt downward inflection? Have you recognized the circumflex whine of self-pity? Or the chaotic flutter of the effusive society belle? On the other hand, observe the orderly wide-ranging melody patterns of the speaker who has thought out his message in keenly discriminating logical sequences and who maintains a sense of clear purpose and controlled intensity.

What, then, can we do to develop meaningful modulations of pitch? If we have developed the basic normal conditions of voice production already discussed, the following exercises may be helpful.

EXERCISES FOR PITCH MODULATION

1. Practice short statements having different intellectual significance and intonation patterns such as one might use in daily conversation—e.g., simple commands or instructions, questions, statements involving a series of items. Accentuate the intonation patterns to bring out the full communicative value. Try the following:

    a. Some days are bright, others gloomy.
    b. The pathway is smooth but narrow.
    c. Why did he spend all his money?
    d. Speak softly, but carry a big stick.
    e. "It is too bad," he said, "that you cannot go."
    f. Both the boys and the girls were invited to this party.
    g. That university is famous in football but infamous in scholarship.
    h. Please send me one head of lettuce, three ripe peaches, a bunch of grapes, and a watermelon.
    i. James, George and John walked, vaulted, swam, and crawled the entire length of the handicap course.
    j. Fourscore and seven years ago our fathers brought forth on this continent a new nation.
    k. Where shall wisdom be found? and where is the place of understanding?

2. Analyze the logical structure of short selections of well-written prose. Discover the central ideas and the main supporting ideas. Notice

which phrases or clauses are subordinated, look for comparisons and contrasts, and follow through any sequences which build up to climax. Practice making these relationships clear in the intonation patterns of your voice. Try the following:

> Charity suffereth long and is kind; charity envieth not; charity vaunteth not itself, is not puffed up, doth not behave itself unseemly, seeketh not her own, is not easily provoked, thinketh no evil; rejoiceth not in iniquity, but rejoiceth in the truth; beareth all things, believeth all things, hopeth all things, endureth all things. Charity never faileth; but whether there be prophecies, they shall fail; whether there be tongues, they shall cease; whether there be knowledge, it shall vanish away.

> I Corinthians 13

> A woman well-bred and well taught, furnished with the additional accomplishments of knowledge and behavior, is a creature without comparison; her society is the emblem of sublimer enjoyments; her person is angelic and her conversation heavenly; she is all softness and sweetness, peace, love, wit, and delight. She is every way suitable to the sublimest wish, and the man that has such a one to his portion has nothing to do but rejoice in her and be thankful.
> On the other hand, suppose her to be the very same woman, and rob her of the benefit of education, and it follows thus:
> If her temper be good, want of education makes her soft and easy. Her wit, for want of teaching, makes her impertinent and talkative. Her knowledge, for want of judgment and experience, makes her fanciful and whimsical. If her temper be bad, want of breeding makes her worse, and she grows haughty, insolent, and loud. If she be passionate, want of manners makes her termagant and a scold, which is much at one with lunatic. If she be proud, want of discretion (which still is breeding) makes her conceited, fantastic, and ridiculous. And from these she degenerates to be turbulent, clangorous, noisy, nasty, and the devil.

> DANIEL DEFOE, "The Education of Women"

> This business of conversation is a very serious matter. There are men whom it weakens one to talk with an hour more than a day's fasting would do. Mark this which I am going to say, for it is as good as a working professional man's advice, and costs you nothing: It is better to lose a pint of blood from your veins than to have a nerve tapped. Nobody measures your nervous force as it runs away, nor bandages your brain and marrow after the operation.
> There are men of *esprit* who are excessively exhausting to some people. They are the talkers who have what may be called *jerky* minds. Their thoughts do not run in the natural order of sequence. They say bright things on all possible subjects, but their zig-zags rack you to death. After a jolting half-hour with one of these jerky

companions, talking with a dull friend affords great relief. It is like taking the cat in your lap after holding a squirrel.

What a comfort a dull but kindly person is, to be sure, at times! A ground-glass shade over a gas-lamp does not bring more solace to our dazzled eyes than such a one to our minds.

OLIVER WENDELL HOLMES, "On Conversation,"
The Autocrat of the Breakfast Table

Our awareness of time has reached such a pitch of intensity that we suffer acutely whenever our travels take us into some corner of the world where people are not interested in minutes and seconds. The unpunctuality of the Orient, for example, is appalling to those who come freshly from a land of fixed meal-times and regular train services. For a modern American or Englishman, waiting is a psychological torture. An Indian accepts the blank hours with resignation, even with satisfaction. He has not lost the fine art of doing nothing. Our notion of time as a collection of minutes, each of which must be filled with some business or amusement, is wholly alien to the Oriental just as it was wholly alien to the Greek. For the man who lives in a pre-industrial world, time moves at a slow and easy pace; he does not care about each minute, for the good reason that he has not been made conscious of the existence of minutes.

ALDOUS HUXLEY, "Time and the Machine,"
The Olive Tree

In your hands, my fellow citizens, more than mine, will rest the final success or failure of our course. Since this country was founded, each generation of Americans has been summoned to give testimony to its national loyalty. The graves of young Americans who answered the call to service surround the globe.

Now the trumpet summons us again—not as a call to bear arms, though arms we need—not as a call to battle, though embattled we are—but a call to bear the burden of a long twilight struggle year in and year out, "rejoicing in hope, patient in tribulation"— a struggle against the common enemies of man: tyranny, poverty, disease and war itself.

Can we forge against these enemies a grand and global alliance, north and south, east and west, that can assure a more fruitful life for all mankind? Will you join in that historic effort?

In the long history of the world, only a few generations have been granted the role of defending freedom in its hour of maximum danger. I do not shrink from this responsibility—I welcome it. I do not believe that any of us would exchange places with any other people or any other generation. The energy, the faith, the devotion which we bring to this endeavor will light our country and all who serve it—and the glow from that fire can truly light the world.

And so, my fellow Americans: ask not what your country can do for you—ask what you can do for your country.

My fellow citizens of the world: ask not what America will do for you, but what together we can do for the freedom of man.

Finally, whether you are citizens of America or citizens of the world, ask of us here the same high standards of strength and sacrifice which we ask of you. With a good conscience our only true reward, with history the final judge of our deeds, let us go forth to lead the land we love, asking His blessing and His help, but knowing that here on earth God's work must truly be our own.

From President John F. Kennedy's Inaugural Address,
"For the Freedom of Man," January 20, 1961

3. Practice reading aloud selections of both prose and poetry involving complex logical relationships.

It is certainly true that birds were not made for cages, and that to be a natural, normal, proper bird, a winged creature ought to be allowed to fly. So man, in order to be man, and no chattel, must be free. A civil society of slaves is nonsense in the statement. Only freemen, as Aristotle teaches, can constitute a State. But freedom does not mean absolute freedom; on the contrary, it rather means only the equal acknowledgement of just and fair restraints. Mere liberty, though a very great thing to a bird, is the first and lowest and smallest condition of human society. Freedom, however much belauded, is, in fact, that quality or function which man shares in common with children, savages, madmen, and wild beasts. All these naturally rejoice only in freedom and disown all restraint. The imposition of restraints upon liberty is the first great act of civilization; and to increase restrictions is, in the general case, to make progress in legislation. . . .

John Stuart Blackie, "Freedom,"
Democracy

With malice toward none; with charity for all; with firmness in the right, as God gives us to see the right, let us strive on to finish the work we are in; to bind up the nation's wounds; to care for him who shall have borne the battle, and for his widow, and his orphan—to do all which may achieve and cherish a just and lasting peace among ourselves, and with all nations.

Lincoln, "The Second Inaugural Address"

Oratory is the art of enchanting the soul, and therefore he who would be an orator has to learn the differences of human souls— they are so many and of such a nature, and from them come the differences between man and man—he will then proceed to divide speeches into their different classes. Such and such persons, he will say, are affected by this or that kind of speech in this or that way, and he will tell you why; he must have a theoretical notion of them first, and then he must see them in action, and be able to follow them with all his senses about him, or he will never get beyond the precepts of his masters. But when he is able to say what persons are persuaded by what arguments, and recognize the individual about whom he used to theorize as actually present to him, and say to himself, "This is he and this is the sort of man who ought to have that argument applied to him in order to convince him of this:"—when he has attained the knowledge of all this, and knows also when he should speak and when he should abstain from speaking, and when he should make use of pithy sayings, pathetic appeals, aggravated effects, and all the other figures of speech;—when, I say, he knows the times and seasons of all these things, then, and not till then, he is perfect and a consummate master of his art.

Plato, Phaedrus

He who knows, and knows he knows,—
He is wise—follow him.
He who knows, and knows not he knows,—
He is asleep—wake him.
He who knows not, and knows not he knows not,—
He is a fool—shun him.
He who knows not, and knows he knows not,—
He is a child—teach him.

Arabian Proverb

All the world's a stage,

And all the men and women merely players:
They have their exits and their entrances;
And one man in his time plays many parts,
His act being seven ages. At first the infant,
Mewling and puking in the nurse's arms.
Then the whining schoolboy, with his satchel
And shining morning face, creeping like snail
Unwillingly to school. And then the lover,
Sighing like furnace, with a woeful ballad
Made to his mistress' eyebrow. Then a soldier,
Full of strange oaths, and bearded like the pard,
Jealous in honour, sudden and quick in quarrel,
Seeking the bubble reputation
Even in the cannon's mouth. And then the justice,
In fair round belly with good capon lin'd,
With eyes severe and beard of formal cut,
Full of wise saws and modern instances;
And so he plays his part. The sixth age shifts
Into the lean and slipper'd pantaloon,
With spectacles on nose and pouch on side,
His youthful hose, well sav'd, a world too wide

For his shrunk shank; and his big manly voice,
Turning again toward childish treble, pipes
And whistles in his sound. Last scene of all,
That ends this strange eventful history,
Is second childishness and mere oblivion,
Sans teeth, sans eyes, sans taste, sans everything.

Shakespeare, As You Like It

4. In one of the expository talks already assigned, study the logical relationships of main and subordinate ideas as shown in the outline and let your voice respond to these relationships as clearly and purposefully as possible.

5. Make recordings of some of these exercises and study your intonation patterns. Do they communicate the full logical significance of the material? How would you change them?

Quality

We have seen (Chapter 14) that quality of tone depends on complexity of vibration and that for the human voice this complexity is determined primarily by two organic processes—vocal chord vibration and the adjustment of the resonating cavities. These activities are influenced by whatever degree of muscular tension and coordination are characteristic of the person, and these in turn are intimately related to his thinking and emotional attitudes.

Of all the vocal modulations, quality is probably the most subtle and difficult to describe or define definitely. We can measure duration and loudness of tones and identify inflections as rising or falling, but we have no accurate means even of naming the nuances of voice quality. We use a variety of figurative terms such as *brilliant, shrill, raspy, gentle, soft, hollow, flat, thin;* but no one has succeeded in defining exactly what is meant by any of these words and the voices to which they refer may actually differ greatly in audible effect.

Vocal quality, however, has great significance as a revealer of personal attitudes and emotions. This is a matter of subtle empathy between speaker and listener. When a speaker is creating rich personal meanings which he feels deeply and genuinely, his muscular tonus and implicit expressive movements influence the functioning of his vocal organs so as to produce a tone complex which, though it may not be named or described exactly, tends to arouse similar attitudes and emotions in a participating listener. Vocal quality thus reveals and communicates the emotional overtones of a speaker's thought. We should think of this expressive function in two ways: First, as a constant personal characteristic; second, as a sensitive and variable indicator of our changing emotional attitudes.

Hear your voice as others hear it.

QUALITY AS A PERSONAL CHARACTERISTIC

Every one of us has a basic timbre of voice which is a distinctive part of his personality. We recognize the voices of our friends even when we cannot see them or understand their words; and though it is true that tempo and loudness and pitch changes are important clues in such recognition, quality is often most significant. This characteristic vocal timbre is determined by many factors, including structure of the larynx and resonating cavities as well as the speaker's fixed habits of muscle tension, breath control, and coordination. Except for the purely structural determinants, these influences are intrinsically related to our habitual mental and emotional responses. Improvement of basic voice quality, therefore, is a complex process which requires mental and emotional enrichment as well as patient and persistent practice to develop coordinated functioning of vocal organs.

Those of us who are emotionally well balanced, who maintain an objective attitude toward the world around us, and who are relaxed and well coordinated, will usually speak in tones characteristically open, well resonated, rich and mellow or perhaps even ringing and brilliant. (Notice how we search for the right words to express a subjective, connotative meaning.) In contrast, however, many of us in the stress of daily life, sometimes because of complex and little realized influences during our early formative years, develop habitually distorted and unpleasant voice qualities. Acoustically such qualities are noises arising from irregularity of vibration, lack of overtones, or discord among overtones. We often become so accustomed to these distorted qualities in ourselves that they seem perfectly natural; but they nevertheless tend to distract a listener's attention and so interfere with communication. The variety of these unpleasant personal voice qualities is as numerous as the people who have them, but certain types are so common as to be almost standard among us. We name and describe a few of these arbitrarily in hope that they may help you to observe and improve your own vocal quality.

Breathiness. The fuzzy, aspirate noise of poorly controlled breath escaping between partially approximated vocal chords and through squeezed and constricted resonating cavities.

Nasality. Improper use of the resonating cavities in the nose. Two varieties are common: (1) excessive nasal resonance, caused by inactivity of the soft palate so that the velar-pharyngeal passage is too large and allows tones to pass through the nose. This robs vowels of their dominant oral resonance and tends to make some consonants, especially the plosives, indistinct. (See section on improving resonance in Chapter 14 and articulation, Chapter 16.) (2) Deficiency of nasal resonance. Caused by obstruction in the nasal passages or excessive tension in the soft palate and upper pharynx which makes the velar-pharyngeal opening too small. The nasal sounds (*m, n,* ŋ) thus robbed of their full resonance, become muffled and pinched and vowels tend to become dull and flat.

Flatness. Deficiency of resonance caused by excessive tension of jaw, tongue, and pharynx, which constricts and narrows the cavities and thus limits the number of overtones. The result is a dull, thin, lifeless quality.

Throatiness. Distortion of resonance caused by excessive tension in pharynx, larynx, and back of tongue, which interferes with vocal-fold vibration and constricts the resonating cavities. The result is a deep, gutteral, rasping quality which sometimes involves lower pitch than is normal.

MODULATION OF QUALITY

Another important phase of expressive voice quality consists of those variations which follow our changing emotional responses. If you speak in happy anticipation of success this morning and in the sadness of failure this afternoon, your voice, unless it is completely unresponsive, will show the difference. If you speak in calmness now and in anger five minutes from now, your voice will change accordingly. Such changes do not eliminate the basic personal quality of the voice nor the chronic mood in which we speak, but they operate within the limits of personal mood and characteristic timbre. Most of these quality changes are quite spontaneous and arise directly out of the mental and emotional attitudes of a speaker. Their subtle expressiveness cannot be imitated or assumed. If you do not feel the emotion but are only pretending, your voice will proclaim the pretense. Ham actors, declaimers, and bombastic politicians are instantly recognized by discerning listeners. Changes in voice quality are primary cues in revealing genuine emotion, although of course other modulations and bodily action also reveal emotion. Monotony of quality may not be as easy to detect as monotony of pitch, but it is none-the-less a sign of limited emotional participation and dull, lifeless imagination.

How then can we improve the communicative values of tone quality? All that we have said so far implies three effective methods:

1. Develop rich imagination and depth of controlled feeling (see Chapters 10 and 11).
2. Establish the basic responsiveness of the voice (see Chapter 14).
3. Improve sensitivity of the ear to quality values.

These are not abilities which can be developed in any sudden spurt. They require patient learning and growth. Some methods of improvement we have already considered. We now add a few more specific procedures which relate directly to voice quality.

EXERCISES FOR VOCAL QUALITY

1. Listen to your classmates and speakers in your community. Describe their voice qualities as accurately as possible. What effect does each voice have on listeners? Does it aid or hinder communication? When defective or unpleasant qualities appear, try to determine what causes them—e.g., organic conditions which hinder vocal fold vibration, limited resonance, excessive tension of jaw and tongue, poor breath control. Can you trace these physiological causes to psychological causes such as lack of purpose, limited self-confidence, lack of emotional participation, or poor emotional control? What remedial measures would you suggest in each case?

2. Listen to a tape recording of your own voice and make an analysis as suggested in Exercise 1 above. Compare this with analyses made by your classmates and instructors. Prepare an outline of methods you will use for improving your vocal quality.

3. Review exercises for breath control, phonation and resonance given in Chapter 14.

4. Practice interpreting selections from literature which portray many types of emotional experience.

5. Engage in discussion with friends on subjects about which you have deep convictions or emotional attitudes.

6. Prepare and deliver to the class a short talk on a subject which involves some variety of emotional attitude. For example: Create in succession its humorous aspect, its dangers, and its values; and ask your classmates to judge how genuinely your voice reveals the attitudes of amusement, apprehension, fear, enthusiasm, confidence, or whatever emotions are appropriate to your subject.

BIBLIOGRAPHICAL NOTE

For Chapters 14 and 15 the following specific sources are acknowledged: S. S. Stevens and Hallowell Davis, *Hearing: Its Psychology and Physiology*, Wiley, 1938; Giles W. Gray, "Phonetic Microtomy: The Minimum Duration of Perceptible Speech Sounds," *Speech Monographs*, 1942, pp. 75–90; Carl Erickson, "Basic Factors in the Human Voice," *Psychological Monographs*, 1926–1927, p. 88; John W. Black, "The Effect of Noise-induced Temporary Deafness upon Vocal Intensity," *Speech Monographs*, March, 1951, pp. 74–77; Wilbert Pronovost, "An Experimental Study of Methods for Determining Natural and Habitual Pitch," *Speech Monographs*, 1942, pp. 111–123; Grant Fairbanks and Wilbert Pronovost, "An Experimental Study of the Pitch Characteristics of the Voice During the Expression of Emotion," *Speech Monographs*, 1939, pp. 87–104.

16

AUDIBLE COMMUNICATION: ARTICULATION AND PRONUNCIATION

Articulation and pronunciation are the aspects of audible communication by which we (1) produce the sound units of our language and (2) join these sounds together in connected and meaningful patterns. We have defined articulation as the process of obstructing and shaping the outgoing stream of breath and tone so as to produce the sequences of sounds which make up spoken discourse (Chapter 14). The word *articulate* has two general meanings—segmented or formed in distinct units; joined or brought together in sequence. Both ideas are implicit in our definition. Articulation includes the production of distinct sound units and their combination in syllables and words. To articulate means to put together in close-knit fashion and that is exactly the way speech sounds are uttered. *Pronunciation* is a broader term, often used to include articulation; but it includes also those more complex processes by which we combine sounds into the standard patterns of utterance which are characteristic of a given linguistic community. Pronunciation involves especially such processes of word formation as syllabication, accent, and the assimilation, juncture, and blending of sounds.

The Sound Units of Utterance

Basic to any understanding of these processes of articulation and pronunciation is some awareness of the various kinds of units into which utterance may be analyzed. We have already considered the units of knowledge which make up spoken discourse (Chapter 6) and the ways in which they are combined into significant statements (Chapter 7) and organized in orderly outline patterns (Chapter 8). A speaker who has established these foundations of fact, inference, and organization is prepared for orderly thinking during utterance. Such thinking finds its audible formulation in pausing and phrasing.

287

THE PHRASE

We have studied the phrase as the smallest of the basic units of thought in discourse (see Chapter 4). When we utter such a unit, the organs of articulation do not make first one sound and then another in a series of fixed positions, but pass through a rapid series of movements each of which tends to merge into those that precede and follow it. This continuity is broken by pauses between breath groups or phrases; but within each phrase the activities of tongue, lips, jaw, and soft palate make an almost continuous flow of movement to and from the obstructing or narrowing positions by which we designate the successive sound units.

In both speech and writing, words are linguistically significant units of meaning; but they are not primarily significant phonetic units. Of course we study words phonetically—that is, we analyze and record the sounds of which they are composed. In normal speech, however, the phrase becomes the major unit which is spoken as a continuity of sound, and in strictly phonetic analysis is broken down directly into syllables with little, if any, attention to the words as such.

THE SYLLABLE

The kinds of sound combinations which make up syllables seem to have no necessary consistency of pattern. A syllable may consist of a consonant followed by a vowel as in *too*, or a vowel followed by a consonant as in *at*, or a vowel with consonants to mark both its boundaries as in *toot*, or a vowel alone with no consonants at all as in *ah*, or a diphthong alone as in *eye*. (Do not be deceived by spelling; we are speaking of sounds.) What is the common basic element which justifies our calling all these different sound combinations syllables? If you listen carefully to an uttered phrase, you will notice that each syllable is produced as a distinct impulse of voice or breath. This is the factor which brings the combination of sounds into unity. The most fully vocalized or sonorous sound in any syllable is its center. This is usually the vowel or diphthong, although certain other sounds, such as [l], [n], or [m], may occasionally constitute syllables.

Even though the consonants or less sonorous sounds do not form syllables by themselves, they nevertheless perform an indispenable function in syllabication. They provide the boundaries. Of course the beginnings and endings of syllables can be and often are indicated by intervals of silence; but if we were entirely dependent on them to separate our syllables, our speech would be hopelessly disjointed and inarticulate, literally not well joined together. In marking boundaries consonants serve not only to make syllables distinct but at the same time to link them together in sequence within each phrase. The fact that the boundary of any syllable may consist of more than one consonant (observe, for example, *sp* in *speak, str* in *stress, nt* in *accent*) does not change the principle.

A *syllable is a sound or combination of sounds produced on a single impulse of breath power.*

PHONEME AND ALLOPHONE

As syllables make up phrases, so individual speech sounds make up syllables. When the sounds are spoken singly or in isolation, their place and manner of formation and their acoustic properties tend to be relatively constant and distinctive. Descriptions of the individual speech sounds are usually given in terms of such stable characteristics. Propositional speech, however, is not a process of forming discrete sound units. When spoken in continuous discourse speech sounds, although retaining their elements of stability, are also quite variable. Every sound is influenced by the sounds which precede and follow it; and since phonetic contexts are continually changing, each sound in utterance is a unique event. Seldom are any two phonetic units exactly alike, even though they may sound alike to a casual listener.

The term *phoneme* is used to indicate this combination of constancy and variability in our speech sounds. A *phoneme is a sound family or group of variables which are near enough alike to be recognized for practical purposes as the same sound, or which have reasonably identical significance in determining the form and meaning of words.*

Consider, for example, the sound of the letter *t* in such words as *top, pot,* and *button.* In all of them the tongue tip is placed against the gums just back of the upper teeth, and breath pressure is built up behind the obstruction; if the sound were spoken in isolation an abrupt release or plosion would follow. Phonetic context, however, changes the action in each word. In *top* the [t] is released into the following vowel [ɑ]. In *pot* the [t] is primarily an obstructing movement which terminates the vowel [ɑ]; usually no releasing movement is heard. The third word, *button,* involves an obstructing movement of the tongue upward from the position for the vowel [ʌ] represented by the letter *u,* to its contact with the upper gums. The tongue then retains this position while the soft palate breaks its contact with the back wall of the throat so that the [t] is released abruptly through the nose. The articulatory action passes directly from [t] into [n].

In these three words, *top, pot,* and *button,* therefore, we have three variations of the sound [t] which are near enough alike to be recognized as members of the same sound family, distinctly different from the members of other phonemes. These variations together with all others which can be recognized audibly, constitute the phoneme /t/. The variables are called allophones of /t/. An *allophone is any distinctive variable within a sound family or phoneme.*

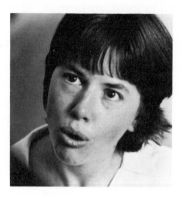

Good speech is clearly articulated.

A basic test of any phoneme is the common distinctiveness of its member allophones in forming words. All the variants of /t/, for example, have the same value in word patterns. Consider the word *tap*, transcribed in phonetic symbols as [tæp]. No matter how variable the pronunciations of different speakers may be, the meaning remains unchanged so long as the sounds can be recognized as falling within their respective phonemes; but if we substitute other phonemes such as /k/, /m/, or /s/, for the /t/, then we shall have entirely different words, *cap* [kæp], *map* [mæp], *sap* [sæp]. To add a different illustration, suppose we change the *e* [i] of *gleam* to *u* [u] as in *gloom*, or the *e* of *beet* to *a* [æ] as in *bat*. The change of phoneme changes word and meaning, whereas variation within any given phoneme makes no basic difference in meaning.

The Phonemes of English

The number of phonemes or recognized sound units in any language will vary according to the fineness of discrimination among the variables in utterance. For most languages and certainly for English the problem is further complicated by unphonetic spelling. Our written alphabet has only 26 letters. The number of sound units in our language is between 40 and 45 depending on how finely they are discriminated. As a result we cannot even approach accurate representation of pronunciation in writing or visual characters. Dictionaries have attempted to meet this problem by using diacritical marks with a system of respelling. Such a system, however, is bound to be complicated and confusing, especially when applied to vowels. For example, at least half a dozen sounds have been listed for the letter *a*, as follows:

ā as in *āle*   ă as in *ădd*
â as in *câre*   ä as in *fäther*
ă as in *ăbove*   à as in *àsk*
ạ as in *ạwl* or *ạll*; also given as ô, as in *lôrd* or *fôrm*.

These symbols are comonly referred to as forms of *a*. This is true, of course, only if we refer to the visual letter. Phonetically or in terms of sounds these various units of utterance are by no means forms of the sound [e] as in *ale*. The vowels in *add*, *arm*, and *ask* may seem to belong to the letter *a* because we have been taught to call them "short *a*," "long *a*," and "intermediate *a*" respectively; but careful utterance with an open ear should easily demonstrate that they do not sound at all like the vowel in *ale*. Analysis of the characteristic sound waves of most of these vowels has shown that each has a distinctive wave pattern of its own quite different from that of any other sound.

Attempts to resolve the confusions which result from the many differences between our written and spoken language have had a long history. Systems of phonetic writing go back at least as far as the thirteenth century. When the International Phonetic Association was founded in 1886, it adopted a simplified system of representing speech sounds by visual characters based on the principle that there should be one and only one symbol for each phoneme. This alphabet, although changed in minor ways to represent various regional dialects or the views of different linguists and phoneticians, has been accepted in its basic form by the great majority of scholars as the standard method of representing speech sounds.

We have already used some of the symbols in preceding paragraphs and shall present them systematically with the descriptions of the phonemes for which they stand. If you begin at once to observe and use them, they can be learned quite easily and will be a real help toward understanding the sound system of English. For sixteen of the phonemes in which there is no possibility of confusion or duplication, familiar letters of the written alphabet are used. Special characters have been adopted only in cases where a single letter represents several sounds, as we have seen with the letter *a*. In order to avoid any possible confusion between written letters and phonetic symbols, phoneticians have adopted the further device of enclosing them in brackets, thus [ ]. When the symbols are used to represent phonemes rather than specific utterances, they are usually enclosed in double bars, thus / /.

Phoneticians have also developed a system of supplementary markings to represent minor variations of our speech sounds, but these we shall leave for more specialized courses in phonetics. For our purposes detailed or narrow phonetic transcription is unnecessary. We shall be content with broad or phonemic transcriptions which use one symbol to stand for all the allophones of any given phoneme. In its full scope the International Phonetic Alphabet, I.P.A. for short, includes the phonemes of the principal European languages; but we shall consider here only the principal phonemes of American pronunciation. For convenience we classify them in three main groups—vowels, consonants, and glides.

VOWELS

Many of us have been taught that there are five or seven vowels in English, *a, e, i, o, u,* and sometimes *w* and *y.* Such a statement is misleading for it does not refer to vowels in the phonetic sense, but to those letters of the written alphabet which in our spelling usually represent vowels. Even in this sense, however, the statement is not accurate, for a complete list of the letters which may represent sounds having the function of vowels should include *l, r, n,* and sometimes *m.* In fact seventeen vowel phonemes have been recognized in our language, although if we ignore some of the finer distinctions, the number may be reduced to fourteen or even twelve.

In the sense in which we shall understand the concept, *a vowel is a speech sound resonated in a relatively open and unobstructed vocal tract and serving as the nucleus or center of a syllable.* We use the word "sound" in order to include the vowels of whispered speech, although vowels are typically vocal tones. In fact, from an acoustic point of view each vowel is a distinct tone quality. Vowel quality, however, is not the same as general voice quality. We are accustomed to thinking of voices as pleasant or unpleasant, gutteral or nasal, pinched or resonant; but most of us are not quite so used to the idea that such sounds as [ɑ], [o], [u] are but different qualities of tone—vowel qualities, not general voice qualities. Experience, however, readily illustrates the difference. All of us have heard voices of unpleasant quality whose vowels were nevertheless clear and easily distinguished; and occasionally we hear a voice of pleasant quality whose vowels are indistinct or muffled. The difference is to be found in the arrangement of partials in complex tones. General voice quality, as we have seen, depends chiefly on the number and harmonic relationship of overtones. (Review the section on the nature of sound in Chapter 14.) Vowel quality, on the other hand, is primarily a matter of relative intensity of overtones. Each vowel is characterized by a concentration of greatest intensities at certain relatively definite overtone levels.

The physiological vowel chart. These acoustic or resonant properties, of course, are determined by the adjustment of the resonance cavities of throat and mouth through which sound waves pass on their way from vocal folds to point of emission at the lips. Each vowel is characterized by a typical size and shape of cavities and their outlet, and by the subtle changes in tension of the tongue and other structures which shape the cavities. For our purposes in speech improvement we need only a general description of the shaping of resonators for each principal vowel phoneme. These facts are summarized in the traditional vowel chart.

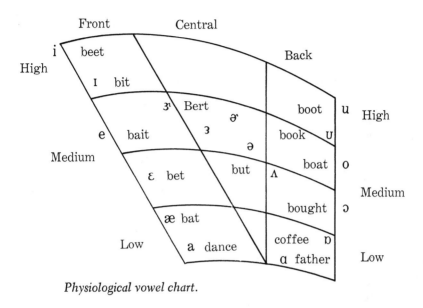

Physiological vowel chart.

This diagram is based on a cross section of the mouth cavity in its middle plane from front to back, and represents approximately the relative height of the highest part of the tongue in forming the resonance cavities for the various vowels. Notice that the word *central* refers to the middle part of the tongue, the word *medium* to the height of its arching. Each position represented is, of course, only a typical or characteristic norm of actually variable positions fo reach phoneme.

The position for [i] as in *beet* indicates that the front of the tongue (not the tip but the part just back of the tip) is high in the mouth, relatively higher than for any other vowel. Observe that such a position divides the entire throat and mouth passageway into two main cavities, a small one in front of the high tongue arch and a much larger cavity including the back part of the mouth and all of the pharynx behind the tongue. Notice also that the arching of the back of the tongue for [u] likewise divides the entire passageway into two cavities which are separated but connected by a narrow channel between the top of the tongue and the back part of the roof of the mouth. You will readily see, however, that in this case the two cavities, one in front of and one behind the tongue, are more nearly equal in size than for the vowel [i]. As with the front vowels, so also the series of back vowels from [u] to [ɑ] involves a progressive lowering of the height of the tongue until for [ɑ] the entire passage constitutes one primary resonance chamber. Symbols in the central-medium part of the chart represent variations of the sound [ɝ] as in *Bert* and [ʌ] as in *but* which will be discussed later.

Position of the lips is not specially indicated in the chart, but can be remembered easily. Back vowels are produced with lip-rounding which is greatest and hence leaves smallest opening for [u] as in *boot*, with progressively less rounding and wider openings for the other back vowels down to [ɑ] in which there is typically no lip-rounding whatever. The [ɝ] as in *Burt* is rounded and its related sounds [ɜ] and [ɚ] may be slightly rounded. All other vowels are produced without lip rounding.

Description of vowel phonemes. Much of this information about vowels is summarized in the brief descriptions which follow.

The terms *tense* and *lax* refer to relatively minor differences in tension. These can be noticed by placing the finger lightly under the chin as one sounds in succession such pairs of vowels as [i] and [ɪ], [e] and [ɛ], and [u] and [ʊ]. These distinctions are not easy to observe for some vowels, and are not well supported by experimental evidence. The differences in tension occur entirely within the limits of the normal tonus and coordination of muscular activity which are necessary for the open throat and resonant tone.

/i/   High front, tense, lips unrounded, as in *beet* [bit]. Other spellings are dec*ei*t, gr*ie*ve, p*eo*ple, Ph*oe*nix, k*ey*, qu*ay*, m*ea*t, mach*i*ne.

/ɪ/   High front, lax, lips unrounded, as in *bit* [bɪt]. Other spellings are *E*ngland, wom*e*n, b*u*sy, m*y*stery, s*ie*ve, b*ui*ld.

      Use: This is the only vowel which retains its full quality in unaccented as well as accented syllables, as in *village* [vɪlɪdʒ] and *limit* [lɪmɪt]. It is often substituted for [ɛ] in careless pronunciation which may sometimes create confusion of meaning, as in [mɪn] for [mɛn] and [gɪt] for [gɛt]. In some unaccented syllables the substitution creates no confusion of meaning and is established usage, as in the second syllables of such words as *hostess* [hostɪs], *college* [kɑlɪdʒ], *roses* [rozɪz].

/e/   Mid front, tense, lips unrounded, as in *bait* [bet]. Other spellings are t*a*ke, g*au*ge, d*ay*, br*ea*k, v*ei*l, conv*ey*, qu*a*ke.

      Use: In American pronunciation this sound is usually diphthongized except before stops, especially voiceless stops, as in *fate* or *make*. (See the section on diphthongs below.)

/ɛ/   Mid front, lax, lips unrounded, as in *bet* [bɛt]. Other spellings are m*a*ny, b*u*ry, h*ea*ther, fr*ie*nd, h*ei*fer, l*eo*pard, s*ay*s.

Use: This vowel is often confused with [ɪ] as in [sɛns] for *since,* and [ʌntɛl] for *until.*

/æ/   Low front, lax, lips unrounded, as in *bat* [bæt]. The spelling is usually the letter *a.*

Use: In General American pronunciation this sound is heard typically in a group of words known as the *ask* and *man* words. See discussion of [a].

/a/   Low front, lax, lips unrounded, as in *ask* [ask], when pronounced by many speakers in Scotland, southern England, and parts of New England. The spelling is always the letter *a.*

Use: This sound is not well established as a distinct phoneme either by experimental studies of vowel qualities or by observations of usage. By some speakers the sound is considered to be a mark of refinement and is used in a group of words spelled with *a* followed by a voiceless fricative as in *ask, path, grass, after, gasp,* or with *a* followed by *m* or *n* plus a consonant as in *command, example, dance, chant.* It does not occur significantly in General American pronunciation.

/ɑ/   Low back, lax, lips unrounded, as in *father* [fɑðɚ]. Other spellings are *ah, top, hearth, sergeant.*

Use: If the muscles of tongue and pharynx are overly tense, [ɑ] may take on some of the quality of [ɒ] or even [ɔ].

/ɒ/   Low back, partially lax, with a slight degree of lip rounding, as in *hot* [hɒt] or *want* [wɒnt], as spoken by many speakers in southern England and in New England and the southern United States. Typical spellings are p*aw,* c*au*ght, *ou*ght, although these words are not always pronounced with [ɒ].

Use: This sound, like [a] is not well standardized in American usage, nor is it clearly distinguished by experimental evidence from [ɑ] on one hand and [ɔ] on the other hand. [ɒ] is not strictly phonemic since change from [ɒ] to [ɑ] in such words as *hot, not, Boston, water,* seldom causes any change or confusion in meaning.

/ɔ/   Low back, tense, rounded, as in *bought* [bɔt]. Other spellings are *a*ll, c*o*st, br*oa*d, l*a*w, c*au*ght.

Use: This sound occurs most typically in words spelled *ar* as in *war, quart;* or preceded by voiceless fricatives as in *soft, cloth,* or by *au* plus *n* as in *daunt, haunt.* In American usage the lips are not always fully rounded; as a result the sound is not clearly distinct from [ɒ] or even from [ɑ], as for example in *laundry* often pronounced [lɑndrɪ] instead of [lɔndrɪ].

/o/ Medium back, tense, lips rounded, as in *boat* [bot]. Other spellings are *go, know, yeoman, though, beau, sew, owe.*

Use: In American pronunciation this sound is typically diphthongized when long or in final position as in *go, sew.* Before stops the extent of dipthongizing is usually so slight as to be negligible, as in *coat, hope.* (See the section on diphthongs below.)

/ʊ/ High back, lax, lips rounded, as in *book* [bʊk]. Other spellings are *wolf, full, could.*

/u/ High back, tense, lips rounded, as in *boot* [but]. Other spellings are *rule, blue, fruit, shoe, group, crew.*

Use: [u] is standard in many words spelled *oo*, such as *choose, fool, moon, proof,* although [ʊ] is well established for such words as *foot, good, wood, stood.* In many words spelled with *u*, such as *duty, suit, chew, mature,* pronunciation varies between [u] and the diphthong [ɪu] or [ju]. (See section on diphthongs.)

/ʌ/ Low-medium, back-central, lax, lips unrounded, as in *but* [bʌt]. The lips though unrounded must be well open if the sound is to be produced distinctly. Other spellings are *come, does, blood, trouble.*

/ə/ Medium central, lax, lips unrounded, as in *above* (first syllable). This sound resembles [ʌ] in acoustic quality, but is more lax and usually much shorter in duration. [ə] is represented in writing by every vowel letter in English and by many vowel combinations.

Use: This is a neutral sound used in almost all of the unstressed syllables of normal conversational speech. Exceptions are syllables which have the vowel [ɚ] (see below), unstressed [ɪ] in the second syllable of such words as *lettuce* and *biscuit* (see discussion of [ɪ] above), and unstressed [e] or [o] which have been reduced from the dipthongs [eɪ] and [oʊ] by loss of accent in such words as *fatality* and *obey.* The symbol [ə], therefore, is used for unaccented syllables to represent a large group of neutral sounds with various subtle degrees of vowel coloring.

If accent is restored to a syllable, the distinctive vowel quality can be heard. Pronounce the following pairs of words and notice that neutral vowels in words in the first column are restored to full vowel value in the parallel accented syllables in words of the second column.

parent	parental
salute	salutation
the boy	*the* boy (meaning the only one)
gentleman	man
tangent	tangential
battalion	battle
ability	able
constitution	constituent

/ɝ/   Medium-high front-central, tense, lips rounded, as in *Burt* [bɝt]. Not only is the front-central part of the tongue arched, but the tip is also inverted, that is, raised toward the roof of the mouth in a position approximately like that for the glide [r]. No glide is involved here, however; the characteristic tongue position is relatively stable. Other spellings are bird, her, world, myrtle, journey, heard.

Use. This phoneme is used in the central and western parts of the United States by those who "sound their r's." The symbol given here is used only for the sound in accented syllables as distinguished from the symbol used in unaccented syllables [ɚ] (see below). Other symbols sometimes used for the accented sound are [r] and [ɜ:]. We shall use [r], however, to represent the consonantal glide (see below), and [ɜ] for a modified form of [ɝ] as indicated below.

Reference to the vowel chart indicates that an overactive pushing of the tongue upward or forward may give [ɝ] a confusing [i] or [ɪ] quality, and that too much lowering or relaxing of the tongue may produce a sound resembling [ʌ].

/ɚ/   High-medium central, relatively lax as compared with [ɝ], as in *further* (second syllable) [fɝðɚ]. Other spellings are similar, actor, tapir, murmur.

Use: This sound is used only in unaccented syllables by those General American speakers who "sound their r's." It may be considered a member of the /ɝ/ phoneme, but is represented by a distinct symbol in order to indicate the important difference between the vowel qualities of stressed and unstressed syllables. See discussions of the consonant glide [r] and diphthongs ending in the off glide [ɚ].

/ɜ/   Medium central, lax, slightly rounded. As compared with [ɝ], the [ɜ] is produced with the tongue slightly lower and retracted and the lips slightly less rounded. Unlike [ɝ] this sound has little or no "r" quality; the tongue tip is raised only slightly or not at all above its position of rest behind the lower front teeth. Typical spellings are the same as those for [ɜ˞], the difference depending entirely on the way the words are pronounced.

Use: This sound and [ɜ˞] may be considered members of the same phoneme, each representing a regional usage. [ɜ] is heard chiefly in southern England and in eastern and southern United States in the speech of those who do not "sound their r's."

CONSONANTS

A consonant is a speech sound produced with some kind or degree of obstruction in the vocal passage so that a characteristic noise element is heard. In "voiced" consonants, tone is also present; but noise is the more important distinguishing feature (see Chapter 14). In all consonants except the subgroup of nasals, the velum or soft palate is raised so as to block the posterior opening into the nasal passages. Consonants, as we have seen, do not by themselves form syllables. They are therefore nonsyllabic, although they serve to accentuate the boundaries of syllables and so add indispensable differentiating elements in word formation.

For our purposes each consonant phoneme may be described adequately by four kinds of information: (1) place at which the vocal passage is obstructed, (2) type or degree of obstruction, (3) manner of release, and (4) presence or absence of voicing. These types of information also give us the bases for recognizing subclasses of consonants:

Anatomical classification. If we think in terms of the organs or structures which form the obstructions, we have the following classes:

1. Bilabial. The obstruction is formed by bringing the two lips firmly together, as in [p], [b] and [m].
2. Labiodental. The lower lip is against the edge of the upper teeth, as in [f] and [v].
3. Lingua-dental. The blade of the tongue is against the edge of the upper teeth, as in [θ] *thin* and [ð] *this*.
4. Lingua-rugal. The tip or front of the tongue is against the upper gums, as in [t], [d], [n], [s] and [z].
5. Lingua-palatal. The central part of the tongue is near to or in contact with the front part of the palate or roof of the mouth just behind the gums, as in [tʃ] *church* and [dʒ] *judge*.
6. Lingua-velar. The back of the tongue is against the velum or soft palate, as in [k], [g] and [ŋ].
7. Glottal. This is formed by near closure or closure of the vocal bands, as in the breath fricative [h] and glottal click or stop [ʔ]. The glottal stop is not part of the sound system of English, but is often heard as a sharp catch or click at the beginnings of vowels in the speech of persons whose voice

production is not well coordinated. (See the exercises on phonation in Chapter 14.)

Physiological classification. If we think in terms of the degree of obstruction and manner of release, we can classify consonants as follows:

1. Stop-plosives [p, b, t, d, k, g]. These sounds are produced by complete obstruction of the vocal tract, with build-up of breath pressure behind the closure and abrupt or plosive release. Observe that such sounds cannot be prolonged, except in a very limited degree; they can only be repeated. When stop-plosives are at the ends of syllables, their audible element is usually the result of abrupt closure instead of release. Speak such words as *Bob, pop, tot, dad, kick, gag,* and notice that the final consonants are typically heard only as abrupt stoppage of breath. As mentioned in the section on phonemes above, there is usually no audible plosion because the breath pressure has ceased to function before the obstruction of the final sound is released. The initial consonants in these words, on the other hand, are heard primarily because of abrupt release of breath pressure.

2. Fricatives [f, v, θ, ð, s, z, ʃ, ʒ, h]. These sounds are formed by partial or incomplete obstruction of the vocal tract and a gradual release in which the outflowing breath produces a friction-like noise; hence the name *fricative.*

3. Affricates [tʃ, dʒ]. These two sounds combine complete obstruction of the vocal tract with release which is in part plosive and in part fricative, i.e., in part abrupt and in part gradual.

4. Nasals [m, n, ŋ]. These sounds are formed by closing the passageway through the mouth and relaxing and lowering the soft palate so as to open the posterior entrance into the nasal passage. Hence they are characterized by dominant resonance in the nasal and nasopharyngeal cavities, and in the English language are the only sounds which are properly nasalized. For [m] with its bilabial closure the entire mouth cavity serves as a closed-end resonator; for [n] with its lingua-rugal closure the mouth cavity is a smaller resonator; and for [ŋ] the lingua-velar closure at the back of the mouth shuts it off entirely as a resonator. Nasals are like vowels in their resonant, tonal characteristic and in the fact that they sometimes serve as syllables. For example, in substandard utterance when [m] follows [p] or [b], it is often syllabic in such words or phrases as [opm̩] for *open* or [dipm̩waɪd] for *deep and wide.* [n] is more often syllabic, especially when it follows one of its cognate lingua-rugal sounds in such words as *button* [bʌtn̩], *kitten* [kɪtn̩], *reason* [rizn̩].

Acoustic classification. The final method of classifying consonants is in terms of voicing.

1. Voiceless [p, t, k, f, θ, s, ʃ, h]. In these sounds the vocal bands are abducted, i.e., the glottis is open and the breath flows past

them without causing vibrations. The moving breath produces a friction-like noise at the point of greatest obstruction which, of course, is different for each sound.

2. Voiced [b, m, d, n, g, ŋ, v, ð, z, ʒ]. For these sounds (except the nasals) the glottis remains partially open so that the outflowing breath produces a friction-like noise as in the voiceless sounds but at the same time the vocal bands are tense and adducted closely enough so that the breath pressure causes them to vibrate. Acoustically, therefore, voiced consonants are combinations of tone and noise. (Review the section on phonation in Chapter 14.)

On the basis of the facts so far given we can now describe the various consonants briefly as follows:

/p/   Voiceless bilabial stop-plosive, as in *pat* [pæt], *apple* [æpl̩], *top* [tɑp].

/b/   Voiced bilabial stop-plosive, as in *bat* [bæt], *above* [əbʌv], *crab* [kræb].

/m/   Voiced bilabial nasal, as in *most* [most], *hammer* [hæmɚ], *beam* [bim]. Notice also the spellings in psa*lm*, la*mb*, anthe*mn*, sha*me*, phleg*m*.

/t/   Voiceless lingua-rugal stop-plosive, as in *tin* [tɪn], *attire* [ətaɪɚ], *cat* [kæt]. Other spellings are *Th*ames, tau*ght*, in*d*ict, tripp*ed*, de*bt*.

/d/   Voiced lingua-rugal stop-plosive, as in *dot* [dɑt], *medal* [mɛdl̩], *add* [æd]. Other spellings are fa*de*, woul*d*, rud*dy*.

/n/   Voiced lingua-rugal nasal, as in *not* [nɑt], *honey* [hʌnɪ], *done* [dʌn]. Other spellings are *pn*eumograph, *gn*at, *kn*owledge, *Wedn*esday.

/k/   Voiceless lingua-velar stop-plosive, as in **can** [kæn], *account* [əkaʊnt], *pack* [pæk]. Other spellings are ta*lk*, bi*ck*er, pla*que*, a*ch*e, lac*qu*er.

/g/   Voiced lingua-velar stop-plosive, as in *goat* [got], *bigger* [bɪgɚ], *egg* [ɛg]. Other spellings are *gh*ost, ro*gue*.

/ŋ/   Voiced lingua-velar nasal, as in *thing* [θɪŋ], *bang* [bæŋ]. It is also spelled with *n* when followed by lingua-velar [k] or [g] as in i*n*k and mi*n*gle. A few words spelled with the letters *ng* are pronounced with both [ŋ] and [g] as in *single* [sɪŋgl̩] or *finger* [fɪŋgɚ], although many words with the same spelling are pronounced without the [g] and with [ŋ] only as in *singer* [sɪŋɚ], *wringer* [rɪŋɚ].

/f/   Voiceless labiodental fricative, as in *fine* [faɪn], *rifle* [raɪf!], *tough* [tʌf]. Other spellings are *p*hantom, cal*f*, wi*fe*.

/v/   Voiced labiodental fricative, as in *vow* [vaʊ], *invest* [ɪnvɛst], *have* [hæv].

/θ/   Voiceless linguadental fricative, as in *thin* [θɪn], *nothing* [nʌθɪŋ], *tooth* [tuθ].

/ð/   Voiced linguadental fricative, as in *these* [ðiz], *father* [fɑðɚ], *loathe* [loð].

/s/   Voiceless lingua-rugal concentrated fricative, as in *see* [si], *assess* [əsɛs], *us* [ʌs]. Other spellings are fa*c*e, loo*s*e, *c*ent, *p*sychology, *s*cience, thi*s*tle.

/z/   Voiced lingua-rugal concentrated fricative, as in *zeal* [zil], *seizing* [sizɪŋ], *buzz* [bʌz]. Other spellings are know*s*, posse*ss*, *cz*ar, the*s*e, ho*s*e.

In the sounds [s] and [z] the sides of the tongue are raised to contact the teeth and gums and the center is depressed to form a channel through which a concentrated stream of breath flows to strike the upper teeth and produce the characteristic high-pitched hiss.

/ʃ/   Voiceless lingua-palatal distributed fricative, as in *shame* [ʃem], *assure* [əʃuɚ], *ash* [æʃ]. Other spellings are *s*ugar, ma*ch*ine, mo*ti*on.

/ʒ/   Voiced lingua-palatal distributed fricative, as in *version* [vɝʒən], *garage* [gərɑʒ], *azure* [æʒuɚ].

In the sounds [ʃ] and [ʒ] the upper surface of the tongue is relatively flat so that the stream of air striking the teeth is broad or distributed. The lips are usually rounded.

/tʃ/   Voiceless lingua-palatal affricate, as in *chair* [tʃɛɚ], *question* [kwɛstʃən], *beach* [bitʃ]. Other spellings are a*ct*ual, na*t*ural, tin*ct*ure.

/dʒ/   Voiced lingua-palatal affricate, as in *jam* [dʒæm], *agile* [ædʒəl], *judge* [dʒʌdʒ].

/h/   Voiceless glottal fricative, as in *had* [hæd], *who* [hu], *ahead* [əhɛd]. This is a highly variable phoneme usually having some of the quality of the nearest vowel.

GLIDES

In its most general sense *glide* refers to the transitory noises which are produced as the organs of articulation move from the position for one sound unit to another in the continuous flow of utterance. These changes at the beginning and end of each sound have been called the "on-glide" and "off-glide."

This general gliding movement of the organs of articulation, however, should not be confused with a more definitely phonemic kind of action. As we shall understand the concept, a glide is a speech sound or phoneme characterized by a continuous gliding movement of some part of the articulating system. More precisely stated: *A glide is a speech sound produced while the articulating organs are moving without interruption from the approximate position for one vowel toward that for another vowel during a single breath pulse.* These typical movements are stable and distinctive enough to occur repeatedly as standard elements in word formation. The element of constancy for each glide phoneme is a distinctive kind of *movement*, just as the element of constancy for phonemes of other classes is a characteristic *position* of the articulating organs.

Descriptions of the glides are usually stated in terms of the positions at which the movements typically begin and end, but the particular articulating organs involved and the direction of movement are also characteristic for each phoneme. There are two subclasses of glides, consonant glides and diphthongs. In their principal characteristics these two groups of phonemes are directly opposite to each other.

Consonant glides. These are characterized by a movement of the articulating organs from a less open to more open position on a single breath pulse. The glide begins at a position which closely approximates one of the high vowels, [i], [ɝ], or [u], but is usually more closely narrowed so as to form a small amount of obstruction which produces a slightly fricative noise at the beginning of the sound. The noise element continues only for an instant, and immediately changes to a resonant vowel-like quality as the movement opens the vocal tract more widely. The greater openness builds up resonance so that there is an increase of stress which reaches its full force in the vowel marking the end of the glide. You can easily observe this by speaking the syllables [jɑ], [rɑ], [wɑ], and noting the increase of intensity as the vocal passage opens.

The primary function of consonant glides in word and phrase formation is to accentuate the boundaries of syllables. Even in words like *cream* [krim], *view* [vju], *splash* [splæʃ], *twin* [twɪn], in which the glides are not actually the first sounds, they are nevertheless parts of the boundaries of the syllables. When sounds having acoustic qualities similar to [j], [r], or [w] occur after vowels or at the ends of syllables, they usually acquire vowel-like characteristics and become the final elements in diphthongs. For these we use vowel symbols. Note, for example, that the movement for [jɑ] reversed is [ɑɪ] or [aɪ], that [rɑ] when reversed is [ɑɝ], that [wɑ] reversed is [ɑu]; and that none of these diphthongs involves any appreciable fricative or consonantal element such as occurs in the consonantal glides. (See the section on diphthongs below.)

/j/   Voiced front-tongue glide, lips unrounded, as in *year, you, yell*. The movement is from the approximate position for [i] or [ɪ] to the position for the vowel which follows. Other spellings are mill*i*on, spec*u*late, v*i*ew, m*ew*, imb*ue*, b*eau*ty.

Use: In some words such as *duty, Jew, suit, chew, news, tune*, usage varies between [ju] and [u]. In other words such as *pewter, few, cuticle, view*, [ju] is clearly established. In certain pairs of words, such as *blew* and *blue, dew* and *do, pure* and *poor, mew* and *moo*, the difference between [ju] and [u] is phonemic, that is, an aid to discrimination between meanings.

/r/   Voiced, tip and front tongue glide; an uninterrupted movement from the position for [ɝ] to whatever vowel follows. The lips are usually protruded and rounded at the beginning of the glide. As with [j], the entire phoneme includes at least as many allophones as there are distinguishable vowel positions on which the glide ends. Typical spelling is *r*, although a few variations occur as *wr* in *write* and *rh* in *rhetoric*.

Use: In the English language there are several sounds (some glides, some fricatives, some trills) which have a characteristic quality like that of the vowel [ɝ]. For convenience they are referred to as *r* sounds. In narrow transcription various symbols are used, but for our purposes most of the variations and fine distinctions may be overlooked. We describe the sound as a glide having the functions of a consonant (i.e., it always forms the boundaries of syllables), and use the symbol [r] to distinguish it from the *r*-colored vowels, [ɝ] and [ɚ].

/w/   Voiced bilabial glide from closely rounded lips to whatever vowel follows. The starting position is approximately that for the vowel [u] but typically a little more closed especially when a high vowel such as [u] or [ʊ] follows.

Use: Many speakers use this voiced [w] instead of the voiceless [wh] in words spelled *wh* as *when, where, why*. In certain paired words, such as *watt* and *what, wear* and *where, wen* and *when*, the distinction is important even though the difference may often be inferred from context.

/ʍ/ or   Voiceless bilabial glide, produced in similar manner to [w]
/wh/   except that the vocal bands do not vibrate until the articulating

organs have reached or almost reached their position for the following vowel.

/l/   Voiced lateral tongue glide, as in *lean, blue, all, parallel*. Notice that in some words spelled with *l* the sound does not actually occur in normal pronunciation, as in *psalm* [sɑm], *calf* [kæf], *walk* [wɔk], *salmon* [sæmən]. The sound is characterized by a narrow tongue with its tip against the upper gum ridge so as to form a divided or bilateral tone passage. The stream of sound waves is thus emitted around the two sides of the tongue. When [l] is at the beginning of a syllable, the glide is toward the position for whatever vowel follows with the tip of the tongue moving down toward its normal position of rest behind the lower front teeth. When [l] is final, the glide is reversed and the tongue moves from the preceding vowel position to its narrowed shape with tip against the upper gums.

Use: In final position [l] is sometimes syllabic, as for example in *cattle* [kætl̩], *bubble* [bʌbl̩], *muddle* [mʌdl̩], *pommel* [pʌml̩], *brothel* [brɑθl̩], *thistle* [θɪsl̩].

Diphthongs. Most of us have been taught to regard a diphthong as a combination of two vowels. The word "diphthong," in fact, means two sounds. Although this is a convenient and useful description, a more accurate statement is the following: A *diphthong is a glide produced on a single breath pulse in one continuous movement from a relatively open vowel position to another less open vowel position.* The decrease in size of resonating cavities results in a decrease of intensity or stress, so that the final element of the sound is an off-glide which is acoustically weaker than the beginning. These sounds are essentially like vowels in resonant quality, absence of noise, and syllabic function.

Theoretically there are as many diphthongs as there are possible movements from more open to less open vowels or vowel variants. In actual utterance, however, only a limited number of them are sufficiently frequent and distinctive to be recognized as phonemes. Many of the other possible movements are merely variant allophones of the significant sounds.

If you look again at the vowel chart, you will see that movements from more open to less open positions are most likely to terminate at or near one of the three highest vowel positions, those for [i], [u], or [ɝ]. More accurately we should say they terminate at the relative positions for [ɪ], [ʊ], or [ɚ] because the final element of a diphthong is the weak or unaccented off-glide. On this basis we recognize 11 distinct diphthongs, which can be classified conveniently according to their endings, as follows:

<table>
<tr><td>

Group I
Ending in [ɪ] or [i]

[aɪ] as in *buy*
[ɔɪ] as in *boy*
[eɪ] as in *bay*

Group II
Ending in [ʊ] or [u]

[oʊ] as in *beau*
[ɑʊ] as in *bough*

</td><td>

Group III
Ending in [ɚ] or [ə]

[ɪɚ] or [ɪə] as in *ear*
[ɛɚ] or [ɛə] as in *air*
[ɑɚ] or [a:] as in *are*
[ɔɚ] or [ɔə[as in *or*
[oɚ] or [oə] as in *oar*
[ʊɚ] or [ʊə] as in *poor*

These are often called "centering diphthongs" because they end in a central vowel [ɚ] or [ə].

</td></tr>
</table>

In regard to [eɪ] and [oʊ] refer back to the discussion of the vowels [e] and [o]. They are usually diphthongized except possibly before stopped consonants. In actual utterance many of our vowels are diphthongized to a slight extent, but these two more than others.

Continuity of Utterance

Now that we have surveyed the various units—phrase, syllable, phoneme—which make up the audible part of our speech, we should study their relationship in the sequence of utterance and the principal ways in which they influence each other. This is obviously a complex subject which we can study here only in most general terms. We shall limit our consideration to four topics which seem to be most important— rhythm, accent, assimilation, and juncture and blending.

RHYTHM

Most of us are inclined to think of rhythm as a regular pattern or beat in the alternation of strong and weak impulses. Musical rhythm, for example, has a high degree of regularity; and there is also a sameness of pattern in the accents of metrical poetry. In propositional speech such as conversation, discussion, public speaking, or any matter-of-fact reading of prose, the regularity tends to disappear but the pattern of weak and strong accents is no less important. In its larger and more general aspect the rhythm of speech is based on the succession of pauses and phrases, but its more specific and detailed aspect is the alternation of strong and weak syllables within the phrases. In normal utterance the phrases vary in length and the pattern of syllabic accent changes constantly. Rhythm in speech does not require regularity, but it does require definiteness in the alternation of contrasting elements—silence and sound, strong syllables and weak. Every speaker should develop at least some sensitivity to the rhythmic patterns of his utterance, whether they are elemental and regular or complex and variable. Speech can scarcely go "trippingly on the tongue," as Shakespeare advised, unless it is well phrased and the accents are properly distributed.

Speak the following words and phrases, for example, and observe the rhythmic variations:

thĕ bóy	[ðə 'bɒɪ]
précèpt	['pri ˌsɛpt]
bánk nóte	['bæŋk 'not]
stárs and strípes	['stɑɚz n̩ 'straɪps]
thĕ póstmăn	[ðə 'post mən]
ìn thĕ mórning	[ˌɪn ðə 'mɒɚnɪŋ]
phì lós ŏ phў	[fɪ 'lɑs ə fɪ]
cŏn gràt ŭ lá tiŏn	[kən ˌgræt ju 'le ʃən]
rĕ spòn sĭ bíl ĭ tў	[rɪ ˌspɑn sə 'bɪl ə tɪ]
ù nĭ vér sĭ tў	[ˌju nə 'vɚ sə tɪ]

Notice the wide differences between strong and weak syllables, and their various patterns of alternation. There are sequences of weak-strong syllables, strong-weak, strong-strong, strong-weak-strong, weak-strong-weak, and various combinations of these in words and phrases of four, five, and six syllables. Observe also the longer and more complex sequences of rhythmic patterns in sentences:

1. Ìn thĕ mórnĭng /   thĕ bóy /
[ˌɪn ðə 'mɒɚnɪŋ /   ðə 'bɒɪ /
toók thĕ stárs ănd strípes /   tŏ thĕ ùnĭvérsĭtў.
'tuk ðə 'stɑɚz n̩ 'straɪps /   tə ðə ˌju nə 'vɚ sə tɪ].

2. Ă sýmphŏnў órchĕstră /   cŏnsísts ŏf twó básĭc élĕmĕnts
[ə 'sɪm fə nɪ 'ɔɚ kəs trə /   kən 'sɪsts əv 'tu 'be sɪk 'ɛl ə mənts].

3. Órătòrў /   ìs the árt /   ŏf ènchántĭng thĕ sóul
['ɒɚ ə ˌtɒɚɪ /   ˌɪz ðə 'ɑɚt /   əv ˌɛn 'tʃæn tɪŋ ðə 'soʊl].

ACCENT

We have already referred to accent in the section on pitch variety of Chapter 15, pointing out that it is a complex factor in which loudness and duration of tone and change of pitch, or at least two of these three variables, are combined. Accented syllables have relatively greater loudness, longer duration, and wider pitch change than un-accented syllables. The proportion of these elements present in any given accented syllable is variable for different speakers and for any single speaker under varied circumstances and in changing contexts of utterance.

The English language and especially our pronunciation in the

United States, is characterized by wide differences in degree of stress. This has two areas of significance. First, as we have already seen, stress is a means of emphasis which helps to show the relative value of words or the difference between more important and less important ideas; this is "sense stress." Second, accent is an important element in the formation of words and phrases. Notice, for example, what happens to a word like *university* if we shift the primary accent and say, *ùn ĭ věr sĭty,* as though it were some peculiar kind of city. Similar confusion of meaning would result from such a drastic change of accent in almost any word or phrase of several syllables.

Actually these two kinds of stress or reasons for stressing usually coincide and reinforce each other. Words of one syllable present no problem, since they receive whatever degree of stress is required by the meaning. Words of several syllables receive their sense stress on whatever syllable has the primary accent in formation of the word. Notice this union of accents in such words as *university, orchestra, elements, oratory,* and *enchanting.*

If we were to indicate all the subtle variations in our pronunciation, we would have to use many different marks. For practical purposes, however, the many variations are reduced to a few main levels each of which includes some range of difference. One basic scheme designates four degrees of accent: (1) primary or strong indicated by the acute stress mark (′); (2) secondary indicated by the circumflex (^); (3) tertiary indicated by the grave (`); and (4) weak or unaccented indicated by the breve (ˇ). In this system the third level is significant primarily for certain special distinctions of meaning as, for example, between such contrasted phrases as *grêen hóuse* (any dwelling of green color) and *gréenhoùse* (a special botanical building); *blŭe bírd* (any bird of blue color) and *blúebìrd* (a particular species). The three-level system used in our illustrations has only one medium or secondary level represented by the grave (`). Primary (′) and weak (ˇ) levels remain as indicated. Notice that all these marks are usually placed directly above the vocalized nucleus of a syllable.

The I.P.A. transcription uses a different system as shown in the illustrations. Strong or primary accent is indicated by a vertical mark just above and in front of the syllable, and secondary accent by a similar mark just below and in front of the syllable. You will observe that no special mark is used for weak syllables. The reason, as set forth in the description of individual vowel sounds, is that the vowels of unaccented syllables are usually reduced to the vowel murmur [ə] or the r-colored [ɚ] so that no special sign is needed.

ASSIMILATION

We have referred several times to the influence which speech sounds exert on each other. Assimilation is the most important of these influences. We might analyze in detail the sequences of movement and the effects which the various kinds of sounds—stops, fricatives, nasals, glides, and vowels both front and back—exert on each other in the continuous flow of utterance; but such detail must be left for specialized courses in phonetics. We shall have to be content with citation of a few typical examples:

1. The word *cats* [kæts] ends in [s] whereas *cads* [kædz] ends in [z] because of the influence of the preceding consonant in each case. Voiceless [t] is followed by voiceless [s], whereas the vocal vibrations of [d] are carried forward into the [z] of *cads*. This is a progressive change in voicing.

2. Have you heard [hæf tu] for *have to?* Anticipation of voiceless [t] changed the vocalized [v] to voiceless [f]. This is a substandard regressive change in voicing.

3. Place of obstruction for a final stopped consonant is usually influenced by a preceding front or back vowel. Notice, for example, that the obstruction for [k] after [i] in *teak* is farther forward than after [ɔ] in *talk*. This is a progressive change in place of obstruction.

4. *Income tax* is sometimes heard as [ɪŋkəm tæks] because the lingua-velar obstruction for [k] is anticipated and so changes the lingua-rugal [n] to lingua-velar [ŋ]. This is a substandard regressive change in place of obstruction.

5. In a word like *Christian* overly meticulous people may take pains to keep the [s] and [t] distinct, thus saying [krɪs tjən] while a more casual speaker will say [krɪs tʃən]. In the casual utterance the [t] and [j] exert a mutual influence on each other and are combined by a reciprocal change in both place of obstruction and manner of release to form [tʃ]. Changes of this kind are found in a number of words such as *virtue* and *nature*. In a similar group of words the fricative [s] or [z] is combined with [j] to form [ʃ] or [ʒ], as in *mission* [mɪʃən) instead of [mɪsjən] or *vision* [vɪʒən] instead of [vɪsjən].

6. Occasionally sounds are lost entirely as a result of assimilation. Observe the standard pronunciations of *cupboard* as [kʌbɚd], *comptroller* as [kəntrolɚ] and *horseshoe* as [hɔɚʃu]. In *cupboard* the [b] has absorbed its voiceless cognate [p]. In *comptroller* anticipation of [t] has changed the sound cluster [mp] to [n]. In *horseshoe* anticipation of [ʃ] often absorbs [s]. Although these instances of elision are acceptable, others such as [sʌmpm̩] for *something*, [gʊbaɪ] for *good-bye*, and [lɛmɪ] for *let me* are substandard.

Observe the varieties of change in these examples. First, there are changes in direction of influence. Assimilation is progressive when a characteristic of one sound is carried forward into a following sound; it is regressive when a characteristic of one sound is anticipated in the formation of a preceding sound; and reciprocal when two successive sounds mutually influence each other. These influences may affect either voicing, place of obstruction, or manner of release. In some instances the change is a minor shift from one allophone to another within the same phoneme, while in other cases an entirely different phoneme is produced. Sometimes the result is a usage which is entirely acceptable; at other times it is substandard. The question of standards will be discussed in a later section.

JUNCTURE AND BLENDING

Juncture deals with the relationship between the closing sound of one syllable and the initiating sound of the following syllable. These relationships are of two kinds, open and closed. Open junctures include pauses between phrases, which we have already studied (see Chapters 4 and 15), and the slight pauses which sometimes must occur between syllables within phrases if the sense is not to be confused. Closed junctures are the normal transitions in which there is unbroken movement from the final sound of one syllable to the initial sound of the next.

A special case of blending or reciprocal assimilation occurs when the successive concluding and initiating sounds of two syllables are both stop-plosives, as in *stopgap*. The first [p] is formed entirely as an obstructing movement which terminates the vowel [ɑ]. Behind the bilabial closure for [p] the back of the tongue is raised to make the obstruction for [g]. Audible plosion is heard only when [g] is released into its following vowel [æ]. The obstructions for [p] and [g] together form a continuous closure during the transition. Each stop-plosive is modified by the presence of the other; the first [p] becomes stop only, while the [g] is plosive only. They have been blended or assimilated to each other so as to form a closed juncture between the two syllables. When the closing and initiating stop-plosives are of the same phoneme, as in the phrases *top part* and *stop-plosive*, the transition between syllables is merely a delayed release of the obstruction. When the boundary between syllables is a fricative, as in *missent*, the transition is merely a slightly prolonged duration. In any such instances the use of an open juncture or pause between the syllables probably would seem overly careful and labored.

An especially significant kind of juncture occurs between two syllables of which the first ends in a consonant and the second begins with a vowel, as in the phrase *it is*. Try repeating this rapidly and you will soon find yourself saying, *i-tis* [ɪ ˈtɪz] instead of *it is* [ɪt ɪz]. Or if you say the word *at* rapidly, you will soon be saying, *ta-ta-ta* [tæ-tæ-tæ]. The consonant [t] has shifted from its obstructing or terminal function in the first syllable to an initial or releasing function in the next syllable. Other kinds of sounds, such as fricatives or nasals, may also blend in this way, as when the phrase *stars and stripes* [stɑɹz n̩ straɪps] becomes [stɑɹ zən straɪps]. In such rapid conversational utterance a certain amount of such blending is inevitable unless our speech is to sound labored and overly meticulous.

We should be aware, however, that in some consonant-vowel

junctures such a degree of blending may easily cause confusion of meaning. Compare *an ice man* with *a nice man*, and *an aim* with *a name*. The place and function of the first [n] makes a real difference in the message communicated. In other cases, such as change of *fried egg* to *frei degg* [fraɪ dɛg], the confusion is not so great but recognition of meaning may still be hindered or at least delayed. In such cases the closed juncture, in which the terminal sound of one syllable becomes the releasing sound of the next, must be replaced by an open juncture or slight pause to keep the syllables distinct. There is similar need for pause or open juncture between two accented syllables such as *play pen* or *handwork*. In every case, of course, maintenance of distinct impulses of breath power and voice for the successive syllables is a basic requirement; but the use of open juncture between the syllables within a phrase is sometimes an important additional dividing element which enhances clarity of meaning.

Standards of Pronunciation

All the complex variations of speech sounds, which we have barely glimpsed in the preceding sections, give urgency to the questions: What is correct pronunciation? How can we know what is right? The answer is that we seldom can know what is right or correct in any final or absolute sense. We should think instead in terms of standard or substandard usage, effective or ineffective forms. The adequacy of any given utterance is dependent upon the circumstances in which it is spoken—the formality or informality of the occasion, the established linguistic customs of the community, the nature of the subject matter, the relationship between speaker and listener or listeners, and their auditory sensitivity and phonetic sophistication. There are standards, indeed, and we should seek them diligently; but they are not to be found in any superior authoritarian body of people or set of rules. Standards evolve along with linguistic development and change.

Many people, because of a desire for some firm and dependable standard elevate the dictionary to a position of supreme authority and quote it with assurance and finality. But what is *the* dictionary? Which one? Many dictionaries are available and they do not always agree. Dictionaries, moreover, by their very nature cannot adequately record words as they are spoken in the continuity of daily use. When words are considered singly with attention directed to them as words, the inevitable tendency is to overlook or minimize the effects of continuity in phrasing. A dictionary word is, in part at least, a formalized word which cannot have the rhythm nor the subtle assimilations and blendings of normal speech.

Modern dictionary makers do not, in fact, pose as arbiters of authoritarian standards. Their primary function is to serve as reporters of usage. They devote years of time, millions of dollars, and more millions of scholarly and expert man hours to collect and interpret specific evidence of language customs, including those of pronunciation. A dictionary "shows as far as possible the pronunciations prevailing in general cultivated conversational usage, both informal and formal, throughout the English speaking world. It does not attempt to dictate what the usage should be."[1]

Dictionaries are invaluable and should be in constant use by every thoughtful person, especially by students of language and speech. We should refer to them for information about new and unfamiliar words and for renewal of our understanding of words already known. Every dictionary should be used in the light of its purposes and scope. Students of speech in the United States, for example, should have access to Kenyon and Knott's A Pronouncing Dictionary of American English. For reliable information about standard pronunciation among the educated classes of southern England, Daniel Jones' An English Pronouncing Dictionary is likewise unique and indispensable.

A primary source of problems in pronunciation is the wide variety of dialects with which English is spoken. The major dialects are generally well recognized. The differences between British and American pronunciation, for example, are matters of common though often inaccurate knowledge; and many of their major subdialects—such as Scottish, Irish, and Welch in the British Isles, and Eastern, Southern and Western in the United States—are also commonly known as are many of the more local dialects within each of these areas.

These impressions about dialect areas in the United States have been confirmed in their general scope, but also extended and made more exact by field studies of linguistic geography initiated by the Modern Language Association in 1928. The terms North, South and Midland have been suggested as more realistic names for area divisions than Eastern, Southern, and General American. Extension of the field work west of the Appalachian Mountains indicates that the dividing lines between these areas may extend to the Mississippi River and even beyond.

Although our regional divisions are significant, the general similarity of our pronunciation and the relative ease with which people in all parts of the country understand each other are even more significant. Major forces are at work which tend to promote uniformity. The great media of mass communication, radio and television, enable us to hear speakers from all parts of the country. Most of our professionals in broadcasting use the General American or Midland standard which is already numerically superior. Rapidly increasing ease and distance of travel are making us more cosmopolitan and tending to merge us into

[1] Webster's Third New International Dictionary, preface, p. 6a.

a single large linguistic community. The outcome is likely to be a continued minimizing of differences; and, we hope, some preserving of those features of all dialects which are most effective for communication and most truly representative of our culture. Probably the General American standard will continue to prevail, but some regional variations and dialects will always be with us.

In broadest terms one standard is primary: Is utterance clearly and immediately understood? This, of course, must assume a listener with normal hearing and desire to listen. It should also assume voice and articulation which achieve precision without strained effort, and flexibility without slovenliness or distortion. Articulation and pronunciation may be inadequate in either of two ways: (1) They may be strained and overly precise so as to call attention to themselves and interfere with communication. Tense and poorly coordinated vocal habits are involved here, as well as failure to observe rhythm and the wide variations in accent which characterize American speech. (2) They may be careless and indistinct. Substandard utterance of this kind involves disorderly phrasing; improper use of assimilation, blending and juncture; as well as inversion, substitution or omission of sounds. The ideal is a happy medium between these two extremes. The best articulation and pronunciation combine precision with ease and flexibility. This is the key to maximum intelligibility.

Distinct articulation as we have seen, depends on (1) good phrasing and orderly sequence of thought units, (2) adequate breath power and control, (3) freedom and flexibility of the articulating organs, and (4) sensitive auditory discrimination. Adequate or standard pronunciation requires in addition (1) choice of the right sound combinations (2) uttered in their standard linguistic order (3) with proper distribution of accent and (4) with such degrees of assimilation and blending and such uses of juncture as will contribute to economy of effort and ease of utterance without reducing clarity or effectiveness of communication.

Effectiveness of communication, however, is primarily a utilitarian standard. To it should be added the pride which all people feel in the unique cultural traditions and practices of their own communities. The distinctive speech of a region or a nation is not the least of such traditions. Standards of pronunciation, like many other conventional habits in social life, are determined by the consensus of practice among the most influential members of a community, whether it be a suburban area, a city, a region set apart by geographical boundaries, or an entire nation. Within any given area the speech habits are most largely influenced by the educated and linguistically sensitive members of the community.

Adequate or good articulation and pronunciation are not to be found engraved on any tablets of stone. They are to be attained only by constant listening to the usage of people around us; by thoughtful study and analysis of what we hear; by frequent reference to dictionary records of pronunciation; and by continued practice and self-evaluation to clarify our own habits and bring them into such agreement with the usage of our communities, local and general, as will meet both aesthetic and utilitarian requirements.

As a beginning of your observations, notice several common kinds of pronunciation habits which are often considered substandard or which interfere with clarity of communication:

1. Substitution of one phoneme for another

/n/ for /ŋ/	as in *talkin'* [tɔkɪn] for *talking* [tɔkɪŋ]
	as in *singin'* [sɪŋɪn] for *singing* [sɪŋɪŋ]
/t/ for /θ/	as in [tɪk] for *thick* [θɪk]
	as in [tɪn] for *thin* [θɪn]
/z/ for /s/	as in [ɪnkriz] for *increase* [ɪnkris]
	as in [əbzɝd] for *absurd* [əbsɝd]
/tʃ/ for /dz/	as in [ɛtʃ] for *edge* [ɛdʒ]
	as in [tʃʌtʃ] for *judge* [dʒʌdʒ]
/w/ for /wh/	as in [waɪt] for *white* [whaɪt]
	as in [waɪl] for *while* [whaɪl]
/θ/ for /ð/	as in [wɪθ] for *with* [wɪð]
	as in [hɪθɚ] for *hither* [hɪðɚ]
/ɪ/ for /ɛ/	as in [mɪn] for *men* [mɛn]
	as in [gɪt] for *get* [gɛt]

2. Addition of sounds or syllables

/g/ as when *singer* [sɪŋɚ] becomes [sɪŋgɚ]
/j/ as when *column* [kɑləm] becomes [kɑljəm]
/ə/ as when *athletic* [æθlɛtɪk] becomes [æθələtɪk]
/h/ as when *vehement* [viəmənt] becomes [vəhimənt]

3. Inversions of sounds

as in [mɑdrən] for *modern* [mɑdɚn]
as in [lɛɚnɪks] for *larynx* [lɛɚɪŋks]

4. Omission of sounds

/d/ as in [fʌnəmɛntl̩] for *fundamental* [fʌndəmɛntl̩]
/g/ as in [rɛkənaɪz] for *recognize* [rɛkəgnaɪz]
/b/ as in [prɑblɪ] for *probably* [prɑbəblɪ]
/k/ as in [æsɛsərɪ] for *accessory* [æksɛsərɪ]

5. Difficult combinations of consonants from which one element is lost in pronunciation

/sts/ as when *tests* becomes [tɛs] or *ghosts* becomes [gos]
thz /ðz/ as when *clothes* [kloðz] becomes [kloz]

tsht /tʃt/ as when *watched* [wɑtʃt] becomes [wɑʃt]
kst /kst/ as when *next* [nɜkst] becomes [nɛks]
ndlz /ndlz/ as when *candles* [kændlz] becomes [kænlz]
dnt /dnt/ as when *didn't* [dɪdnt] becomes [dɪnt]

EXERCISES

1. The following selection includes all the phonemes of our English sound system and many common sound combinations. Make a recording and study your articulation, phrasing, accent, and uses of assimilation, juncture, and blending. Do you notice any habits which interfere with clarity of meaning or are substandard in usage?

It is a pleasure to visit the little town named Homedale, which is not far south of here. Life in Homedale is peaceful and quiet. There are only five stores and one garage along the main street of this little town. Most of the things needed by people who live there can be found in these few places of business. Perhaps the one and only drugstore in Homedale is the busiest place in town. It is the very hub of activity. No doubt the reason is that the greatest variety of things is to be found there. Among the items supplied for sale are children's toys and other playthings. Also there are books both large and small, dishes, cups, saucers, perfumes, zippers and kitchen articles of every sort. In fact unless you look closely you will never find the little smooth counter back in the corner where drugs are sold. Along one wall is the soda fountain. The old druggist known as "Judge" Philip has a wife who takes great pride in her mixtures of ice cream, charged water and flavoring. She is affectionately known as "Maw" Philip. Her sodas always fizz and gurgle. They are very delightful to her many young customers who come during the noon-hour lunch period and after school. So you see, Homedale's drugstore is the center of buzzing activity.

2. In similar manner record one of the selections given for practice in Chapters 10 or 15 or restudy any recording of your speech made earlier in the course, and evaluate your habits of articulation and pronunciation.

3. For practice in transcription as well as assistance in analyzing your patterns of utterance, transcribe one of your recordings in I.P.A. symbols.

4. Practice pairs of words to clarify the distinctions between vowel and glide phonemes, especially those which are often confused or substituted for each other or which you find confused in your own pronunciation. Begin with the following pairs and build up your own extended list from vowel substitutions which you hear in others or discover in your own utterance.

/i/–/ɪ/

beet [bit]–bit [bɪt]
feet [fit]–fit [fɪt]
greet [grit]–grit [grɪt]

/ɪ/–/ɛ/

mit [mɪt]–met [mɛt]
bit [bɪt]–bet [bɛt]
sit [sɪt]–set [sɛt]

/ɑ/–/ɔ/

tot [tɑt]–taught [tɔt]
cot [kɑt]–caught [kɔt]
not [nɑt]–naught [nɔt]

/u/–/ʊ/

boot [but]–book [bʊk]
lute [lut]–look [lʊk]
coot [kut]–cook [kʊk]

/ʌ/–/ɝ/

but [bʌt]–Bert [bɝt]
cut [kʌt]–curt [kɝt]
shut [ʃʌt]–shirt [ʃɝt]

/ɪu/–/u/

chew [tʃɪu]–choose [tʃuz]
news [nɪuz]–noose [nus]
beauty [bɪutɪ]–booty [butɪ]

/e/–/ɛ/

bait [bet]–bet [bɛt]
date [det]–debt [dɛt]
gate [get]–get [gɛt]

/æ/–/ɑ/

cat [kæt]–cot [kɑt]
map [mæp]–mop [mɑp]
flap [flæp]–flop [flɑp]

/ɔ/–/o/

bought [bɔt]–boat [bot]
flaw [flɔ]–float [flot]
raw [rɔ]–wrote [rot]

/ʊ/–/ʌ/

put [pʊt]–putt [pʌt]
took [tʊk]–tuck [tʌk]
could [kʊd]–cud [kʌd]

/ɑu/–/ɒɪ/

bough [bɑu]–boy [bɒɪ]
owl [ɑul]–oil [ɒɪl]
towel [tɑul]–toil [tɒɪl]

/ɛɚ/–/ɑɚ/

fair [fɛɚ]–far [fɑɚ]
dare [dɛɚ]–dark [dɑɚk]
care [kɛɚ]–car [kɑɚ]

5. Repeat the following as *precisely* and as *rapidly* as you can:

How much wood would a wood chuck chuck if a wood chuck could chuck wood?

Lester likes lemons lovelier while Peter prefers peppers peeled. Still Sue savours sweets silently, as Aggie articulates adages addicts admire.

The baby buggy, bulging badly, barged between Bob and Barbara.

Ten tins tied together tightly tipped the trailer. Dazed, ditched Don dragged drearily dextrally.

Can cotton candy coat clean, cold combs? Golly, guesses gone goofy gum great geniuses.

6. Stand about 5 feet from a classmate and pronounce various words *without sound.* You must exaggerate the words so that the eyewitness can attempt to read your lips. Graduate from words of a single syllable, to polysyllabic words, then phrases, then sentences. Finally, speak (without sound) sentences in a "normal" manner. Repeat at least 5 examples of each category.

7. Study the pronunciations of words in the following groups, comparing the sounds given in two or three different dictionaries. Include at least Kenyon and Knott's A *Pronouncing Dictionary of American English* and

Webster's Third New International Dictionary. If you find variant pronunciations, which of them are most frequently used or considered standard in your community or region? What typical fault of pronunciation is most common for the words in each group?

Group I

actually	geography	pumpkin	gentlemen
arctic	government	recognize	president
candidate	library	suggest	chocolate
diamond	poem	usual	library
figure	probably	violent	temperature

Group II

across	girl	often	sword
car	grievous	preventive	toward
calm	height	mayoralty	umbrella
film	blackguard	salmon	obtrusive
forehead	mischievous	subtle	Washington

Group III

amenable	financier	diphthong	pronunciation
apparatus	gesture	experiment	sacrilegious
breeches	heinous	just	status
catch	hiccough	penalize	virile
February	Italian	process	zoology

Group IV

abdomen	exquisite	integral	pianist
aspirant	formidable	infamous	preferable
combatant	incomparable	irreparable	resources
decadent	impious	lamentable	superfluous
demonstrate	industry	maintenance	theatre

SUPPLEMENTARY READINGS

Bronstein, Arthur J., *The Pronunciation of American English*, Appleton-Century-Crofts, 1960.

Carrell, James A., and William R. Tiffany, *Phonetics: Theory and Application to Speech Improvement*, McGraw-Hill, 1960.

Thomas, Charles K., *The Phonetics of American English*, 2nd ed., Ronald, 1958.

Trager, G. L., and H. L. Smith, Jr., *An Outline of English Structure*, American Council of Learned Societies, 1957.

Wise, Claude M., *Applied Phonetics*, Prentice-Hall, 1957.

Practice Manuals

Brigance, William N., and Florence M. Henderson, *A Drill Manual for Improving Speech*, 3rd ed., Lippincott, 1955.

Fairbanks, Grant, *Voice and Articulation Drillbook*, 2nd ed., Harper & Row, 1960.

Gordon, Morton J., and Helene H. Wong, *A Manual for Speech Improvement*, Prentice-Hall, 1961.

Reference Works

Jones, Daniel, *An English Pronouncing Dictionary*, Dutton, 1956.

Kenyon, John S., and Thomas A. Knott, *A Pronouncing Dictionary of American English*, Merriam, 1944.

Kurath, Hans, and Raven I. McDavid, Jr., *The Pronunciation of English in the Atlantic States Based Upon the Collections of the Linguistic Atlas of the Eastern United States*, University of Michigan Press, 1961.

The Principles of the Internal Phonetic Association, London, University College, 1949.

Webster's Third New International Dictionary, Merriam, 1961.

17

THE USE OF LANGUAGE

by Thomas R. Nilsen

Joseph Conrad, speaking with some poetic license, uttered a profound truth when he said, "Give me the right word and the right accent and I will move the world."[1] During the past generation we have seen such simple phrases as "we have nothing to fear but fear itself," and "blood, toil, tears and sweat," capture men's minds and move them to work and fight against great odds. We have seen other simple words, *cold war, iron curtain, New Deal,* somehow epitomize complex patterns of ideas and sharpen men's awareness of their problems and responsibilities. Most of us will never be Roosevelts or Churchills in our ability to choose the right word for the right time, but all of us can learn to make significantly better use of words, enriching our thought and feeling and making our communicatian with others more rewarding.

Understanding Our Language

LANGUAGE AS SYMBOLIC BEHAVIOR

Humans and subhumans, people and animals, live in the same physical world and have many of the same kinds of physical needs; they must respond to similar patterns of stimuli, and in many ways their responses are similar. They eat when they are hungry, they run or fight when challenged, they sleep, they reproduce, they die. But human beings do many more things and do them in different ways. For example, many people when sitting down to a meal say grace before eating. They do so because the food and the eating of it have a meaning beyond the taste and the satisfaction of tissue needs. We say they are acting symbolically because they attach a significance to the eating beyond its immediate practical value; the prayer acknowledges this deeper meaning. Words themselves are symbols, representing ideas, objects, relations, processes and all the infinitude of things it is possible to experience. Through the use of words we deal with all these whether or not they

[1] Joseph Conrad, A *Personal Record*, Doubleday, 1925, p. xiv.

318

are actually present—separating, grouping, relating, testing, sharing, re-cording—building up bodies of knowledge and creating a culture. If we could not use words, we could only respond to the immediate objects of sense and then only within an extremely limited range of action; we could not accumulate experience by conceptualizing it and storing it in our memory. Without language symbols life would be solitary and poor indeed.

Language also includes the large collection of words that make up the common vocabulary of any particular cultural or national group, such as the French language. To make communication possible, to make a culture possible, a common set of word symbols must be de-veloped and preserved within any given linguistic community. All human societies of which there is any record have developed languages capable of expressing all the principal ideas of their various cultures.

THE INNER AND OUTER ASPECTS OF LANGUAGE

By the inner aspect of language we mean the intellectual and emotional life we carry on by silent talking to ourselves. Without lan-guage we could not relate our many and varied experiences to each other in meaningful wholes. Reasoning is a process of selecting and arranging in various orders, the words which represent our experiences. Such a process makes possible inference and the drawing of conclusions upon which future action can be based. How well and clearly we reason de-pends in part upon the kind of words we use. If we use words that are vague or that unduly stir our emotions, we cannot think as clearly and accurately as we can when we use words that are specific, that refer to something definite, and that we can relate significantly to other words.

Not only the clarity of our reasoning, but also the richness of our experience at the emotional level depends in large part upon our use of words. Perhaps we cannot put some of our feelings into words any more than we can put into words our sensation of "red." Certain basic sensations must be experienced directly if they are to be meaning-ful to us. We do know, however, that emotional experiences can be enriched when expressed in words. When Elizabeth Barrett Browning wrote

> How do I love thee? Let me count the ways.
> I love thee to the depth and breadth and height
> My soul can reach, when feeling out of sight
> For the ends of being and ideal grace.
> I love thee to the level of every day's
> Most quiet need, by sun and candlelight,

she no doubt enhanced her own feelings and at the same time gave to many others a heightened appreciation of the emotion of love. Though we may not write verse, our experiences are more meaningful and enjoyable when we verbalize them.

The outer aspect of language refers to our use of words for the purpose of evoking response in others. To evoke responses in others we usually complete our thoughts in more definite and organized form than we do when talking silently to ourselves. Thus the outward utterance becomes valuable as a more definite formulation and expression *for ourselves* of the meaning we intend. Its adequacy for our listeners, however, is equally important. If communication is to be effective, we must select those words which will be most meaningful to our listeners, keeping in mind their varied experiences—educational, social, professional—and their probable attitudes toward our ideas.

We realize that our bodily actions and vocal characteristics also play a vital part in evoking responses from others; and that our supporting materials, reasoning processes, and methods of organization are basic to the entire process. All these matters, however, are dealt with in other sections of this book. We are here concerned with such choice and use of words as will communicate our meanings most fully and accurately.

THE MEANINGS OF WORDS

We can think of meaning as a set of relationships among things, words, and ideas. Whenever we make a statement, three factors are involved: the words used, the thing (referent) referred to by the words, and the speaker's idea of the thing referred to. The more simple, objective and measurable the thing referred to, the more the meaning of the word can be pinned down—that is to say, the more easily the speaker's meaning and the meaning aroused in the listener can be brought into congruence through reference to the object itself. The more intangible or complex the referent, the more difficult it is to arouse the intended conceptions in the mind of the listener.

Since so many of the words we use refer to that which is intangible or complex, we are constantly faced with the difficulty of communicating accurate meanings, of using words that are clear and explicit. Mutual understanding of what is meant by such terms as *delinquency, happiness, morality, attitudes, politics, religion, social welfare,* is often very difficult to achieve. If, for example, we were to use the term *socialized medicine* in a classroom speech, we would find many different conceptions of what in practice constitutes socialized medicine, and many different views about its possible effects. In addition, there would be many different degrees of intensity of attitude toward the concept. Evoking in the mind of the listener, then, a conception similar to that of the speaker requires most careful consideration of the meanings the listeners may find in the terms used. We can only touch on the problem here, suggesting some of the difficulties it involves, and presenting a few suggestions for using words so that the possibility of misunderstanding is reduced.

Except for scientific or technical terms, the words in our language necessarily have multiple meanings. If we tried to create a language with a distinct word for every possible event, object, relation and experience, our vocabularies would become impossibly large and unwieldy.

For any given individual, words have only such meaning as he has had experience with them, and, directly or indirectly, with what they

The map is not the territory; the word is not the thing.—Korzybski.

represent. In the everyday activities of living, words become associated with the objects and events of our experience and with ideas and feelings; and we build a vocabulary which enables us to talk with others, to interact and cooperate with them, and, in general, to relate ourselves to the world around us. Since people in any given culture experience many things in common they come to have many words in common. (Review section on development of your speech in Chapter 2.)

No two people, of course, have exactly the same or similar experiences, and consequently no two words have exactly the same meaning for any two people. Moreover, the very fact that each person is a separate nervous system means that no matter how similar the environmental stimuli appear to be, the response of one individual will never be quite like the response of another. Even though there are large areas of common experience, there are also areas of unique experience and of unique response. Thus, words have both common or denotative, and unique or connotative meanings. The common qualities of our experience underlie denotative or dictionary meanings, while the unique qualities of experience underlie connotative meanings.

The main sources of word meaning are (1) dictionary definitions, (2) context, both verbal and nonverbal, and (3) individual experience associated with the word.

Dictionary definitions. Dictionaries are source books of meaning, and we should use them diligently and often. We should recognize, however, that while dictionaries are a very useful tool they should be used with discretion. A well known authority on English usage gives the following suggestions:

(a) A dictionary does not *require* or *forbid* a particular meaning of a word but *records* the uses that have been found for it. Now and then a word is in the process of acquiring a new meaning or somewhat altering its usual sense. (b) The dictionary definition is for the most part a record of the denotation of a word and often cannot give its connotation. For this reason it is safest not to use a word unless you have heard or read it and so know it in part from experience, at least what suggestion it carries if it is not a simple factual word. (c) Finally and most important, the words of the definition are not the meaning of the word, but they, and perhaps an illustration, are to help let you see what in the world of objects or ideas the word refers to.[2]

Context as a determinant of meaning. The immediate context in which a word is used plays a large part in suggesting the intended meaning. Verbal context is the most obvious and immediate. The word *run*, for example, has two distinct meanings in the following sentences: "He can run around the block in two minutes"; "She has a run in her stocking." The words forming the context leave no doubt as to what is intended. Other verbal contexts may not delimit meaning as sharply. In "The run is good this year," the context formed by the sentence does not indicate whether the run is of fish or sap. The verbal context provided by related sentences might be sufficient, or the larger social and physical context might suggest the meaning intended. "The run is good this year" spoken in Vermont probably would refer to sap. The same sentence spoken in an Alaskan seacoast town would no doubt refer to fish. Since most of the words we use have more than one meaning, our phrases, sentences, and paragraphs should be structured so that the

[2] Porter G. Perrin, *Writer's Guide and Index to English*, Scott, Foresman, 1950, p. 315. Compare this statement with the comment on dictionaries in the section on standards of pronunciation, Chapter 16.

context both verbal and physical will reveal the meanings as clearly as possible.

Individual experience as a determinant of meaning. Suppose you had lived in a family where the father owned and managed a business of moderate size. Suppose that during all the years of your childhood and youth your father had had genuine troubles with an irresponsible union which often made unrealistic wage demands and sought a presumptuous share of authority in the affairs of the business. The meaning of *labor union* to you would have been shaped through the years by the tensions revealed in your father's behavior, the conversations of the family and close associates, and the sense of conflict with employees, as well as by various direct statements heard and read. Suppose, on the other hand, you had lived in a family where the father was a skilled workman, who belonged to a responsible union that made realistic wage demands, respected management prerogatives and encouraged good work among its members. Imagine too, that some of the wage increases negotiated by the union brought your family some much wanted amenities, orthodontia for you perhaps, or a regular vacation for the family—things not other wise possible. The meaning of *labor union* to you would be the result of such experiences.

We can easily understand how difficult it would be for two people, with such contrasting experiences, to share the meaning of *unionism*. Difficulties of this kind, however, confront us constantly as we talk about events, movements, institutions, ideas, policies, and people. No amount of looking in dictionaries and encyclopedias for definitions and descriptions can provide the kind of meaning we get from our experiences. It behooves us as speakers to be keenly sensitive to the way in which the experiences of our listeners may cause them to perceive meanings different from those we intend to convey. As listeners we must be careful to take into consideration the way in which our own interpretations of words may enter into and modify the meanings intended by other people.

Functions and Purposes of Language

We should recall again that symbols, particularly language symbols, are the medium in and through which we have most of our intellectual and our more highly developed emotional experiences and by which we interact with other people. Since we have many different kinds of experiences and engage in various forms of interaction with others, it is apparent that language serves many functions. (Review the discussion of speech purposes in Chapter 8.)

These functions may be enumerated in many different ways.

Aiken, for example, lists eleven functions:

> To accomplish the purposes both of individual and of social life it is, at the very least, necessary that we be able to do the following things with words: (1) identify objects, (2) describe their characteristics, (3) predict their causes and effects, (4) infer from such descriptions and predictions what means are necessary to accomplish our ends and what ends are worth entertaining seriously, (5) express individual and collective attitudes and decisions, (6) adjudicate differences in attitude, (7) clarify aims, (8) commend, exhort, and persuade others to acts which we approve or deem desirable, (9) make promises, (10) assign responsibilities, (11) authorize, regularize, and correct behavior, and this on a variety of levels.[3]

Werkmeister, on the other hand, classifies the many and varied functions of words in six main types:

> Logical: When language conveys information or when it is used to reason from data to a conclusion, it is used logically [see Chapter 7, on inference].
>
> Expressive: We may reveal our emotions directly and explicitly or indirectly and vaguely, but express them we must and will. The oral word is our most adequate means of such expression.
>
> Poetic: When the experience of emotion is deep, but its expression controlled and infused with creative thought, we speak poetically. The thought content is enhanced and enriched by the poetic form.
>
> Evocative: Language is used evocatively when it brings out response or induces action by others. We may ask for help, give orders, exhort or plead; and sometimes persuade indirectly by telling a story, describing a need, or pointing to possible satisfactions.
>
> Ceremonial: Language is used in rituals, liturgy, prayer, eulogies, dedications, patriotic addresses, and anniversary speeches. There is even a ceremonial element in the informal utterances by which we greet people, pass the time of day, or exchange casual chitchat.
>
> Mixed: Only rarely is any use of language confined strictly to one purpose or function. Most of the time two or more functions are served by any single utterance. The uses of language are usually complex.[4]

If we are aware of the various functions of language, we can put many statements into better perspective. A man, for example, who is intensely concerned about the issue of prayer in the public schools may speak more expressively than logically, or at least his deep emotion may have a marked influence on the logic of his discourse. People feel strongly about many issues in the areas of labor, education, racial problems, politics, and social movements; and public discussion of these issues often involves intense feeling.

Apparent aims, moreover, are not always real aims. A basic expressive purpose may often be concealed beneath a facade of informa-

[3] Henry D. Aiken, *Reason and Conduct*, Knopf, 1962, p. 38.
[4] Adapted from W. H. Werkmeister, *An Introduction to Critical Thinking*, Johnsen Publishing Company, 1948, pp. 4–17.

tion; an evocative function may be hidden by the garments of logic; sometimes a poetic or ceremonial utterance may be used to hide a persuasive function. Many political speeches, for example, are primarily ceremonial. Representatives of one party are expected to warn of the danger to the nation if the other party comes to power, to extol the virtues of their candidates, and condemn the limitations of opposing candidates. Such speaking may be expressive and perhaps evocative of response at the ballot box, but we shall grossly misinterpret its purpose and function in our political system if we look upon it as primarily informative or logical. Accurate and truthful it should be, of course, but dissemination of fact and logic often is not its primary purpose.

These considerations remind us that ethical questions are involved in our uses of language. Such questions arise whenever our utterances affect other people. All of us are aware of the moral problems involved in slander, obscenity, outright lies, or rabble-rousing language. Ethical values, however, are often violated in more subtle ways. Inaccurate or loosely used words may distort the facts of an issue. Statements, though factual, may deceive if some important information is concealed. Incomplete or out-of-context quotations may easily misrepresent another person's point of view. We influence others not only by what we explicitly urge them to do, but also by our method of urging. We can use language objectively to foster informed, critical thinking; or we can arouse uncritical responses by emphasizing narrow, personal advantage or by distorting information.

No speaker, of course, should be held solely responsible for the reactions of his listeners. In the communicative process they, too, have responsibility for interpreting a speaker's meaning as accurately and honestly as possible. If we accept the basic values of our culture, if we believe that people should be self-determining in so far as reasonably possible, if we believe in making informed and rational choices, then certainly all of us, both speakers and listeners, are obligated to use informed and rational discourse. The fact that we see this principle violated frequently in our society—in advertising, in political campaigns, in the promotion of individual and group interests—does not make it any less valid or urgent. Individuals are debased in the degree that they are deceived or cajoled into uncritical and highly emotional responses on issues of public concern. If we are to develop thoughtful, self-determining citizens, indeed if we are to maintain our democratic society, responsible use of language is a necessity.

Improving Our Use of Language

During the first century A.D., the Roman rhetorician Quintilian said that a speaker should take care not merely that his listeners understand, but that they should not be able to misunderstand.[5] The United States Army echoes and extends this thought in its statement that an order which can be misunderstood will be misunderstood. In all phases of life there will be misunderstandings at times, but at least we can do our best to minimize them by careful selection and use of words.

CHOICE OF WORDS

There are no set rules for choice of words. Much depends upon the subject matter, the listeners, and the situation. There are times when accuracy of meaning is at a premium, as when we report on an experiment. At other times interestingness and richness of association may be more important. Choosing words is an art not reducible to formula. There are, however, some helpful guidelines. In selecting words for effective communication we should observe their (1) clarity, (2) interest, and (3) force or emphasis. These aspects of language are by no means mutually exclusive; the factors, for example, which contribute to clarity often enhance interest and add force. We should, however, focus briefly on each criterion in order to make its significance more apparent.

Clarity. For our purposes clarity is the most important attribute of discourse. People will not long attend to what they do not understand. The first prerequisite for clarity in the use of language is that the speaker himself must know precisely what he wishes to express. Our listeners certainly can get no more accurate conception of what we say than we ourselves have.

A second prerequisite for clarity is an adequate foundation of specific facts. For lack of details we may lose the wholeness of our meanings. Man's nervous system is so constituted that it tends to construct organized patterns out of partial or disorganized materials. If we do not readily and clearly perceive a "whole," we attempt to fill in the picture from our own knowledge and experience. When, for example, we see or hear of someone acting strangely, we try to assign causes for his behavior; if we see or hear of an accident, we begin to conjecture how it might have happened. We are ill at ease until a situation makes sense to us, and we often supply our own meanings to give it sense even though we may turn out to be in error. Obviously no speaker can mention all the details about anything. We must be selective but we should select those items which will most clearly and accurately characterize our referents.

A speaker who knows clearly what he wants to say and has assembled a meaningful body of facts will already have found words which embody his thought adequately for himself. He should then take care that his words will arouse the identical meanings in his listeners. Two

[5] *Education of the Orator,* Book VIII, chap. II.

criteria are especially important: (1) His words must be as accurate as possible in their referential value, and (2) they must be adequately defined, especially if there is any possibility of misunderstanding.

Accuracy in the meaning of a word depends primarily on the specific nature of its reference. Words are specific when they outline or delimit the referent so sharply that it is unmistakably identified. Definite titles, accurate numbers, qualified nouns, words of vivid imagery, synonyms which suggest distinctive shades of meaning, the particular rather than the general—all of these are means of achieving greater accuracy.

In this connection three concepts are often confused—vagueness, ambiguity, and generality. A vague term is imprecise; the referent is indefinite, obscure, not sharply outlined; the meaning is hazy like a picture out of focus. Such words as *conservative* and *liberal*, for example, are vague; their boundary lines are seldom clearly drawn; the range of possible referents is large and indeterminate. An ambiguous term, on the other hand, may be in perfectly clear focus but lack clarity because there is no positive indication which of two or more perfectly clear alternative referents is intended. The word as used has more than one possible interpretation; classification of the referent is uncertain. Sometimes this ambiguity arises because an antecedent is confused, as in "He told his brother that he was working too hard." We simply cannot tell to what person the third pronoun refers. In contrast to both vagueness and ambiguity is generality. A general term is one which refers definitely and properly to a class of things. When we use the word *tree* to refer to the entire class of trees, there need be no misunderstanding if we remember that such a general term does not give the distinguishing characteristics of any particular trees, and if we take care not to lump different classes of referents together carelessly under the same general term. (Review the section on levels of abstraction in Chapter 7.) To make our language more accurate, then, we should describe our referents exactly to avoid vagueness, classify them definitely to avoid ambiguity, and use general terms only when generalities are appropriate.

Accurate definition is a major requirement for clear understanding of words. Definition is a process of setting up limitations and making distinctions, reducing the number of referents and delimiting their scope. Three methods are most useful: (1) Giving synonyms for the term defined, (2) pointing out examples of its referents, and (3) stating the characteristics by virtue of which a referent is a member of a class. Suppose, for instance, we are to define *discussion*. First, we might suggest synonyms such as *purposive conversation* or *conference*. Next we might give examples citing such radio and television programs as "Northwestern Reviewing Stand" and "Open End" and group meetings within our own community. Finally we might state the characteristics of discussion as "Cooperative deliberation . . . by persons thinking and conversing together in face-to-face or coacting groups under the direction of a leader."[6]

Among these means of definition the use of synonyms is perhaps the most convenient, although not always the most adequate. Definition by example relates a word most directly to reality, but the example may not be typical. The naming of distinctive characteristics sets the referent apart from all related things. The face-to-face feature of the situation and the presence of a leader are such items. Some combination of these methods will best serve a listener's understanding.

The detail and rigor of a definition should be in proportion to the need for accuracy and the possibilities of misunderstanding. Words obviously unusual or unfamiliar to your listeners should be defined. Sometimes even familiar words need defining just because we tend to take them for granted. Such general terms as *religion, progressive education, right to work, conservatism, socialism,* and *un-American* may cause endless misunderstandings. We have a special obligation to let a listener know in what sense we use them.

Interest. The interestingness of discourse is a product of many factors, including the occasion, the subject, the personality of the speaker, and the kind of material used to develop his thought. Material is interesting to a listener which touches his own most vital needs or which has elements of uncertainty, conflict, or novelty. Unusual themes, however, should always be linked somehow with familiar experiences of the listener. Words are interesting when they reflect all these qualities and, in addition, are varied, personal, and vivid.

Variety in choice of words contributes to interest as well as to clarity. Many of us do not even begin to use the full range of our vocabularies; we overwork a few words when a little thought might suggest varied synonyms. A simple word like *walk* has many substitutes, such as *trudge, amble, hike, plod, stroll,* which would enliven our speech and enrich its meaning. We tell more about a fellow student when we say, "He trudged home after the exam," than when we say, "He walked home after the exam."

Rapport between speaker and listener is also vital to continued interest, and therefore vital to effective communication. One of the most important ways of promoting rapport is the use of personal words, *we, you, I, us.* They provide a sense of the speaker's interest in his listeners, a feeling that he and they are on a level of equality, and a recognition of the cooperative nature of the process of communication. Personal words, however, should not be overused. In some situations an excess of such informality might suggest ulterior motives on the part of the speaker, an intent to ingratiate and manipulate. The occasion

[6] James H. McBurney and Kenneth G. Hance, *Discussion in Human Affairs,* Harper & Row, 1950, p. 10.

should always be taken into account, lest undue familiarity violate good taste.

Words are vivid when they name and describe the qualities of objects, people, and events in such clear images that we can see them in the mind's eye. When a speaker tells, for example, of the large number of traffic accidents resulting in serious injury or death, and drives the point home by describing a scene—the twisted metal, the shattered glass, the strangely awkward bodies, the contorted faces—then images leap to the mind, intensifying the meaning as no piling up of statistics could do. Statistics, of course, are essential to an adequate grasp of the scope of the accident problem, but the concrete words bring us to grips with that problem in human terms.

Vividness is especially enhanced by use of figurative language. Such language imbues an idea with the sensory quality of an event or object close to our experience; it paints a picture. By means of figures of speech abstract ideas are related to images, and concepts to sensory experiences. The most common forms of figurative language are metaphors and similes. A metaphor is a figure of speech in which two things are declared identical in order to suggest a quality in one which is clearly apparent in the other:

> He is a walking computer.
> He is a gadfly.
> The president was a rock in that crisis!
> College is an intellectual hot house.

A simile is a figure of speech in which two thought units are related by the words *like* or *as*:

> His mind works like a computer.
> A general in the field is like a quarterback calling signals.
> International politics is very like an international chess game.

The force of figurative language can be felt in these excerpts from politcial campaign speeches: "The real question is whether a platform represents the clicking of a ghost's typewriter . . . or the beating of a human heart." And again: "In times like this the brush of politics is dipped pretty deep into vats of paint, black and white, and seldom any other shades. And everything that is put on display is painted in these rather sharp tones."[7]

Force. By force is meant the impact of words, the emphasis they carry. Words which evoke images have more impact than abstract words, and specific words more than general words. Notice the difference between "Many trees were growing on the side of the hill" and "A small forest of pines and hemlocks clung to the rugged hillside."

---

[7] *Major Campaign Speeches of Adlai E. Stevenson,* Random House, 1952, pp. 31 and 282.

Again short words tend to have more force than long words, and terse statements more than longer sentences. Compare "He did not tell the truth" with "He lied."

In sentence structure force is often gained by the use of short and balanced or antithetical clauses, as in this statement: "Where we have erred let there be no denial; where we have wronged the public trust, let there be no excuses. Self-criticism is the secret weapon of democracy, and candor and confession are good for the soul."[8] A series of short phrases can hit hard: "A University is a community of scholars. It is not a kindergarten; it is not a club; not a reform school; it is not a political party; it is not an agency of propaganda. A University is a community of scholars."[9]

All of us are familiar with certain pithy statements that have become a part of our folklore: "Give me liberty or give me death" and "Never . . . was so much owed by so many to so few." Our discourse obviously cannot be made up entirely of short epigrammatic phrases; such phrases usually make their impact by epitomizing ideas which have already been developed at some length. Nevertheless the pungent, easily remembered phrase captures the meaning and preserves its vividness in men's minds.

What to avoid. To the positive criteria of clearness, interest, and force let us now add certain warnings or negative criteria. Some kinds of words are to be avoided or used with caution—trite words, euphemisms, slang, and loaded words. If we follow the main principles already given, we probably would not choose such words in any case, but a brief comment may help to reveal their inadequacy.

Words are trite when they have been overused and thus have become too familiar. If your listeners can finish a phrase or sentence which you begin, then beware! "Where there is life there is _____." "Honesty is the best _____." Such phrases as "his heart is pure gold," "life is a merry-go-round," "strong as a lion" add little or nothing to meaning. Their very triteness can make listeners recoil.

Words are euphemistic which "pretty up" a meaning. Sometimes to avoid the unpleasant implications of a term we try to use fancy substitutes such as *passed away* for *dead*, *mortician* for *undertaker*, *custodial engineer* for *janitor*. Well-chosen euphemisms may sometimes be appropriate, but for the most part they dissipate the force of our language.

Slang consists of words used out of context or in a bizarre and unusual manner to gain a startling effect. Such words are borrowed from one area of thought or action and applied to another in an effort to gain novelty or emphasis, as in "He struck out" for "He failed to

[8] *Ibid.*, p. 5.
[9] Robert Hutchins, "What is a University," *Vital Speeches*, May 20, 1935, p. 547.

qualify for the job," or "He hit the books" for "He studied." "Park your bags here" is slang, while "Park your car here" is not. Slang may consist of shortened, overworked, or newly coined words. It may also be figurative as in "He's an egghead" or "He's a pain in the neck." The possibilities are endless. There is no rule by which to determine how much slang is permissible, although it certainly should be avoided in the more formal kinds of speaking. Informal situations allow us much greater freedom. Well-chosen slang expressions can add color and verve to our speech but they should be used with care.

Loaded words carry a large freight of emotion; they arouse strong feelings. *Socialism, atheism, radical,* are words that may evoke unthinking rejection of ideas. Words or phrases such as *The Grand Old Party, altruistic,* and *scientific* may sometimes evoke unthinking acceptance. Highly emotional terms are the enemy of sound judgment. Use them with care.

BUILDING A BETTER VOCABULARY

If our words are to evoke the responses we seek from listeners, we must have an adequate vocabulary upon which to draw. Each of us should be constantly enlarging his stock of words. The words we learn should have significant meaning for us. The more thoroughly one understands a word and knows the various ways in which it is used and the associations it calls up, the more valuable it becomes—valuable, indeed, not only for the purpose of communicating to others, but also for receiving communications. The need for an *understanding* of words points to certain methods of vocabulary building.

Wide reading of challenging material. By such reading we not only discover new words, but new usages for familiar words and new contexts that add significant meaning. When you meet a new word, consult your dictionary, of course; but for all words not fully understood, old as well as new, pause in your reading to notice the particular use and gather as much significance as possible from the context. If each time you meet a word you pause to relate it to your experience and to enjoy its flavor, the successive encounters will enrich the meaning. Your interest in both ideas and words and your command of them will grow with the breadth and depth of such reading and meditation.

Learning word roots and prefixes. As you know, a great many words in the English language are based on words from other languages, mostly Greek and Latin. If you know the roots and prefixes most frequently used in English words, you can very rapidly increase your vocabulary and build up a sense of the meaning. How many words can you think of that use the following roots: *philos* (loving); *logy* (science or branch of knowledge); *anthropo* (man or mankind); *tele* (far or far off); *pathos* (disease, suffering); and *soph* (wisdom). A few of the derivatives are *philosophy, pathology, anthropology, telescope, pathetic, sophisticated.* How about the Latin roots: *capere, tenere, mittere, ducere?* Are these as familiar? Can you list a few of their derivatives?

Some years ago James I. Brown compiled a list of 14 of the most important Greek and Latin roots and 20 of the most frequently used prefixes.[10] Taken together these language units, says Brown, are the key to more than 14,000 of our common English words. The list follows. Look up each root word or prefix in the dictionary; then write down as many words derived from each as you can. Check all your words in the dictionary and begin to use them in your everyday discourse.

Words	Prefix	Common Meaning	Root	Common Meaning
1. Precept	pre-	before	capere	take, seize
2. Detain	de-	away, from	tenere	hold, have
3. Intermittent	inter-	between	mittere	send
4. Offer	ob-	against	ferre	bear, carry
5. Insist	in-	into	stare	stand
6. Monograph	mono-	alone, one	graphein	write
7. Epilogue	epi-	upon	legein	say, study of
8. Aspect	ad-	to, towards	specere	see
9. Uncomplicated	un-	not	plicare	fold
	com-	together with		
10. Nonextended	non-	not	tendere	stretch
	ex-	out of		
11. Reproduction	re-	back, again	ducere	lead
	pro-	forward		
12. Indisposed	in-	not	ponere	put, place
	dis-	apart from		
13. Oversufficient	over-	above	facere	make, do
	sub-	under		
14. Mistranscribe	mis-	wrong	scribere	write
	trans-	across, beyond		

IMPROVING THE ARRANGEMENT OF WORDS

Words convey their full meaning only when put together in phrases, sentences, paragraphs, and series of paragraphs; and our method of arranging them is vitally important for effective communication.

The phrase. In our consideration of orderly utterance in Chapter 4 we defined a phrase as any group of words expressing a single thought unit, and we referred to phrasing and pausing again in the section on duration in Chapter 14. We saw that phrases are basic units of meaningful speech. "The tall fir trees" is a phrase; so is "in the distance." "The tall fir trees in the distance" is also a phrase although it

[10] By permission. From *Word Study,* copyright 1949, by G. & C. Merriam Company, Publishers of the Merriam-Webster Dictionaries. These words are treated in book form in James I. Brown's *Building a Better Vocabulary,* Ronald, 1959, and *Programmed Vocabulary: Steps Toward Improved Word Power,* Appleton-Century-Crofts.

expresses a more complex idea. Grammatically speaking, of course, a phrase is distinguished from a clause by the absence of a predicate or verb. Clauses are thought units or subordinate parts of sentences which always include a verb or predicative element. Both phrases and clauses should be clear and distinct so that the individual thought units are meaningful; and further, they should be so related to each other that the larger predicative or propositional meanings can be readily grasped.

The sentence. A sentence is a group of words that asserts, requests, questions, commands, or exclaims about something. It may be spoken as one phrase unit or several, depending on its length and complexity; but to be clear and complete in meaning it must have both subject and predicate, clearly implied if not explicitly stated. (Refer to the discussion of predication in the section on types of relationships in Chapter 7.) Although the reference to fir trees in the phrases given above is clear enough, they leave us expecting more; they do not seem complete. If we add a phrase which asserts or predicates something, such as "are shrouded in fog," the meaning is rounded out and we experience a sense of completeness.

For clarity in speech, sentences should be relatively short, usually with no more than three or four phrases or units of meaning. An occasional longer sentence, of course, can give desirable variety and emphasis. The structure of sentences should be simple so that their meaning is immediately clear. The relationship between subject and predicate should be consistent and obvious. The direction of thought should be stated early, and closely related words or phrases should be close together. Modifiers should be attached to the ideas they modify and not left hanging so that a listener must search for the relationship.

The paragraph. Sentences are combined into larger units of meaning to make paragraphs. All the sentences in a paragraph should have a clear and definite relationship to its central idea. In terms of structure a good paragraph has three characteristics—unity, coherence and emphasis. Unity refers to the "oneness" of thought, the degree to which all the statements develop the one main idea which is the theme of the paragraph. Coherence is a matter of the relationships among the sentences, the degree to which they are tied together and build on each other in the development of the thought. Emphasis is achieved partly by placement of ideas; items which are first or last in a series are usually considered most important. In oral discourse emphasis is also achieved by bodily action and vocal changes in pitch, loudness, and rate (see Chapters 13 and 15).

You will have better success in constructing good paragraphs if you think of them more as unified and coherent groups of facts and ideas than as groups of sentences. In each paragraph there should be a central idea or theme, declared in a single topic sentence and systematically amplified, explained, and developed. If the ideas and facts are logically related so that all contribute directly to the central meaning, the paragraph will have sound structure.

The structuring of paragraphs is closely related to the organization of thought. Review Chapter 8, especially the section on synthesis. The level at which items in an outline should be regarded as topic sentences of paragraphs will depend on the range and complexity of material. At the very least in a short discourse each main point of the outline, labeled by a Roman numeral, should be regarded as a distinct unit of thought and developed in an oral paragraph. In longer discourses lower-order items should be developed as separate paragraphs, especially if they involve considerable factual material or expansion of thought. Division of an outline into paragraphs of discourse is a matter of judgment, depending primarily on the scope of the subject, complexity of thought sequence, and receptivity of the listener. Do not make your paragraphs too long and inclusive; listeners have difficulty keeping in mind large clusters of ideas. To avoid excessive length of paragraphs subdivide the larger units and develop the subthemes separately. Let your paragraphs, moreover, be clearly marked and separated by transitions. Your listeners constantly need the guidance of clear signposts as you move from one to another of your larger units of discourse. (Refer again to the section on transitional cues at the end of Chapter 4.)

IMPROVING ORAL STYLE

Style is the choice and arrangement of words. The improvement of style, therefore, requires integration of everything we have said about both choice and arrangement.

Listeners need successive statements that fit together so they can see the connections quickly and easily. They enjoy the systematic movement of ideas toward a definite objective and the satisfaction in knowing that a speaker has a clear purpose. Moreover, they like variety in words and sentences. They are attracted by novelty, but not by strangeness or bizarre effects; a touch of familiarity gives new ideas greater force. A speaker's words should flow easily; listeners dislike the feeling that he has to grope for the right word or that he is trying for effect. They like to feel, finally, that he is talking directly to them.

These characteristics may be understood more thoroughly if we compare oral discourse with writing. A writer is far removed from his readers, and frequently does not even know who they may be. A speaker is typically face to face with his listeners; if not, he speaks to their imagined presence. A reader has his own time and leisure to reread and ponder; a listener must understand as the discourse proceeds or lose the connections and train of thought. This circumstance requires a speaker to be instantly intelligible. To this end he should use more familiar and explicit words, form shorter and simpler sentences, repeat and reiterate his key ideas more often, and give his listener more frequent transitional words to serve as guideposts to the progress of his thought. Oral style tends to be relatively less compact and more diffuse, less terse and more discursive, less formal and more intimately personal than written style.

Writing and speaking, though widely different in some ways, are nevertheless companion processes which contribute jointly to our mastery of language. We should write and rewrite, speak and repeat, phrase and rephrase again and again in order to improve selection and structure, sound and sense. All of us, of course, must improve our concepts of good style if we are to evaluate our own use of language adequately. We need to read widely in good literature, listen frequently to good speeches, and constantly strive to understand and be sensitive to the qualities that make for excellence in both speaking and writing. As we become more discriminating and our command of language improves, we shall find ample reward in more effective and more satisfying oral communication.

EXERCISES

1. Select a word each day, preferably a noun or verb, and write down as many synonyms for it as you can. Practice using these synonyms wherever appropriate in your everyday conversation.

2. Make a list of worn out figures of speech, e.g., *cold as ice, strong as a lion, pretty as a picture.* Substitute fresh and unusual words, descriptive comparisons or vivid figures of speech.

3. Browse through a few volumes of collected speeches or the magazine *Vital Speeches*, and select a number of paragraphs that use language unusually well. Analyze them to discover what made the language effective. Consider such questions as the following:

Was the language well adapted to the type of thought? Was it immediately clear? Were the words specific or general? Did they arouse vivid images? Were the sentences long or short? Simple or complex? Varied or monotonous in type and length? Were transitional words and phrases used effectively to guide you from idea to idea?

4. Select some paragraphs from one of your recorded classroom speeches and rewrite them several times, improving the word choice and arrangement to the utmost of your ability. Check your recorded speeches carefully for common errors in language. List any that you find, and write corrections.

SUPPLEMENTARY READINGS

Brown, James I., *Building a Better Vocabulary*, Ronald, 1959.
Brown, James I., *Programmed Vocabulary: Steps Toward Improved Word Power*, Appleton-Century-Crofts, 1964.

Evans, Bergen, and Cornelia Evans, A *Dictionary of Contemporary American Usage*, Random House, 1957.

Flesch, Rudolph, *How to Test Readability*, Harper & Row, 1951.

Hayakawa, S. I., *Language in Thought and Action*, 2nd ed., Harcourt, Brace & World, 1964.

Lee, Irving J., *Language Habits in Human Affairs*, Harper & Row, 1941.

Strunk, William J., and E. B. White, *The Elements of Style*, Macmillan, 1959.

BIBLIOGRAPHICAL NOTES

In addition to works specifically cited in footnotes, the following sources have been used in preparing this chapter: Charles Morris, *The Open Self*, Prentice-Hall, 1948; C. K. Ogden and I. A. Richards, *The Meaning of Meaning*, Harcourt, Brace & World, 1923; I. A. Richards, *Practical Criticism*, Harcourt, Brace & World, 1929; John C. Sherwood, *Discourse of Reason: A Brief Handbook of Semantics and Logic*, Harper & Row, 1960; and Viscount Samuel, *Practical Ethics*, Oxford University Press, 1935.

IV

FORMS AND USES
OF SPEECH

The Ways We Speak: An Overview of the Forms

We have been studying speech from a general point of view, concentrating most of our attention on those elements which are inherent and necessary in any or all kinds of speaking. The situations in which speech occurs, however, are highly variable. Reasons for meeting and talking together range from chance encounter on the street to formal assembly as in legislature or court. Factors of time and place change. Speakers and listeners differ in alertness, orientation, knowledge, and purpose. The extent of vocabulary commonly understood by speaker and listener is highly variable. The intellectual or cultural climate often changes. Inevitably such variations in factors of the speaking situation give rise to varied patterns of interaction. As a result we use many forms of speech which are as variable as the situations in which we find ourselves in this social world.

Some occasions call upon us to present our own thoughts. When friends or acquaintances meet casually there is the informal exchange of conversation. When a few people with a common problem come together around the conference table, informal group discussion is in order. Whenever one man has knowledge or conviction which other people assemble to hear, public speaking occurs. When there is a clash of opinion on issues of group, community or civic welfare, public discussion and debate follow. Activities such as these, in which thoughts, attitudes, and symbolic processes are primarily created, formulated, and arranged by the speakers themselves, we call original speaking.

Interpretative speaking, on the other hand, includes all utterance in which the sequence of thought, some part of the social and emotional attitudes and imaginative enrichment, and frequently also the form of words have been selected and composed prior to the time of utterance and usually by someone other than the speaker, who then uses visible action and audible voice to give the material a fresh and dynamic significance. An interpretative speaker, whether he is storyteller, oral reader, or actor, serves as a kind of middleman in literary or dramatic communication.

Finally, there are situations in which we communicate by means of special transmitting equipment to large audiences widely scattered in location. In terms of speaker behavior, broadcast speaking is primarily like any other speaking, most often like interpretative speaking, except that the studio situation and the instruments of mass transmission impose certain special requirements and limitations on speakers.

Although these various forms of speech have the same kinds of interacting forces, as we have seen, they differ widely in the specific nature of these forces. Speaker, listener, physical and social setting, subject matter, and symbolic or linguistic forms, though always present, are never quite the same in any two kinds of speaking. Let us summarize the principal ways in which these situations may vary.

1. Primary variables among speakers:
   Special training and qualifications
   Purposes or reasons for speaking
   Typical relationships to listeners
   Extent and type of immediate preparation for speaking
   Characteristic types of action, voice, and language used

2. Differences among listeners:
   Reasons for listening
   Particular relationship to or attitude toward a speaker
   Habitual responses or established attitudes toward subject
      and theme
   The number present or the size and cohesiveness of the
      listening group

3. Variations in the settings in which speakers and listeners meet:
   The extent to which the location is especialy chosen or
      prepared
   Typical acoustic and spatial characteristics
   The general intellectual, social and political "climate"
   Specific events and circumstances which immediately precede
      or accompany the speaking

4. The subjects of spoken discourse differ significantly:
   Types of material, whether primarily factual, imaginative,
      logical or motivational
   Sources of information
   Degree of specialization
   Patterns of organization in which the material is cast

5. The symbolic or linguistic processes of speech are distinctive:
   Types of bodily action and vocal expression
   Typical standards of pronunciation
   Level of vocabulary and degree of its specialization
   Grammatical and stylistic usage

A complete and full-rounded description of any single act of speech should include specific information about all or most of these features; but the distinctiveness of each form of speaking can usually be defined in terms of a limited number of its most significant characteristics. We shall concentrate attention on the types of speech that are (1) most important in daily life, (2) offer the greatest opportunities for speech improvement, and (3) are most easily adapted to classroom practice. Experience indicates that conversations, group discussion, short talks, and oral readings best meet these criteria. Our final step in the study of basic speech improvement, therefore, will be to turn our attention to these most fundamental and convenient kinds of speaking, the principal elements of these activities, and the particular contributions they can make to speech development.

18

CONVERSATION

Of all the ways we speak, conversation is undoubtedly the most used and probably the most significant. Conversation, in fact, is so much a part of our daily living that we are sometimes inclined to take it as a matter of course. Its very frequency and informality easily give rise to carelessness and ineptitude and make it difficult to study systematically. Nevertheless as the Educational Policies Commission has said: "There seems to be no good reason why this ability, so useful for disseminating information and increasing the value and satisfaction of social contacts, should not be more generally included as a definite aim of instruction in American schools."[1]

Conversation is a form of original speaking characterized by informality of relationships between the participants. It varies from random small talk, at one extreme, to serious and persuasive interview at the other extreme. It is neither aimless chatter, harangue, nor monologue. As an elementary social process, conversation includes such polite formalities as greetings, introductions, casual dinner-table talk, and the forever popular "bull" session. At a slightly more formal level, interview is a form of conversation distinguished by serious purpose and advance planning (see Chapter 6). Telephoning is a special kind of activity in which the auditory medium alone must carry the message. In a practical work-a-day sense conversation reaches its highest point in such business activities as dictating, reporting, conferring, and selling. In a more subjective and subtle sense we may even include within the scope of conversation that internal kind of talking to one's self which we have already described as a primary form of thinking (see Chapter 4).

In all these widely varied forms, however, conversation is always primarily a process of mutual stimulation and adjustment between two or a very few persons. It is an elementary meeting of minds, an interaction of personalities. Joost A. M. Meerloo says that talking to each other is loving each other. In its most typical form conversation occurs in unplanned and unstructured situations which involve (1) a high degree of social and psychological rapport between the participants, (2) intensely communicative attitudes, and (3) frequent interchange of the roles of speaker and listener.

[1] *The Purposes of Education in American Democracy*, National Education Association, 1938, pp. 54–55.

Although conversation may be at times both impressive and profound, its proper aim is neither to make an impression nor display profundity. Conversation may seek to win converts or influence votes, but its typical purposes are simpler and more elemental. We exchange greetings, seek recognition, share experiences, inquire and give information. The subjects of our discourse should be neither trivial nor labored, but (1) meaningful to the person engaged, (2) provocative and stimulating, and (3) intensely personal although above personalities. We talk about everything from amusements to the latest news item, politics, love, and perhaps even theology. Whatever the subjects, however, our conversations should be an empathic sharing of life and its significant problems and concerns. The truest conversation is a communion of kindred spirits. Conclusions may indeed be reached in our more serious discourses, but as Robert Louis Stevenson reminded us, "That is not the profit. The profit is in the exercise, and above all in the experience."[2]

Conversation satisfies our deep need for human association. The word itself comes from the Latin *conversari*, meaning to associate with. By means of talk we build and strengthen our friendships, and in so doing we can find something of our own uniqueness and the confidence to express it. An understanding listener not only satisfies our need for acceptance; he can also enlarge our stock of information and provide an exercise in enriched thinking. Solitary study is forever in danger of getting lost in the labyrinth of its own limited outlook and aberrations. Conversation helps to mature and integrate our thought by exposing it to the reaction of another intelligence. Conference indeed makes a ready man, as Francis Bacon said; but it does even more. Nothing can so quickly expose crooked thinking as the interplay of keen minds. Talk, even though it be casual and light, can provide a check on thought and aid in the quest for truth. Conversation not only enhances social enjoyment; it promotes intellectual growth, and indeed the whole range of personal development.

Such high values, of course, do not arise from talk that is careless or petty or dull. We are thinking of that kind of conversation which, even though it may be light and casual in tone, is nevertheless the product of outgoing and honest minds whose mutual impact stirs the fires of interest and imagination.

CHARACTERISTICS OF THE GOOD CONVERSATIONALIST

Genuine liking for people. A friendly, outgoing attitude, good-humored and light-hearted, neither flippant nor conceited is coupled with a willingness to meet others as equals in the exchange of knowledge and opinion. The conversationalist talks *with* people, not *to* or *at* them.

Sensitivity to the feelings and viewpoints of others. Spineless yielding of opinion or conviction is not required, but good manners and

2 "Talk and Talkers," *Memories and Portraits*, Scribner, 1904, p. 154.

Conversation is thinking together.

unfailing courtesy are necessary plus a willingness to accept another man's experience at his own evaluation and as a possible means of enlarging our own insights. The ideal courtesy, especially when we are dealing with conceited persons who do not share it, may require no small endowment of fortitude, humility, and humor.

Balance between self-assertion and receptivity. The well-adjusted talker has no lack of confidence to affirm his own ideas or of willingness to listen to his respondent. He is sensitive to the distribution of time and reasonable in exchange of roles from speaker to listener and back again.

Wide-ranging interests and knowledge. None of us can approach the broad and philosophical wisdom which Cicero ascribed to his ideal orator, but we can develop a responsive interest in all the varied kinds of knowledge held by our companions along the way. Indeed we can do more. Instead of "merely using with lifeless talent the topics offered by others," we can, as DeQuincey suggested, attempt to raise such a continual succession of topics as will contribute to the brilliance of conversation; and we can do this without restricting in any way our companion's freedom to make an equal contribution.

Sense of relevance and continuity. Conversation should indeed be free and flexible in its forward movement, but the interacting ideas should have such coherence that each arises out of its predecessor and leads on inevitably to its consequent. As Olive Heseltine said, "The function of conversation is to make some area of thought more interesting and manageable."[3]

[3] Olive Heseltine, *Conversation*, Methuen, 1927, p. 2.

343

Mastery of the contemplative attitude and leisurely pace. The thoughtful pause gives time for depth and enrichment of meaning. A relaxed, deliberate manner is basic to imagination and emotional balance, recall of knowledge and past experience, orderly phrasing and coherent sequence, and the attainment of utterance that is both easy and vigorous. Hurry produces little if any enrichment of thought. Public discourse may at times become hasty and precipitate, but the height of stimulating conversation is most fully realized in a quiet and meditative spirit.

THE IMPROVEMENT OF CONVERSATION

Planned and purposeful exercises in discourse with one or two fellow students involve some hazards and difficulties, but if we can combine thoughtful planning and preparation with a spontaneous quality in the exercise itself, we may open some doors which might otherwise remain closed or only slightly ajar.

Conversation, for example, can serve as a medium for understanding ourselves and developing sensitive and tactful relationships with others—in a word, as a means of developing the attitudes of communication (see Chapter 5). For the timid, conversation can ease the transition from painful silence to self-confidence, and provide opportunities for achieving balance and control in emotional participation. Conversation, rightly used, can give us practice in marshalling our knowledge, bringing it into organized coherence, and adapting it to the interests and feelings of other people and to the tone and spirit of speech occasions. Finally, conversation is a proving ground in which we can exercise the simpler nuances of voice and action and thus develop our command of the symbolic techniques of expression.

Any attempt to lay down a formula for improving speech by means of conversation is sure to be inadequate. If it does not harden into a dogmatic and inflexible set of rules, it is in danger of evaporating into vague and windy platitudes. Nevertheless, we should look for means of improvement. Review the discussion of the interview in Chapter 6, and then study the following additional suggestions concerning the subject matter, attitudes, and the visible and audible elements in conversation.

The subjects of conversation. Try to find the interests and areas of knowledge which you and your companion hold in common. Use tactful questions, especially to draw out a timid person. Respond constructively to your companion's ideas. Differ with him if you must, but in any case try to extend and interpret the subject which he begins. Avoid talking about yourself. You are undoubtedly the most fascinating of subjects—for you; but your respondent may not have the same degree of fascination. Answer his queries about yourself briefly but then toss a question back to him. In some situations the small affairs of daily life may be suitable grist for the conversational mill, but be careful it does not grind too long on the trivial. Avoid broad generalizations and high level abstractions. Let your conversation be rich in vivid detail and relevant illustration or anecdote.

Attitudes in conversation.   Be courteous, give attention, look at your companion. Be confident, respect your own ideas, do not apologize for them. Avoid self-aggrandizement. True conversation is both an exploration of ideas and an excursion in mutual enjoyment; it is not a contest for dominance, and has no place for idea-possessiveness. Even if you are in the presence of a loquacious egotist, who has none of the give-and-take spirit of conversation, maintain your own modesty. If he is so conceited as to ruin companionship and the quest for ideas, leave him.

Be careful not to humiliate your respondent. Avoid a superior attitude and any expression which might suggest it, such as "Do you see?" or "Have you learned that . . . ?" Be slow to interrupt. If you do flag the man down, try to catch him tactfully at a transition point—if you can find one. Maintain good humor, but be careful not to use witticisms which may have an unexpected caustic quality. Humor, badly placed or phrased, can easily become a cutting double edge. If disagreements arise, keep them in friendly spirit or move on to other subjects or—move on.

Visible and audible elements.   Be relaxed but alert and poised in body; do not slouch. Use deliberate pacing; pause. Conversation should be well phrased. Let variety of attitude and interest beget variety in action and voice. Be sure your voice and articulation are pleasant and distinct. Use plain and simple language. Technical or unusual words are in order only when you are sure your listeners understand them. Cultivate the art of easy transition. (See also standards and techniques studied in Part III.)

EXERCISES

1. Write a report and evaluation of a recent conversation in which you engaged. Choose one that was spontaneous, not planned for this assignment, relatively brief (5 to 10 minutes), and recent enough to be quite well remembered. Include in your report (1) a statement about the setting and circumstances, (2) the other person or persons involved (not their names but their general character status and relationship to you and to each other), (3) the subject of the conversation, and (4) a record of the sequence of remarks.

When you have finished the descriptive report, evaluate your part in the conversation in the light of the principles and methods suggested in this chapter and in any supplementary reading your instructor assigns. Suggest ways in which you might have improved your participation. Rewrite any of your statements or questions which in afterthought seem inadequate or inept.

2. Listen quietly and as unobtrusively as possible to several conversations among your friends. Observe the progression of thought. What are the opening topics? Are they developed with any degree of continuity? Are they factual or opinionated? Emotional or matter-of-fact? How frequently do the participants change from topic to topic? Is there any use of orderly transitions? Is there any degree of consistent purpose in each conversation? On the basis of your observations what conclusions would you draw about the thoughtfulness of conversation? If you had been a participant, how would you have improved the talks you listened to?

3. Join your classmates in choosing, with the guidance of your instructor, a few subjects for conversation (perhaps important news events or campus problems or significant books) about which you can talk with real interest. After a day or two during which you can inform yourself about the subject to which you are individually assigned, plan and carry out a conversational procedure such as the following:

Let the class be divided into small groups of three to five members; and let each group retire to a conference room, lounge, or corner of the classroom. One member in each group should be designated to start conversation by asking a question to which another member should reply immediately. The questioner should then follow with another inquiry which grows directly out of the reply, and then another and another, each question to be a direct follow-up of the preceding reply. The questioner should not be allowed to make statements but only to raise questions. When he has completed a series of successive inquiries on the same subject in a period of 5 to 7 minutes, another student should take the role of questioner. He may continue the former subject if it still is vital for the group, or he may begin another. This should continue until each member has had opportunity both to question and reply. More than one student may join in the replies to a given questioner; and any member may contribute supplementary questions so long as they do not disrupt a questioner's line of inquiry or encroach unduly on his time.

The entire procedure, though planned in its general course, should be flexible and spontaneous in performance. If the sessions can be recorded, each group might then make an evaluation of its own activity. If recording is not possible, one student might be assigned to act as recorder and observer and then as resource person for the group's self-evaluation.

4. During your preparation for any one of the exercises in discussion or extempore speaking (see Chapters 19 and 20) in which an interview would be a useful and appropriate means of fact-finding, plan to confer with some available authority in the subject field of your assignment. After study of the principles of interviewing given in Chapter 6 and in this chapter, prepare a written analysis of the information needed and a description of your intended method of approaching your interviewee. Present the plan to your instructor for his advice and suggestions before you actually seek an appointment with your man (or woman). After the interview evaluate your methods on the basis of his responses, suggest ways in which your procedure

might have been improved, and summarize the information gained. Hand the report to your instructor for his comment and evaluation.

    5. Prepare and present to the class a brief talk on one of the following topics:

> Humor as an Element of Conversation
> The Art of Asking Questions
> How to Be a Bore
> Should Conversation Be Competitive?
> The Conversational Bully
> The Virtues of Silence
> The Best Conversationalist I Ever Knew
> Conversation as a Developer of Personality
> Conversation and Public Speaking
> The Kinds of Conversation

A round of talks by an entire class on these and similar subjects might be used as the basis for a review and discussion of the principles of conversation.

SUPPLEMENTARY READINGS

Bacon, Francis, "Of Studies" and "Of Discourse" in *Essays*, edition of 1625.

Bingham, Walter V., and Bruce Moore, *How to Interview*, 4th ed., Harper & Row, 1959.

DeQuincey, Thomas, "Conversation," *Logic of Political Economy and Other Papers*, C. Black, 1863.

Meerloo, Joost A. M., *Conversation and Communication*, International Universities Press, Inc., 1952.

Nutley, Grace Stewart, *How to Carry On a Conversation*, Sterling Publishing Company, 1953.

Oliver, Robert T., *Conversation—The Development and Expression of Personality*, Charles C Thomas, 1961.

Pear, T. H., *The Psychology of Conversation*, Nelson, 1939.

Priestley, J. B., *Talking*, Harper & Row, 1926.

Taft, Henry W., *Kindred Arts: Conversation and Public Speaking*, Macmillan, 1929.

Wiksell, Wesley (ed.), *Your Conversation: As Observed by Eminent Authorities*, Stephens College, 1938.

Wright, Milton, *The Art of Conversation*, McGraw-Hill, 1936.

19

DISCUSSION

Discussion is one kind of original speaking, which we have already defined as speaking in which the participants create and formulate their own thoughts and methods of utterance. Discussion may be further distinguished as *an orderly process of co-operative deliberation designed to exchange, evaluate, and/or integrate knowledge and opinion on a given subject or to work toward solution of a common problem.*

Discussion shares the casual informality, close interpersonal relationships, and frequent exchange of speaker and listener roles characteristic of conversation; but differs from it in the larger number of people involved, their more complex interpersonal relations, and the greater degree of planned, purposeful, and orderly procedure. The typical member of a discussion group comes in the spirit of inquiry ready to pool his resources of knowledge and opinion with those of his colleagues in a search for the best possible conclusion or decision. (The typical public speaker, in contrast, comes to his task with purpose and theme chosen, and usually with listeners assembled to hear his message.)

In its broadest scope discussion is often understood to include debate, but more precise concepts distinguish between the two activities. Debate is a form of controversial public address in which opposing speakers meet face to face and speak under definite rules of procedure. Speakers in discussion typically have less rigidly prescribed procedure and engage each other in a manner more cooperative than competitive or controversial. The typical starting point of debate is a statement or question: "Resolved that . . . etc." or "Shall we adopt this proposal or belief?" The typical starting point for discussion is a question such as "How can we understand this subject better?" "What is the nature of this problem?" or "What shall we do about this problem?" The typical debater is an advocate who speaks to defend his convictions and bring others to his point of view; the typical discussant is an inquirer who has not arrived at a definite opinion but is still in process of exploring a subject or problem to find the best possible solution.

The formulation of a question or resolution for debate requires some preliminary *discussion* of the nature of a difficulty and recognition of one or more available solutions. If opponents of a proposed solution can secure its defeat, or if the advocates secure adoption and it fails to remove the difficulty or do what is needed, the problem is again thrown back into the arena of general discussion until another definite proposal is put forward. Then pro and con debate is again the necessary procedure. A series of successive debates on successive proposals may thus proceed until an effective remedy for the problem is found.

TYPES OF DISCUSSION

The total process of understanding our group and community problems and finding solutions for them usually employs a wide range of discussion activities. In general they fall into two classes: (1) informal round-table conference, and (2) public discussion. The round-table type of discussion typically involves more than the two or three people of a private conversation, but still a number small enough that each person can be aware of and react to every other member. The limits for such a relationship range from four or five to fifteen or possibly twenty people. Meetings are usually prearranged and proceed under a leader according to a method which is essentially cooperative rather than competitive. In social and community activities we see discussion of this kind functioning in such different situations as study groups, committee meetings, cooperative investigations, classrooms, and problem-solving sessions. The small-group method is often adapted to larger meetings by dividing the members into "buzz" groups of four to six or eight members in order to bring everyone actively into the process of group thinking. The results of such smaller sessions may then be brought together in a panel or symposium consisting of a representative from each group.

The second general type, public discussion, occurs when the number of people assembled is too large for direct, face-to-face interaction. There are several subforms depending on the way in which the procedure is organized:

1. Panel discussion. A small number of speakers (usually three to six) converse together in the presence of an audience. The members of the panel talk *to* each other *for* the listeners.

2. Symposium. Several speakers (usually three or four) address an audience on a common topic. In a planned. symposium there is preliminary division of the subject so that the speakers present a more or less coherent sequence of material.

3. Forum. A subject or problem is presented by one or more speakers. The presentation is followed by a period of comment or questions from the audience. There are several kinds of forums—lecture, panel, symposium—according to the kind of initial presentation.

4. Colloquy. This is a special type of forum in which a panel from the audience is supplemented by a panel of experts in the subject field who serve as resource persons to provide facts and opinions as needed.

5. Public hearing. A committee, usually either administrative or legislative, holds a public meeting to gather information and opinion on some question of public policy by hearing and questioning experts and interested citizens.

6. Conference or institute. A continuous series of meetings is organized to consider a single large problem or subject field. Such programs require careful advance planning and arrangement of detail, and utilize lectures as well as a variety of discussion methods.

You will observe that these types of public discussion, except perhaps the panel, are actually specialized ways of using public speaking.

A panel discussion is semiformal.

All of them involve in some degree a formal speaker-audience relationship with a designated speaker or speakers taking the leading role and dominating the procedure. It is not our purpose to study these various forms of public discussion in any detail. Our primary interest is in the less formal small-group processes, although of course some of the general principles we shall study apply to all kinds of discussion, public as well as private.

LEVELS AND VALUES OF DISCUSSION

Discussion in all its various forms, both public and private, is a basic and indispensable process in the democratic way of life. It operates at all the major levels of decision-making.

The first level reaches decisions by the method of majority vote. This method is most used in all our larger political and civic affairs. Problems are discussed and issues debated publicly, and decisions reached at the ballot box or by vote of representatives in policy-making assemblies. Within the framework of basic law and civic institutions the widest range of discussion and debate should be used. The method depends, of course, on preservation of the citizen's franchise and protection of the rights of minorities. It is essentially controversial, but must operate within a framework of basic law and institutions which are cooperative. If democracy is to operate successfully, minorities must be willing to accept majority decisions and majorities must be careful not to override basic rights and freedoms. Minorities often grow into majorities and may change tomorrow the decision of today. Any given decision, however, is reached primarily by means of public discussion and debate, although a vast network of smaller committee and conference discussion may often provide a foundation for the public decision.

A second level of the democratic process reaches decisions through compromise. By this method citizens or their representatives yield some part of their convictions or preferences for the sake of unanimity. This, of course, is not completely separate from the level of majority decision. Compromise proposals, developed during the discussion of a problem or difficulty, may provide the specific issues which are settled by majority vote. The work of conference committees between the two houses of a legislative body, for example, is often the only way in which they can agree on the formulation of a bill. The processes of compromise operate not so much by public discussion as in conferences and committee hearings in which bases for agreement are developed.

A third level of discussion aims to solve problems by means of consensus. Its method is cooperative investigation and thought, and its ideal goal is complete agreement. Members of the discussion group come together without prior commitment but with minds open to find the best possible conclusions. Such a method requires a high degree of objectivity and emotional balance, and a willingness on the part of every member to pool his resources of knowledge and opinion with those of every other member and to accept the facts fully without prejudice or preconception. We must recognize, of course, that such a method is idealistic and does not fit all kinds of situations or problems. It requires time for the slow maturing of thought, and can be carried out only in small groups whose members are in good rapport. Whenever a genuine consensus is attained, however, the decision is likely to prove both sound and workable because it is a product of group thinking to which all have contributed and which all therefore accept and support. Even though the hard realities of life's problems and the peculiarities of human nature may limit the usefulness of consensus as an independent method, it embodies attitudes and ideals which should permeate all methods of discussion and all levels of decision.

These broad aspects of the decision-making process suggest the range within which the forms of discussion operate. They are the processes by which people live and work together in organized groups and solve their problems cooperatively. That the various forms of discussion differ in methods and techniques is obvious, yet all of them embody certain fundamental principles and procedures. In spirit and method all the forms of discussion involve a basic element of cooperation and pooling of resources. All of them aim to achieve one or both of two fundamental purposes—(1) inquiry or the discovery and synthesis of information, and (2) problem-solution or the discovery of ways to remove difficulties or inadequacies in life situations and processes. All the forms of discussion require some kind and degree of leadership, and all of them use problem-solving method in some part.

For the student seeking basic speech improvement, discussion has special values. Together with other forms of speaking, especially conversation, it offers opportunities for improvement of communicative attitudes, ease and emotional balance, facility in marshaling knowledge and adapting it to listener and situation, and the light touch and quick rejoinder. The study of discussion, moreover, has distinctive values of its own. Beyond all other forms of speech, discussion requires cooperative attitudes and tactful response to other people. Open-mindedness, tolerance and objectivity are essential. Interaction with other minds provides stimulation and guidance toward logical thinking. Finally discussion offers an unsurpassed opportunity for study of the problem-solving method of thought.

REQUIREMENTS OF DISCUSSION

Effective procedures differ as widely as the various forms; but certain principles and techniques are fundamental, especially for the round-table, panel and problem-solving types.

The right kind of setting is important. If possible, the size of the room should be in harmony with the size of the group, and the seating arrangement should provide face-to-face relationship of all the members (preferably around a table or in a circle). Unless the members are already well acquainted, name tags or other easy means of identification should be provided. Materials for note-taking should be handy. Charts, maps, pictures and a blackboard, if needed, should be arranged in advance so as to provide easy view for all members (see the section on visual aids in Chapter 13).

The subject or problem should be so clearly worded that there can be no doubt or confusion about it. If this has not been done before the meeting, it should be one of the first items on the agenda. Very few rigid rules can be prescribed for wording discussion questions because they are as variable as the types of problems. Some call for investigation of facts, others for analysis and interpretation of them. Some problems center in attitude and belief, others in a program for action. Some require a search for adequate policies, others for means of implementing policy. The form of wording should grow out of the nature of the problem and should be adapted to the qualifications of the group and the time available for discussion. Only a few general principles can be suggested.

Question form should be used in order to emphasize the exploratory nature of the process. Let the wording be as simple and direct as possible. Technical or highly specialized language should be used only if the nature of the subject requires and the members of the discussion group understand it. Avoid loading the questions with prejudicial words such as qualifying adjectives or phrases which imply argument. Better say, "How should the tax laws of our state be revised?" instead of "What can be done about our confused and unjust tax laws?" The existence of confused or unjust laws is a point to be investigated or proved, not assumed. Better say, "What can we do to reduce cheating at our university?" than "In view of the arbitrary action of the faculty, should the student body try to do anything about cheating?" Any action by the faculty, whatever its nature, should not be assumed in the statement of question, but should be brought into the discussion as a demonstrable point of fact.

The breadth and scope of a question, moreover, should be consistent with the aims and qualifications of the discussants and the time available. For students the question, "How can we best describe an educated man?" may be a valuable means of formulating educational goals; but so generalized a wording probably would be entirely inadequate for a group of citizens trying to analyze a difficulty in the public educational system. Open field questions such as, "What should be our attitude on the civil rights issue?" have the merit of opening an entire problem area, but may lead nowhere if a group is working within time limits. A more specific question such as, "What should be our attitude on the proposed open housing ordinance in our city?" would be more likely to yield definite results.

If only exploration of a situation or difficulty is required the question should be phrased in a form such as: "How should we define _____?" "What are the causes of _____?" "Is the present system or policy adequate?" On the other hand problem-solving questions should take some such form as: "How best can we _____?" "What should be our attitude toward _____?" "What policy shall we adopt for _____?" If some part of a problem has already been explored, a given discussion may be confined to one or two of the remaining aspects, such as searching for possible courses of action, setting up criteria for judgment, or considering ways and means to put into effect a course of action already chosen. (See the outline of the problem-solving pattern on pp. 166–167.) Questions or resolutions which propose any single belief or action, as we have seen, are usually more suitable for debate than for discussion because they call for advocacy rather than exploration.

The procedure or pattern of the discussion should be governed by its purpose. We have already studied the most basic patterns (see Chapter 9). If the group is seeking information or a broader outlook in some social or cultural area, the subject matter may fall easily into a topical or chronological pattern. If the purpose is to analyze and understand a problem, the causal or logical patterns may be needed. The most basic procedure for serious discussion, however, is the problem-solving method. It consists of five indispensable levels or stages of thought:

1. Awareness of a difficulty
2. Analysis of its nature and causes
3. Suggestion of possible solutions
4. Evaluation of solutions
5. Acceptance and application of that solution which is chosen as best

Such an order of thoughtful procedure may be useful in almost any kind of discourse, even in a simple exchange of information; but its most significant application is in problem-solving. Here the order of steps should be followed consistently as given, because each level provides an indispensable foundation for the steps which follow. Obviously awareness of a difficulty must precede its analysis, which is a necessary preliminary to the search for solutions. Just as obviously an evaluation of proposed solutions must precede the choice and implementation of any one of them. Problem-solving is a basic method which includes the most essential thought processes—fact-finding, analysis, evaluation, synthesis, motivation, imaginative projection, emotional balance, and memory—but the five main steps outline an orderly pattern in which all these processes of thought should function.

Finally, the interpersonal relations of discussion are derived from attitudes toward self, toward the subject or problem, and toward other members of the group. (Review the section on attitudes and speech in Chapter 5.) The adequate discussant is a person of emotional verve and balance. He has a modest kind of self-confidence which may be characterized as objective. He sees himself realistically in relation to other members of his group. In respect to the subject or problem, the ideal discussant strives for complete intellectual honesty. His knowledge is wide-ranging and well verified. He makes a thorough attempt to discover and escape his own bias. In relation to his colleagues in the discussion process, the primary attitude of every participant should be a readiness to think cooperatively. He will have convictions and declare them frankly, but he will also search for ways of integrating his thought into the consensus of group thinking. The spirit of discussion is neither competitive nor combative, but a genuine "working with."

If we are to implement these ideals and principles effectively in practice, the following attitudes and techniques are necessary:

From the standpoint of *attitude,* the successful participant in discussion

Is an open-minded seeker of the best solution for problems.

Does not come to the meeting as an advocate with his mind made up to support one proposal or point of view.

Is willing to accept verified facts even if they run counter to his bias.

From the standpoint of *knowledge,* the successful participant in discussion

Distinguishes between the facts he *knows* and opinions he *believes.*

Is willing to carry on thorough search for facts.

Insists on careful verification of every alleged fact.

From the standpoint of *procedure,* the successful participant in discussion

Has the ability to listen. Listening involves a genuine attempt to understand the viewpoints of others.

Avoids personalities and name-calling.

States his own ideas tentatively as contributions to group thinking.

Says frankly and honestly what he believes and *why* and *how* he arrived at it.

Speaks up freely but is careful not to dominate the discussion.

When he does speak, makes his utterance as direct, concise, simple, and conversational, as possible.

Speaks relevantly to the point and purpose of the discussion and adheres to an orderly sequence of logical procedure.

LEADERSHIP

Discussion requires leadership as well as participation. Two general concepts of leadership are important. First, there is the designated or nominal leader who serves as chairman or moderator. His main functions are to see that the setting is properly arranged, get the meeting started, introduce the members or speakers, conduct the procedure in orderly manner, and bring it to appropriate close. The second concept of leadership refers to anyone who is influential in directing the course of group thinking. The nominal or designated leader may not always be the actual leader. In this informal sense leadership may rest with one most influential person or may change from moment to moment so that any individual member may lead at one moment and become just another participant the next moment. Groups in which such distributed leadership operates are often called "leaderless groups" although the term is not strictly accurate because in such a case every member accepts a large measure of responsibility for the progress of the discussion.

From another point of view there are as many kinds of leaders as there are types and functions of group activity. First, we recognize the expert who has information to give. As resource person he may exert strong influence on group thought; if he assumes more than a basic informative role, he may become authoritarian and disrupt the co-operative nature of discussion. Another type of leader is the proponent or compeller who has decided in advance what direction the group thinking should take and exerts subtle but strong pressure. Some group conferences in business or military affairs are of this authoritarian type; the commander or boss knows what he wants and calls a meeting to let his subordinates "discover" it for themselves. A third type of leader is the representative or spokesman, who keeps his ear to the ground and formulates group opinion just one step ahead of the members. He is an expert on trends. Then of course there is the chairman whose function is merely to preside; he introduces speakers, enforces time limits, and in symposium or forum may summarize the speakers' con-tributions. In policy-making bodies he usually follows rules of parlia-mentary procedure. Finally there is the type of leader who is a group builder, whose method is evocative and even creative. He attempts to stimulate, guide and crystallize group thinking so as to achieve some degree of that integration which results in consensus.

Each of these different kinds of leaders serves an essential func-tion in one or more of the various types of discussion processes. Some groups need instruction; others require an interpreter of trends. Some situations call for a firm authoritarian hand; others need only a chair-man. The group builder, however, is the kind of leader in whom we are most interested. He is the type needed especially in the small, informal, cooperative group which hopes to arrive at consensus. His ideal qualifi-cations are those of a paragon—mental alertness, objective attitude, ability to analyze and synthesize, emotional balance and control, tact, patience, sense of humor, humility, and social vision. He refuses to assume the role of expert or authority, or to become a protagonist when differences of opinion arise. He keeps his own personality in the back-ground, but has the strength of character to wield a strong guiding influence when the group wanders from its major purpose. He con-centrates always on the goal to be attained. Some of his more important functions and activities are the following:

To get a meeting started

  Create a spirit of friendliness and good will.
  State the purpose of the meeting.

State the problem or difficulty (as far as it is known).

Outline any special plans, procedures, or rules for the meeting.

Show the importance of the matter to be discussed.

Present some leading question or questions.

To encourage general participation

Stimulate the timid members.

Curb the overly talkative members.

Call for information he knows members possess (with care not to embarrass the timid ones).

Avoid the listener-learner attitude.

Encourage a cooperative attitude.

To keep the discussion on the track

Hold the group to an orderly procedure.

Allow flexibility and variation as the group's thinking proceeds.

Keep perspective and view of the goal.

Make occasional summaries of progress, preferably at transition points.

To see that all conclusions are based on verified information

Ask for sources of information.

Point out the need for investigation whenever it arises.

Provide for committees or individuals to make the investigations.

To maintain balance in the discussion

See to it that all aspects, possible solutions, and points of view are considered.

Recognize and summarize agreements.

Encourage matter-of-fact exploration of disagreements.

To crystallize results by bringing agreements into focus

Agreements on fact.

Agreements on purpose and principle.

Agreements on needs the solution must meet.

Agreement on solution chosen.

Perhaps even agreement that certain points are matters of persistent and unshakable disagreement.

Two of the most important techniques a leader may use in carrying out these functions are questions and summaries.

Questions are an important means of suggestion rather than domination on the part of a leader. Some questions may be exploratory, calling for facts; others may be evocative, bringing out opinions; still others may be evaluative, asking for judgments of the worth of facts or opinions. Whatever their function, questions should not be loaded; they should not point to any given answer as in "Might it not be . . . ?" The phrasing of questions should be clear and definite, as simple as possible, and clearly related to points under discussion. A wise leader will use them with caution so that the deliberations of his group do not become merely a question and answer period.

Summaries are less evocative than questions, but more positive in their contribution to group thinking. In a sense they serve a purpose in small group conference similar to parliamentary devices and voting procedures in larger meetings. Summaries mark the main transitions and stages in progress of a group's deliberations. One of the surest marks of the wise and mature leader is the sensitivity to realize when his group's thinking is ready to be summarized and carried forward to its next stage. Every summary should represent actual progress fairly, should crystallize achievement up to that point, and should be subject to review by the entire membership. An ideal summary will also stimulate further discussion or lead on to the next step in procedure.

We have not attempted to present a full or adequate treatment of the forms and techniques of discussion, but merely to summarize the most elemental and necessary principles we should observe if the practice of discussion is to contribute to our basic speech improvement. The highest test of success in group discussion is not merely the number or difficulty of problems solved, even though solution of problems is the ultimate goal. The highest test is the emergence of a sense of group unity, a cohesive will to think and act together. In so far as we attain this end, we shall have made real progress in developing our speech as a process of social life.

EXERCISES

1. Prepare a list of questions which you would like to use for an assignment in group discussion. Keep in mind the standards for choice of subjects and wording. Consider especially the timeliness and importance of the problems you choose; their breadth or scope in relation to circumstances of the discussion, especially the time limits; and the avoidance of prejudicial terms and phrases in your statement (see Introduction for the Student).

2. Listen to a panel discussion and prepare a critical evaluation of it. Prior to listening join your fellow students in developing an outline or list of the standards you should apply. In the evaluation observe not only the points your outline includes, but be alert also to discover other important elements of procedure by the discussion group. Write the evaluation and hand it to your instructor. If a televised discussion program can be brought into the classroom, it will provide an excellent opportunity for evaluation by means of class discussion.

3. With the class divided into groups of five to seven members, let each group choose an exploratory type of question (see Introduction for the Student), and engage in a series of two or more round-table or conference type discussions. At its first session each group should choose a

leader, analyze the phases of its problem, and determine the kinds of information needed. Each member should be given primary, though not necessarily exclusive, responsibility for fact-finding on one of the aspects or issues of the question. The later session or sessions should attempt to synthesize the findings and reach a consensus or agreement on the facts of the situation. For each group an observer should be appointed to take the lead in post-session evaluations of the procedure.

4. Again divide the class into small discussion groups, each of which should plan and present before the rest of the class a panel discussion of the problem-solving or action-determining type. Each group should hold a preliminary planning session to choose a leader, select a problem, make tentative analysis of the issues involved, and assign to each member primary responsibility for fact-finding on some one issue or aspect of the problem. Each member should prepare an outline similar to Example 34 in Chapter 9 as a summary of his thought and preparation for the panel. The series of panel discussions thus prepared and presented by the various groups should be the basis for observation and evaluation of discussion techniques and procedures by the entire class.

SUPPLEMENTARY READINGS

Barnlund, Dean C., and Franklin S. Haiman, *The Dynamics of Discussion*, Houghton Mifflin, 1960.

Chase, Stuart, and Marian Tyler, *Roads to Agreement: Successful Methods in the Science of Human Relations*, Harper & Row, 1951.

Crowell, Laura, *Discussion: Method of Democracy*, Scott, Foresman, 1963.

Elliott, Harrison S., *The Process of Group Thinking*, Association Press, 1932.

Ewbank, Henry Lee, and J. Jeffery Auer, *Discussion and Debate: Tools of a Democracy*, 2nd ed., Appleton-Century-Crofts, 1951.

Kemp, C. Gratton, *Perspectives on the Group Process*, Houghton Mifflin, 1964.

Lee, Irving J., *How To Talk With People*, Harper & Row, 1952.

McBurney, James H., and Kenneth G. Hance, *Discussion in Human Affairs*, Harper & Row, 1950.

Ross, Murray G., and Charles E. Hendry, *New Understandings of Leadership*, Association Press, 1957.

20

PUBLIC ADDRESS

The study of rhetoric began among the ancient Greeks as long ago as the fifth century before Christ, when men faced the necessity of defending their civic and property rights in court and sought the help of logographers and rhetors. The development of democratic institutions, especially in Athens, provided an impetus for continued study of speaking, which has been carried on in various ways to the present day. As a result, the principles of public speaking probably are more highly developed than those of any other form of speech. All students of speech, whether their interests are in discussion, phonetics, semantics, oral reading, or any other special aspect, have a rich heritage in the rhetoric of public address.

Public speaking is traditionally the form of speech most used in public life; the primary form of oral instruction in classrooms, lecture halls, and over the great media of mass communication; and the principal means of oral persuasion by which public problems are debated, decisions made, and policies formulated.

Public address is a type of original speaking in which one person is the dominant stimulating factor, carrying on a sustained discourse directly to a given audience in a specific setting for the purpose of arousing a definite and usually predetermined response.

The basic types of public speaking were recognized and described by Aristotle in the fourth century before Christ. First he listed the deliberative or policy-making speech. A deliberative speaker, he said, looks to the future and gives counsel or advice about proposed or possible courses of action. The primary method is persuasive and the aim is to secure advantage or avoid disadvantage. Next Aristotle described the forensic or courtroom speech. A forensic speaker looks to the past and attempts to influence judgments about the guilt or innocence of persons in relation to acts already done. The primary methods are accusation and defense and the outcome is justice or injustice. Finally, Aristotle recognized the demonstrative or ceremonial kind of speaking. A ceremonial speaker serves a present occasion, although he may draw material from the past or refer to the future. The materials are praise or blame, humor or sentiment; and the primary aim is to honor (or dishonor) a person or event and sometimes even such an object as monument or building.

Through the centuries, these basic forms have been developed in greater variety. Under the deliberative type, for example, we now recognize a difference between legislative addresses made in policy-making or representative bodies and campaign speeches made before general public audiences. In modern courtroom practice we distinguish between the pleas of attorneys and a judge's instructions to a jury. Demonstrative speeches we have developed into commemorative types, such as dedications and eulogies, and occasional or courtesy types such as speeches of introduction, welcome, farewell, reponse, presentation, acceptance and after-dinner speeches, all of which serve occasions.

Changing modes of thought and social conditions during the centuries have also given rise to new forms. The Christian Church has developed the sermon or pulpit speech. The rise of universities and spread of popular education brought forth the lecture or expository speech. The growth of modern big business and industrial organization led to recognition of the special field of business speaking. Our purpose is not to study all these various forms of public speaking, but to consider those fundamental characteristics which are comon to all of them and which will contribute most significantly to our basic speech improvement.

Distinctive Features of Public Speaking

Probably the most significant elements of public speaking are to be found in its (1) purposes, (2) speaker-listener relationships, (3) systematic organization, (4) sustained development and proof, and (5) special adaptations of the media of symbolic formulation and expression, that is of action, voice and language.

The purposes of public address have been variously named, but are generally thought of as falling into five principal levels: to entertain, amuse or arouse interest; to instruct or inform; to inspire or stimulate; to influence attitude or belief; to motivate or move to action. (Study the relation of this list to the more general speech purposes given in Chapter 8.) A speaker is expected to determine in advance not only what *kind* of response he desires from his hearers, but the *specific* response. If his purpose is to entertain the listener, is the reaction to be subtle empathy or overt laughter? If instruction is the aim, exactly what subject matter is to be understood? If the listener is to be inspired, what specific persons, events, or objects are to be appreciated? If belief is to be influenced, what convictions or doctrines of faith are to be accepted? If overt behavior is to be motivated, exactly what action is sought?

Other forms of speech seldom require such specific determination of purpose in advance. Conversation, for example, tends to be more casual and may have a rapidly shifting variety of purposes. Discussion typically has a more general goal which depends on exploratory and cooperative processes for its specific result, which no one participant, therefore, can formulate in advance.

In public speaking the responses of listeners are relatively silent; the transmission of auditory stimuli is largely a one-way process. Interaction occurs, of course, as in all speech; but the feedback from audience to speaker is not only visual but, since overt movement of audiences is necessarily limited, primarily empathic.

Public speaking requires systematic structuring of ideas prior to utterance. A public speaker needs to decide in advance, whenever possible, what particular pattern of organization—topical, chronological, causal, logical, or problem-solving—best fits his purpose and material (review Chapter 9). Whatever its basic pattern, the plan of the speech should be arranged in three parts—introduction, body, and conclusion—and should observe also the other basic requirements of good outlining (review Chapter 8).

Public speeches require also thorough and systematic use of the methods for developing thought. If statistics or statements by authorities are available and pertinent, the wise speaker will use them. He will define, enumerate, compare, and sometimes repeat and raise questions to give his material more attention value. A listener needs images based on daily experience to give substance and body to general propositions. A speaker, therefore, should make full use of examples or specific instances and illustrations drawn from knowledge already familiar. Whether he aims to enlighten understanding, win assent, or merely stimulate, a public speaker will need to search out the entire factual bases of his theme, and consider the impact of his own personality and of the imaginative and emotional elements of his material as well as the soundness of his inferences (review Chapters 6, 7, 10, and 11).

The presence of a group of listeners, instead of one or a few, requires more thoughtful choice of language and more extended use of voice and action than are needed in more casual kinds of utterance. In a public speaking situation the dangers of misunderstanding are enhanced because listeners do not have freedom to respond immediately and specifically as statements are made. The speaker, therefore, should choose his words with unusual care. As the size of audiences increases, the auditory elements must be transmitted in greater range. The pauses will need to be longer, the phrasing more definite, the vocal power more vigorous, and all the variables of voice increased in range and flexibility. A speaker's quality of tone becomes especially important if he is to be heard at a distance, for the noise elements (i.e., irregular vibrations) in unpleasant voice qualities tend to damp each other out by interference. Pleasant tone qualities with their regular vibrations, on the other hand, are more easily heard at greater distances. (Review the section on nature of sound in Chapter 14.) Finally in an enlarged speaking situation the variations of pitch and loudness must show the various degrees of emphasis more clearly than in the private uses of speech.

The Practice of Public Speaking

Any kind of thoughtful and well-prepared audience speaking—whether sales talk, eulogy, after-dinner speech, informative lecture or persuasive argument—can be valuable for the development of speech abilities; but two elementary kinds of speaking involve the most fundamental processes common to the various types and therefore seem most useful for our purposes: (1) the expository talk, or speech to inform and (2) the argumentative or persuasive speech.

THE SPEECH TO INFORM

Under this heading fall several specific kinds of talks—announcements, reports, instructions, classroom lectures, descriptions, book reviews, biographies, and historical narratives. In some ways an expository talk is closely similar to many of the demonstrative and occasional forms. These various kinds, of course, involve some differences; but in such basic characteristics as purpose, theme, organization, methods of development, and use of symbolic processes, they are all fundamentally similar.

Subject. The subject of a speech to inform is frequently suggested, if not demanded, by the nature of the occasion. Lecturers before organized groups usually are invited because they have special knowledge of subjects interesting or valuable to members of the organization. Similarly a classroom audience has assembled for a definite kind of learning, and a professor is under obligation to adhere to the subject systematically —except, of course, that he should be allowed to tell his favorite jokes. As a student of speech you should choose for informative talks those subjects which come from your own areas of study and interest and which you can relate to the knowledge and interests of your classmates.

Purpose. The purpose of an expository talk, of course, is always to give information, to systematize and clarify confused or obscure facts, or to deepen understanding of an area of knowledge. A speaker may include some remarks about the value or importance of his material if necessary and, if there should be a question about the reliability of some of the facts, an argument to establish their credibility. Otherwise he should have no need for motivating or persuasive argument. He should be willing to let his hearers decide what application to make of his information.

We should always remember that the function of a conclusion

A public speaker must adjust to the setting.

is to bring to effective close the identical theme which has been developed, not to suggest some partially new line of thought or purpose. For example, if a speaker who explains the make-up of a symphony orchestra (see Example 29 in Chapter 9) closes with an invitation to attend a concert, he has in effect declared a new purpose and theme which have not actually been developed. An expository address is seldom concluded effectively by sudden change to persuasive purpose at the close; and just as obviously a persuasive purpose cannot be accomplished in the closing moments of an address otherwise expository. Consistency of purpose is one of the marks of an able speaker.

Organization. The organization of an expository talk is usually topical, although some other patterns may be used if they fit the subject matter (see Chapter 9). A chronological sequence, for example, is especially suitable for historical subjects and those dealing with processes. The causal pattern and the problem-solving pattern may also be used.

The only pattern which does not fit a speech to inform is the logical. In such a speech the "because" relationship between main and supporting points simply does not exist—not if the talk is truly expository. The speaker is not giving reasons why we should accept his point of view; he is not trying to win assent. His main points are not issues to be argued, but simply major parts of his theme arrived at by subdividing the subject; and the subpoints should be component parts or details of the higher level points under which they stand. These various divisions or points, as we have seen (see section on topical pattern in Chapter 9), may be based on whatever elements are inherent in the subject, such as spatial, part-whole, substance-quality, basic questions, or any other; but so long as they represent a way of dividing the subject, the pattern is topical.

Whatever plan of organization is adopted, however, should be followed consistently. A shift from one kind of pattern to another in the midst of an explanation can be as confusing as a change of purpose. The introduction to a speech to inform, moreover, should arouse interest in the subject and forecast the plan of presentation, and may include some remarks on the importance of the material or the ways in which it may be used. The conclusion should bring into focus the central feature or key idea of the entire discourse, and may epitomize its pattern of organization.

Development. The development of a speech to inform should use methods which will attain maximum clarity and vividness. Select only those items of fact and principle which are necessary to the explanation; omit minor and unimportant details. The precept is easy to state, less easy to follow. What is *necessary* material? How can one distinguish between essential and nonessential? These are questions for which there is no sure formula. A speaker must exercise his judgment on the basis of the total speaking situation, with special attention to the background and receptivity of his audience. Certain methods, however, have stood the test of time and experience.

First, use examples, concrete instances, and illustrations (review Chapter 17). No one can follow a chain of general or abstract statements for long unless he can see them in terms of specific details and vivid imagery. Notice, for example, that the student who spoke on Samuel Adams (see Example 28 in Chapter 8) did not merely tell us that Adams was prominent in early protests which led to the Revolution, but described also his specific activities and gave names and dates. These are the kinds of materials which give definite meaning to a theme.

Second, in choosing materials for developing an explanation maintain balance between that which is new and informative and that which is already familiar. Your listeners are seeking increased knowledge, but they will surely find difficulty understanding information which is new to them unless it is related to that which they already know. Read Thomas Huxley's essay, "The Method of Scientific Investigation," and observe how simply he explains complex mental processes by reference to familiar, everyday experiences—the tasting of an apple, the discovery that a teapot and spoons are missing, an open window nearby, the mark of a dirty hand, the impress of a hobnailed shoe, and the argument with a friend. Notice also his references to definite places—Somersetshire, Devonshire, Normandy, and North America. The explanation is effective because it uses familiar experience to clarify that which is new and unfamiliar.

Symbolic processes. A talk to inform should make distinctive use of bodily action, voice, articulation, pronunciation, and the choice and combination of words. These, as we know, are the media by which a speaker's ideas can be brought effectively into his listener's experience.

We saw in Chapter 13 that the whole body should be balanced, alert and controlled in action. Be as easy and informal as possible, but let your action also be energetic enough to enliven your subject and keep the listeners alert. For expository speaking representative or descriptive gestures are especially useful. The hand, for example, can point, divide, measure, shape, caress, show direction, accept, or reject. The head can affirm or deny. The eye and face can indicate relative distance or breadth of view. We have also studied the values and uses of visual aids. These are especially important for expository speaking. Remember to maintain direct eye contact with your listeners; do not let the chart or map or picture get between you and them.

Adequate pausing and definite phrasing are indispensable. Get on with the explanation, of course, but give people time to understand. Give yourself time also to realize the relationships and relative importance of successive divisions and units of your discourse, so that your vocal modulations will show the right degrees of emphasis. The differences between main and subordinate ideas should be made unmistakably clear. Each successive new idea should be given emphasis according to its relative importance (review Chapter 15).

Let your statements be simple and direct. Choose a short and simple word whenever it will serve your meaning as well as a longer one. Define unfamiliar terms. Words which are to clarify and explain should be concrete, specific, vivid, and above all else, as exact and accurate as possible (review Chapter 17).

THE PERSUASIVE OR ARGUMENTATIVE SPEECH

We know, of course, that persuasive speaking is of basic importance in a democratic society. We hear persuasion in political campaign addresses, debates in legislative assemblies and other policy-making bodies, general speeches of advocacy before community audiences, courtroom arguments, sales talks, some sermons, and indeed in any and every kind of public speaking which aims to influence directly the beliefs and actions of men. Conversation and discussion may frequently involve arguments on particular points; and even expository speeches, as we have seen, may at times need to convince listeners of the importance of the subject or the reliability of sources.

These various kinds of persuasive speeches have certain differences. Some speeches are primarily logical in method, others primarily motivating. Some are plain and matter-of-fact in style, others highly figurative. The very words *persuasion* and *argument* have different meanings. The first usually refers to speaking in which emotional appeal and motivation are dominant, the other to a closely reasoned logical discourse. The differences are so relative, however, that we shall use the terms as synonyms. In such basic elements as subject, purpose, patterns of organization, methods of development, and some symbolic processes, all these kinds of speaking have fundamental similarities. Our present concern is with these elements of likeness.

Subjects. The subjects of persuasive speaking are typically controversial. Differences of attitude or behavior may not be direct and open; they may consist of nothing more than neutrality of belief or lassitude in action. Nevertheless, whenever two or more people do not believe or act in full unison, there is a setting for persuasive talk. The subjects may range all the way from the simplest practices of daily living to affairs of state or matters of conscience and worship.

Purposes. The basic purposes of persuasive speaking are (1) to influence attitudes, (2) to induce belief in a policy or article of faith, and (3) to move to action. These are not so much different kinds of response as they are differences in level or degree or immediacy of overt response. An attitude, as we have seen (Chapter 5), is an internal readiness for a given kind of action; belief is more a matter of intellectual assent. Both are primarily subjective and covert, while action springs from motivation and takes the form of overt and evident response. All actions, however, are the result of some attitude or belief which they translate into outward and visible behavior; and a belief or attitude which does not lead to action at some appropriate time is too weak and insignificant to be important for our study of speech.

Organization. The logical plan is best adapted to persuasive speaking (review Chapter 9). Other patterns may be used, especially problem-solving if the speaker advocates a policy or plan of action. Topical patterns, though sometimes used in speeches of advocacy, are not really well adapted either to the purpose or to the kind of proof required. Topics, as we have seen, are only subdivisions of subject matter, not impelling reasons why listeners should accept or believe or act in accord with a speaker's theme. A speaker who aims to win assent should not be content merely to divide his subject into parts and elaborate the detail of each part, as he might do in an expository talk. If he wishes to persuade he must give reasons; he should use the "because" relationship between main and subordinate statements so that each lower order point will directly support the statement under which it stands. The reasons, if they are effective, will be based on the kind of analysis which finds the issues in controversy (see the section on analysis in Chapter 8).

Refer to Example 33 in Chapter 9 and observe that the speaker did not divide his subject on the basis of kinds of facts or areas of knowledge—economic, political, social, or any other. Instead he based his opposition to federal farm price supports on their operation. He challenged their effectiveness, pointed out the harmful results, and suggested other possible remedies. If instead of opposing, he had been among those who were advocating farm price supports, he might have had to consider not only the questions about operation but also the difficulties and dangers which created the need for some kind of assistance to farmers—unless, of course, that need had already been clearly established.

Men who think carefully about a proposed policy or solution will require that any speaker who attempts to persuade them shall consider at least four basic issues—the needs to be met, the potential effectiveness of the proposal in meeting those needs, the possible side effects, and the relative merits of other available measures or courses of action. (Notice that these issues closely parallel the steps in problem-solving which are presented in Chapter 9 and referred to again in Chapter 19.) Analysis should reveal which of these basic aspects of a problem are important in a given case. If a speaker examines the reasons put forward by those who advocate a given belief or action and then examines the objections of those who oppose or doubt, he will soon discover the crucial issues in controversy. These should be the main headings of his argument. In persuasive address, moreover, the introduction should not only declare the theme and possibly forecast its method of development, but should also give whatever information is necessary for understanding the argument and arouse the listener's interest so that his attention is polarized for the main body of the talk. The conclusion should reiterate the main theme and bring the motivating appeals to their highest possible level of impelling effectiveness. (Review the sections on introduction and conclusion in Chapter 8 and study the examples in both Chapters 8 and 9.)

Development. The methods of development best suited to persuasion rest on two foundations—logical reasoning from well-verified facts (review Chapters 6 and 7) and motivating appeal based on human needs (review the section on motives in Chapter 5). Back of these methods, of course, lie analysis of issues to discover the main points of controversy in any given case, and analysis of the audience to discover which of the basic human needs provide the most active means of motivation. Man is a creature of both reason and emotion. An argumentative speaker, therefore, should learn to use reason as a basis for his motivating appeals while using emotional appeals to energize his inferences. Persuasion is most effective when motivation is based on fact and logic, and when reasoning is alive with motivation (see Chapter 11, on the speaker's emotions).

In this process any and all types of information may be important; but statements of principle, statistical evidence, and the opinions of authorities are especially appropriate. The methods of enumeration, analogy, and scientific generalization, which function so largely in expository speaking, are no less important in persuasion; but persuasive method should go beyond inductive processes to utilize the broad principles and judgments which grow out of induction.

Fundamentally involved in all these principles of persuasion are the methods of arousing interest and holding attention. Persuasive speakers cannot safely assume that listeners are inherently interested and willing to believe or act as proposed. He who argues must not only appeal to basic human needs, as we have said, but he must also make these appeals effective through clearness of purpose, factual development, orderly sequence, intensity of feeling, vividness of imagery, variety in symbolic processes (action, voice, words), and dynamic forward movement.

Symbolic process. Those especially appropriate for persuasive speaking should arise from the mental and emotional drive of deep conviction. Sincerity in itself is not enough. It must be based on thorough analysis, logical reasoning, imaginative enrichment, and emotional control.

The bodily actions of convincing speech should be vigorous and well-poised. Stance will be less in repose, more actively inclined toward the listeners. Eye contact is highly important. Instead of the descriptive gestures of expository speaking, persuasive speech needs more the direct and purposeful gestures—the pointing finger, the sidewise thrust of rejection, or the accepting movement of open hands.

The tempo of persuasive speech should be forward moving, though not hurried. Conviction and feeling should find their expression in rich vocal quality and well-controlled intensity. Language should be vivid and emotionally charged. The relationships of coordination and subordination between successive ideas and statements should be clearly revealed in vocal variety and positive use of transitional words and phrases. (Review Chapter 15, vocal expression; and Chapter 17, the use of language in speech; in addition to the section on orderly utterance in Chapter 4.)

EXERCISES

For each of the following talks you should prepare an outline (as described in Chapter 8) and hand it to your instructor for his approval at least two or three days before you are scheduled to speak. This not only will give you the benefit of his suggestions regarding your speech plan, but also will give you some time to assimilate and master the thought sequence after the plan is complete.

1. Prepare a short talk in which you explain the structure of a physical object or social institution. See Introduction for the Student for examples of this kind of subject. Give special thought to the kinds of factual material you will need and to the sources in which it will be found (see Chapter 6 and the Appendix). Divide the material you are to use into subpoints according to the basic parts of the subject (Chapter 9, section on topical pattern), arrange details in orderly sequence, and prepare your outline. In your oral

presentation give special attention to phrasing, pausing and the use of transitional cues. If you plan to use visual aids of any kind, refer to Chapter 13, section on visual aids.

2. In like manner prepare a talk to explain a process or mode of action. Give special attention to the functional kind of relationships (Chapter 7) and to chronological and causal patterns of organization (Chapter 9). Use whichever of these two patterns of organization best fits your subject. Give special attention to freedom and poise in bodily action; and if you use visual aids, plan them carefully (Chapter 13).

3. In like manner prepare an informative talk on a significant event in history. This should be more than simple narrative; it should include some exposition of the background and meaning of the event. If so treated, this exercise could be used as the occasion for emphasizing the imaginative aspect of thought, especially as creative thinking exemplified in your method of preparation (Chapter 10). Your instructor may ask you to submit a written report of experience or procedure during each of the four stages of preparation.

4. Prepare an inspirational talk in which you explain the most significant aspect of the life and work of some outstanding personality, either an historical character or someone on your campus or in the community. If you choose a living person of your acquaintance, you can take the opportunity to apply techniques of interviewing (see Chapter 6). In any event this assignment affords an excellent opportunity to give special attention to emotional participation (Chapter 11) and to the use of language (Chapter 17) as additional elements in your cumulative practice of the basic aspects of speech.

5. Concluding this series of expository talks, prepare and present to the class a talk explaining a concept or general idea. As background review the nature of concepts (Chapter 6), the conceptual or subjective viewpoint and methods of induction (Chapter 7), analysis and synthesis (Chapter 8). This talk should be an appropriate occasion to give special attention to the use of illustrations and to clarity and interestingness in use of language.

6. Prepare and present to the class an oral argument on some controversial matter of conduct or belief about which you have a conviction. Let your purpose be to secure acceptance of your belief or point of view. Analyze the issues involved and determine which of these is most important for your particular audience. Since the time for classroom speeches is usually limited, you should devote your talk to the one or two most important issues. Give special attention to logical relationships of ideas and pattern of organization and to the factual basis of your proof. Decide also how you will introduce and conclude the talk, and complete your outline. Throughout the preparation and delivery you should bear in mind, of course, the characteristics of argumentative speaking as discussed in this chapter.

7. Present another argumentative or persuasive talk, if possible on the same general theme or closely related subject used in the exercise just preceding. Make whatever changes in evidence and logical methods are suggested by evaluations of the preceding talk, but in addition this time direct your speech purpose specifically toward securing some definite action or

response from your listeners. With this purpose before you, proceed with the following steps for development of your speech outline: (*a*) Ask yourself what attitudes and beliefs or what past experiences of your listeners might inhibit the kind of response you desire. (*b*) Consider what kinds of motivation are most likely to overcome these barriers (see Chapter 5). (*c*) Formulate appeals to these motives in the most vivid and compelling references you can find to the past experience and future welfare of your listeners. (*d*) Organize these appeals in relation to the factual and logical foundations developed in the preceding talk.

SUPPLEMENTARY READINGS

Aristotle, *The Rhetoric*. Several good translations are available but that by Lane Cooper, Appleton-Century-Crofts, 1960, is probably most suitable for college undergraduates.

Brigance, William Norwood, *Speech: Its Techniques and Disciplines in a Free Society*, 2nd ed., Appleton-Century-Crofts, 1961.

Bryant, Donald C., and Karl R. Wallace, *Oral Communication*, 3rd ed., Appleton-Century-Crofts, 1962.

Minnick, Wayne C., *The Art of Persuasion*, Houghton Mifflin, 1957.

Monroe, Alan H., *Principles and Types of Speech*, 3rd ed., Scott, Foresman, 1949.

Oliver, Robert T., *The Psychology of Persuasive Speech*, Longmans, 1957.

Weaver, Andrew T., and Ordson G. Ness, *An Introduction to Public Speaking*, Odyssey, 1961.

21

ORAL READING

We have already said that interpretation is a kind of speech in which some elements, especially the sequence of thought, are fully prepared before actual utterance. Oral reading and acting are forms of interpretation in which the words also are composed prior to the speaking. In primitive societies legends and folk tales are often transmitted orally from generation to generation and may acquire a relatively fixed form long before they are actually written down. In our culture, however, an interpreter usually speaks material which has been written previously, usually by someone else.

An interpreter is more re-creative than creative in his thought, even though some element of creativity is always present. Storytellers, for example, are free to change wording so long as they recall the form and spirit of the narrative accurately. Readers and actors, although they have some freedom to interpret their material, are bound to adhere faithfully to the verbatim text as well as to its purpose and thought sequence. These circumstances, however, should not conceal the interpreter's communicative function. Some educators have considered reading aloud to be like the "arty" elocution which was common in our country during the past century. They forgot, if indeed they ever knew, that sound traditions of *elocutio* and *pronunciatio* were vital parts of ancient classical Greek and Roman education. Other educators have thought of oral reading as the slow and laborious process by which primary school pupils learn to recognize and pronounce words of the printed page. Neither of these concepts of reading recognizes its communicative nature.

The development of printing and improved methods of illustration, and the later development of silent moving pictures with their explanatory lines, pointed away from oral reading and directly to silent reading as the primary need in a society flooded with visual material. Rapid increase in population and in the complexities of life, together with compulsory school attendance laws, accelerated the growth of mass education. Time for classroom exercises in speaking or reading aloud seemed increasingly difficult to find. So the pedagogues, having condemned elocution, put oral reading out of the curriculum, and emphasized speed and more speed in silent reading. Eye-mindedness was emphasized for several generations of pupils, most of whom lost whatever ear-minded sensitivity they may have had for the communicative values of reading aloud.

Then came another revolution in social conditions—the movies became talkies. Radio made oral reading the primary medium of mass communication. Television emphasized the importance of the visual symbols of bodily action. While these technological changes were developing, linguists and anthropologists "discovered" that language is primarily oral and writing but a copy of the spoken word. Our educational system has not yet restored oral reading to its adequate place; but listening and ear-mindedness are re-emphasized, and the fundamental relationship between the eye appeal of bodily action and the ear appeal of voice and articulation is more generally understood. In schools and colleges verse choirs and choral speaking groups have been popular; reader theaters are developing group reading; and courses in oral interpretation are well attended.

The usefulness of reading aloud in daily life is apparent. Businessmen read reports, announcements, news items, and instructions of many kinds. In organized groups we hear the reading of minutes and resolutions. Law-making and policy-formulating bodies hear committee reports and pass bills through series of readings. In the classroom we quote documents, literary works, and other sources of information. Broadcasting is primarily oral reading. Even in labor-management controversies mediators sometimes ask that contracts be read aloud by the parties around the bargaining table.

Oral reading also serves artistic and cultural purposes. We read literature aloud for the enjoyment of beauty and the self-realization which comes from creative activity. Literature is read before public audiences as a means of entertainment and a performing art which enriches community life. Monologists like Ruth Draper and Cornelia Otis Skinner and such actors as Charles Boyer, Sir Cedric Hardwicke, and Charles Laughton have toured the country with programs of platform reading. We recognize reading aloud as that form of speech which most directly translates the written word back into its primary linguistic oral form and most adequately expresses the deeply human values of literature.

The Nature of Oral Reading

With this background we can now formulate a definition: *Oral reading is the art of re-creating and communicating the meaning of a piece of writing by translating its visual symbols into the visual-auditory speech symbols of bodily movement and sound.*

Compared with original speaking, a reader's message may be more aesthetic and literary and, if he is impersonating, may be spoken indirectly *for* instead of directly *to* listeners. The original speaker concentrates his attention on the task of communicating his own purpose and thought directly to the audience and receiving reaction as a direct feedback. The interaction is essentially two-sided. The oral reading situation, on the other hand, is characteristically three-sided. The reader is not communicating his own thought, but serving as transmitter of another man's message. The listener's responses, therefore, are or should be directed primarily to that third entity, the author's material, and only secondarily to the reader. Speaker and listeners are together sharing whatever of information and inspiration is in the material. Empathy between speaker and listener is important in all kinds of speaking, but in this special sense it is the soul of oral reading.

We should notice also the differences between acting and oral reading. Acting is primarily an art of character portrayal and is properly used only in impersonations or stage plays. Oral reading, on the other hand, takes for its province the whole wide world of literature, including essays, speeches, lyric and epic poetry, and narrative in any of its forms, as well as monologues and plays.

The most fundamental difference between acting and reading is found in attitude and point of view. An actor lives in the play; he properly speaks only *to* his fellow actors in the scene. Actors identify themselves completely with their material and maintain a considerable sense of aesthetic distance between themselves and the audience. An oral reader, on the other hand, identifies himself more completely with his listeners. He is, in effect, one of their number who in order to be seen and heard more effectively stands or sits facing the others and speaks directly to them. He must understand his author's message, assimilate its spirit, and create its imagery; but at the same time must maintain a partially detached attitude as though to say, "Look at this literature as a work of art. This is how it impresses me, and this is the evaluation I put upon it." This difference between reader and actor is probably exemplified most clearly in their interpretation of character. The actor impersonates, that is, he identifies himself with the character as completely as possible, and uses costume and make-up to create the most realistic illusion possible. The oral reader, on the other hand, makes no attempt to create the outward appearance of characters, but is content to suggest their personalities by subtle nuances of voice and action. The reader maintains a sense of greater aesthetic distance in relation to his material, but is closer and more direct in relation to his listeners.

As a result the oral reader's techniques must be more subtle and suggestive. He should not use action and voice in quite such broad and sweeping forms as can the actor or the original speaker. He is typically restrained in movement and depends more on minute changes of stance and facial expression and delicate nuances of vocal modulation. The reader maintains always the attitude of direct communicative relation-

*Oral reading
often sparks
conversation.*

ship to his listeners, even though he may and usually does speak with book or manuscript in hand. His book should be merely a guide, not a barrier between himself and the listeners nor a crutch to support wavering and uncertain mastery of material.

Oral Reading and Speech Improvement

Oral reading permits an acquaintance with factual and literary material which will contribute to every speaker's resources. Interpretative reading of great literature provides a vicarious experience which enriches imagination and emotion, develops greater sensitivity to the finer nuances of style, and stimulates the more subtle empathic responses of body and voice. Common work-a-day reading provides practice in pausing, phrasing, articulation, and pronunciation; but great literature stimulates the deeper responsiveness of body and voice and helps build a more discriminating command of expressive-communicative techniques.

Students seeking basic speech improvement should use the material of oral reading especially as a means of developing (1) wide range of knowledge, (2) skill in analysis and synthesis of thought, (3) deeper sensitivity to the imaginative and emotional values of life, (4) increased vocabulary and command of language, and (5) a more discriminating and responsive mastery of the bodily and vocal techniques of speech. In our study and practice we should consider choice of material, method of preparation, the actual reading performance, and its final evaluation.

375

CHOICE OF MATERIAL

For first practice in reading aloud you should choose selections which are related to your own interests and experience and which will broaden your knowledge or deepen your insight and at the same time will be interesting and stimulating to your listeners. Since the classroom audience is made up of students like yourself, the choice of such materials should not be difficult. Anthologies of literature are full of appropriate selections and are easily available in your college library. Look for essays which contain vital information; speeches which stir your convictions; narrative which holds your interest intensely; poetry, especially lyric or simple narrative poetry, which appeals to your feeling and imagination. Sometimes you will spontaneously discover some inspiring or challenging selection from your casual reading of newspapers, magazines, or even textbooks.

Avoid long and difficult types of material, complex character impersonations, and strongly rhyming "sing-song" poetry. Interpretation of the more difficult forms of literature is a valuable and challenging study, but should be undertaken in more advanced courses. For classroom practice your selections should be relatively short, depending of course on size of the class and time available. Except for brief anecdotes or short lyric poems, you will almost always need to select some portion of a longer work. Try to choose an excerpt which has unity of both idea and mood. If such a selection is to be meaningful to your listeners, you may need to explain briefly the larger context from which it is taken or summarize the preceding material and explain the author's point of view and purpose. Preparation of introductory remarks is discussed below.

PREPARATION

As a background for this section, review what we have said about memorizing in Chapter 12, especially the latter part in which the techniques of remembering are summarized. A reader should come to his communicative task with thorough mastery of the material. Although he will not need to memorize verbatim, he should assimilate the thought content, the emotional mood, and the imaginative elements so thoroughly that he will not be bound to his book or manuscript, but will use it only as a guide while he communicates the author's message directly to his listeners. Preparation should include the following methods of study and practice:

Study the selection as a whole so that you will be familiar with the context from which your excerpt is taken.

1. Read first for pleasure.
2. Be sure you understand the author's purpose.

3. Find the main theme or central idea—first of the entire selection, then of the part you are to read.
4. Analyze the logical.sequence and organization of thought.
5. Try to assimilate the mood, i.e., the imaginative and emotional values.
6. Notice any changes in mood or point of view.
7. Observe the relationships of large units, paragraphs or stanzas, to each other.

Study the details, especially of the part you have selected to read.

1. Study the sentences and phrase units, i.e., the sequence of detailed thought units.
2. Study the word meanings including their connotations and allusions.
3. Find the key words both logical and emotional.
4. Visualize the images and figures of speech.
5. Study the relationships of ideas—coordinate, subordinate, echo.
   a. What main ideas support the theme?
   b. What subordinate ideas support each main idea?
   c. Do you find any use of contrast? Of comparison?
6. Make an outline of your selection.

Practice reading your selection aloud, especially if you are preparing for audience reading.

1. Imagine your listeners before you, and practice just as you will want to sit or stand before them with copy of your lines in hand.
2. Train yourself to maintain contact with your listeners; learn to use the book or manuscript without letting it get between you and them.
3. Begin early enough to allow time for adequate thought assimilation and distribute your practice so as to allow appropriate intervals of rest. (See Chapter 12 on the speaker's memory.)

Prepare appropriate introductory or concluding remarks whenever they will aid the total communicative process. Your listeners may need to know the following:

1. Definitions of unfamiliar terms.
2. Context from which your selection was taken.
3. Something about the author and his reasons for writing.
4. Something about the time or circumstances in which the material was written.
5. The application or interpretation you would make of the author's message.

Such introductory or concluding remarks should be thought out carefully and spoken extemporaneously. If you write them word for word, destroy the manuscript; speak from notes if you must, but trust your creative memory.

PRESENTATION

All that we have said about use of symbolic processes in Part III should now be reviewed and applied to the actual process of communicating the author's message to your listeners. Balance and freedom in bodily action, responsiveness and flexibility in vocal response, ease and clarity in articulation—these are the technical media by which you will communicate.

When you actually face your listeners, observe the following minimum requirements:
1. Use the book or manuscript as a guide but maintain direct communicative attitude toward your listener.
2. Maintain an alert and easy stance, but be reserved in overt action.
3. Take time to pause in recognition of phrase units, but adjust your tempo to the spirit of the material.
4. Adapt your voice to the size of your audience and conditions of the setting, but let variety in vocal modulation reflect the changing patterns of your thought.

Throughout the reading maintain active realization of the purpose and theme of your selection. Remember that reading aloud is communication, not exhibition.

EVALUATION

Review the section on the listener as critic, Chapter 3. Evaluation of oral reading, as of all speech, should be realistic, definite, balanced, and constructive. In order to apply these general standards specifically to reading aloud, consider the following questions:

Was the reading of the selection clearly understandable? Was it true to the author's intention? Did the reader show quiet confidence born of adequate preparation? Did he maintain communicative attitude? Did the reading hold attention? Was it lively, or monotonous and dull? Did it sound like talk? Did the interpretation reveal the total meaning including subtle changes in mood and attitude? Were voice and action adequately adjusted to the size of audience and conditions of the setting? Did the reading give you a sense of increased knowledge and/or renewed inspiration?

EXERCISES

1. Read aloud to the class a short selection of prose, chosen from a published speech or essay. You should analyze and assimilate the thought of the selection carefully in advance of the presentation, with special at-

tention to the recognition and phrasing of thought units and the use of pausing and transitional cues.

Prepare a brief explanation about the author or original speaker of your selection, the occasion of its delivery or place of publication, and the larger context of thought from which it is taken, together with any other explanations or definitions which may help your listeners to understand the message. Give this information extemporaneously, preferably without notes, as an introduction to your reading. Your instructor may arrange to record this exercise so that you can hear and analyze your own utterance.

2. Choose a short poem or selection of imaginative and literary prose, assimilate the thought content, prepare any introductory or concluding comment which will aid the listener's understanding, and read the selection aloud to the class together with your extemporized comment. Give particular attention to the imaginative and emotional aspects of the author's message and to the vocal and articulatory aspects of interpretation. (Refer to Chapters 10, 11, 15, and 16.)

SUPPLEMENTARY READINGS

Cunningham, Cornelius C., *Making Words Come Alive*, Wm. C. Brown Company, 1951.

Dolman, John, Jr., *The Art of Reading Aloud*, Harper & Row, 1956.

Grimes, Wilma H., and Alethea Smith Mattingly, *Interpretation: Writer, Reader, Audience*, Wadsworth Publishing Company, Inc., 1961.

Johnson, Gertrude E. (ed.), *Studies in the Art of Interpretation*, Appleton-Century-Crofts, 1940.

Lee, Charlotte I., *Oral Interpretation*, 2nd ed., Houghton Mifflin, 1959.

Lowery, Sara, and Gertrude E. Johnson, *Interpretative Reading*, Appleton-Century-Crofts, 1942.

Parrish, Wayland Maxfield, *Reading Aloud*, 2nd ed., Nelson, 1941.

APPENDIX

SOURCES OF INFORMATION

MAGAZINE INDEXES

Readers' Guide to Periodical Literature, 1900 to date, H. W. Wilson.
Cumulative monthly, annually, and biennially. Probably the most useful
general index to recent periodicals. Supplemented by many indexes in
special fields, e.g.:

Agricultural Index	*Education Index*
Applied Science and Technology Index	*Engineering Index*
Art Index	*Index to Legal Periodicals*
Biography Index	*Industrial Arts Index*
Business Periodicals Index	*International Index*

Poole's Index to Periodical Literature, 1802–1881, Houghton Mifflin, 1891;
supplements to 1906. Indexes 470 English and American periodicals.
References are given by subject and title with authors' names in parentheses after titles. Only volume and page numbers are given, but a table
in the front of each volume gives corresponding dates.

Annual Magazine Subject-Index, 1907–1949, The F. W. Faxon Co.

Subject-Index to Periodicals, 1915 to date, Library Association. Chiefly
British plus a few American and continental publications.

Psychological Index, annual, 1894–1935, Psychological Review Co.

Psychological Abstracts, 1927 to date, American Psychological Association.

Index to the Quarterly Journal of Speech, vols. I–XL, 1915–1954, comp. by
Giles W. Gray, Wm. C. Brown Co., 1956.

NEWSPAPER INDEXES AND DIRECTORIES

New York Times Index, 1913 to date; semimonthly and annual cumulations.

Official Index, London Times, 1906 to date, quarterly cumulation since
July, 1914.

American Newspapers, 1821–1936, 2nd ed., ed. by Winifred Gregory,
H. W. Wilson, 1943. Union list of serials in libraries of United States
and Canada.

Ayer's Directory of Newspapers and Periodicals, annual since 1880, Ayer.
Papers in the United States and Canada, circulation figures, editors and

publishers, frequencies of issue, size of pages, prices, dates of establishment, politics, and other information.

Ulrich's Periodicals Directory, 9th ed., ed. by Eileen C. Graves, Bowker, 1959.

BIBLIOGRAPHIES AND BOOKLISTS

Professional and Trade Lists: Books, Pamphlets, Documents

Bibliographic Index: A Cumulative Bibliography of Bibliographies, 1938 to date, H. W. Wilson.

Book Review Digest, 1905 to date, H. W. Wilson.

Cumulative Book Index, 1898 to date, H. W. Wilson. A world list of books in the English language; supplements the *United States Catalogue*.

Essay and General Literature Index, 1900 to date, H. W. Wilson.

Public Affairs Information Service Bulletin, 1915 to date, Public Affairs Information Service. Weekly, annual cumulation. Indexes books, pamphlets, documents and periodicals in political and social sciences.

Publishers' Weekly, 1872 to date. American trade book journal, lists currently published books.

United States Catalogue, 4 eds., 1899–1928, H. W. Wilson; supplements, 1906, 1912–1917, 1918–1921, 1921–1924. A list of all books in print in the English language.

Vertical File Service Catalogue, 1932–1934, H. W. Wilson. Monthly, annual cumulation. Annotated subject catalogue of pamphlets, booklets, leaflets, circulars, folders, maps, charts, and mimeographed bulletins.

Bibliographies Issued by Government Agencies

Ames, John G., *Comprehensive Index to the Publications of the United States Government*, 1881–1893, Government Printing Office, 1905.

Bureau of Labor Statistics, *Subject Index of Bulletins*, 1915–1959, Bulletin No. 1281, U.S. Department of Labor.

Library of Congress, Processing Department, *Monthly Check List of State Publications*, 1910 to date, Government Printing Office. Includes publications of possessions and territories as well as of states.

Poore, Benjamin Perley, *A Descriptive Catalogue of the Government Publications of the United States*, 1774–1881, Government Printing Office, 1885.

U.S. Bureau of the Census, *Census Publications; catalog and subject guide*, Government Printing Office, 1945 to date. Quarterly, annual cumulation.

U.S. Superintendent of Documents, *United States Government Publications: Monthly Catalog*, 1895 to date, Government Printing Office; supplements, 1941–1942, 1943–1944, 1945–1946.

U.S. Superintendent of Documents, *Price Lists*, Nos. 1–85, Government Printing Office. Lists pamphlets and brochures issued by government agencies on a wide variety of subjects.

Special Speech Bibliographies

Phelps, Edith M. (comp.), *Debate Index*, rev. ed. (*The Reference Shelf*, vol. 12, No. 9) H. W. Wilson, 1939; *Supplement* (*The Reference Shelf*, vol. 14, No. 9), Julia E. Johnsen, comp., H. W. Wilson, 1941.

Sutton, Roberta Briggs, *Speech Index: An Index to Sixty-four Collections of World Famous Orations and Speeches for Various Occasions*, H. W. Wilson, 1935; *Supplement*, 1935–1955, Scarecrow Press, 1956.

Thonssen, Lester, and Elizabeth Fatherson, *Bibliography of Speech Education*, H. W. Wilson, 1939; *Supplement*, 1939–1948 by Lester Thonssen, Mary Margaret Robb, and Dorothea Thonssen, H. W. Wilson, 1950.

REFERENCE WORKS

Winchell, Constance (ed.), *Guide to Reference Books*, 7th ed., American Library Association, 1951; supplements, 1950–1952, 1953–1955, 1956–1958.

General Encyclopedias

Encyclopedia Americana, 30 vols., Americana Corporation, 1951; *Americana Annual*, 1923 to date.

Encyclopaedia Britannica, 24 vols., 1960; 11th ed., 1910–1911, 28 vols., generally considered most scholarly of all. *Britannica Book of the Year*, 1938 to date.

Collier's Encyclopedia, 20 vols., Collier, 1957.

Dictionaries and Encyclopedias in Special Fields

Black, Henry C., *Black's Law Dictionary*, 4th ed., West, 1951.

Cambridge History of American Literature, 4 vols., ed. by William P. Trent et al., Putnam, 1917–1921.

Cambridge History of English Literature, 15 vols., ed. by A. W. Ward and A. R. Waller, Cambridge University Press, 1907–1927.

Dictionary of American History, 5 vols., 2nd ed., ed. by James Truslow Adams, Scribner, 1942.

Dictionary of Education, 2nd ed., ed. by Carter V. Good, McGraw-Hill, 1959.

Dictionary of Philosophy and Psychology, 3 vols., ed. by J. M. Baldwin, Macmillan, 1901–1905.

Encyclopedia of Religion and Ethics, 12 vols., ed. by James Hastings, Scribner, 1908–1927.

Encyclopedia of the Social Sciences, 15 vols., ed. by E. R. A. Seligman, Macmillan, 1930–1935.

Everyman's United Nations, 6th ed., U.N. Office of Public Information, 1959. Structure, functions, and work of the organization and related agencies, 1945–1958.

Oxford Classical Dictionary, ed. by M. Cary et al., Oxford University Press, 1957.

Van Nostrand's Scientific Encyclopedia, 3rd ed., Van Nostrand, 1958.

Yearbooks and Almanacs

The Annual Register of World Events, 1758 to date, Longmans.

Congressional Quarterly Almanac, annual, 1945 to date. Washington, Congressional Quarterly, Inc. Cumulation based on Congressional Quarterly *Weekly Report*. See also C. Q. *Quarterly Index*. A basic summary of facts about the activities of the United States Congress.

Europa: The Encyclopedia of Europe, 1946 to date, Europa Publications.

Statesman's Yearbook, Macmillan, 1864 to date, statistical and historical annual of states of the world.

World Almanac, 1885 to date, World-Telegram. Wide range of statistical and other information plus a list of organizations in the United States many of which publish material in their special fields.

World Aviation Annual, 1948 to date, ed. by J. Parker Van Zandt, Aviation Research Institute. '

Yearbook of the United Nations, 1947 to date, U.N. Department of Public Information.

Biographical Works

American Men of Science, 10th ed., 4 vols., ed. by Jaques Cattell, Bowker, 1960–1961.

Current Biography, monthly, annual cumulation, 1940 to date, H. W. Wilson.

Dictionary of American Biography, 20 vols., ed. by Allen Johnson and Dumas Malone, Scribner, 1928–1937; supplement 1, 1944; supplement 2, 1958.

Dictionary of National Biography, 22 vols., ed. by Leslie Stephen and Sidney Lee, Macmillan, 1908–1909; supplements to 1950.

Directory of American Scholars, 3rd ed., ed. by Jaques Cattell, Bowker, 1957.

Leaders in Education, 3rd ed., ed. by Jaques Cattell and E. E. Ross, Science Press, 1948.

Twentieth Century Authors, ed. by Stanley J. Kunitz and Vineta Colby, H. W. Wilson, 1942; supplement, 1955.

Who's Who (English), annual, 1849 to date, A. & C. Black and Macmillan.

Who's Who in America, monthly, biennial cumulation, 1899 to date, The A. N. Marquis Co. Additional volumes of the *Who's Who* series are available in special fields, e.g.:

    Who's Who of American Women

    Who's Who in Art

    Who's Who in Engineering

    Who's Who in the Midwest

    Who's Who in the Theatre

Who's Who in Transportation and Communication
Who's Who in the United Nations

Government Documents

Bureau of the Census, *Statistical Abstract of the United States*, annual, 1878 to date, Government Printing Office.

Bureau of Foreign and Domestic Commerce, *Survey of Current Business*, monthly, 1921 to date, Government Printing Office.

Department of Agriculture, *Agricultural Statistics*, annual, 1936 to date, Government Printing Office.

Department of State, *Bulletin*, Government Printing Office. Official record of United States foreign policy; issued weekly by the Office of Public Services, Bureau of Public Affairs, since 1939.

Federal Reserve Bulletin, monthly, 1915 to date, Board of Governors of the Federal Reserve System.

United States Congress, *Congressional Edition or Serial Set*. A collection of all publications whose printing is authorized by Congress, except the Congressional Record. Includes Senate and House journals, reports of committees, and documents, in addition to many reports of executive departments and independent bodies. A complete index with some overlapping will be found in the following:

> U.S. Superintendent of Documents, *Check List of Public Documents*, 3rd ed., 1789–1909, Government Printing Office, 1911.
>
> ―――――――, *Catalog of the Public Documents of Congress and of All Departments of the Government of the United States*, 1893–1940, Government Printing Office, 1896–1945.
>
> ―――――――, *Numerical Lists and Schedule of Volumes of the Reports and Documents of the 73rd Congress*, Government Printing Office, 1934 to date. Continued for successive sessions of Congress, usually in a separate volume for each session.
>
> United States Congress, *Official Congressional Directory for the Use of the U.S. Congress*, 1809 to date, irregular, Government Printing Office. For each session of Congress the directory lists personnel of all agencies of the Federal Government.
>
> United States Congress, *Congressional Record*, Government Printing Office, 1873 to date.
>
> Documents of state, county and city governments. Commissions, boards, committees, and administrative officers issue reports in many fields. Lists of these usually can be obtained from state libraries or from state directors of information and research. State directories or manuals, often under such titles as *Blue Book*, *Red Book*, or *Yearbook* may be obtained from similar sources, although you should consult your local library first.

Publications of Professional and Research Organizations

Encyclopedia of Associations, 3rd ed.; vol. I, National Organizations of the U.S.; vol. II, Geographic and Executive Index; Gale Research Company,

1961. General list of organizations. Check lists of publications are given for most of the organizations reported.

Brookings Institution, *Brookings Publications*, Washington, D.C. A check list issued annually. Material especially useful in the fields of economics, politics and foreign affairs.

National Association of Manufacturers, Research Department, *National Fact Book*, Washington, D.C. Current statistical service.

Foreign Policy Association, *Headline Series*, Washington, D.C. Summaries and analyses of all aspects of United States foreign policy.

Directory of University Research Bureaus and Institutes, Gale Research Company, 1960.

ACADEMIC ASSOCIATIONS

Almost every subject field in college and university curricula is represented by one or more professional organizations which publish journals or other materials in their areas of study. (See *Encyclopedia of Associations* above.) Students of speech should know some of the important professional organizations in their field.

Speech Association of America. The parent association from which most of the others have sprung. Interested in all aspects of speech.

American Speech and Hearing Association. Speech and hearing therapy and speech science.

American Educational Theatre Association. Drama.

National Society for the Study of Communication. All forms of communication.

Western Speech Association

Central States Speech Association

Southern Speech Association

Speech Association of the Eastern States

Miscellaneous Special Sources

MANUSCRIPT COLLECTIONS

Includes diaries, letters, and original documents. These are especially important for subjects of local and historical interest.

MICROFILM, MICROCARD, AND PHOTOSTAT COLLECTIONS

These are increasingly useful for making rare and out-of-print material easily available.

COLLECTIONS OF SPEECHES

American Forum: Speeches on Historic Issues, 1788–1900; and *Contemporary Forum: American Speeches on Twentieth Century Issues*, ed. by Ernest J. Wrage and Barnet Baskerville, Harper & Row, 1960 and 1962.

Representative American Speeches, ed. by A. Craig Baird, annual since 1937–1938, H. W. Wilson.

Vital Speeches of the Day, twice a month since 1934, City News Publishing Co.

BOOKS OF QUOTATIONS

Bartlett, John, *Familiar Quotations*, 13th ed., Little, Brown, 1955.
The Oxford Dictionary of Quotations, 2nd ed., Oxford University Press, 1953.

HANDBOOKS FOR DEBATERS

National University Extension Association, Committee on Debate Materials and Interstate Cooperation, *Discussion and Debate Manual*, ed. by Bower Aly, annual since 1934.
The Reference Shelf, 1922 to date, H. W. Wilson. Each number is devoted to a single controversial question and includes selected articles and a bibliography.
University Debaters Annual, 1915–1951, H. W. Wilson. Verbatim copies of selected college and university debates, including bibliographies of subjects debated.

ANTHOLOGIES

Benét, William Rose, and Conrad Aiken (eds.), *An Anthology of Famous English and American Poetry*, Modern Library, 1945.
Jones, Howard Mumford, Richard M. Ludwig, and Marvin B. Perry, Jr., *Modern Minds: An Anthology of Ideas*, 2nd ed., Heath, 1954.
Locke, Louis G., William M. Gibson, and George Arms, *Readings for Liberal Education*; 4th ed.; vol I, *Toward Liberal Education*; vol. II, *Introduction to Literature*; Holt, Rinehart and Winston, 1962.

SOURCE BOOKS OF SUBJECTS AND TOPICS

Arnold, Carroll D., Douglas Ehninger, and John C. Gerber (eds.), *The Speaker's Resource Book*, Scott, Foresman, 1961.
Black, Edwin, and Harry P. Kerr (eds.), *American Issues: A Source-book for Speech Topics*, Harcourt, Brace & World, 1961.
Bryson, Lyman (ed.), *An Outline of Man's Knowledge of the Modern World*, McGraw-Hill, 1960.
St. Onge, Keith R. *Creative Speech*, Wadsworth Publishing Company, Inc., 1964. Especially Part II, "Ideas in Practice."

INDEX

INDEX